THE MEMOIRS

OF

Herbert Hoover

The Great Depression
1929-1941

THE MACMILLAN COMPANY: NEW YORK

1952

HERBERT HOOVER

INTRODUCTION

—————————— ⟨⟨⟨⟨⟩⟩⟩⟩ ——————————

The central difficulty during my term as President was, obviously, the world-wide "Great Depression." Domestically it first appeared in late 1929, eight months after my inauguration, and continued in the United States not only during my term but for eight years more, until the start of the Second World War in 1941.

That fateful eleven-year period is the subject of this volume of my Memoirs. I have divided it into three major parts:

> The Great Depression
> The Presidential Election of 1932
> The Aftermath

As in the previous two volumes of my Memoirs, I have treated the material topically rather than chronologically, so as to present a clearer picture of the events, policies and forces in motion at the time.

I wrote the sections on the Depression and the Election of 1932, for the most part, less than three years after I left the White House. Later I clarified and condensed some parts, in particular eliminating documents which had become public. These I have indicated by references. The section on the Election of 1932 is more detailed than would be necessary but for the fact that this election was a turning point in American life —and possibly in that of the world.

The section entitled The Aftermath, concerning the continuation of the Depression from Mr. Roosevelt's inauguration in 1933 until 1941, was written from 1942 to 1944. I have included here, from later dates, some quotations which bear on this period.

Throughout I have endeavored to treat persons and events with the

⸜ of a post-mortem. While occasionally mentioning my own ⸜, I have rested criticism of Mr. Roosevelt's policies by other persons ⸜n statements of his sometime associates rather than on quotations ⸜f his Republican opponents.

As this volume will demonstrate, the "Great Depression" did not start in the United States. To be sure, we were due for some economic readjustment as a result of the orgy of stock speculation in 1928–1929. This orgy was not a consequence of my administrative policies. In the main it was the result of the Federal Reserve Board's pre-1928 enormous inflation of credit at the request of European bankers which, as this narrative shows, I persistently tried to stop, but I was overruled. Aside from the inevitable collapse of this Mississippi Bubble, some secondary economic forces also contributed to the October, 1929, events. But even this slump started in foreign countries before it occurred in the United States, and their difficulties were themselves a contributing factor to the stock market crash. Our domestic difficulties standing alone would have produced no more than the usual type of economic readjustment which had re-occurred at intervals in our history.

Eighteen months later, by early 1931, we were convalescing from our own ills when an economic hurricane struck us from abroad. The whole financial and economic structure of Europe collapsed at this time as a result of the delayed consequences of the First World War, the Versailles Treaty, and internal policies.

The immediate effect of Central Europe's collapse was the terrible unsettlement of all economically sensitive nations everywhere. Among the dire consequences were Britain's suspension of payments to foreigners, abandonment of the gold standard by scores of nations, trade wars, political revolutions in more than a dozen countries outside of Europe, and disaster for the American economy.

The eventual effect of this gigantic catastrophe was to kindle political and social revolutions in all the defeated nations of Central and Eastern Europe. Communism reached its dread hand into those areas, and Fascist dictators arose as the antidote. In the end, these forces were to plunge the world into a Second World War.

It is easy for the reader to look back and say that from the very beginning we should have anticipated the European storm and enacted in advance unprecedented measures to counteract it.

America had never before been confronted with such a domestic and foreign storm and, therefore, had little exp which it could be guided.

Whatever our apprehensions may have been, it can be said at once that neither the American people nor the Congress would have approved such unprecedented measures before these ill winds began to strike our shores. It is not given to mortals clearly to foresee the violence or the emergence of hidden forces of destruction. As a measure of proof of public and Congressional unconcern, I may recall that I had repeatedly, yet without success, urged the reorganization of our whole banking system during the two years before the European storm revealed that weakness to our people.

General Prosperity had been a great ally in my election in 1928. General Depression, who superseded, was in some part responsible for my defeat in 1932. The recovery which began in July steadily increased over that summer, but not sufficiently to overcome that particular political opponent.

I give more attention to the campaign of 1932 than might be otherwise desirable, because I then accurately forecast that attempts would be made to revolutionize the American way of life. The effort to crossbreed some features of Fascism and Socialism with our American free system speedily developed in the Roosevelt administration. The result was that America failed to keep pace with world recovery. Instead we continued with subnormal levels of lessened productivity, high unemployment, and costly relief measures until our man power and industries were absorbed by the war eight years later, in 1941.

That our administration policies were right is amply evidenced by the fact that after the world turned toward recovery in July, 1932, the twelve nations retaining their free economies, and pursuing our policies, fully recovered, within two or three years, to levels above the boom year of 1929.

All this will be illuminated in detail and conclusively proved in this volume.

I would be remiss if I did not acknowledge the devoted assistance I have received from my friends and my staff, particularly I should mention Dr. Arthur Kemp, Bernice Miller, Loretta Camp, and Madeline Kelly.

CONTENTS

ILLUSTRATIONS

The Great Depression

CHAPTER 1

THE ORIGINS OF THE GREAT DEPRESSION

In the large sense the primary cause of the Great Depression was the war of 1914–1918. Without the war there would have been no depression of such dimensions. There might have been a normal cyclical recession; but, with the usual timing, even that readjustment probably would not have taken place at that particular period, nor would it have been a "Great Depression." [1]

The Great Depression was a two-stage process of several phases. We had a normal recession due to domestic causes beginning with the stock-market slump in October, 1929, but we were on the way out of it when the European difficulties rose to hurricane force and struck us in April, 1931. Thus the *Great* Depression did not really begin in the United States until the European collapse.

THE DEPRESSION WAS NOT STARTED IN THE UNITED STATES

It has been asserted that the American stock-market slump pulled down the world. That was not the fact.

A study by the National Bureau of Economic Research states: "Several countries entered the phase of recession in 1927 and 1928, long before the date usually taken as marking the crisis in the United States, that of the Wall Street crash of October, 1929." [2]

---

[1] In confirmation of this paragraph the reader should refer to a consensus of European opinion given in a footnote on page 63 n.

[2] Willard L. Thorp, "The Depression As Depicted by Business," National Bureau of Economic Research *News Bulletin*, No. 43, Sept. 19, 1932.

[2]

The report enumerates Bolivia, Australia, Germany, Brazil and Bulgaria as having entered the depression phase before the . can stock market crash.

The Report of the Agent General for Reparations Payments as to Germany states:[3]

A considerable increase has taken place since the beginning of 1929 in the number of business concerns in difficulties. Business failures during the first five months of the year were about 20 per cent more numerous than in the corresponding part of 1928. . . .

German stock prices had fallen sharply by the summer of 1929.

Great Britain, Canada, Holland, Sweden, and Japan also had entered a business recession prior to the stock-market crash. On this Leonard P. Ayres, an eminent economist, states:

Wholesale commodity prices had been falling in England and Canada since the beginning of 1925, and serious declines got under way in a long list of other countries in 1928 and early in 1929. The market prices of stocks turned down in Germany in the summer of 1928; in Great Britain and the Netherlands early in the spring of 1929, and in Sweden in the summer of that year. Industrial activity began to decline in Canada and in Italy in the spring of 1929, and in Japan in the summer of the same year.[4]

France also had shown weakness prior to the slump in the United States. The French index of common-stock prices had dropped from 543 in January, to 491 in June.

Large areas of the world are not very sensitive to economic tides—such as China, Russia, Central Asia, and Central Africa. Eliminating these countries, the economic situation began to decline in more than four-fifths of the economically sensitive peoples of the world before it began in the United States.

We could not but be affected by the degenerative forces moving elsewhere in the world. Our immediate weak spot was the orgy of stock speculation which began to slump in October, 1929. The inflation

[3] *Federal Reserve Bulletin,* September, 1929, p. 622.

[4] Leonard P. Ayres, *The Chief Cause of This and Other Depressions,* Cleveland, 1935, pp. 11–13.

which led to the orgy was a contributory cause of our own difficulties. Secondary causes arose from eight years of increasing productivity. By our energies in invention and enterprise, we had raised our per capita productivity to levels never hitherto known in the world. Various economic studies showed that in the twenties our productivity per person increased by over 30 per cent—a ratio without parallel. As a result of distortions in this advance, some readjustments were due.

The depth of our recession during the first seventeen months did not constitute a major depression, and our internal strength enabled us to begin a strong convalescence during the first three months of 1931. Had no external influences struck us, it is certain that we should have passed out of the slump shortly.

THE GREAT STORM CENTER WAS IN EUROPE

The great center of the storm was Europe. That storm moved slowly until the spring of 1931, when it burst into a financial hurricane. At that moment the enormous war destruction, the economic consequences of the Treaty of Versailles, revolutions, unbalanced budgets, hugely increased armaments, inflation, the gigantic overproduction of rubber, coffee, and other commodities, through overstimulation from artificial controls, and a score of other aftermaths of the war which I give in detail later, finally broke through all efforts to fend off their explosive forces. The wounds of Europe were so deep that the total collapse of most European economies in mid-1931 plunged us into depths not witnessed since our depressions of 1820, 1837, and 1872.

It is of some economic interest that the time of the European depression indicated the approximate ten-year rhythm of economic collapse which followed the Napoleonic Wars and the American and European wars of the 1860's and 1870's.[5]

[5] An overwhelming mass of literature has been written about the cause of the Great Depression. For brevity's sake, the writers may be divided into two major groups: (1) those searching for a single responsible cause, condition, or person; and (2) those who searched patiently and objectively for the truth, recognized the obvious falsity of a single cause for a highly complex phenomenon, and were unwilling to compromise devotion to scientific truth for the sake of some temporary political advantages.

There are, of course, many subdivisions within each group. Those who sought a single cause or person as a scapegoat seemed to find in me an ideal subject. Fortunately, most of this species will be forgotten much sooner and more completely than the

DOMESTIC IMPULSES TO OUR SLUMP

In after years I often had reason to recall the scriptural text: "There ariseth a little cloud out of the sea, like a man's hand. Say unto Ahab, Prepare thy chariot, and get thee down, that the rain stop thee not."

One of these clouds was an American wave of optimism, born of continued progress over the decade, which the Federal Reserve Board transformed into the stock-exchange Mississippi Bubble. Another of the little clouds arose from the fact that the segment of our economy based on catching up with the war lag was coming to its terminal, particularly in the construction industries. Still another, a by-product of our enormous increase in individual productivity, was a need for readjustment of commodity prices between groups.

Our reconstruction from the war had proceeded with such steady success, and the other impulses to progress were so very great that, with the growing optimism, they gave birth to a foolish idea called the "New Economic Era." That notion spread over the whole country. We were assured that we were in a new period where the old laws of economics no longer applied.

MY WARNINGS AGAINST SPECULATION AND CREDIT INFLATION

During 1925, I began to be alarmed over the growing tide of speculation and gave warnings as to the dangers of this mood. In a press statement on New Year's day, 1926, I said:

There are some phases of the situation which require caution . . . real estate and stock speculation and its possible extension into commodities with inevitable inflation; the overextension of installment buying; the extortion by foreign government-fostered monopolies dominating our raw material imports; the continued economic instability of certain foreign countries; the

---

searchers for truth. Of these latter I recommend Charles S. Tippetts, Headmaster of Mercersburg Academy and formerly Dean of the School of Business Administration of the University of Pittsburgh; Garfield V. Cox of the University of Chicago; Rufus S. Tucker, formerly of Brookings Institution; Leonard P. Ayres of the Cleveland Trust Company; Arthur F. Burns, W. C. Mitchell and Willard L. Thorp of the National Bureau of Economic Research; Joseph Schumpeter of Harvard University; and, on the international nature of the depression, Gottfried Haberler and Lionel Robbins. Many others, too numerous to mention, have tried to contribute objectively to an understanding of the forces in motion.

lag in recovery of certain major agricultural products; the instability of the coal industry; the uncertainties of some important labor relationships—all these are matters of concern. . . .

This fever of speculation is also widespread in real estate and, unless our financial policies are guided with courage and wisdom, this speculation may yet reflect into the commodity markets, thereby reversing the cautious buying policies of recent years. Psychology plays a large part in business movements, and overoptimism can only land us on the shores of overdepression. Not since 1920 have we required a better informed or more capable administration of credit facilities than now if we are to continue an uninterrupted high plane of prosperity. In any event there should be no abatement of caution in the placing of forward orders, particularly in view of the great increase in sales of a great variety of merchandise on the installment basis.

The *New York Times* (January 1, 1926) and the New York *Financial Chronicle* (January 2nd) both endorsed this caution. During 1926 I continued to issue warnings that the reckless speculation would undermine our prosperity (for instance, at Staunton, Virginia, March 21st and Caldwell, Idaho, August 17th).

THE FEDERAL RESERVE INFLATION OF CREDIT

My Annual Report as Secretary of Commerce, published in midyear of 1926, said:

No one doubts the extreme importance of credit and currency movement in the "business cycle." Disturbances from this quarter may at once interfere with the fundamental business of producing goods and distributing them. Many previous crises have arisen through the credit machinery and through no fault of either the producer or consumer. . . .

That the Federal Reserve System should be so managed as to result in stimulation of speculation and overexpansion has received universal disapproval.

Behind these alarms was my knowledge that the Federal Reserve Board had deliberately created credit inflation. The Reserve System had been established early in the Wilson administration on December 23, 1913. The act was largely fathered by Senator Carter Glass and was hailed by him, President Wilson, and Secretary of the Treasury William G. McAdoo as the remedy to the whole problem of booms, slumps, and panics. They asserted that, by the control of discount rates, open market operations, and currency issues, business crises could be eliminated. They contended that raising rediscount rates and restriction of credit through the sale of government securities by the Reserve Banks ("open market operations") would curb all speculation, and that the opposite actions by the Reserve Banks would stimulate business activity. A few of their expressions were:

> We shall have no more financial panics. . . . Panics are impossible. . . . Business men can now proceed in perfect confidence that they will no longer put their property in peril. . . . Now the business man may work out his destiny without living in terror of panic and hard times. . . . Panics in the future are unthinkable. . . . Never again can panic come to the American people.

A contribution to optimism and the belief in the "New Era" was the illusion that the economic system was thus completely immune from financial crises. Bankers, accepting this illusion, neglected many of their own responsibilities.

THE CREDIT INFLATION OF 1925–1926

The Federal Reserve Board, during 1925, had undertaken credit expansion by open market operations and by lowering discount rates. It had been led into this action by Governor Benjamin Strong of the New York Federal Reserve Bank upon the urging of Montagu Norman, head of the Bank of England, Hjalmar Schacht of the Reichsbank, and Charles Rist of the Bank of France, who came to New York and Washington to press this expansion. It was direct inflation.

One reason for the action lay in the British resumption of gold convertibility of sterling in 1925 at the prewar rate of $4.86 to the pound.[6]

---

[6] The eminent British economist Lionel Robbins, in *The Great Depression*, Macmillan & Co., London, 1934, asks why inflation took place; and he proceeds (p. 52):

"The answer seems to be that it was the direct outcome of misdirected management on the part of the Federal Reserve authorities—an error of management, however, which Englishmen at any rate have no right to speak of with reproach, for it seems almost certain that it was carried out very largely with the intent to ease our position.

"The situation seems to have been roughly as follows. By the spring of 1927 the upward movement of business in the United States, which started in 1925, showed signs of coming to a conclusion. A moderate depression was in sight. There is no reason to

This was a fictitious rate. The exchange, after the war, had dipped as low as $3.60. The natural market rates were the real measure of the pound as determined by world markets. These lower values represented the weight of the great domestic debts, the war inflation, and the price levels in Britain. I believe it was national pride more than economic sense that had induced the British to resume the prewar gold content of the pound. Having adopted the higher content, they at once found themselves in difficulty supporting its exchange value, as this rate fixed the price of their exports too high, slackened their trade balances, and weakened their gold reserves. They invented the idea that the United States should expand credit and maintain lower interest rates than Britain so that she could attract capital and thus foreign exchange in her direction.

The other European central bankers were in difficulties because of their own government inflations from unbalanced budgets, military and public works expenditures, and bureaucratic expansion. It was also to their benefit to have cheap money in the United States which they could borrow through the high interest rates they offered. Their ills required an altogether different remedy than "cheap money" in the United States.

The consequences of the Federal Reserve Board action were disastrous to our economy. It induced unwise investment in European loans and bank advances. Worse still, it stimulated speculation in common stocks on American exchanges by making large funds available to those who wanted to borrow on small margins. The immediate proof

---

suppose that this depression would have been of very great duration or of unusual severity. It was a normal cyclical movement.

"Meantime, however, events in England had produced a position of unusual difficulty and uncertainty. In 1925 the British authorities had restored the Gold Standard at a parity which, in the light of subsequent events, is now generally admitted to have been too high. The consequences were not long in appearing. Exports fell off. Imports increased. The Gold Standard was in peril. The effects of the over-valued exchange made themselves felt with greatest severity in the coal trade. Throughout 1926 there raged labour disputes, which were the direct consequence of these troubles—first the general strike, then a strike in the coal-fields which dragged out for over six months, still further endangering the trade balance. By 1927 the position was one of great danger. International assistance was sought. And in the summer of that year, partly in order to help us, partly in order to ease the domestic position, the authorities of the Federal Reserve System took the momentous step of forcing a régime of cheap money."

was that during 1925 alone loans to stock brokers had increased from $1,160,000,000 to $2,800,000,000, and common stocks had risen 40 per cent.

In November, 1925, it was confirmed to me by Adolph Miller, a member of the Reserve Board, that Strong and his European allies proposed still more "easy money policies," which included continued manipulation of the discount rates and open market operations—more inflation.

At once, as Secretary of Commerce, I protested to Daniel Crissinger, Governor of the Board, that such action would further stimulate speculation and was not the remedy for Europe's ills anyway. Crissinger was a political appointee from Marion, Ohio, utterly devoid of global economic or banking sense. The other members of the Board, except Adolph Miller, were mediocrities, and Governor Strong was a mental annex to Europe. I got nowhere. President Coolidge insisted that the Board had been set up by Congress as an agency independent of the administration, and that we had no right to interfere.

I was so alarmed, however, that I took up the matter with members of the Senate Banking and Currency Committee—the legislative father of the Board. I hoped to make the Board stop, look, and listen. I especially interested Senator Irvine Lenroot, who undertook to write to the Board asking for information.[7] In one of my memoranda to the Senator, upon which he based his correspondence, I said: "The effects of these proposed policies upon the United States mean inflation with inevitable collapse which will bring the greatest calamities upon our farmers, our workers, and legitimate business."

A lively correspondence ensued, wherein I aided the Senator. The initial letter which I drafted for the Senator to sign, and which he dispatched on December 23, 1925, contained these important passages:

I am much disturbed over the continued expansion of speculation on the New York Stock Exchange ever since the time I addressed the Board. It

[7] In preparing this material, I asked Mr. Lawrence Richey to obtain from Senator Lenroot copies of his correspondence and any memoranda which I might have given him relating to this matter. His covering letter to Mr. Richey of May 3, 1933, said:

"I may add that my letters were written after conversation with, and at the suggestion of, ex-President Hoover who furnished me with the data and assisted in their preparation."

not appear to me that the speculative purchase of large amounts of ities upon credit can be otherwise than dangerous, because it absorbs the credit funds of the country; because of the tendency of speculative fevers to extend into the commodities; and also because it must result in a collapse which will carry losses into every part of the country. . . .

. . . This gigantic expansion of credit upon which it has been carried . . . lends gravity to the situation, for its inevitable collapse would be even more dangerous to commerce and industry by virtue of its widespread character. . . . This large movement in the New York stock market has not been one of realignment of values under new investment but one of sheer speculation. . . . "Street" loans have increased nearly one billion dollars since this movement began and have now reached the gigantic total of nearly $2,700,000,000, or about 40 per cent more than any amount hitherto known in our credit history. Nor is it likely that this represents anything like all the credit being used in this outbreak of speculation. . . . We should make certain that the . . . Federal Reserve System is not a contributor to this expansion either directly or indirectly. . . . There has been a very considerable expansion . . . in security holdings of the Federal Reserve System . . . paralleling the last outburst of speculation in stocks. . . . There is connection between the credit released by the Federal Reserve System and this great increase . . . in street loans . . . because advances from the Federal Reserve are capable of great pyramiding.

What with the Senator's hints of public exposure and the opposition of Mr. Miller and myself, the proposed further inflation of credit was dropped for a while.

THE FEDERAL RESERVE CREDIT INFLATION OF 1927

However, in the spring of 1927 the same European bankers returned to the United States and with Governor Strong were most urgent that the policies of inflation of credit be resumed. They argued that the economic situation in Europe demanded more of this medicine. The United States was not in need of credit expansion. Our industry and commerce were amply supplied. What Europe needed was not credit but disarmament, balancing of budgets, harder work, and more production. But these bankers won over the majority of the Board to their proposals. A determined policy aimed at further inflating credit was entered upon over Adolph Miller's opposition.

Unfortunately at that time I was in the South managing the relief of the great Mississippi flood. When I returned in August from that job, I heard for the first time from Mr. Miller of the Board's secret action. I saw Crissinger at once. Together with Mr. James, another member of the Board, he argued against my "parochial view" of world affairs but assured me they would not let the situation get out of hand.

After my interview with Crissinger I gave him a memorandum, the gist of which indicates my views at the time:

The safety of continued prosperity will depend on caution and resistance to expansion of credit which will further stimulate speculation. . . . Our banking system can check the dangers of speculative credits. . . . The real test will be whether we can hold this prosperity without an era of speculation and extravagance with its inevitable debacle. . . . Unless our financial policies are guided with courage and wisdom this speculation . . . can only land us on the shores of depression. . . . Not since 1920 have we required . . . a more capable administration of credit facilities than now . . . inflation of credit is not the answer to European difficulties. They are far deeper than that.

At this time, again I urged President Coolidge, as I had done eighteen months before, to send for Crissinger and express alarm at the situation. Mr. Coolidge, a strict legalist, again insisted that the Reserve Board had been created by the Congress entirely independent of the Executive and that he could not interfere. The Secretary of the Treasury, Mr. Mellon, also declined and seemed to think my anxiety was alarmist and my interference unwarranted.

THE MISSISSIPPI BUBBLE OF 1927–1929

One trouble with every inflationary creation of credit is that it acts like a delayed time bomb. There is an interval of indefinite and sometimes considerable length between the injection of the stimulant and the resulting speculation. Likewise, there is an interval of a similarly indefinite length of time between the injection of the remedial serum and the lowering of the speculative fever. Once the fever gets under way it generates its own toxics.

This renewed action to inflate credit was begun by the Reserve Banks

y open market operations, and the discount rate was lowered
ist. The fever of speculation began to get out of hand fourteen
j later in the autumn of 1928. The vital relationship of this
Feu. al Reserve expansion of credit to the stock-market orgy is easily
shown.

The theoretical ratio of credit expansion through the Reserve Banks
was about ten to one when it reached the borrower. This action,
when the country was already in an optimistic mood, was greedily
seized upon by the gambling public. Speculation quickly expanded as I
had prophesied that it would. The increased tempo of the speculative
activity appeared in the increase in bank debits to individual depositors'
accounts in 141 cities—from $53,600,000,000 at the end of June, 1927, to
$82,400,000,000 eighteen months later. The volume of bank deposits
increased only slightly, illustrating the increasing turnover which typi-
fies a speculative orgy. But a more vivid proof of the inflation came
from loans to New York stockbrokers and bankers on stocks. These
rose from $3,560,000,000 in June, 1927, to $5,500,000,000 in September,
1928, to more than $8,500,000,000 in September, 1929. The effect upon
common stocks is shown in the *Federal Reserve Bulletins* by the ascent
of the index of common-stock prices from 114 in June, 1927, to 216 in
September, 1929. The prices had thus about doubled.

That commerce, industry, and agriculture gained little from the inflation is easily shown by the indexes of business, which also demonstrate
that the movement was primarily one of stock speculation and promotion, not one of expansion in the volume of business or increase in
commodity prices. Between June, 1927, and June, 1929, wholesale commodity prices rose from 94.1 to 95.2; factory employment, from 99.5 to
102.7; freight-car loading, from 104 to 108; and department store sales
(adjusted index), from 106 to 113.

The concurrent measures of the European central banks spread speculation over the other principal economic centers of the world.

There is an interesting commentary on the attempts of Mr. Miller
and myself to inject some sanity and protection of American interests
into the Reserve System. A member of the Board, Charles Hamlin,
kept a diary which is now in the Library of Congress. His record of my
intervention in the matter is far from complimentary. He confirms that

I had sought the intervention of Coolidge and Mellon. But he amply confirms my opinion of Crissinger.

It does not follow that these international banking policies were inaugurated for the personal profit of the gentlemen concerned or for that of their friends. Undoubtedly, they were acting in the hope of preventing European difficulties. But certainly, the huge budget deficits, currency inflation, vast increase in armaments, and growing military alliances which were at the root of the trouble were not to be cured by a poultice of inflated credit from the United States. I do not attribute the whole of the stock boom to mismanagement of the Federal Reserve System. But the policies adopted by that System must assume the greater responsibility.

The fact that action of such gigantic moment may be set on foot in a democracy, without adequate public consideration or check, emphasizes the dangers of undue powers in the hands of mere individuals, governmental or private.[8]

[8] An interesting summary of the contribution of Federal Reserve policies to the boom appeared five years later in the magazine *Sphere* of July, 1935, summarizing public statements by Adolph Miller, a member of the Reserve Board at that time:

"Mr. Miller, of the Federal Reserve Board, states that the easy credit policy of 1927, which was father and mother to the subsequent 1929 collapse, was originated by Governor Strong, of the New York Federal Reserve Bank, and that it did not represent a policy either developed or imposed by the Board on the Reserve Banks against their will.

"The policy was the result of a visit to this country of the Governors of foreign central banks, who unequivocally stated in New York that unless the United States did adopt it there would be an economic collapse in Europe. It was a European policy, adopted by the United States.

". . . Mr. Miller states that after waiting for the individual Reserve Banks to initiate a policy of safety, the Board, in February, 1929, took matters into its own hands, adopted a policy of 'direct pressure' and issued a 'warning' to the public. It did so, says Mr. Miller, because its anxiety over the situation had become very great. That was one month before Mr. Hoover was inaugurated as President.

"The fact seems to be that the Board, in January, 1928, intended to curb the speculation, but was overridden by President Coolidge, who issued his famous statement from the White House that the speculation was not dangerous and merely reflected the growing wealth and power of the United States.

"The Board only began issuing warnings when Mr. Hoover was about to take office; and it was safe to do so then because the Board knew that Mr. Hoover, from 1926 on, had been protesting that the money policy of the Reserve System was certain to bring about disaster and calamity. Mr. Hoover, before and after he took office, was struggling desperately to curb credit extravagance. He wanted to deflate the utter extravagance then rampant, and his every influence in the Presidency was in that direction. The rec-

It was difficult for the public to believe that such griefs and tragedies lay hidden in so obscure a process as credit inflation when forced on an already optimistic people. It set the stage for wicked manipulations and promotions of stocks. Its collapse brought hunger and despair to millions of homes. It destroyed the savings of millions of families.

It also furnished ammunition to radicals for attacks on the whole American system. The exhibition of waste, fraud, and greed which flowed from this artificial credit inflation appears in their literature as a typical phenomenon of our free civilization; whereas it was the exception.

There are crimes far worse than murder for which men should be reviled and punished.

SECONDARY CAUSES OF OUR MARKET BOOM

There were some secondary causes contributing to the boom.

In 1928 the Committee on Economic Changes, which I had appointed under the chairmanship of Mr. Arch Shaw, gave a warning of another but much smaller cloud coming out of the economic sea. They stated that from our very increase in efficiency we might get some readjustments. They reported that, from an increase in production efficiency of some 30 per cent per person during the 1920's, very little had gone to decrease prices of industrial products. The average price level had remained about the same from 1922 to 1929. The Committee found that about three-fourths of the gains from increased efficiency and decreasing costs had gone to increased industrial wages and one-fourth to increased profits. The buying power of the industrial workers had been increased, and increased profits had become a stimulant to speculation. But as labor and business absorbed the benefits of increased efficiency, such other groups as the farmers and the "white-collar" classes benefited only by a small increase in buying power. Therefore, these groups could not absorb the increased production of industry. To put it another way, had there been a decrease in price levels, the nonindustrial groups could have bought more goods, thus sustaining production.

ord will show that he became the victim of a policy that was anathema to him the whole time it was in operation. Had the Administration listened to him in 1926, Mr. Miller would not now have to be apologizing for a whole series of disastrous developments."

In consequence, during the late twenties, we ran into relatively distorted production of some industrial goods, and a readjustment of income between groups had become necessary.

There were some other secondary economic pressures also present. During the war, building construction, industrial equipment, and capital goods generally had to be suspended to make way for war supplies and war labor. Coming out of the war, we had two capital goods economies—one carrying on the immediate need of a growing population and industry, and the other busily catching up with the war suspensions, a sort of super-layer on construction economy. For instance, we needed, say, 400,000 new dwellings annually for population growth and for the replacement of worn-out buildings. We were compelled to increase construction to about 800,000 houses to catch up with losses during the war and to meet the current demand. This super-layer of construction applied in many directions other than just housing, for example to power, railways, highways, and many capital goods. But when we had caught up with the lag that whole segment of our economy slumped. The halt came in 1928–1929, and would itself have required some economic adjustment had there been no other troubles. This phenomenon may offer some explanation for the previous postwar ten-year cycle of depressions.

Another of our domestic ills was a weak banking system, unable to take shocks, which I describe more fully later on.

But, standing alone, even the stock speculation, the other domestic readjustments, and our weak banking system, could not have created the degree of ultimate wreckage that occurred in the United States, had we not had the panic in Europe. The prospect of that collapse was the apparition that stood beside all of us who knew something of the situation. And fear of it had to guide many of our steps in the earlier stages.

The "New Era" economic philosophy was due for a jolt.

CHAPTER 2

∽♦∿♦∿♦∿

WE ATTEMPT TO STOP THE ORGY OF SPECULATION

By the last months of 1928, Benjamin Strong of the Federal Reserve Bank of New York had died and Daniel Crissinger of the Federal Reserve Board had resigned. Roy Young had been appointed by President Coolidge to the Governorship of the Reserve Board. Young was an able, courageous, and cooperative man. Prior to my inauguration as President I conferred several times with him and found him fully alive to the situation. He agreed to use the full powers of the Board to strangle the speculative movement.

On February 7, 1929, the Board issued public notice of drastic "direct action" to the banks to restrain indirect use of Federal Reserve credits for speculative loans. But the stimulant had been too successful. The fever was beyond control.

Moreover, the effect of the Board's action was greatly minimized by an unfortunate press statement by President Coolidge, a few days before he left office, in which he assured the country that its prosperity was "absolutely sound," and that stocks were "cheap at current prices."

The stock boom was blowing great guns when I came into the White House. Being fully alive to the danger inherent in this South Sea Bubble and its inevitable reaction, my first interest was to get it under restraint. It was obvious that there had to be vast liquidation of paper values, and especially a liquidation of the mental attitude of people mesmerized by the idea of speculation as a basis of living and of national progress.

The initial difficulty was a lack of government authority, except such as could be exerted by the Federal Reserve System. To ask Congress for

powers to interfere in the stock market was futile and, in any ev\
the President to dictate the price of stocks was an expansion of ⸺
dential power without any established constitutional basis.

I, therefore, resolved to attack the problem from several direction⸺
in addition to securing cooperation from the Federal Reserve System.

To create a spirit of caution in the public, I sent individually for the
editors and publishers of major newspapers and magazines and requested them systematically to warn the country against speculation
and the unduly high price of stocks. Most of them responded with
strong editorials. This had no appreciable effect, however.

Secretary of the Treasury Mellon and others, at my request, issued
repeated statements urging the public to convert their stocks into bonds
and advising other forms of caution. This also had no effect.

My second line of attack, six weeks after my inauguration, was to
request Henry M. Robinson, President of the First Security National
Bank of Los Angeles, to go to New York and to talk in my name to the
promoters and bankers behind the market. He fully agreed with me as
to the dangers of the situation. But the New York bankers all scoffed at
the idea that the market was not "sound." They were certain this was a
"New Era," to which old economic experience did not apply. To prove
it, Thomas Lamont of Morgan's wrote me a long memorandum which
makes curious reading today.

My third effort was to send for Richard Whitney, the President of
the New York Stock Exchange, and urge that the Exchange itself curb
the manipulation of stocks. I informed him that I had no desire to
stretch the powers of the Federal government by legislation to regulate
the Stock Exchange—that authority rested only in the Governor of
New York, Franklin D. Roosevelt. I stated that I preferred to let
American institutions and the states govern themselves, and that the
Exchange had full power under its charter to control its own members
and to prevent it from being used for manipulation against the public
interest. Mr. Whitney made profuse promises, but did nothing.[1]

Through the use of some Federal powers in post-office fraud matters
we did stop a flock of bucket-shop operators.

A dispute arose between Governor Young of the Federal Reserve

[1] He was subsequently sent to the penitentiary for mishandling trust funds.

Board and important banks as to whether or not the discount rates should be raised as a brake on speculation. Governor Young contended that to raise the rate simply gave the banks larger returns by penalizing commercial business. He contended that the banks could curb loans for speculation, just by simply refusing to make such loans.

I held with the Governor, who now proceeded by direct action. He issued orders to the Reserve Banks to refuse rediscounts to banks which were lending largely on stocks. Their practice was to rediscount their commercial bills at the Reserve Banks, then loan the proceeds to the market.

At one moment the Federal Reserve Board's action forced money rates for speculative purposes up to 20 per cent per annum. But people who dreamed of 100 per cent profit in a week were not deterred by an interest rate of 20 per cent a year. Mr. Young fully demonstrated the futility of the idea upon which the Reserve System had been founded that it could control booms. Control of interest rates could not stop them. When the public becomes mad with greed and is rubbing the Aladdin's lamp of sudden fortune, no little matter of interest rates is effective.

We did at one time almost secure a stranglehold on the stock market when the Reserve Banks had so tightened the call-loan situation that a moment arrived when there was no money available to the market. A break seemed inevitable. But Charles E. Mitchell, President of the National City Bank of New York, announced that in this emergency his bank would furnish the deficient credit.

Senator Glass expressed my feelings when he said of Mr. Mitchell:

He avows his superior obligation to a frantic stock market over against the obligations of his oath as a director of the New York Federal Reserve Bank. . . .

Mr. Mitchell's proclamation is a challenge to the authority and the announced policy of the Federal Reserve Board. The challenge ought to be promptly met and courageously dealt with.

The Board should ask for the immediate resignation of Mr. Mitchell as a Class A director of the New York Federal Reserve Bank. . . .

ۗle country has been aghast for months and months at the pectacle of excessive stock gambling, and when the Federal Re-ᑛ mildly seeks to abate the danger by an administrative policy, fully sanctioned by law, rather than by a prohibitive advance in rediscount rates, which might penalize the legitimate business of the entire country, an officer of the System issues a defiance and engages in an attempt to vitiate the policy of the Federal Reserve Board.[2]

The Federal Reserve Board on August 6th finally increased the discount rate to 6 per cent. It had no effect whatsoever on this Mississippi Bubble.

All our efforts to secure an orderly readjustment covered six months and perhaps served somewhat to slow up the orgy. The real trouble was that the bellboys, the waiters, and the host of unknowing people, as well as the financial community, had become so obsessed with the constant press reports of great winnings that the movement was uncontrollable.

The stock-market slump on October 29, 1929, came seven months after I entered the White House.

When the inevitable black morning of their dream dawned, the exponents of the "New Era" were surprised. Promptly we had a flood of reassuring statements to the anxious speculators from economists, bankers, the press, and labor leaders. Professor Irving Fisher of Yale said that stocks had not even reached their full values. Charles E. Mitchell of the National City Bank announced that "the reaction had outrun itself." The *New York Times* praised the soundness of the financial structure. Mr. Rockefeller, Mr. Morgan, Mr. Raskob all announced that they were buying stocks. William Green of the American Federation of Labor declared, "In a few months we will be back to normal." A left-wing economist, Stuart Chase, said, "The stock market will not affect general prosperity."

I am not a pessimistic soul, but I was not impressed by any of this optimism. The press insistently urged that I make a statement. Obviously, as President, I had no business to make things worse in the middle of a crash. Loath to speak of the stock market, I offered as encouragement a short statement on our progress in the productive system and the long-view strength of the country.

The normal business cycle periodically must readjust disequilibriums which are a part of the rhythm of any growing free economy. But this

[2] *New York Times,* March 29, 1929.

was more than rhythms. Our overpriced stocks and real estate were bound to come down; and the degree of down is influenced by the degree of up—which means a descent from overvalue to undervalue. The boom had lifted securities and real estate far up and, to this degree, was to deepen further the slump by the downward swing.

Within a few weeks the slump began seriously to affect industrial employment and farm prices, confronting us with problems of the first order.

CHAPTER 3

OUR WEAK AMERICAN BANKING SYSTEM

Before I proceed with this narrative, I must describe in some detail a weakness which increased our difficulties. Our banking system was the weakest link in our whole economic system.

As I have said, the American people had been living for some years under an illusion of the absolute security to be had from the Federal Reserve System. We were slow to realize other dangers in our banking system. These dangers were present in our inexpressibly feeble and badly organized deposit banking, credit, and security promotion structure, enhanced by lack of scruples among some leaders.

As I look back over our whole era of boom and slump, and our passage through the valley of the shadow after the European panic, I feel that our own banking and financial system was the worst part of the dismal tragedy with which I had to deal.

I can truthfully say that I recognized some of the weaknesses of the system from the first. Time and again from my first Annual Message to Congress, I urged the Congress to reform the banking laws to make depositors safe.

The public had become callous to bank failures because we had had over 4,000 such failures in the eight good years before the depression. More than 10,000 deposit institutions were to disappear in the five years after 1929, despite governmental props under the banking system. Their mortality rate was about 40 times that of industrial and commercial firms. But our people were so used to bank failures that it took a major storm to arouse public demand for reorganization.

Among all our banking ills, I give a few of outstanding importance.

1. Our banking system was the outgrowth of a muddle of good and

bad laws and the high spirit of enterprise in our people. There were 52 different bank regulatory systems, one for National Banks, one for the other member banks of the Federal Reserve System, and forty-nine others for state banks and the District of Columbia. The Federal regulatory systems were much better than those of the states. The Federal inspection system was good, as far as it went, but the states' systems shaded all the way from good to purely political. The Federal Reserve and National Bank inspections covered only a minority of the number of banks.

2. There were too many banks. In 1929 there were about 25,000 commercial banks, trust companies, and savings banks entrusted with the people's deposits. Of the commercial banks, 7,500 were National Banks and 14,300 state. There simply were not enough capable bankers to go around among 25,000 banks. And there were some very evil ones in some large banks.

3. Of these deposit institutions, more than 3,500 had less than $100,000 capital and, of these, some 1,500 had less than $25,000 capital. A safe banking life, including payment of bank salaries, simply could not be led on such capital.

4. All commercial banks were permitted to loan excessive amounts of demand deposits on long-term mortgages and to invest in long-term bonds. When stress came, long-term assets could not be quickly liquidated, and depositors' demands had to be met by calling in the short-term business loans. That paralyzed business and employment. The supposed restriction on withdrawal of "time" deposits and their use for long-term lending amounted to nothing, for if the banker refused to cash a time deposit before due date, his bank fell under suspicion.

5. Our agricultural areas must have mortgage capital from the great centers to buy farms and equipment. They must have seasonal capital to raise livestock, to plant, harvest, and market the ground crops. In the normal working of the banking system, the banks and loan concerns in the farm area borrowed seasonally from the nearest cities. These cities borrowed in turn from New York and other large centers. The moment depression came, the city banks drew in funds from their country correspondents or refused to furnish their usual needs. The insurance companies abruptly ceased lending on mortgages, and fore-

closed wholesale those in default. As a result, farmers and small business men were the immediate victims.

6. Only one-third of the total number of banks were members of the Federal Reserve System, and therefore only one-third had the safety valve of rediscount privilege with the Reserve Banks. Moreover, the rediscount privilege was limited to short-term commercial paper. Those banks also had no method of realizing on mortgages. In the slump they could sell many bond holdings in the market, but only at a loss and often for less than their true value.

7. The theory of the Federal Reserve System can well be repeated here. The idea was that speculation could be checked by increasing interest rates, and restricting credit by open-market operations; and on the other hand, that business could be activated by decreasing interest rates and expanding credit by open-market operations. Experience had amply demonstrated that decreased rates and open-market operations could stimulate speculation in good times; but we were soon to prove that they could not activate business in bad times. Thus these activities proved incapable of either checking booms or checking depression. And the system stimulated a false sense of security which in itself led to excesses.

8. Many of the larger banks had "affiliates" through which they speculated in stocks and engaged in stock promotion, indirectly using their depositors' money with ultimately great losses.

9. Nor was our financial weakness solely in the banks. Throughout the whole business of providing capital for our economic life there ran a pollution—the habit of making money by manipulation and promotion of securities. And that promotion too often disregarded the merits of the goods it sold. In addition, the financial world, instead of providing merely the lubricants of commerce and industry, had often set itself up to milk the system. Worse still, instead of being financial advisers to commerce and industry, the financiers had, in many cases, set themselves up to dictate the management of it.

That the fault lay not in our economic system as a whole, but in the singular weakness of the banking system, is evidenced by the fact that the 5,100 banks which failed in the three-year depression period represented 25 per cent of the number of banks. Yet in the same period the failure of industrial enterprise represented only 1.5 per cent of the number of concerns.

That it was possible, by proper organization and inspection, to have a banking system in which depositors were safe was demonstrated by Britain, Canada, Australia, and South Africa, where no consequential bank failure took place in the depression. Their governments gave no guarantees to depositors. Their economic shocks were as great as ours —or worse. But their banks did not try to manage industry or to promote stocks, and the British had evolved methods of restraining a large part of their irresponsible promoters without burning down the house.

If we had possessed adequate banking laws and a sound financial system, we should never have needed the Reconstruction Finance Corporation, the Home Loan Banks, and the half-dozen other government props to credit, which we were compelled to introduce later on.

It is not out of place to present here my opinion of the whole financial system, written on February 17, 1933, to my friend Arch W. Shaw. It was written after the three years' ordeal with banks and before the bank panic of March which greeted Mr. Roosevelt's inauguration. It was intended to be a sort of last will and testament on our economic system:

Dear Mr. Shaw:

I have your request that I should state in writing what I said to you a few days ago as to the broad conclusions I have formed from experience of the last four years as to the functioning of our economic system. It is, of course, impossible in the time I have left at my disposal or within the reach of a short statement, to cover all phases of the problem.

Our whole economic system naturally divides itself into production, distribution, and finance. By finance I mean every phase of investment, banking, and credit. And at once I may say that the major fault in the system as it stands is in the financial system.

As to production, our system of stimulated individual effort, by its creation of enterprise, development of skill, and discoveries in science and invention, has resulted in production of the greatest quantity of commodities and services of the most infinite variety that were ever known in the history of man. . . . We can say, without qualification, that the motivation of production based on private initiative has proved the very mother of plenty. It has faults, for humanity is not without faults. Difficulties arise from overexpansion and adjustment to the march of labor-saving devices, but in broad result it stands in sharp contrast with the failure of the system of production, as in its greater exemplar—Russia—where after fifteen years of trial, in a land of as great natural resources as ours, that system has never produced in a single year an adequate supply of even the barest necessities in food and clothing for its people.

In the larger sense our system of distribution in normal times is sufficient and effective. Our transportation and communication is rapid and universal. The trades distribute the necessities of life at profits which represent a remarkably small percentage of their value.

The system moves supplies of everything into remotest villages and crossroads; it feeds and clothes great cities each. day with the regularity and assurance which cause never a thought or anxiety. The diffusion of commodities and services in a social sense has faults. In normal times out of our 120,000,000 people there are a few millions who conscientiously work and strive, yet do not receive that minimum of commodities and services to which they have a just right as earnest members of the community.

There is another fringe of a few hundred thousand who receive more than they deserve for the effort they make. But taxes are furnishing rapid correction in this quarter. . . . The enlarging social sense of our people is furnishing the impulse to correction of faults. . . . It is not to be brought about by destruction of the system.

The last four years have shown unquestionably that it is mainly the third element of our system—that is, finance—which has failed and produced by far the largest part of the demoralization of our systems of production and distribution with its thousand tragedies which wring the heart of the nation. I am not insensible to the disturbing war inheritances, of our expansion of production, nor to the effect of increased labor-saving devices on employment, but these are minor notes of discord compared to that arising from failure of the financial system. This failure has been evidenced in two directions: that is, the lack of organization for domestic purposes and the weakness . . . through which we have been infinitely more demoralized by repeated shocks from abroad.

The credit system in all its phases should be merely a lubricant to the systems of production and distribution. It is not its function to control these systems. That it should be so badly organized, that the volume of currency and credit, whether long or short term, should expand and shrink irrespective of the needs of production and distribution; that its stability should be the particular creature of emotional fear or optimism; that it should be insecure; that it should dominate and not be subordinate to production and distribution—all this is intolerable if we are to maintain our civilization. Yet these things have happened on a gigantic scale. We could have weathered through these failures with some losses and could have secured reorganization as we went along. . . . The rain of blows from abroad, however, on the system of such weakness has wholly prostrated us by a second phase of this depression which came from a collapse of the financial systems in Europe.

In this system I am not referring to individual banks or financial institutions. Many of them have shown distinguished courage and ability. On the contrary, I am referring to the system itself, which is so organized, or so lacking in organization, that it fails in its primary function of stable and steady service to the production and distribution system. In an emergency its very mechanism increases the jeopardy and paralyzes action of the community.

Clearly we must secure sound organization of our financial system as a prerequisite of the functioning of the whole economic system. The first steps in that system are sound currency, economy in government, balanced governmental budgets, whether national or local. The second step is an adequate separation of commercial banking from investment banking, whether in mortgages, bonds or other forms of long-term securities. The third step is to secure effective coordination between national and state systems. We cannot endure fifty odd separate regulatory systems which are both conflicting and weakening. We must accept the large view that the mismanagement, instability, and bad functioning of any single institution affects the stability of some part of production and distribution and a multitude of other financial institutions. Therefore there must be cooperation within the financial system enforced by control and regulation by the government, that will assure that this segment of our economic system does not, through faulty organization and action, bring our people again to these tragedies of unemployment and loss of homes which are today a stigma upon national life. We cannot endure that enormous sums of the people's savings shall be poured out either at home or abroad without making the promoter responsible for his every statement. We cannot endure that men will either manipulate the savings of the people so abundantly evidenced in recent exposures.

That it has been necessary for the government, through emergency action to protect us (while holding a wealth of gold) from being taken off the gold standard, to erect gigantic credit institutions with the full pledge of government credit to save the nation from chaos through this failure of the financial system, that it is necessary for us to devise schemes of clearing-house protections and to install such temporary devices throughout the nation, is full proof of all I have said. That is the big question. If we can solve this, then we can take in hand the faults of the production and distribution systems— and many problems in the social and political system. But this financial system simply must be made to function first.

There is a phase of all this that must cause anxiety to every American. Democracy cannot survive unless it is master in its own house. The economic system cannot survive unless there are real restraints upon unbridled greed or dishonest reach for power. Greed and dishonesty are not attributes solely of our system—they are human and will infect socialism or any ism. But if our production and distribution systems are to function we must have effective restraints on manipulation, greed, and dishonesty. Our Democracy has proved its ability to put its unruly occupants under control, but never until their conduct has been a public scandal and a stench. For instance, you will recollect my own opposition to government operation of electric power, for that is a violation of the very fundamentals of our system; but parallel with it I asked and preached for regulation of it to protect the public from its financial manipulation. We gained the Power Commission, but Congress refused it the regulatory authority we asked.

I have time and again warned, asked, and urged the reorganization of the banking system. The inertia of the Democracy is never more marked than in promotion of what seem abstract or indirect ideas. The recent scandals are the result. Democracy, always lagging, will no doubt now act and may act destructively to the system, for it is mad. It is this lag, the failure to act in time for prevention which I fear most in the sane advancement of economic life. For an outraged people may destroy the whole economic system rather than reconstruct and control the segment which has failed in its function. I trust the new Administration will recognize the difference between crime and economic functioning; between constructive prevention and organization as contrasted with destruction.

During these four years I have been fighting to preserve this fundamental system of production and distribution from destruction through collapse and bad functioning of the financial system. Time only can tell if we have succeeded. Success means higher and higher standards of living, greater comfort, more opportunity for intellectual, moral, and spiritual development. Failure means a new form of the Middle Ages.

If we succeed in the job of preservation, certainly the next effort before the country is to reorganize the financial system so that all this will not happen again. We must organize for advance in the other directions, but that is another subject.

CHAPTER 4

FEDERAL GOVERNMENT RESPONSIBILITIES AND FUNCTIONS IN ECONOMIC CRISES

With the October–November stock-market crash the primary question at once arose as to whether the President and the Federal government should undertake to mitigate and remedy the evils stemming from it. No President before had ever believed there was a governmental responsibility in such cases. No matter what the urging on previous occasions, Presidents steadfastly had maintained that the Federal government was apart from such eruptions; they had always been left to blow themselves out. Presidents Van Buren, Grant, Cleveland and Theodore Roosevelt had all remained aloof. A few helpful gestures, however, had been made in the past. On one such occasion it was in the form of a little currency relief; on another, the deposit of Federal money in some banks; and there was the crisis when Cleveland announced his fidelity to the gold standard to steady a panicky public.

Because of this lack of governmental experience, therefore, we had to pioneer a new field. As a matter of fact there was little economic knowledge to guide us. The previous great postwar depression of the 1870's had left almost no real economic information except as to consequences in prices, production, and employment. I may reiterate that it is not given even to Presidents to see the future. Economic storms do not develop all at once, and they change without notice. In my three years of the slump and depression they changed repeatedly for the worse—and with the speed of lightning. We could have done better— in retrospect.

The break in the stock market in late October, 1929, was followed by succeeding slumps until, by the end of November, industrial stocks had fallen to 60 per cent of their high point. Even so, the business world refused, for some time after the crash, to believe that the danger was any more than that of run-of-the-mill, temporary slumps such as had occurred at three- to seven-year intervals in the past.

However, we in the administration took a more serious view of the immediate future, partly because of our knowledge of the fearful inflation of stock-market credit, and, in the longer view, because of our fear of the situation of European economy. I perhaps knew the weaknesses of the latter better than most people from my experience in Europe during 1919 and my knowledge of the economic consequences of the Versailles Treaty.

Two schools of thought quickly developed within our administration discussions.

First was the "leave it alone liquidationists" headed by Secretary of the Treasury Mellon, who felt that government must keep its hands off and let the slump liquidate itself. Mr. Mellon had only one formula: "Liquidate labor, liquidate stocks, liquidate the farmers, liquidate real estate." He insisted that, when the people get an inflation brainstorm, the only way to get it out of their blood is to let it collapse. He held that even a panic was not altogether a bad thing. He said: "It will purge the rottenness out of the system. High costs of living and high living will come down. People will work harder, live a more moral life. Values will be adjusted, and enterprising people will pick up the wrecks from less competent people." He often used the expression, "There is a mighty lot of real estate lying around the United States which does not know who owns it," referring to excessive mortgages.

At great length, Mr. Mellon recounted to me his recollection of the great depression of the seventies which followed the Civil War. (He started in his father's bank a few years after that time.) He told of the tens of thousands of farms that had been foreclosed; of railroads that had almost wholly gone into the hands of receivers; of the few banks that had come through unscathed; of many men who were jobless and mobs that roamed the streets. He told me that his father had gone to England during that time and had cut short his visit when he received word that the orders for steel were pouring toward the closed furnaces; by the time he got back, confidence was growing on every hand; suddenly the panic had ended, and in twelve months the whole system was again working at full speed.

I, of course, reminded the Secretary that back in the seventies an untold amount of suffering did take place which might have been prevented; that our economy had been far simpler sixty years ago, when we were 75 per cent an agricultural people contrasted with 30 per cent now; that unemployment during the earlier crisis had been mitigated by the return of large numbers of the unemployed to relatives on the farms; and that farm economy itself had been largely self-contained. But he shook his head with the observation that human nature had not changed in sixty years.

Secretary Mellon was not hard-hearted. In fact he was generous and sympathetic with all suffering. He felt there would be less suffering if his course were pursued. The real trouble with him was that he insisted that this was just an ordinary boom–slump and would not take the European situation seriously. And he, like the rest of us, underestimated the weakness in our banking system.

But other members of the Administration, also having economic responsibilities—Under Secretary of the Treasury Mills, Governor Young of the Reserve Board, Secretary of Commerce Lamont and Secretary of Agriculture Hyde—believed with me that we should use the powers of government to cushion the situation. To our minds, the prime needs were to prevent bank panics such as had marked the earlier slumps, to mitigate the privation among the unemployed and the farmers which would certainly ensue. Panic had always left a trail of unnecessary bankruptcies which injured the productive forces of the country. But, even more important, the damage from a panic would include huge losses by innocent people, in their honestly invested savings, their businesses, their homes, and their farms.

The record will show that we went into action within ten days and were steadily organizing each week and month thereafter to meet the changing tides—mostly for the worse. In this earlier stage we determined that the Federal government should use all of its powers:

(a) to avoid the bank depositors' and credit panics which had so generally accompanied previous violent slumps;

(b) to cushion slowly, by various devices, the inevitable liquidation of false values so as to prevent widespread bankruptcy and the losses of homes and productive power;

(c) to give aid to agriculture;

(d) to mitigate unemployment and to relieve those in actual distress;

(e) to prevent industrial conflict and social disorder;

(f) to preserve the financial strength of the United States government, our credit and our currency, as the economic Gibraltar of the earth—in other words, to assure that America should meet every foreign debt, and keep the dollar ringing true on every counter in the world;

(g) to advance much-needed economic and social reforms as fast as could be, without such drastic action as would intensify the illness of an already sick nation;

(h) to sustain the morale and courage of the people in order that their initiative should remain unimpaired, and to secure from the people themselves every effort for their own salvation;

(i) to adhere rigidly to the Constitution and the fundamental liberties of the people.

While fearful, we could not know at this early stage to what extent the European situation might affect us.

SUSTAINING MORALE IN THE PEOPLE

One of the duties of the times was to maintain confidence of our people in the future. With the powerful spiritual and economic strength of the United States, this could be only a passing phase in the life of the nation. There was a multitude of gloomy prophets who depicted that the era of progress was exhausted, that our way of life was nearing an end, that our social and political system was disappearing. The minor but shrill notes of the Socialists and Communists added other discords. All these tones of gloom and discouragement grew louder and louder as the depression deepened.

Some indication of our efforts to counteract these forces can be given in a few quotations.

In a radio address on February 12, 1931, I said:

It is appropriate that I should speak from this room in the White House where Lincoln strived and accomplished his great service to our country.

His invisible presence dominates these halls, ever recalling that infinite patience and that indomitable will which fought and won the fight for those firmer foundations and greater strength to government by the people. From these windows he looked out upon that great granite shaft which was then in construction to mark the country's eternal tribute to the courage and uncompromising strength of the founder of the Union of states.

Here are the very chairs in which he meditated upon his problems. Above the mantelpiece hangs his portrait with his Cabinet, and upon this fireplace is written:

"In this room Abraham Lincoln signed the Emancipation Proclamation of January 1, 1863, whereby 4,000,000 slaves were given their freedom and slavery forever prohibited in these United States."

It was here that he toiled by day and by night that this Union created by the fathers might be preserved and that slavery might be ended. . . .

The Federal government has assumed many new responsibilities since Lincoln's time, and will probably assume more in the future. . . .

Due to lack of caution in business and to the impact of forces from an outside world, one-half of which is involved in social and political revolution, the march of our prosperity has been retarded. We are projected into temporary unemployment, losses, and hardships. In a nation rich in resources, many people were faced with hunger and cold through no fault of their own. Our national resources are not only material supplies and material wealth but a spiritual and moral wealth in kindliness, in compassion, in a sense of obligation of neighbor to neighbor and a realization of responsibility by industry, by business, and the community for its social security and its social welfare.

The evidence of our ability to solve great problems outside of government action and the degree of moral strength with which we emerge from this period will be determined by whether the individuals and the local communities continue to meet their responsibilities. . . .

Victory over this depression and over our other difficulties will be won by the resolution of our people to fight their own battles in their own communities, by stimulating their ingenuity to solve their own problems, by taking new courage to be masters of their own destiny in the struggle of life. . . .

In an address at Valley Forge on May 30, 1931, I said:

. . . It was not the glory of battle for which these fields are remembered. No great battle was fought here. It was not the pomp of victory, for no martial triumph was won here. It was not the scene where peace was signed by which independence of a great nation was won. It was not the tombs of courageous men who, facing the enemy, gave the supreme sacrifice for their country to which we bow in reverence. A thousand other fields mark the courage, the glory, the valor, the skill, the martial triumph of our race. Yet the instinct and the judgment of our people after the abrasion of the years have appraised this place as a foremost shrine in the War of Independence. . . . It is a shrine to the things of the spirit and of the soul.

It was the transcendent fortitude and steadfastness of these men who in adversity and in suffering through the darkest hour of our history held faithful to an ideal. Here men endured that a nation might live.

*   *   *

. . . The American people are going through another Valley Forge at this time. To each and every one of us it is an hour of unusual stress and trial. You have each one your special cause of anxiety. So, too, have I. The whole nation is beset with difficulties. . . . These temporary reverses in the march of progress have been in part the penalty of excesses of greed, of failure of crops, and the malign inheritances of the Great War and a storm of other world forces beyond our control. Their far-reaching effects have fallen heavily upon many who were in no wise concerned with their causes. Many have lost the savings of a lifetime, many are unemployed, all know the misgivings of doubt and grave concern for the future.

No one who reviews the past and realizes the vast strength of our people can doubt that this, like a score of similar experiences in our history, is a passing trial. From it will come a greater knowledge of the weaknesses of our system, and from this knowledge must come the courage and wisdom to improve and strengthen us for the future. Numerous are the temptations under the distress of the day to turn aside from our true national purposes and from wise national policies and fundamental ideals of the men who builded our Republic. Never was the lure of the rosy path to every panacea and of easy ways to imagined security more tempting. . . .

The Revolution, of which Valley Forge was the darkest but perhaps the most glorious moment, was fought not alone for national independence but to retain our freedom to continue unhampered the most promising social experiment in all human history. . . . It brought America to a greatness unparalleled in the history of the world.

* * *

Valley Forge met such a challenge to steadfastness in times and terms of war. Our test is to meet this challenge in times and terms of peace. It is the same challenge. It is the same test of steadfastness of will, of clarity of thought, of resolution of character, of fixity of purpose, of loyalty to ideals, and of unshaken conviction that they will prevail. We are enduring sufferings, and we are assailed by temptations. We, too, are writing a new chapter in American history. If we weaken, as Washington did not, we shall be writing the introduction to the decline of American character and the fall of American institutions. If we are firm and farsighted, as were Washington and his men, we shall be writing the introduction to a yet more glorious epoch in our Nation's progress.

* * *

Freedom was won here by fortitude, not by the flash of the sword. Valley Forge is our American synonym for the trial of human character through privation and suffering, and it is the symbol of the triumph of the American soul. If those few thousand men endured that long winter of privation and suffering, humiliated by the despair of their countrymen, and deprived of support save their own indomitable will, yet held their countrymen to the faith, and by that holding held fast the freedom of America, what right have we to be of little faith?

In an address at Indianapolis on June 15, 1931, I said:

For the first time in history the Federal government has taken an extensive and positive part in mitigating the effects of depression and expediting recovery. I have conceived that if we would preserve our democracy this leadership must take the part not of attempted dictatorship, but of organizing cooperation in the constructive forces of the community and of stimulating every element of initiative and self-reliance in the country. There is no sudden stroke of either governmental or private action which can dissolve these world difficulties; patient constructive action in a multitude of directions is the strategy of success. This battle is upon a thousand fronts. . . . Some . . . people . . . demand abrupt change . . . in our American system. . . . Others have indomitable confidence that by some legerdemain we can legislate ourselves out of a world-wide depression. Such views are as accurate as the belief we can exorcise a Caribbean hurricane by statutory law. . . .

With the sweep of the economic hurricane from Europe, voices in the country vehemently demanded more violent action by the Federal government. Many of them were advocating collectivist ideas gleaned from the Socialists, the Communists, and the Fascists. Some even cried for dictatorship. I expressed my views on various occasions, but a summing up on August 11, 1932, will indicate what they were:

The function of the Federal government in these times is to use its reserve powers and its strength for the protection of citizens and local governments by supporting our institutions against forces beyond their control. It is not the function of the government to relieve individuals of their responsibilities to their neighbors, or to relieve private institutions of their responsibilities to the public, or of local government to the states, or of state governments to the Federal government. In giving that protection and that aid the Federal government must insist that all of them meet their responsibilities in full. It is vital that the programs of the government shall not compete with or replace any of them but shall add to their initiative and their strength. It is vital that by the use of public revenues and public credit in emergency the Nation shall be strengthened and not weakened.

. . . It does not follow, because our difficulties are stupendous, because there are some souls timorous enough to doubt the validity and effectiveness of our ideals and our system, that we must turn to a state-controlled or state-directed social or economic system in order to cure our troubles. That is not liberalism; it is tyranny. It is the regimentation of men under autocratic bureaucracy with all its extinction of liberty, of hope, and of opportunity. No man of understanding says that our system works perfectly. It does not. The human race is not perfect. Nevertheless, the movement of a true civilization is toward freedom rather than regimentation. This is our ideal.

Ofttimes the tendency of democracy in presence of national danger is to strike blindly, to listen to demagogues and slogans, all of which would destroy and would not save. We have refused to be stampeded into such courses. . . .

Our emergency measures of the last three years form a definite strategy dominated in the background by these American principles and ideals, and forming a continuous campaign waged against the forces of destruction on an ever widening or constantly shifting front.

Thus we have held that the Federal government should in the presence of great national danger use its powers to give leadership to the initiative, the courage, and the fortitude of the people themselves; but it must insist upon individual, community, and state responsibility . . . to supplement and strengthen the initiative and enterprise of the people. That they must, directly or indirectly, serve all the people. Above all, that they should be set up in such form that, once the emergency is passed, they can and must be demobilized and withdrawn, leaving our governmental, economic, and social structure strong and wholesome.

We have not feared boldly to adopt unprecedented measures to meet the unprecedented violence of the storm. . . .

These programs, unparalleled in the history of depressions in any country and in any time, to care for distress, to provide employment, to aid agriculture, to maintain the financial stability of the country, to safeguard the savings of the people, to protect their homes, are not in the past tense—they are in action. . . .

CHAPTER 5

A SUMMARY OF THE EVOLUTION OF THE DEPRESSION

To provide a clear economic perspective of the depression, I will summarize its different phases—as they were definitely different—and then give a detailed account of each. The depression divided itself roughly into six successive periods, or phases. Each phase began with new destructive forces; each had its own acute crisis. As each developed we undertook new measures to ward it off, to cushion its effects and to restore the constructive forces in our economic life. Except for the last phase, each ended in an upturn and a brief hope that the worst was over.

THE FIVE PHASES DURING MY ADMINISTRATION

The first phase spanned the seventeen months from the stock-market crash in October, 1929, to April, 1931. This was a period of a comparatively mild domestic readjustment, such as the country had experienced before. Unemployment of the family breadwinners rose to about 2,000,000, or probably not more than 1,000,000 over the normal. By January, 1931, we had paid the price for our own economic misdeeds and were convalescing. We made steady upward progress from January until April, 1931, when the earthquake of financial panic reached us from Central Europe.

The second phase of the depression comprised the four months from April through July, 1931, when we suffered the first quake from the financial eruption in Continental Europe. This was a period when heavy blows rained on our convalescing economic system. The remedies we applied, however, stopped the development of panic, and again we had a flash of hope for recovery. That hope lasted less than a month. This was merely a preliminary to a still greater shock from abroad.

The depression's third phase also covered about four months, but the shocks were more severe than the previous ones. They began with the difficulties of the British in August, 1931, which culminated in their abandonment of the gold standard and their suspension of payments of most foreign obligations, public and private. During this period a score of countries abandoned the gold standard. The number of families in the United States without employed breadwinners increased to about 4,000,000. Purchases of our farm products from Europe practically ceased; prices of farm products slumped badly; banks were toppling all around us; and foreigners, showing their fear that we would not hold to the gold standard, began to withdraw gold from us. Our citizens began hoarding currency and gold.

We immediately initiated a series of measures—which I will give in detail later—that again prevented panic. Our difficulties and the paralyzing fears of our own people once more began to relax, with a few rays of sunlight appearing about mid-November, 1931.

The fourth period of the depression swept in in early December, 1931, and lasted eleven months. It brought an irregular but general descent to the bottom of the depression pit, which was reached in June, 1932. It was in this period that a Democratic Congress bent on the political destruction of the Republican administration added to the impact of the blows from Europe and the weakness of our own banking system. We narrowly escaped being forced off the gold standard by drains from abroad. Farmers were pushed into even deeper distress and the unemployed increased, until about 7,000,000 families were without breadwinners.

Eventually we forced great legislative and other measures through this opposition Congress, which turned away panic and started us on the road to real recovery around July, 1932. That upturn lasted four months, until the Republicans were worsted in the Maine elections in the latter part of September.

The fifth period of the depression began with the election on November 5, 1932. Recovery was interrupted in the United States by public apprehension over the heterodox economics, currency tinkering, and other policies announced by the New Dealers. The unwillingness of Mr. Roosevelt as President-elect to cooperate in meeting the situation finally culminated in a bank depositors' panic of February, 1933.

The sixth phase of the depression began with the inauguration of the New Deal. The rest of the world turned to recovery in July, 1932, and only the United States marched in the opposite direction with the election of 1932. If the New Dealers had carried on our policies instead of deliberately wrecking them and then trying to make America over into a collectivist system, we should have made complete recovery in eighteen months after 1932, as did all the dozen other nations with a free economy. We continued in the sixth phase of the depression until war intervened in 1941.

Each of the five phases of the depression is discussed in detail in the subsequent chapters.

CHAPTER 6

FIRST PHASE OF THE DEPRESSION—
OCTOBER, 1929, TO APRIL, 1931

As stated, the first phase of the depression lasted seventeen months from the stock-market crash in October, 1929, to the European collapse in April, 1931.

For clearer presentation, I deal with these measures topically rather than chronologically, and I have divided them roughly into:

> Liquidation of Stock-Exchange Loans
> Measures to Restore Employment by
>   Indirect Relief of the Unemployed
> Measures to Support Agriculture
> Direct Relief of Distress
> The Economic Movement During the First Phase

LIQUIDATION OF STOCK-EXCHANGE LOANS

The immediate phenomenon to be dealt with was the liquidation of the loans on stocks, which amounted to more than $8,000,000,000 on the New York Stock Exchange alone, together with the problems of unemployment and agriculture.

Governor Young and the Federal Reserve Banks, in constant conference with myself, Secretary Mellon, and Under Secretary Mills, established cooperative measures to cushion the drastic liquidation down to $3,000,000,000. Most of the large banks had participated in the loan orgy. Had the liquidation been conducted with less skill, panic could have resulted which would have injured millions of innocent depositors.

MEASURES TO RESTORE EMPLOYMENT AND RELIEF

During the first phase of the depression, unemployment reached such threatening dimensions that relief of distress was imperative.

At the outset I must clarify a distinction between "direct relief" and "indirect relief." "Direct relief," as used here, means relief given directly to individuals or families through charitable, local, county, municipal, or state action. "Indirect relief" comprises Federal and state public works, together with stimulation of private construction, "spreading of work," restriction of immigration, government financial measures to support private employment, and action in the foreign field.

Less than a month after the crash, we began to organize indirect relief. On November 18th, I instructed Secretary of Commerce Lamont to set up an organization of experienced men to assure as much public and private construction work as possible. The next day, with the Secretary, I called the major railway presidents to the White House. At the end of our meeting they issued a statement that the railways would continue and even expand their construction and maintenance programs over the next year.

A few days later I invited the public utility leaders to confer and secured their promise to continue and expand their construction activities. We made similar arrangements with the larger manufacturers.

On November 23rd, I wired the governors and mayors, asking their cooperation to expand public works. They responded with full assurances. To stimulate Federal public works, I instructed the departments to expedite our own program, for which we had some $420,000,000 available. In addition, I instructed the Postmaster General and the Shipping Board to expedite all the ship construction possible under the authority which we possessed in that field. A month later, in my message to Congress, I recommended further Federal appropriations for these purposes.

As a result, we were assured that many billions of dollars would be spent and many thousands employed on capital improvement during the first phase of the depression.

MAINTENANCE OF WAGES AND AVOIDANCE OF STRIKES

With a view to developing programs to aid the unemployed aside from construction work, on November 21st, I assembled a meeting of leading industrialists at the White House. I felt that a most important part of our recovery in this period rested on the maintenance of wages and avoidance of strikes. Many of the leaders were not at first impressed with the gravity of the situation but became more seriously concerned as the meeting proceeded. My secretary, Walter Newton, made a note on what took place:

The President . . . outlined the situation. He said that he would not have called them were it not that he viewed the crisis more seriously than a mere stock market crash; that no one could measure the problem before us or the depth of the disaster; that the depression must last for some time; and that there were two or three millions unemployed by the sudden suspension of many activities. He warned them that we could expect a long and difficult period at best; that there must be much liquidation of inflated values, debts and prices with heavy penalties on the nation; that no one could at this time measure the destructive forces we must meet, since the stock boom and collapse were world-wide; that Europe was still under the influence of the destructive aftermath of the war.

The President further proceeded to point out that our immediate duty was to consider the human problem of unemployment and distress; that our second problem was to maintain social order and industrial peace; the third was orderly liquidation and the prevention of panic, and the final readjustment of new concepts of living. He explained that immediate "liquidation" of labor had been the industrial policy of previous depressions; that his every instinct was opposed to both the term and the policy, for labor was not a commodity. It represented human homes. Moreover, from an economic viewpoint such action would deepen the depression by suddenly reducing purchasing power and, as a still worse consequence, it would bring about industrial strife, bitterness, disorder, and fear. He put forward his own view that, in our modern economy and on account of the intensified competition from shrinkage in demand and the inevitable loss of profits due to a depression, the cost of living would fall even if wages were temporarily maintained. Hence if wages were reduced subsequently, and then no more and no faster than the cost of living had previously fallen, the burden would not fall primarily on labor, and values could be "stepped down." Thereby great hard-

ships and economic and social difficulties would be avoided. In any event
the first shock must fall on profits and not on wages.

President Hoover held the fundamental view that wages should be maintained for the present; that planned construction work should be maintained
by industry, and governmental agencies even should increase construction
to give as much employment as possible; that the available work should be
spread among all employees by temporarily shortening the work-week of
individuals; and that each industry should look after distress among its own
employees. By these means industry would help to "cushion down" the
situation.

A discussion followed in which the industrial representatives expressed
major agreement. The program was accepted subject to its approval by labor
leaders and the agreement by them that they would initiate no strikes or
demands for increased pay during the present situation. It was also agreed
that those present would sponsor a larger meeting of industrial leaders in
Washington on December 5th to further organize the program of co-operation by industry as a whole.[1]

The same afternoon I conferred with the outstanding labor leaders
and secured their adherence to the program. This required the patriotic
withdrawal of some wage demands which already had been made.

In the meantime, various business organizations had been called by
the United States Chamber of Commerce to confer in Washington on
the situation. The purpose was to gain wider support of the industrialists' undertaking of two weeks earlier. On December 5th I addressed
these groups, and after a reserved review of the situation, so as not to
add to public alarm, I said:

. . . The cure for such storms is action; the cure for unemployment is to
find jobs. . . .

All of these efforts have one end—to assure employment . . .

The very fact that you gentlemen come together for these broad purposes
represents an advance in the whole conception of the relationship of business
to public welfare. You represent the business of the United States, undertaking through your own voluntary action to contribute something very
definite to the advancement of stability and progress in our economic life.
This is a far cry from the arbitrary and dog-eat-dog attitude of the business

[1] This note is also quoted in Myers and Newton, *The Hoover Administration*, pp.
26–27.

world of some thirty or forty years ago. And this is not dictation or interference by the government with business. It is a request from the government that you co-operate in prudent measures to solve a national problem. A great responsibility and a great opportunity rest upon the business and economic organization of the country. The task is one fitted to its fine initiative and courage.

Those conferences in Washington established four understandings vital to the recovery program: (a) no strikes or lockouts that leaders could prevent; (b) wage rates not to be reduced except as the cost of living fell; (c) within their resources, employers to look after the relief of their own employees; (d) where possible, a sharing of work. The three last provisions were currently referred to in our discussions as the "employers' direct relief." As all this was voluntary, we did not expect a 100 per cent compliance; but we did receive an astonishing support.[2]

THE WAGE AGREEMENT HELD

Throughout my whole administration, the wage agreement held up fairly well in the organized trades and industrial good will developed in a most gratifying and inspiring way. Our real difficulty was with the unorganized trades. In their case, it was a matter of constantly urging employers to support the plan in the national interest. However, most of the nonunion employers complied.

We had abundant evidence that labor leaders appreciated our efforts. The publication of the American Federation of Labor (*American Federationist*) said on January 1, 1930:

The President's conference has given industrial leaders a new sense of their responsibilities. . . . Never before have they been called upon to act together . . . in earlier recessions they have acted individually to protect their own interests and . . . have intensified depression.

On October 6, 1930, William Green, president of the American Federation of Labor, said:

At that conference [the President] suggested that peace be preserved in industry and that wages be maintained during the period of unemployment through which we are passing. The great influence which he exercised upon

[2] These relief measures by employers had a profound effect. At one time we estimated that 2,000,000 workers were being kept from becoming a public charge either through dividing the work or through direct relief by employers.

that occasion served to maintain wage standards and to prevent a general reduction of wages. As we emerge from this distressing period of unemployment we are permitted to understand and appreciate the value of the service which the President rendered the wage earners of the country and industry when he convened the White House conference to which I have just referred.

In a public address on October 6th to the American Federation of Labor I reviewed these measures and expressed my satisfaction with the spirit shown by both labor leaders and employers.

In the 1931 convention of the American Federation of Labor, held at Vancouver, the executive council in its report again expressed appreciation of my efforts and of the substantial success attending them, and stated:

. . . In the full year of 1921 there were ninety-two wage cuts per hundred firms reporting to the Bureau of Labor Statistics, while in the full year of 1930 there were only seven firms per hundred firms reporting.

Although wage cuts have increased in 1931, there still has been no widespread tendency toward a liquidation of wages such as we experienced in 1921.

In the first seven months of 1931 the number of cuts reported per hundred firms was twelve compared to fifty-four in 1921.

These accomplishments in the creating of industrial good will were evidenced by the sharp decrease in labor conflicts. We had fewer strikes and lockouts than in any other four years of recent history.[3]

[3] The Department of Labor record of man-days lost by strikes and lockouts:

| 1929 | 9,975,000 | 1931 | 6,386,000 |
| 1930 | 2,730,000 | 1932 | 6,462,000 |

The high figure for 1929 was influenced by attitudes prior to the good-will program.
The record of Mr. Roosevelt's administration was one of stimulating labor conflict instead of seeking to find healing measures. His record of man-days lost in strikes and lockouts was:

1933	16,872,000	1937	28,425,000
1934	19,592,000	1938	9,148,000
1935	15,456,000	1939	17,812,000
1936	13,902,000	1940	6,701,000

The comparative record cannot be attributed to the reluctance of men to strike because of unemployment fears, for unemployment in just as large a degree continued during the Roosevelt period.

FEDERAL EMPLOYMENT AGENCIES

Another vital factor in our employment and indirect relief program was the Federal employment service. In April, 1930, I asked the Congressional leaders to increase our appropriations for expansion of this service, and it was done. The Federal service concerned itself with interstate problems and coordination of the state services. Senator Wagner of New York, however, promptly brought in a bill which would have transferred the control of Federal offices to the states and local governments. It would have put workers' jobs in control of political machines, such as Tammany in New York, or the Hague gang of Jersey City. Therefore, I vetoed it, and on March 7, 1931, I explained my stand in a statement disclosing the above facts. I directed the Secretary of Labor to submit a bill to the Congressional committees which would set up more coordination between the Federal and state agencies in interstate job placements; although supported by the labor leaders, it was ditched by the Democratic opposition. However, we reorganized the service on lines of expanded voluntary cooperation with state and local agencies. The effect of this reorganization appeared in the increase in placements. Together with cooperating state and municipal employment offices 1,104,136 persons were placed in 1931. The record showed 2,174,179 were placed in 1932. The service to agricultural seasonal workers expanded from 559,571 workers in 1929 to 886,605 in 1932.

RESTRICTION OF IMMIGRATION

In order to cope successfully with the unemployment problem, I felt it necessary to restrict immigration. Early in the administration I had completed the steps necessary to put in force a law passed during President Coolidge's administration restricting immigration by quotas from each country outside the Western Hemisphere. That law also provided that entrance might be refused to immigrants likely to become public charges. In view of the large amount of unemployment at the time, I concluded that directly or indirectly all immigrants were a public charge at the moment—either they themselves went on relief as soon as they landed, or, if they did get jobs, they forced others onto relief. I, therefore, stopped all immigration with some minor exceptions as to tourists, students, and professional men and women, and I made the order apply even to the non-quota countries. This was put into effect on September 9, 1930.

We held to this policy throughout my administration. Reports issued from time to time showed that the persons departing exceeded those arriving by several hundred per cent.

The following figures show the results of this order even more clearly:

	Immigrants	Emigrants
1929	279,678	69,203
1930	241,700	50,661
1931	97,139	61,882
1932	35,576	103,295

DEPORTATIONS

While the deportation of convicted aliens, illegal entries, and other undesirables does not pertain to unemployment I mention it here because the law was administered by the Labor Department, which enforced it rigidly. The results were:

| | Deportations | |
	Fiscal Year	Number
Hoover Administration.....	1930	16,631
	1931	18,142
	1932	19,426
	1933	19,865 [4]

Labor policies as a whole came up in the Presidential campaign of 1932 and I shall review them in that connection.

A CENSUS OF THE UNEMPLOYED

In order to find out exactly how much unemployment there was at the time, in April, 1930, six months after the market slump, I ordered the first accurate house-to-house census of unemployed ever made in the

[4] How quickly the attitude of the administration changed is shown by the following table of the first four years of Roosevelt:

| | Deportations | |
	Fiscal Year	Number
Roosevelt Administration	1934	8,879
	1935	8,319
	1936	9,195

United States. This became the base by which, with the application of statistical indexes, the subsequent estimates of unemployment were made during my administration.

Although this house-to-house census seemed simple on the face of it, it turned out to be most complicated. The enumerators found themselves faced with a dozen different situations. They had to list the shiftless citizen who had no intention of living by work as unemployed. A household of four adults capable of work, of whom only the father had ever worked for pay, might be listed as only one unemployed; but the number could be stretched to enumerate the other three, especially since they might tell the census taker that they wanted work. Other perplexing cases included persons out of work but not looking for a job; persons in the seasonal trades resting—as usual—between seasons; persons laid off temporarily or laying off voluntarily; persons idle for short periods between a job lost and one for which they had been engaged. While listed as unemployed, these groups were not in distress, but their number was so large that they constituted an important part of the estimates.

This census showed on paper that 2,429,000 persons were out of jobs and that 758,000 still retained their jobs but were laid off temporarily without pay—a total of 3,187,000. But a rough review of the facts indicated that probably 500,000 to 1,000,000 of these persons did not intend to work under any circumstances, while another 500,000 to 1,000,000 represented "between-jobbers," mostly in the seasonal trades. Even in highly prosperous times like 1927–1929, when there was no distress, the pool of unemployed averaged about 1,500,000.

We also found that there was an average of 1.7 breadwinners to each family. One breadwinner, generally speaking, was enough to keep a household from want; therefore, in each ten families which needed no relief, there might yet be seven unemployed persons. Also many families without one employed member had savings or other income which would keep them going for the time being—although, of course, this class would constantly diminish as the depression went on.

These statistics on unemployment did not indicate with accuracy the degree of destitution. In considering all the factors, we concluded that there were about 1,000,000 families without breadwinners in April, 1930.

The Census Bureau and the Bureau of Labor Statistics estimated that the average monthly total labor force during 1930 was 50,080,000 persons. The unemployed would be about 6 per cent. The relief measures we had taken proved sufficient for that time.

MEASURES TO SUPPORT AGRICULTURE

Immediately after the stock-market slump, I called a White House conference of leading farm organizations (November, 1929), to discuss measures to meet its effect upon agriculture. The fall in prices did not begin to develop seriously until the following January (1930), when export orders for farm products began to drop and credits with which to carry them in storage became restricted.

At the time of the 1929 market crash, the 1929 crop was partially marketed. The farmers had raised the crop at costs which, if not realized in selling the remainder, would be ruinous. The Federal Farm Board had already been created, upon my recommendation, with a capital of $500,000,000 and wide powers generally to aid agriculture. It had a strong chairman in Alexander Legge, who had been for many years president of the International Harvester Company and could hardly be classed as a radical.

FARM BOARD SUPPORT OF PRICES

We now determined that the Farm Board should give indirect support to prices which had seriously declined. Some action was taken in January, 1930, and on February 3rd to support a floor under prices of both wheat and cotton by loans and purchases. Criticism of these operations in the eastern press drove Chairman Legge to make a characteristic statement on February 25th:

Some objection has developed in the grain trade against the action of the Farm Board. . . .

In connection with these objections I should like to make this statement as a conservative business man, addressed to the conservative business men of the country.

The country as a whole was thrown into depression through the collapse of speculation on the New York Stock Exchange. The action of the President in securing co-operation of the business world absolutely prevented this collapse from developing into a panic and has enormously mitigated its effects upon employment and business, including agriculture.

The cooperation of the great employers of the country in upholding wages, and therefore the buying power of the public, the action of the railways, the public utilities, the industries, the Federal Government, the States, the municipalities in undertaking great programs of construction, are greatly mitigating unemployment and giving protection to the workman and stability to business.

The farmer also was the victim of this collapse. His products and his labor were jeopardized the same as the other workers through the currents started in considerable part from the same causes. His only direct support in this emergency is the Farm Board, through powers conferred upon it. The Board is endeavoring through finance of the farmer's own organizations to help restore stability and expedite recovery from a crisis which the farmer did not create and for which he is not responsible.

The measures taken are purely emergency measures on a par with those taken by other business agencies of the country, and I am confident that the Board deserves and will receive the support of all thinking business men in its endeavor to contribute its part toward the swift recovery of the country as a whole from this situation.

The Farm Board eased the farmers over the 1929–30 winter marketing hump and the bulk of the 1929 crop harvest was marketed at fair prices. At the end of April it withdrew support to allow prices to reach their natural level as a guide to the farmers for the following planting season.

RELIEF OF THE GREAT DROUGHT

While the outlook was generally improving during the first seven months of 1930, another calamity hit us in August—a drought throughout large agricultural sections of the Midwest and South. About a million farm families and twenty million animals were affected. The first result was an acute shortage of feed for animals. I secured at once from the railroads half-rates on feedstuffs shipped into stricken sections, and I directed an expansion in Federal highway construction in those localities to aid farmers with supplementary employment. I also called a meeting at the White House of governors of the states concerned, to devise other relief measures. This conference decided (August 15th) that the situation could be brought under control, and distress alleviated by an appropriation from Congress for seed loans to the farmers, by direct relief to needy families through the Red Cross, by persuading the banks and insurance companies to extend mortgages and interest, and by systematically handling highway and other public works to give farmers cash employment. All these things were done. I secured an immediate appropriation from the Red Cross of $5,000,000 which we subsequently increased by a popular appeal to $15,000,000. We furnished seed to the farmers through the Department of Agriculture.

The problem of marketing farm products arose again with the harvest of 1930. That autumn the Farm Board renewed its support of prices until the following April (1931), when again it allowed prices to readjust themselves to natural levels. During the marketing season of the 1930 crop, we, for instance, held the prices of wheat 25 to 30 cents a bushel above the European markets.

The *New York Times* of November 19, 1930, reported the directors of the Chicago Board of Trade as confirming that these actions had alone prevented widespread panic in the agricultural markets. The Board of Trade had not hitherto been friendly or very cooperative. The Farm Board lost about $100,000,000 in stabilization operations over these two winters, but we saved many times that amount to the farmers. This was not a perfect solution, but it did cushion the blows that agriculture was taking.

STOPPING SOVIET SHORT SALES OF WHEAT

An interesting but momentarily alarming side issue arose late in September, 1930. We were informed that the Soviet government had been selling large amounts of wheat short on the Chicago market. Investigation confirmed this and I demanded that the Chicago Board of Trade and other markets prohibit transactions by foreign governments. In order to secure this action by them for the protection of our farmers, I was compelled to threaten Federal control. Soon thereafter the Communist government began dumping large amounts of wheat upon the European markets and broke the price several cents a bushel. The Soviets, out of their short selling in Chicago, however, took a considerable sum which would otherwise have gone to our American farmer.

DIRECT RELIEF OF DISTRESS

I have already described such measures of indirect relief as public and private construction and the "employers' relief."

Fearful of the inevitable increase of unemployment and distress during the winter of 1930–1931, however, and wanting to be sure of no failure in their care, I initiated a relief program by setting up the President's Committee for Unemployment Relief. I appointed Colonel Arthur Woods, former Police Commissioner of New York, as chairman, with a committee of thirty leading citizens to assist him. I requested the governors of the states to cooperate by forming nonpartisan committees of responsible men and women, in each state, these committees in turn to organize such committees in each municipality and county. This was carried out in each locality where unemployment existed. We thus set up some 3,000 nonpartisan committees of devoted, intelligent men and women. They were given the primary responsibility to see that no one went hungry or cold. In October, 1930, Colonel Woods reported to me that his organization was functioning everywhere.

On January 2, 1931, our government departments estimated the total unemployed at 6,050,000. This, with the usual deductions demonstrated in our previous census and taking account of the fact that this was the low point in seasonal work, indicated about 2,300,000 families without employed breadwinners. I directed Colonel Woods to check these estimates and to make a complete survey of the work load of his committees by his own independent agents. He confirmed the department's estimates as approximately correct and reported that needs were being well cared for by the local county and municipal committees and by the "indirect relief."

In a conference with the national committee and the state committees, I insisted that the first obligation of direct relief rested on local communities, and that they should not call upon the state and Federal governments until the load overtaxed their capacities. I said that if Federal aid became necessary we would act through the state committees in supplementing state appropriations, and would insist that both Federal and state aid be supplemented by the local authorities; also that the whole should be administered by the nonpartisan committee system as the only method by which waste, politics, and graft could be prevented. I added emphatically that direct relief to individuals from the Federal government would bring an inevitable train of corruption and waste such as our nation had never witnessed.[5]

As a result of surveys, the state committees reported it unnecessary at that time for the state governments to make substantial appropriations for relief other than public works, and likewise no call was involved upon the Federal government except for our "indirect relief."

PRESSURE FOR DIRECT PERSONAL FEDERAL RELIEF OR DOLES

Early in 1931 came much public discussion and conflict as to the method of relieving distress. Should direct personal relief be organized and administered upon a local community and state basis, or should the Federal government take over the whole direct operation with doles and other devices?

The gist of this discussion was not a question of relief or no relief. It was solely a dispute over the *method* of organization.

During the winter season of 1931, the Senate Democrats, aided by Senator Borah and by all the radical groups in the country, demanded appropriations for direct Federal doles to individuals in distress. Both our relief committees and the Red Cross, looking after the Midwest drought distress, reported that such action was not needed. Hoping that I could keep relief measures out of politics, I called individually to the White House Senator Robinson and Representative Garner, the Democratic Senate and House leaders, also Senator Borah representing the "left wingers," and the Republican leaders. I went over the groundwork of relief for both agriculture and unemployed, our "indirect" relief measures, and our system of direct relief to those in distress through our committees and the Red Cross. *I insisted that if the local committees became exhausted they should apply to the state committee, and this in turn to the state government; that if these resources were exhausted, then and then only should the Federal government contribute*

[5] Years later this was proved all too true.

to state aid and that to be administered by the system of nonpartisan committees. I insisted that if Federal action followed any other course it would destroy local responsibility and introduce graft, politics, waste, and mismanagement. Constant repetition of this thesis became a sort of patter with me. I did not, however, satisfy my political opponents. They saw great political grist in emotional appeals to presumed sympathy— or human greed.

An ugly incident offered an opportunity to some Democratic members of Congress and to Senator Borah. They gladly seized upon it. In the relief of the Arkansas drought–sufferers, the Red Cross, in August, 1930, had properly insisted on delivering relief directly to the Negro and white tenant families. The plantation owners insisted upon distributing it, obviously to keep these dependents under control. I backed the Red Cross in refusing. An alleged riot by "starving people" in February, 1931, attacked the local Red Cross and was greatly exploited in the Congress. When I sent my military aide, Colonel Hodges, to investigate the "riot," he found that it was a fake.

The opposition in Congress continued its efforts to force various Federal doles by amendments to a bill for seed-loan appropriations, which I had recommended for the drought areas. I was now proved "heartless," to the great exultation of my opponents. Senator Borah assailed me mercilessly. On February 3, 1931, I issued a public statement saying:

Certain senators have issued a public statement to the effect that unless the President and the House of Representatives agree to appropriations from the Federal Treasury for charitable purposes they will force an extra session of Congress.

I do not wish to add acrimony to a discussion, but would rather state this case as I see its fundamentals.

This is not an issue as to whether people shall go hungry or cold in the United States. It is solely a question of the best method by which hunger and cold shall be prevented. It is a question as to whether the American people, on one hand, will maintain the spirit of charity and mutual self-help through voluntary giving and the responsibility of local government as distinguished, on the other hand, from appropriations out of the Federal Treasury.... If we start appropriations of this character we have not only impaired something infinitely valuable in the life of the American people but have struck at the roots of self-government. . . .

And there is a practical problem in all this. The help being daily extended by neighbors, by local and national agencies, by municipalities, by industry and a great multitude of organizations throughout the country today is many times any appropriation yet proposed. The opening of the doors of the Federal Treasury is likely to stifle this giving and thus destroy far more resources than the proposed charity from the Federal government.

The basis of successful relief in national distress is to mobilize and organize the infinite number of agencies of self-help in the community. That has been the American way of relieving distress among our own people, and the country is successfully meeting its problem in the American way today.

I then reviewed our various measures of unemployment and drought relief and the reports from governors and other leaders that it was working most satisfactorily. I continued:

I have indeed spent much of my life in fighting hardship and starvation both abroad and in the Southern states. I do not feel that I should be charged with lack of human sympathy for those who suffer. . . . In all the organizations with which I have been connected over these many years, the foundation has been to summon the maximum of self-help. I am proud to have sought the help of Congress in the past for nations who were so disorganized by war and anarchy. . . . But even these appropriations were but a tithe of that which was coincidentally mobilized from the public charity of the United States and foreign countries. There is no such paralysis in the United States and I am confident that our people have the resources, the initiative, the courage, the stamina and kindliness of spirit to meet this situation in the way they have met their problems over generations.

. . . *I am willing to pledge myself* that if the time should ever come that the voluntary agencies of the country together with the local and state governments are unable to find resources with which to prevent hunger and suffering in my country, *I will ask the aid of every resource of the Federal government because I would no more see starvation amongst our countrymen than would any Senator or Congressman.* . . .

The American people are doing their job today.

Despite and contrary to all the smearing, we got through the first phase of the depression until the spring of 1931 and no one went hungry or cold—if our committees knew of it.

LEGISLATIVE ACTION

The December 1929–1930 session of Congress, upon my recommendation, increased public works appropriations and authorized seed loans to the drought areas. It failed, however, to accept my recommendations on the much needed reform of the banking laws, and most other reforms.[6]

ECONOMIC MOVEMENT DURING
THE FIRST PHASE OF THE DEPRESSION

In my message of December 3, 1929, to the regular session of Congress, I did not wish to add alarms to the already rising fears. Therefore, I gave a guarded discussion of the economic situation arising out of the crash of six weeks previously, and reviewed the steps taken to protect the situation.[7]

Our various measures taken in late 1929 and early 1930 soon began to have encouraging effects. The *New York Times* announced on February 12, 1930, that the country had begun to recover. The economic indexes confirmed this hope.

On February 18th, Myers and Newton point out:

In the Cabinet discussion it was agreed that the danger of a banking panic from the stock collapse definitely had passed. The stockholders' loans of eight and a half billion had been liquidated to three billion with the help of the Federal Reserve System. It was obvious that . . . although the banks had sustained great losses from customers' withdrawals and the depreciation of securities, uneasiness among depositors generally had been prevented.

The President now was able to announce to the press that the preliminary shock of the collapse had abated; also that the Department of Labor index of all employment, which had dropped from 93.3 in October to 86.0 at the end of December, had by this date increased to 92.8, which indicated the return of several hundred thousand men to work. The governors' reports and independent surveys showed that in thirty-six States no important distress had developed from unemployment, and that in the other twelve States measures put in operation by private and local authorities were meeting the

[6] Ample evidence of this is given in Chapter 40.
[7] *The State Papers and Other Public Writings of Herbert Hoover*, Vol. I, pp. 138–166.

situation. The danger of a general panic in finance and industry had been averted.

During the next six weeks the economic indexes continued to grow still more favorable. There were significant increases in the demands for steel and other raw materials. Construction work generally was reviving, even surpassing the normal. In addition, our fears as to Europe had not yet materialized.

In consequence of these favorable indications, on May 1st (1930), I addressed the United States Chamber of Commerce, the major purpose being to express appreciation of the cooperation we had received from the business world and to urge its continuance. I indulged in some moderate optimism saying, "We are not through the difficulties of our situation," but "I am convinced we have passed the worst and with continued effort we shall rapidly recover."

Presidents cannot be pessimistic in times of national difficulties. They must be encouraging. However, this bit of optimism was later distorted by our opponents to make me say, "Prosperity is just around the corner," which I never did say. It was no doubt a political mistake on my part to open the way for such an attack if things went wrong— which they did.[8] During the remainder of 1930 the country was steadily and successfully readjusting itself despite some adversities and much licking of wounds.

In addition to the mid-western drought calamity, the Congressional election in November, 1930, went against us. General Prosperity gave way to General Depression as a campaign issue. The result of the election was a Democratic majority in the House and an effective opposing coalition in the Senate. The Democratic-controlled Congress was not to come into session until a year later. Prices of commodities and securities fell sharply with the election. I tried to patch up this threat to public morale by an agreement to "cooperate" with the Democratic leaders.

My message to the short session of Congress on December 2, 1930,

[8] President Roosevelt likewise became optimistic at various times from 1934 to 1937. With the slumps which followed, he was subjected to the same unkind remarks. His most unfortunate phrase at a moment of temporary recovery was "We planned it that way." But it went sour again.

again reviewed at length the economic situation and our actions. Some paragraphs of summary deserve to be quoted here:

In the larger view the major forces of the depression now lie outside of the United States, and our recuperation has been retarded by the unwarranted degree of fear and apprehension created by these outside forces.

The extent of the depression is indicated by the following approximate percentages of activity during the past three months as compared with the highly prosperous year of 1928:

Value of department-store sales..............	93% of 1928
Volume of manufacturing production........	80% of 1928
Volume of mineral production..............	90% of 1928
Volume of factory employment..............	84% of 1928
Total of bank deposits	105% of 1928
Wholesale prices—all commodities...........	83% of 1928
Cost of living............................	94% of 1928

Various other indexes indicate total decrease of activity from 1928 of from 15 to 20 per cent.[9]

RECOVERY STARTS

Early in 1931 the situation improved sharply. There were many evidences of progress. The *New York Times* on March 23 concluded that the depression had passed bottom, that we were on our way out; and this view was supported by the press generally. All the business indexes at the end of March showed sharp rises in employment, pay rolls, prices of commodities and securities, and industrial production beyond the usual seasonal movements.

The bank failures during the first three months of 1931 were inconsequential, and foreign confidence in our strength was unimpaired, as indicated by the increasing volume of deposits in our banks from abroad.

The Federal Reserve Board's report at the end of March indicated a strong movement to recovery. During this first quarter of 1931, they showed:

[9] The full text appears in *The State Papers and Other Public Writings of Herbert Hoover*, Vol. I, pp. 428–440.

Industrial production..........increased 12 per cent
Pay rolls ....increased 10 per cent
Common stocks...............increased 11 per cent
Construction contracts.........increased 25 per cent

The need for direct relief sharply decreased. A survey by our committees at the end of March showed that 120 cities had ended their relief measures as they were no longer necessary. The percentage of unemployed to the total labor force had apparently decreased by about 25 per cent.

Had there been no other malign forces in the world, the American depression to all appearances had run its course. The public mind was recovering from its mania of extravagance and speculation. There had been no panics. Significant reforms had taken place in business management. Our cushioning measures had made the industrial effects of the slump less severe than those of some previous slumps. We had sustained agriculture and cared for the destitute.

But we were scarcely to set our feet on the floor from our economic sickbed when Europe struck us a stunning blow. We were soon to learn that there was a delayed bomb in financial Europe.

CHAPTER 7

SECOND PHASE OF THE DEPRESSION— APRIL TO AUGUST, 1931

In the spring of 1931, just as we had begun to entertain well founded hopes that we were on the way out of the depression, our latent fears of Europe were realized in a gigantic explosion which shook the whole foundations of the world's economic, political, and social structure. At last the malign forces arising from economic consequences of the war, the Versailles Treaty, the postwar military alliances with their double prewar armament, their frantic public works programs to meet unemployment, their unbalanced budgets and the inflations, all tore their systems asunder.

Out of their war inheritances came even deeper explosive forces. Dissolution of the old Central European empires had created twelve new states, each erecting trade barriers against the others. Austria had been reduced to a gigantic poorhouse, and her only hope was economic union with Germany. Russia had been economically isolated by the Communist revolution, and no longer exported a large volume of raw materials and food in exchange for Eastern European manufactures. As a result, many countries had to seek new sources of raw materials and food supplies and, in turn, sell their goods in new markets. Thus the older channels of commerce were dislocated and restricted. Contributing to the European collapse was the huge overproduction of several commodities. This surplus was induced by cartels which had artificially increased prices and thus stimulated production. High prices stifled consumption. In the meantime, great bubbles of speculation sprang up in foreign countries in the stocks of corporations which were producers of these commodities—of which rubber and coffee were examples. The collapse in prices created side depressions affecting all South Asia (and incidentally Britain and Holland) and all northern Latin America.

European statesmen did not have the courage to meet the real issues. They continued to assert, even after the explosion, that the remedy lay in more credits, more government expenditures, more deficits, and more inflation.

All these things we had known and long feared. But the violence of these forces we did not know. And there were still other hidden explosive materials. They only gradually appeared. In retrospect, it is evident that the inflationary action of our Federal Reserve System in 1925 and 1927, undertaken at the instance of foreign bankers, had contributed to delay their crisis, but in the end created a time bomb through immense short-term borrowing of Central European banks from banks all over the rest of the world.

Like the Sarajevo incident of 1914 which lighted the fuse of the First World War, the agreement between Germany and Austria for a customs union, which was announced on March 21, 1931, touched off the European explosion. The French and British governments interpreted this as a start toward repudiation of the Versailles Treaty, one of the keystones of which was the political separation of Germany and Austria.

A customs union of a small state of 6,000,000 people and a great state of 60,000,000 people was scarcely a serious menace. But France and Britain at once declared that it would not be permitted. On the surface, this was just another exhibition of European power politics. But underneath, in order to bring pressure to bear, the Bank of France and other French banks presented for payment the short-term bills which they held from Austrian and German banks. It was the last push against an already tottering economic structure in Europe. The full amount of these French-held bills is not known, but it was estimated at $300,000,000. Other holders of European bank obligations became frightened.

THE PANIC IN AUSTRIA AND GERMANY

Austria and Germany began frantic efforts to secure foreign exchange and gold. To accomplish the purpose, they began to curb imports; to control capital movements, they started borrowing from every source they could find.

Apprehension began to run like mercury through the financial world. It spread through the world's markets all during the first half of April. Security and commodity markets in the United States began to slump. I directed the Department of Commerce and the Treasury to inquire at home and abroad as to the situation in each country. They reported steady European selling of American securities in our markets, some flight of capital from Europe to us, and a sharp decrease in orders for our export commodities. European insiders were apparently protecting themselves from something sinister to come.[2]

[2] Four years after this was written I made a journey over Europe in the winter months of 1938, visiting fourteen countries, and discussed the causes of the great European debacle of 1931 with statesmen and economists of Belgium, France, Switzerland, Austria, Germany, Poland, the Baltic States, Sweden, and Britain.

The sum of two score views of leading men was well summed up at a meeting I had in Vienna with President Miklas, Finance Minister Neumayer, President Kienböck of the Austrian National Bank and three University economics professors. I had asked their views as to the underlying causes of the European economic collapse in 1931 which had been touched off from Vienna. In a note I made at the time, the Austrians said in sum:

"There were several primary and a number of secondary causes. The primary causes were, first, the weakening of the economic structure of every nation in Europe by the war; second, the economic consequences of the Treaty of Versailles which had divided the Danube Valley among five states, each of which had set up trade barriers by tariffs, discriminatory rail rates, quotas, etc., and thus weakened and impoverished the productivity of that whole great area. This had impoverished and paralyzed the great financial and trade center of Vienna with its skills and former resources. Third, the reparations and intergovernmental war debts which distorted all finance and exchange and through pressures had forced the export of goods into unnatural channels. Fourth, the economic isolation of Russia by the Communist destruction of her productivity, thus stopping the flow of food and raw materials into Europe and closing a large part of the market for European manufactured goods in Russia. Fifth, immediately after the Treaty and despite the League, military alliances and power politics had steadily increased armaments with their inevitable unbalanced budgets. Sixth, the rise of the school (the totalitarian liberals) which believed governments could produce employment and increase productivity by bureaucratic control and dictation of business with the consequent fright to business. From this followed hesitation and increasing unemployment. Seventh, the attempts of governments to provide for this unemployment by public works

In speaking before the Gridiron Club on April 27, 1931, I could not refrain from showing apprehension, for I said:

... If, by the grace of God, we have passed the worst of this storm, the future months will be easy. If we shall be called upon to endure more of this period, we must gird ourselves for even greater effort ... So far our people have responded with courage and steadfastness. If we can maintain this courage and resolution we shall have written this new chapter in national life in terms to which our whole idealism has aspired. May God grant to us the spirit and strength to carry through to the end.

World commodities and securities continued to decline in the markets. On May 7th, our Ambassador to Germany, Frederic M. Sackett, arrived in Washington on an urgent mission. His purpose was to inform me that Chancellor of Germany Brüning had disclosed to him a detailed account of the disastrous financial crisis then developing in his country. Mr. Brüning had outlined the increasing economic strain as shown by the flight of capital, currency difficulties, unemployment, drying up of credits from abroad, pressures for payment of debts, and refusal to give renewals of accounts due from German banks to foreigners. The Chancellor had also set forth the danger from the Communist and Nazi elements, and the old military groups, now rallying to Hitler, all bent on destroying the representative government. However, Mr. Sackett thought that there was no danger of political or economic crisis in Germany before autumn.

Aside from any economic repercussions which might affect us, it

---

drove budgets into further deficits with a train of foreign and domestic borrowing, kiting of bills and disguised inflation. From all this flowed government controls of imports and exports in an effort to protect currencies and gold reserves, all of which created more unemployment. The whole of the process was an aftermath of the World War and the Treaty of Versailles. If there had been no war, there would have been no world depression.

"The crack started at its weakest point, that is, in Austria, and was widened when the French demanded payment of short-term bills as a pressure measure to prevent the proposed economic union with Germany in 1931."

It did not occur to these gentlemen in Europe that I was personally responsible for the world-wide depression as Mr. Roosevelt so repeatedly charged.

The Austrians, of course, laid great emphasis upon the Treaty of Versailles as a cause. And, in fact, many of us had protested in 1918 that it would make Vienna the center of poverty in Europe with political and social instability which was bound to radiate woe and disturbance to all Europe.

seemed to me that the United States had a broad interest in supporting the efforts of liberal-minded men in Germany, Austria, and Eastern Europe to sustain their representative governments against the political forces besetting them. These democratic governments were the foundation of any hope of lasting peace in Europe.

I informed the Ambassador of my convictions and assured him of my desire to help, although I had the direst forebodings of the economic effect their situation might have upon the United States.

The first important American press notice of the situation in Europe was a May 13th dispatch from Vienna, disclosing that Austria's largest private bank, the Kreditanstalt, was in such trouble that depositors were rioting outside its offices. On May 15th, our Budapest legation reported great excitement and runs on banks in Hungary over rumors of financial difficulties. On May 18th, one of our leading banks informed me that it was selling $100,000,000 worth of American securities for a European client. Foreign orders for our wheat and cotton almost ceased, and as a result, our prices of commodities and securities were steadily falling.

On May 20th, I called in Federal Reserve Board officials to discuss our threatened economy. They intimated that I was seeing ghosts so far as the United States was concerned, and declared that nothing was going on that they and our banks could not easily handle.

In the remaining days of May the crisis developed even more acutely. Various efforts of a patch-up kind were undertaken to sustain the Austrian National Bank, which was now also in trouble. Temporary loans were made under the leadership of the Federal Reserve Bank of New York and the Bank of England. The French, however, refused to participate in these efforts. During the last few days of May and the first days of June, German difficulties had also become so evident that they were being openly discussed in the American press. The situation had developed far more quickly than Ambassador Sackett anticipated.

EXCHANGE AND GOLD IN MID-1931

I must digress here to discuss certain phenomena of international exchange, finance, and gold in order to make subsequent events clear.

When the European crisis began, the currencies of the world were generally based upon convertibility into gold of a definite weight and fineness for each currency, and the central banking institutions of each country held substantial gold reserves to protect convertibility and foreign exchange. The ebb and flow of trade and credit necessarily resulted in some movement of gold from one country to another to settle balances. World monetary relations were, therefore, simple and direct.

The interlocked functions for which gold was used—currency, deposit reserves, and settlement of international balances—were, at the time of this 1931 crisis, thrown into utter confusion by interferences of frantic governments. The Central European states, trying to attract to themselves a movement of gold and capital, raised interest rates. That failed, however, and then they tried to stop by law the flight of capital and the outward movement of gold to pay debts or to buy imports. Then they restricted imports and devised stimulants to exports, in order to create a surplus of foreign exchange in their favor. Although not initially acknowledged, this was in effect an abandonment of the gold standard, beginning in Central Europe, which was to disturb the world, including ourselves, with shocks for many a year to come. The whole process was a terrible destruction of world trade. No merchant could know what he might receive in payment by the time his goods were delivered. Risks, thus multiplied, further hampered trade.

At this time—June, 1931—the European press cried out that by our economic policies the United States was sucking up the world's gold, thereby undermining exchanges, currencies, and their gold standards. This was not only untrue, but it was the usual Europeans' practice of blaming Uncle Sam for their own failures. When questioned by the press on this, I replied that our gold stock in two years had been increased by about $600,000,000 to its present volume of about $5,000,-000,000, but that this increase had come from domestic and foreign sources other than Europe—from which, on balance, we had received very little. In the same period the European gold stocks had increased by $1,500,000,000. I stated that some flight of capital had now started from Europe to us because of the citizens' lack of confidence in the currencies of their own countries. This flight of capital and the movements of gold from one country to another were subsequently to give us great anxiety. Gold coming into the United States was absorbed at once into our currency and credit structure. When it was withdrawn, it tended to cause a shrinkage in the volume of credit or even endanger our currency coverage. We were especially pregnable to such movement because of the large foreign deposits in our banks: deposits not only those of foreign individuals and banks, but also of foreign governments. During the years prior to 1931, our banks had accumulated a good deal of gold from many smaller nations who sent the reserves behind their currencies with confidence that dollars were as good as gold. By this device they earned interest on their currency reserves.

We were later to see our own citizens yielding to spasms of fright and exporting their capital, which moved gold from under our currency and credit structure. To stop gold exports would be in effect a refusal to pay our debts in gold and thus would amount to a repudiation of the gold standard.

During this new stage of the depression, the refugee gold and the foreign government reserve deposits were constantly driven by fear hither and yon over the world. We were to see currencies demoralized and governments embarrassed as fear drove the gold from one country to another. In fact, there was a mass of gold and short-term credit which behaved like a loose cannon on the deck of the world in a tempest-tossed era.

I SECURE A MORATORIUM ON INTERGOVERNMENTAL PAYMENTS

As the strain increased in all international payments and exchange, I asked Secretaries Stimson and Mellon (May 11, 1931) to study some method of relieving the pressure through relaxation of the huge worldwide intergovernmental payments for reparations and war debts. These payments totalled more than $1,000,000,000 a year between governments, of which we annually received about $250,000,000 by way of payments on our war debts.

The Secretaries were unable to make any suggestion. On the 5th of June I called them and Under Secretary Mills to the White House and suggested that, in order to ease the situation, I should propose to all governments a moratorium of a year on all intergovernmental payments. In payments to the United States this would give actual relief for eighteen months, as installments had just been paid. Mr. Mellon objected that it was Europe's mess, and that we should not involve the United States. Messrs. Stimson and Mills supported my idea. As Mr. Mellon was leaving for Europe next day on a vacation, I suggested that he look into the situation abroad. I was also relieved to be able to deal directly with Mr. Mills, who would be acting Secretary of the Treasury and had a younger and more vigorous mind than Mr. Mellon.

The next day the German Finance Minister visited London. He informed the British government and also publicly stated that the Austrian panic was infecting Germany, but implied that he did not expect an acute crisis for sixty days. But people do not wait for a disaster sixty days away. In the following week runs were begun upon all German banks, both by citizens and by foreign banks, the latter demanding payment of outstanding German trade bills and acceptances.

I had previously agreed to make two addresses in the Midwest and was so compelled to be away from the Capital for a few days. As Congress was not in session, I requested midwestern Congressional leaders to meet me on the train, where I outlined my proposals for the moratorium. I wished to secure their support if Congressional action should become necessary.

When I returned to Washington on June 18th, Mr. Mellon, now in Europe, had reversed his views and was telephoning frantically that action must be taken at once or American financial safety would be seriously involved. I also found an official appeal from President von Hindenburg stating that the Weimar Republic was in danger of collapse. The full text of Hindenburg's message was:

Mr. President:

The need of the German people which has reached a climax compels me to adopt the unusual step of addressing you personally.

The German people has lived through years of great hardship, culminating in the past winter, and the economic recovery hoped for in the Spring of this year has not taken place. I have, therefore, now taken steps, in virtue of the extraordinary powers conferred upon me by the German Constitution, to insure the carrying out of the most urgent tasks confronting the Government and to secure the necessary means of subsistence for the unemployed. These measures radically affect all economic and social conditions and entail the greatest sacrifices on the part of all classes of the population. All possibilities of improving the situation by domestic measures without relief from abroad are exhausted. The economic crisis from which the whole world is suffering hits particularly hard the German nation which has been deprived of its reserves by the consequences of the war. As the developments of the last few days show, the whole world lacks confidence in the ability of the German economic system to work under the existing burdens. Large credits received by us from foreign countries have been withdrawn. Even in the course of the last few days the Reichsbank has had to hand over to foreign countries one third of its reserves of gold and foreign currency. The inevitable consequence of these developments must be a further serious restriction of economic life and an increase in the numbers of unemployed who already amount to more than one third of the total number of industrial workers. The efficiency, will to work, and discipline of the German people justify confidence in the strict observance of the great fixed private obligations and loans with which Germany is burdened. But, in order to maintain its course and the confidence of the world in its capacity, Germany has urgent need of relief. The relief must come at once if we are to avoid serious misfortune for ourselves and others. The German people must continue to have the possibility of working under tolerable living conditions. Such relief would be to the benefit of all countries in its material and moral effect on the whole crisis. It would improve the situation in other countries and materially reduce the danger to Germany due to internal and external tension caused by distress and despair.

You, Mr. President, as the representative of the great American people, are in a position to take the steps by which an immediate change in the situation threatening Germany and the rest of the world could be brought about.

VON HINDENBURG

I spent the two days after my return to Washington interviewing and telephoning Congressional leaders and ranking members of committees in both houses and both parties, seeking their approval of my moratorium proposals. Senator Robinson and Speaker Garner, Democratic leaders of the Senate and House, refused to take any position, but Senator Glass and some other important Democratic members did agree.

As soon as I was sure of enough Democratic votes in addition to the Republican to pass legislation, I instructed the Secretary of State to communicate the proposal to the different governments.

Although I had urgently impressed upon all members of Congress that the subject must be confidential until we had had time to lay it before the other governments, Senator King of Utah told it "off the record" to reporters with the result that a garbled and antagonistic account went out to the press both at home and abroad. I was, therefore, compelled either to risk displeasing the other governments by not giving them the courtesy of a few days for consultation or, alternatively, to have my proposal discussed by their peoples in a garbled and destructive form.[2] Therefore, on the 20th of June I issued a statement to the press for release the following morning:

The American Government proposes the postponement during one year of all payments on intergovernmental debts, reparations and relief debts, both principal and interest, of course, not including obligations of governments held by private parties. Subject to confirmation by Congress, the American Government will postpone all payments upon the debts of foreign governments to the American Government payable during the fiscal year beginning July 1st next, conditional on a like postponement for one year of all payments on intergovernmental debts owing the important creditor powers.

The statement then gave the names of members of Congress who had approved, and continued:

The purpose of this action is to give the forthcoming year to the economic recovery of the world and to help free the recuperative forces already in motion in the United States from retarding influences from abroad.

The world-wide depression has affected the countries of Europe more severely than our own. . . . The fabric of intergovernmental debts, supportable in normal times, weighs heavily in the midst of this depression.

From a variety of causes arising out of the depression such as the fall in the price of foreign commodities and the lack of confidence in economic and political stability abroad there is an abnormal movement of gold into the United States which is lowering the credit stability of many foreign countries. These and the other difficulties abroad diminish buying power for our exports and in a measure are the cause of our continued unemployment and continued lower prices to our farmers.

Wise and timely action should contribute to relieve the pressure of these adverse forces in foreign countries and should assist in the reestablishment of confidence, thus forwarding political peace and economic stability in the world.

[2] Walter Lippmann and other opposition pundits hauled me over the coals repeatedly for this lack of international courtesy.

. . . The essence of this proposition is to give time to permit debtor governments to recover their national prosperity. I am suggesting to the American people that they be wise creditors in their own interest and be good neighbors.

A flood of propaganda had come from Europe urging that we cancel the war debts. Therefore I stated that no such proposal was involved, and gave reasons for noncancellation, continuing:

I wish further to add that while this action has no bearing on the conference for limitation of land armaments to be held next February, inasmuch as the burden of competitive armaments has contributed to bring about this depression, we trust that by this evidence of our desire to assist we shall have contributed to the good will which is so necessary in the solution of this major question.[3]

The American press at once hailed the proposal in the most glowing terms. Prices of farm products and securities rose at once, retail trade expanded, and men were called back to work. On the 29th of June the *New York Times* summarized the situation:

Great results [are] already achieved . . . that a severe financial crisis was hanging over Germany is fully established . . . that danger . . . not only to Germany but of all Europe and the United States was removed. . . . We cannot but wonder with the rest of the world at the happy revulsion of feeling which everywhere followed. . . .

During this period and subsequent weeks, I was in hourly touch with our representatives in London, Paris, Berlin, and Vienna by transatlantic telephone, and they were in similar close touch with one another. It was the first time that such extensive use had been made of the telephone by our government officials. Mechanical devices prevented the conversations from being tapped; and the telephone afforded far better understanding and much quicker contact than were possible with the slow coding and decoding of formally phrased cables.

Within a week, fifteen of the governments concerned had accepted the proposals unconditionally; the only important opponent was the

[3] "Only an intervention 'in extremis' by President Hoover and his proposal for a moratorium saved Germany" (June 20, 1931), wrote André François-Poncet, the French Ambassador. See his memoirs, *The Fateful Years*, Harcourt, Brace & Co., New York, 1949, p. 5.

French. They still vibrated from hideous wrongs done them by Germany and were slow to lend any helping hand to their brutal enemy. That government raised a host of technical and fictitious difficulties and continued to produce fresh ones as fast as we met them. They kept this up for more than three weeks. Discouragement and destructive forces again began to haunt the world. Further runs on Central and Eastern European banks became prevalent, and further gold poured out of Europe.

Finally on July 5th, I instructed our Ambassador to France, Walter Edge, to inform the French government that I had secured enough support for the proposal and did not require the inclusion of France. They might therefore continue to exact payments from other governments as they fell due, while the other countries would continue to exact payments due from France. It happened that this would leave France (including her payments to the United States) little better off on balance than if she accepted the moratorium, and would isolate her from world cooperation.

In the meantime, the French private institutions had withdrawn most of their banking and commercial loans from other parts of Europe and did not stand to lose on this account. But the withdrawals had made the general situation more acute. Upon receipt of my final message, the French Cabinet very heatedly reversed itself and accepted the plan, with a few minor reservations. However, irreparable damage had been done to the morale of the whole economic world by its delays and its propaganda.

On July 6th, I announced to the press the completion of the agreement, and I breathed easier in the hope that it might still save the situation. There was again a momentary lift in the economic world—but it lasted less than a week.

THE TIME BOMB, AND THE STANDSTILL AGREEMENT

During the French delay, the spirit of panic had gained force and the drains upon Germany, Hungary, and Eastern European countries severely depleted the gold reserves against their currency. But something worse was impelling the crisis. By July 15, 1931, practically all Austrian, German, Hungarian, and European banks farther east had been closed. Various meetings between government representatives were taking place in Europe, but they got precisely nowhere.

In the meantime, Secretary of State Stimson had gone to the South of France on a holiday, and Under Secretary William R. Castle was acting Secretary. I suggested through him to the British government that they call a conference in London on the European financial situation. I requested Messrs. Mellon and Stimson to attend. The meeting was set for the 20th of July. On the 16th and 17th, however, at an intermediate meeting in Paris of various government representatives, including Secretary Stimson, it was proposed by the French that the British, French, and American governments should lend Germany $500,000,000. I informed Secretary Stimson (who urged it) by telephone that the United States government could not join in such a plan, as in my view it would be totally ineffective even if Congress were called into session and approved it.

With these bank closings in Central Europe, I naturally wanted to know if American banks had any loans to or deposits in the banks of this crisis area. I first telephoned Henry Robinson, chairman of a large California bank, who had had much experience in international banking. He told me that many of our banks had bought German trade bills and "bank acceptances," both sixty- and ninety-day paper. The trade bills were supposed to be secured by bills of lading covering goods shipped, and to be payable on delivery of the goods. The bank acceptances were simply "kited" bills without any collateral. Robinson expressed great alarm.

I at once inquired of the Federal Reserve officials what amounts of these bills were held by American banks and business houses. After some inquiry, they informed me that our banks held only $400,000,000 or $500,000,000 of them, and that they could be easily handled. Worrying over the matter during that night I was somehow not satisfied with this report, and in the morning I directed the Comptroller of the Currency to secure an accurate report on such American holdings direct from the banks. Twenty-four hours later I received the appalling news that the total American bank holdings probably exceeded $1,700,000,-000; that certain banks having over $1,000,000,000 of deposits held amounts of these bills which, in case of loss, might affect their capital or surplus and create great public fears. Here was one consequence of the Reserve Board maintaining artificially low interest rates and expanded credit in the United States from mid-1927 to mid-1929 at the urging of European bankers. Some of our bankers had been yielding to sheer greed for the 6 or 7 per cent interest offered by banks in the European panic area.

Worse still, the Comptroller informed me that these European banks were already in default on many bank acceptances and were frantically endeavoring to secure renewals. He thought the "acceptances" comprised a major part of American bank holdings and informed me that some of the "trade bills" did not have the collateral documents attached.

When the Comptroller's information began to come in, I sent for Secretary Mills who was also fearful, and requested him to ask his friends in the Bank of England by telephone what they knew about the volume of these bills. In a day or two they replied, in alarm, that there might be $2,000,000,000 in the banks of Britain and the Dominions, together with Sweden, Norway, Switzerland, Holland and Denmark. They also stated that there were quantities in Latin-American and Asian banks. They said the German and other Eastern European banks were frantically trying to renew the bank acceptances and were being refused.

It looked at this time as if Germany, Austria, Hungary, and other Eastern European countries had as much as $5,000,000,000 of these short-term bills afloat. The Germans had also, over the years since the war, floated many long-term loans by their governments, their municipalities, and their business houses.[4] It looked as if the German total external debt alone, excluding reparations but including long-term debt, might possibly exceed $5,000,000,000. They not only had paid all their reparation instalments to the Allies out of this borrowed money, but had paid for reconstruction of German industry and their budget deficits. It was obvious that they and the others could not meet their short-term obligations, at least for the present.

Thus, the explosive mine which underlay the economic system of

---

[4] The Secretary of State and I, as Secretary of Commerce, had frequently protested at the German bond issues in the United States on the ground that their payment was second to reparations, and that they were being used to pay the Allies.

the world was now coming clearly into view. It was now evident why the European crisis had been so long delayed. They had kited bills to A in order to pay B and their internal deficits.

I don't know that I have ever received a worse shock. The haunting prospect of wholesale bank failures and the necessity of saying not a word to the American people as to the cause and the danger, lest I precipitate runs on our banks, left me little sleep.

The situation was no longer one of helping foreign countries to the indirect benefit of everybody. It was now a question of saving ourselves.

That day, July 19th, I came to the conclusion that, in view of the confusion among leaders in Europe, we must take a strong hand if we were to save our situation as well as theirs. I had in mind a new and drastic solution. I called in Secretaries Mills and Castle, Senator Dwight Morrow, and our Ambassador to England, Charles G. Dawes, who was then in Washington. They fully agreed to my proposals.

I cabled Secretaries Stimson and Mellon my plan, which was for a "standstill" agreement among all banks everywhere holding German and Central European short-term obligations. As my cable outlining the plan might become public, it had to be carefully phrased so as not to fire further alarms as to the already tense Central European situation. The cable read:

The essence of the problem is the restoration of confidence in Germany's economic life, both in Germany and abroad.

1. On the political side, the United States hopes that, through mutual good will and understanding, the European nations may eliminate all friction, so that the world may rely upon the political stability of Europe.

2. On the economic side, the present emergency is strictly a short-term credit crisis. Fundamental pressure on German economy during the period of depression has been relieved by the joint action of the creditor powers in suspending all payments upon governmental debts during the period of one year. But Germany has financed her economic activities to a very great extent through the medium of short-term foreign credits. There is no reason to doubt the soundness of the basis upon which these credits rest, but the general uncertainty which has prevailed for the last few weeks resulted in such a loss of confidence that the German banking and credit structure was subjected to a very severe strain. This strain took two very definite forms,

both of which resulted in a drain of banking resources and the depletion of German gold and foreign exchange holdings.

In the first place there was a flight from the mark within Germany. In the second place there was a withdrawal of foreign deposits and a curtailment on the part of foreign banks of outstanding lines of credit.

(a) As to the first, namely, the internal flight from the mark, this can be and is being successfully combated by the vigorous action of the German Government and the Reichsbank. Once unreasonable fear has been eliminated, it is certain that the patriotism of the German people can be relied on to prevent the destruction of the credit of their own country.

(b) As to the external credits, we believe that the first approach to this problem is the development of a program that will permit the maintenance for an adequate period of time of the present outstanding lines of credit. In this connection it is our understanding that this volume of credit, together with the freed reparations and the natural gain from the allayment of the panic, should be adequate to meet the needs of German economic life for the immediate moment.

On the other hand, it must be apparent that, unless provision is made for the maintenance of these credits, an attempt to provide new ones, whether of short- or long-term character, would be ineffective. In the development of such a program the governments of the countries having principal banking centers, including the United States, Belgium, France, Great Britain, Holland, Italy, Japan, and Switzerland, and other important banking centers, might well undertake to encourage their bankers so to organize as to permit the maintenance for an adequate period of time of present-day outstanding lines of credit to Germany.

The responsibility for working out the details of such a program and the methods of making it effective with due regard to the protection of the banks and the needs of German economy should be left to the banking communities of the respective countries and the central banks could, we believe, be relied on to furnish the necessary leadership, cooperation and direction.

Such voluntary arrangements should be supplemented, for the time being, by strict control of all foreign exchange transactions by the Reichsbank so that the integrity of the program can be maintained and the banks that are participating can be assured that there would be no arbitrary withdrawal either from within or without Germany.

3. It is our belief that if such a program could be made promptly effective

it would result in an immediate restoration of confidence and that in a comparatively short time the necessity for restrictions of this character would disappear and normal conditions would once more prevail. There is all the more ground for faith in such a result in view of the fact that the United States debt suspension program has now become effective and that the events which succeeded the announcement of that program clearly demonstrate that relief from payment of intergovernmental debts established in the minds of the business world the basis for renewed confidence.

4. A committee should be selected by the Bank for International Settlements or created by some other appropriate method to secure cooperation on the following question:

(a) In consultation with the banking interests in the different countries, to provide for the renewal of the present volume of outstanding short-term credits from those countries.

(b) In making an inquiry into the immediate further needs in credit of Germany.

(c) In the development during the course of the next six or eight months of plans for a conversion of some proportion of the short-term credits to long-term credits.

My telephone conversations with Secretaries Stimson and Mellon were far less optimistic about Germany's ability to pay than this cable might indicate. I insisted on the complete necessity of what I called a "Stand-still" agreement.

The Secretaries, in reply, objected to placing this plan before the London Conference lest we appear to be dictating its policies. The Conference met, and the French again proposed a joint loan of $500,000,000 to Germany to be participated in by several governments. Mellon and Stimson again strongly urged this measure upon me. I replied that this was a banker-made crisis, and that the bankers must shoulder the burden of solution, not our taxpayers; moreover, that the amount proposed would not be a drop in the bucket. It was merely partial relief of banks at government expense. Or even if a loan to Germany was provided by American, British, and French and other banks themselves, it would be a wholly inadequate solution. I again informed them by telephone in detail of the situation as to German and other Central European short-term obligations in the United

States and abroad. I also stated that such a loan would not even take care of the American situation alone.

At this point I instructed Mr. Mills to ask a friend in the Bank of England by telephone what their idea was of the French loan proposal. He quickly learned that the Bank of England did not approve of such a loan. Also, the British Treasury officials had no faith that it would meet the crisis. The affair began to take the color of the usual attempt of European political officials to make us the first to refuse something and therefore the scapegoat for anything that happened. Indeed, one reason given to me by Messrs. Stimson and Mellon for American governmental support of a loan was fear of just that. I finally telephoned them emphatically that we would not participate in such a loan and that I was publishing the gist of the standstill proposal to the world that very minute. They protested against the publication as undiplomatic. I issued it nevertheless.

The next day the Conference, with the now public proposal in front of it, adopted the essence of my plan and delegated the Bank for International Settlements at Berne to carry it out. Its success depended on bankers of all countries holding the bills and agreeing further that they would accept pari-passu payments on unsecured bills when payment could be extracted by the Bank for International Settlements.

A group of our New York banks informed me that they could not agree to the stand-still plan and that the only solution was for our government to participate in a large international loan to Germany and other countries. My nerves were perhaps overstrained when I replied that, if they did not accept within twenty-four hours, I would expose their banking conduct to the American people. They agreed.

On July 23rd I made a statement expressing satisfaction with the acceptance of my plan by the Conference.

THE GIGANTIC CENTRAL EUROPEAN KITING OF BILLS—AND ITS DISASTERS

We believed that the amount of these short-term bills afloat could not exceed $5,000,000,000. But the European financial bomb was far bigger than our estimates showed. That became clear a year later when the Bank for International Settlements made a long detailed report, which said in part:

When at the end of March, 1931, the Bank for International Settlements closed its books for the first financial year, the world-wide depression, although characterized by an unusually sharp fall in prices, still showed in most respects the main tendencies of an ordinary depression. On the capital markets there was a large supply of short-term funds at declining rates . . . government credit had not yet been seriously weakened. . . .

[But] it is now possible to estimate that the total amount of short-term international [private] indebtedness which existed at the beginning of 1931 aggregated more than $10,000,000,000. At that time the magnitude of this indebtedness was not known . . . central banks began to realize . . . a danger and they endeavored . . . to strengthen their reserves of foreign exchange. . . . The menace . . . did not appear as self-evident as it does today. . . . [it was] almost certain to break the situation at some point. The liquidation in a single year [was] of more than six billion of short-term indebtedness . . . of the balance . . . still outstanding, a substantial part has in fact become blocked. . . .

It is unnecessary to emphasize the havoc wrought . . . or to dwell upon the stagnation that resulted. . . . Each contributed their part to the persistent fall in prices . . . [and] accentuated the deflationary forces which are oppressing world economy. . . . In an effort to cope with the situation . . . new forces, themselves dislocating, were introduced into the international economic system of the world . . . a whole series of steps designed to arbitrarily arrest the continuation of transfers and to protect home currencies, such as exchange control, standstill agreements, restrictions on imports and exchange [and] suspension of the gold standard . . . with consequent depreciation of currencies . . . [also] to control capital movements and especially to prevent the flight of capital . . . further to control imports . . . [with] allotted foreign exchange for import of "necessary" raw material . . . governments have established import quotas or clearing arrangements. Exchange control . . . forces trade into a kind of strait-jacket. . . . This interference offers no solution . . . [but] aggravates [it].

No greater proof of one cause of the hurricane that swept our shores is needed than this statement. It is also obvious that I was right when I maintained that half a billion of government money would have been only a drop in this ten-billion-dollar bucket.

EFFECTS ON THE UNITED STATES

During the period from April to August, 1931, we lost all the economic gains of the first three months of that year and more. Industrial production decreased by 15 per cent; construction contracts by 20 per cent; farm prices dropped 10 per cent on the average and more in the export commodities. Common stocks had fallen 20 per cent.[6]

A MOMENTARY START AT RECOVERY AGAIN

However, with the combined moratorium on intergovernmental payments and the standstill agreement, we had avoided a panic in the United States. With both these measures, the world breathed more easily again, and recovery began to show itself in the market places. It was only a momentary breathing spell, for the larger forces mentioned by the Bank for International Settlements had now begun to gnaw like wolves into the financial vitals of Britain.

When this economic earthquake spread to our shores, Americans were to learn about the economic interdependence of nations through a poignant experience which knocked at every cottage door.

[6] The Federal Reserve Board indexes show something of the changes during this second stage of the depression:

	Common Stock Prices	Industrial Production	Dept. Store Sales	Factory Pay-rolls	Farm Prices	Merchandise Exports ($ Millions)	Construction Contracts
April	109	90	106	74	70	215	82
May	98	89	97	72	67	204	78
June	95	83	95	68	65	187	74
July	98	80	91	64	65	181	68
August	96	78	88	64	64	165	63

CHAPTER 8

THIRD PHASE OF THE DEPRESSION—
AUGUST TO NOVEMBER, 1931

EFFECTS OF THE BRITISH COLLAPSE

Our breathing spell was short. We had scarcely begun to hope that Central Europe had struck bottom when we received a new and worse blow from Britain.

The first indication came with the beginning of French withdrawals of their considerable gold deposits from London, July 24, 1931. The French also had more than $800,000,000 in deposits payable in gold in American banks. These French withdrawals from Britain were at once interpreted as a lack of confidence in the stability of British currency and credit. Quickly a run on Britain started from other countries. The British at that time were bankers for the world, holding large deposits from all countries and in turn making loans to other countries. In addition they held the huge amounts of German and other Eastern European short-term bills. Confronted by withdrawals from every quarter and unrealizable loans to Central Europe, the British financial situation was akin to that of a bank faced with depositors' demands, but unable to call in its loans and turn them into cash.

The Bank of England tried to stop the run and attract capital—and thus gold to Britain—by the usual device of raising interest rates. That device does not work in times of fear, and, in this instance, had little effect except to spread more fear. On August 1st, the British government inquired if our government had any objection to their negotiating a $250,000,000 private bank loan, largely in the United States. This we encouraged, and it was completed at once by our banks. On

August 5th came a further severe break in British exchange, and on the 26th the British government inquired of us if we would approve another $400,000,000 loan from our banks. We did approve, and the loan was made. Both loans, however, mostly served to create more fear.

Economic earthquakes also have political effects. During the last week in August, revolutions stemming from economic shocks took place in several South American countries. This gave no boost to world confidence. Then, suddenly, a new shudder of fear was sent through the world from report of a mutiny in the British Navy on September 14th.

Finally, on September 21st, the Bank of England defaulted on payments to foreigners. Most security and commodity markets in Europe closed at once. Quickly Denmark, Sweden, Norway, Holland, Bolivia, and India refused gold payment. Greece, Italy, Germany, Austria, and Hungary already had imposed such restrictions on exchange which amounted to the same thing.[1]

In spite of this setback, the United States kept open and doing business on all its exchanges, paying gold dollars over the international counter. But it seemed to me that the bottom was fast dropping out of the economic world. Certainly it dropped out of commodity prices in the United States. Failures among our weak and improperly run banks flamed up, and insensate runs on good banks began in a number of places. Our banks in interior cities were asking for more and more help. Bankers began to make the situation worse by fears of their own. Unable to liquidate long-term loans, they called in or restricted the short-term loans so necessary to industry and commerce.

At this time foreigners concluded that the United States would be the next bulwark of international stability to collapse. They began to withdraw their deposits from our banks in gold. By the end of October we were to lose about $700,000,000 from our gold supply. This cramped our volume of credit and increased our bank demands on their borrowers. To add to our troubles, domestic hoarding of gold and cur-

---

[1] There have been elaborate attempts to prove that the British debacle was the result of having established too high a convertibility or any convertibility of their currency into gold. At best that is only a partial explanation. Certainly their huge loans on feeble security (which we also made) contributed to their difficulties.

rency by our citizens began. Our exports to the world dropped to about one-third of the 1929 rate. Worse still, our exports of principal farm products to Europe had now dropped to almost zero, further demoralizing commodity prices. Our unemployment swelled.

In the five months from April to September the price of wheat had dropped to 55 cents from 74 cents per bushel; the price of cotton to 6 cents per pound.

The ordeal we were passing through is well indicated by the comparison of the Federal Reserve Board's economic indexes of this time (the end of September, 1931) with those of the previous April, when the European panics began. The indexes showed that in this period there was a

Fall in industrial production	18	per cent
Fall in factory pay rolls	20	per cent
Fall in construction contracts	30	per cent
Fall in common stocks	40	per cent

THE AMERICAN LEGION ABANDONS A CASH BONUS AT MY REQUEST

In the midst of this nightmare the American Legion announced its annual convention and its purpose of seeking payment of the "bonus" of $3,400,000,000 in cash from the Federal government. I went to Detroit on September 21st, stayed one hour and addressed the convention. As a result I staved off that blow—for a while.

In mid-September I held an off-the-record press conference. Presidential secretary Walter Newton's note of this meeting states:

The President asked the press to use its utmost exertion to keep the country "steady in the boat," to which the press responded helpfully. He gave an outline of the situation, both its dangers and the tendency of news statements to overestimate these dangers and to make the situation worse. . . . He stated that the world again was faced with a crisis as great as that of June, but with the difference that the economic situation in Great Britain was fundamentally stronger than had been that of Central Europe. No doubt the British crisis seriously weakened the whole economic fabric of the world. All now depended upon the United States. We now were the Verdun of world stability.[2]

[2] Myers and Newton, *The Hoover Administration,* Charles Scribner's Sons, New York, 1936, pp. 120–121.

WE DETERMINE ON MORE UNPRECEDENTED ACTIONS

With the Bank of England's collapse, I determined that bold action must be taken if panic were not to extend to the United States. We were dealing not alone with tangibles, such as unemployment, falling prices, movement of gold, exchange goods, bank deposits, loans, and commodities, but with fear. And fear had grown in virulence because of the greatly increased speed of communication over the world. Our people began postponing purchases and new enterprises—all of which added to our difficulties. It was easy to expound upon the unlimited resources of the United States, its stocks of food, its production and its skills, and the evanescent character of our difficulties; but, when fear strikes, such comfort has little effect. Our job was to dissipate fear as well as to deal with tangible things.

I determined first to try to mobilize our private institutions and, if that failed, to summon every resource of the Federal government. The center of our weakness now was obviously in our banking and financial system—the element most sensitive to fear. And one of our difficulties was that we did not know in advance how weak it was.

At this time I was faced with a practical Democratic control of the Congress, whose antagonism no man could measure or conciliate. The skirmishing preliminary to the Presidential campaign of 1932 had begun. Out of power for three administrations, the Democrats at last saw a chance for victory. They were hot with partisanship, and many of them would not have regretted if demoralization extended through the election.

THE NATIONAL CREDIT ASSOCIATION

During September I had called to the White House for a confidential meeting the Advisory Council of the Federal Reserve Board, consisting of twenty-four bankers, together with the Board itself and Treasury officials. The British had not yet collapsed, but already the signs were ominous enough in our banking world. I suggested that our banks create a central pool of credit of $500,000,000, with powers to borrow another billion, to be administered by their own committee to rescue banks throughout the country which were under pressure. We also tentatively discussed a government corporation for the purpose. I requested that they organize the banks in each Federal Reserve District to make loans on assets of closed banks and thus relieve depositors. This they agreed to do.

On October 2, 1931, eleven days after the British collapse, through Mr. Mellon, I called the heads of the leading banking, insurance, and loan agencies, together with leading Federal officials, to meet with me on the evening of the 4th. I also asked the Congressional leaders of both parties and the chairmen of the committees concerned to a similar meeting on the evening of October 6th. I was by no means sure that the financial institutions either would or could take up the burden. In case they failed, I intended to arrange for a special session of Congress, or in any event, to inform the Congressional leaders of the situation.

To avoid public alarm and press speculation, the meeting with the forty banking and insurance leaders was held in Mr. Mellon's home. It attracted no public notice.

After general discussion of the situation, I presented a program in two parts—one concerning relief for general banking, and the other, relief from mortgage pressure on farms, homes, and real estate generally. In order to avoid confusing the two subjects, I gave the two programs separately.

To the banking group, I proposed a stop to policies of "getting liquid" by needless calling of loans, and urged that they try to furnish full credit to industrial concerns and to other banks under pressure, all as a vital necessity to maintaining employment and prices. I pointed out that the city banks were recalling the advances which they seasonally made to the country banks to finance the crops and thus adding to the pressures.

I proposed that the banks set up a corporation with $500,000,000 paid-in capital, to help banks in need and to loan against the assets of closed banks, so as to melt large amounts of frozen deposits and generally stiffen public confidence. I suggested that this new corporation should have powers to borrow another billion dollars in addition to its capital. On the assurance of Governor Meyer, I promised that the Federal Reserve Banks would assist them to the utmost of their powers.

I informed the conference that I had called a meeting of the Congressional leaders for two days later, declaring that I could take no risks of failure to meet the situation, but urging that American private enterprise demonstrate its ability to protect both the country and itself.

A few of the group evinced enthusiasm for my ideas. But they constantly reverted to a proposal that the government do it—despite my urgings that such a course should be avoided if private enterprise were to perform its own functions.

We had a long and sometimes not too pleasant discussion in which some of them in courteous terms gave me some unnecessary elementary instruction in the principles of banking and insurance.

Finally, however, the banking group agreed to call a meeting of all New York banks the next day to see whether they could not effect my proposal.

To the insurance and real estate loan groups I proposed that we establish a system of mortgage discount banks, the details of which I give later. They were considerably less than enthusiastic. However, I requested them to meet with me and a larger group of their representatives at the White House three days later.

I returned to the White House after midnight more depressed than ever before.

I had long since arranged to attend the World Series at Philadelphia the next day. Although I like baseball, I kept this engagement only because I felt that my presence at a sporting event might be a gesture of reassurance to a country suffering from a severe attack of "jitters."

The bankers having asked that I place my proposals as to a bank guarantee corporation in writing for their meeting, I dictated and signed a letter on the train en route to the game, explaining both the proposals and the reasons for them:

October 5, 1931

Honorable George Harrison
Federal Reserve Bank
New York City

Dear Mr. Harrison:

The request which I laid before the leading New York bankers last night for cooperation in unity of national action to assure credit security can, in the light of our discussion, be simplified to the following concrete measures:

1. They are to take the lead in immediate formulation of a national institution with a capital of $500,000,000. The function of this institution to be:

(*a*) The rediscount of bank assets not now eligible in the Federal Reserve System in order to assure the stability of banks throughout the country from attack by unreasoning depositors. That is to prevent bank failures.

(*b*) Loans against the assets of closed banks to enable them to pay some early dividend to depositors and thus revive many business activities and relieve families from destitution.

2. It is proposed that the capital be underwritten by the banks of the United States as a national effort, possibly with the support of the industrials. New York being the financial center of the nation must of necessity assume both the initiative and the major burden. The effort should be participated in by the country at large by appropriate organization.

3. As I said last night, we are in a degenerating vicious cycle. Economic events of Europe have demoralized our farm produce and security prices. This has given rise to an unsettlement of public mind. There have been in some localities foolish alarm over the stability of our credit structure and considerable withdrawals of currency. In consequence, bankers in many other parts of the country in fear of the possibility of such unreasoning demands of depositors have deemed it necessary to place their assets in such liquid form as to enable them to meet drains and runs. To do this they sell securities and restrict credit. The sale of securities demoralizes their price and jeopardizes other banks. The restriction on credit has grown greatly in the past few weeks. There are a multitude of complaints that farmers cannot secure loans for their livestock feeding or to carry their commodities until the markets improve. There are a multitude of complaints of business men that they cannot secure the usual credit to carry their operations on a normal basis and must discharge labor. There are complaints of manufacturers who use agricultural and other raw materials that they cannot secure credits beyond day to day needs with which to lay in their customary seasonal supplies. The effect of this is to thrust on the back of the farmer the load of carrying the nation's stocks. The whole cumulative effect is today to decrease prices of commodities and securities and to spread the relations of the debtor and creditor.

4. The only real way to break this cycle is to restore confidence in the people at large. To do this requires major unified action that will give confidence to the country. It is this that I have asked of the New York bankers.

5. I stated that if the New York banks will undertake to comply with this

request, I will seek to secure assurance from the leaders of appropriate committees in Congress of both political parties to support my recommendation at the next session for

(*a*) The extension of rediscount eligibility in the Federal Reserve System.

(*b*) If necessity requires, to re-create the War Finance Corporation with available funds sufficient for any emergency in our credit system.

(*c*) To strengthen the Federal Farm Loan Bank System.

Yours faithfully,

HERBERT HOOVER

I was not able to work up much enthusiasm over the ball game, and in the midst of it I was handed a note informing me of the sudden death of Senator Dwight Morrow. He had proved a great pillar of strength in the Senate and his death was a great loss to the country and to me. I left the ball park with the chant of the crowd ringing in my ears: "We want beer!"

That evening the bankers' committee reported that they would form the National Credit Association as requested.

STRENGTHENING THE FEDERAL LAND BANKS

Believing that we would secure little real cooperation from the insurance and other real estate loan agencies in farm mortgages, I sent for Chairman Bestor of the Federal Farm Loan Board and with him worked out a method for further liberalizing the suspensions of foreclosures on farm loans by the Federal Land Banks. We also formulated a plan that I would present to the meeting of the Congressional leaders by which the government would advance more capital to these banks to enable them to expand their loans by $1,000,000,000 and thus aid farmers who were being pressed from other quarters to pay off mortgages.

THE CONGRESSIONAL MEETING

On the evening of October 6th I met the Congressional group at the White House. They comprised thirty-two leading Senators and Congressmen, in political makeup about equally Republican and Democratic. Congress was not in session, but the group included the majority and minority ranking members of the committees concerned.

I recounted the various steps we had taken and frankly presented the world situation confronting us. I pointed out the drop of 70 per cent in our exports; that our tax collections had fallen by 50 per cent; that we were faced with a huge deficit and must expect new taxes, more reliable than those dependent upon personal income. I had prepared in advance a memorandum which I read to them. In summary, it said:

The nations of Europe have not found peace. Hates and fears dominate their relations. War injuries have permitted no abatement. The multitude of small democracies created by the Treaty of Versailles have developed excessive nationalism. They have created a maze of trade barriers between each other. Underneath all is the social turmoil of communism and fascism gnawing at the vitals of young democracies. The armies of Europe have doubled since the demobilization. They have wasted the substance which should have gone into productive work upon these huge armies and massive fortifications. They have lived in a maze of changing military alliances and they have vibrated with enmities and fears. They have borrowed from any foreign country willing to lend, and at any rates of interest, in order to carry unbalanced budgets.

The Treaty of Versailles imposed impossible reparations upon the former enemy states. . . . [I described the way the Germans and others had paid reparations by foreign loans and a flood of short-term bills.]

The Allied countries of the Continent—France, Italy and Belgium—are obliged periodically to reduce their impossible debts by devices of inflation and devaluation. Nineteen countries in the world, in two years, have gone through revolutions or violent social disturbances. Whether or not Germany and Central Europe will avoid Russian infiltrated communism or some other "ism," is still in the balance, and that does not contribute to a revival of world confidence.

The British, while more prudent, are suffering deeply from the shocks of the financial collapse on the Continent. Their abandonment of the gold standard and of payment of their external obligations has struck a blow at the foundations of world economy. The procession of countries which followed Britain off the gold standard has left the United States and France as the only major countries still holding to it without modification.

The instability of currencies, the now almost world-wide restrictions on exchange, the rationing of imports to protect these currencies and the default of bad debts, have cut deeper and deeper into world trade.

We are finding ourselves in much the same position as the British, but in lesser degree. Long-term loans which we made to Europe and the mass of kited bills bought from them are affecting us sadly with each new default. Like the British, we too are increasingly unable to collect moneys due us from abroad. Extensive deposits in our banks owned by foreigners are demand liabilities on our gold reserves and are becoming increasingly dangerous. After the British abandoned the gold standard, even the dollar came under suspicion. Out of an unreasoning fear, gold is being withdrawn from our monetary stocks and bank reserves. These devitalizing drains and the threat of them hang like a Damoclean sword over our credit structure. Banks, fearing the worst, called industrial and commercial loans, and beyond all this the dwindling European consumption of goods has decreased purchases of our farm products and other commodities and demoralized our prices, production and employment.

We are now faced with the problem, not of saving Germany or Britain, but of saving ourselves.

Mr. Mills added further explanations, including our impending deficit, the hoarding of currency, the current drain on our gold reserves, and the necessity to expand the functions of the Federal Reserve System in order to offset the shrinkage in credit.

I presented a program for Congressional action if the bankers' movement did not suffice. I hoped those present would approve my program in order to restore confidence which was rapidly degenerating into panic.

The group seemed stunned. Only Garner and Borah reserved approval. The others seemed shocked at the revelation that our government for the first time in peacetime history might have to intervene to support private enterprise. In order to have some definite conclusions, and for public announcement, I already had dictated the outlines of a memorandum for the legislators to consider, which we might issue to the press as expressing our views. There was strong opposition to a Federal charter for the system of mortgage discount banks, and, in order to get agreement on a statement, I substituted the expansion of the Federal Land Banks. After much discussion and changing of some particulars, the press statement was agreed upon at one o'clock in the morning and handed to the press. It ran as follows:

The prolongation of the depression by the succession of events in Europe, affecting as they have both commodity and security prices, has produced in some localities in the United States an apprehension wholly unjustified in view of the thousand-fold resources we have for meeting any demand. Foolish alarm in these sections has been accompanied by wholly unjustifiable withdrawal of currency from the banks. Such action results in limiting the ability of the banks in these localities to extend credit to business men and farmers for the normal conduct of business, but beyond this to be prepared to meet the possibility of unreasoning demands of depositors the banks are compelled to place their assets in liquid form by sales of securities and restriction of credits, so as to enable them to meet unnecessary and unjustified drains. This affects the conduct of banking further afield. It is unnecessary to specify the unfortunate consequences of such a situation in the districts affected both in its further effect on national prices of agricultural products, upon securities and upon the normal conduct of business and employment of labor. It is a deflationary factor and a definite impediment to agricultural and business recovery.

There is no justification for any such situation in view of . . . the strong position of our Federal Reserve System. Our difficulty is a diffusion of resources and the primary need is to mobilize them in such a way as to restore in a number of localities the confidence of the banker in his ability to continue normal business and to dispel any conceivable doubt in the mind of those who do business with him.

In order to deal with this wholly abnormal situation and to bring about an early restoration of confidence, unity of action on the part of our bankers and cooperative action on the part of the government are essential. Therefore, I propose the following definite program of action, to which I ask our citizens to give their full cooperation:

1. To mobilize the banking resources of the country to meet these conditions, I requested the bankers of the nation to form a national institution of at least $500,000,000. The purpose of this institution to be the rediscount of banking assets not now eligible for rediscount at the Federal Reserve Banks in order to assure our banks, being sound, that they may attain liquidity in case of necessity, and thereby enable them to continue their business without the restriction of credits or the sacrifice of their assets. I have submitted my proposal to the leading bankers of New York. I have been advised by them that it will receive their support, and that at my request they will assume the leadership in the formation of such an organization. The members of the

New York City Clearing House Association have unanimously agreed to contribute their share by pledging $150,000,000, which is two per cent of their net demand and time deposits. I have been assured from other large centers, as far as I have been able to reach, of their support also. I consider that it is in the national interest, including the interest of all individual banks and depositors, that all the banks of the country should support this movement to their full responsibility. It is a movement of national assurance and of unity of action in an American way to assist business, employment, and agriculture.

2. On September 8th, I requested the Governors of the Federal Reserve Banks to endeavor to secure the cooperation of the bankers of their territory to make some advances on the security of the assets of closed banks or to take over some of these assets in order that the receivers of those banks may pay some dividends to their depositors in advance of what would otherwise be the case pending liquidation. Such a measure will contribute to free many business activities and to relieve many families from hardship over the forthcoming winter, and in a measure reverse the process of deflation involved in the tying up of deposits. Several of the districts have already made considerable progress to this end, and I request that it should be taken up vigorously as a community responsibility.

3. In order that the above program of unification and solidarity of action may be carried out and that all parts of the country be enlisted, I request the Governors of the Federal Reserve Banks in each district to secure the appointment of working committees of bankers for each Reserve District to cooperate with the New York group and in carrying out the other activities which I have mentioned.

4. I shall propose to the Congress that the eligibility provisions of the Federal Reserve Act should be broadened in order to give greater liquidity to the assets of the banks, and thus a greater assurance to the bankers in the granting of credits by enabling them to obtain legitimate accommodation on sound security in times of stress. . . .

5. Furthermore, if necessity requires, I will recommend the creation of a finance corporation similar in character and purpose to the War Finance Corporation, with available funds sufficient for any legitimate call in support of credit.

6. I shall recommend to Congress the subscription of further capital stock by the government to the Federal Farm Loan Land Banks (as was done at their founding) to strengthen their resources so that, on the one hand, the

farmer may be assured of such accommodation as he may require and, on the other hand, their credit may be of such high character that they may obtain their funds at low rates of interest.

7. I have submitted the above mentioned proposals which require legislation to the members of Congress, whose attendance I was able to secure on short notice at the evening's meeting—being largely the members of committees particularly concerned—and they approve of them in principle.

8. Premier Laval of France is visiting the United States. It is my purpose to discuss with him the question of such further arrangements as are imperative during the period of the depression in respect to intergovernmental debts. The policy of the American Government in this matter is well known, and was set out by me in public statement on June 20th in announcing the American proposal for a year's postponement of debt payments. Our problem in this respect is one of such adjustment during the period of depression as will at the same time aid our own and world recovery. This being a subject first of negotiation with foreign governments was not submitted for determination at this evening's conference.

9. The times call for unity of action on the part of our people. We have met with great difficulties not of our own making. It requires determination to overcome these difficulties and above all to restore and maintain confidence. Our people owe it not only to themselves and in their own interest, but they can by such an example of stability and purpose give hope and confidence in our own country and to the rest of the world.

Premier Laval had requested an invitation to visit the United States. After the invitation had been extended, a fog of statements arose from Paris that he would propose a reduction in the war debts. The number "8" paragraph above was introduced by me in an attempt to satisfy Senator Borah.

MEETING OF REAL ESTATE LENDING AGENCIES

The conference to discuss further the mortgage situation took place next day (October 7th) at the White House.

To the insurance and real estate loan group represented at the meeting in Mr. Mellon's apartment, I had proposed that they announce a suspension of mortgage foreclosures on the homes and farms of responsible people.

I proposed a system of mortgage discount banks, a plan which I had developed some years before, when Secretary of Commerce. The proposal provided that we establish a national system of twelve mortgage discount banks somewhat comparable to the Federal Reserve Banks (which served only commercial loans). I fashioned it partially after the French system, which had been successful over many years. I suggested that it have a central institution and twelve subsidiary institutions with, say, $50,000,000 initial capital each, to be advanced by the government but ultimately absorbed by the insurance companies, banks, and various lending institutions. These branch mortgage banks were to issue debentures—after the fashion of the Federal Land Banks. It was to discount live mortgages up to 85 per cent of the face value upon the guarantee of the discounter. I proposed some smaller ratio on defaulted mortgages to be based on the value of the property. I proposed also that the central mortgage bank stand behind the branch banks and issue debentures to the public to secure further capital if necessary. All this was designed to protect especially savings banks, insurance companies and ease overloads of mortgages from commercial banks.

I suggested that the debentures would be a prime security as they would have behind them (a) the property, (b) the mortgage, (c) the guarantee of the discounter, (d) the capital of the discount bank. In the French case, these debentures had for many years ranked next to government bonds for private investment.

I pointed out that the mixture of short- and long-term functions in our commercial banks was to a considerable degree the immediate cause of our bank failures. The banks could not realize on their mortgage loans to meet depositors' withdrawals and so had to call in commercial loans, thus paralyzing business and employment. I related the situation in building and loan associations and savings banks, where depositors were withdrawing their savings in order to live, and thus paralyzing the ability of these concerns to make renewals or new loans.

I urged that the discount institution would have many constructive objectives. It would save homes and farms from foreclosure. It would thaw the frozen real estate loan market. It would restore the liquidity of several billion dollars in assets of banks and other institutions; and by making mortgage money liquid, it would make possible the resumption of much home and building construction and thus aid employment.

The idea was not well received, except by the building and loan associations and some savings banks.

One leading insurance president objected that it would result in lower interest rates and thus reduce the policyholders' income. It did not seem to me that this was much of an answer to the people about to lose their homes, who, in most cases, were also policyholders.

In the face of this opposition and that of the Congressional leaders the previous evening, it seemed to be unlikely that I should get the Democratic Congress to set up so radical a system. I therefore reduced this idea to a system of Home Loan Banks, for here I could secure the powerful support of the savings banks and the building and loan associations.

RELIEF OF AGRICULTURE AND OF UNEMPLOYMENT

To ease the agricultural strains I again set the Federal Farm Board to the task of lifting farm prices over the hump of the marketing season from August, 1931, to April, 1932. They gradually overcame a considerable part of the disastrous falls of the summer.

Beginning in July, we strengthened our relief measures throughout the country so that they could carry the additional load of unemployment distress already upon us, which would be, no doubt, still greater during the forthcoming winter of 1931–1932. I give the details of this expanded organization in the next chapter.

LAVAL'S VISIT

At the end of October, Premier Pierre Laval of France made his visit to the United States. His real purpose was to urge a reduction of the French war-debt payments. As France had enough gold on deposit in the United States to cover future debt payments for five or six years, I was not very enthusiastic about that part of his errand. I assured him that the whole basis of American war-debt settlements was capacity to pay. At the same time I urged him to relax some of the unnecessarily severe restrictions on Germany, in the interest of maintaining the German democratic regime.

We issued a joint statement on October 24th, which consisted mostly of expressions of good will. The only paragraph of importance was:

Our especial emphasis has been upon the more important means through which the efforts of our governments could be exerted toward restoration of economic stability and confidence. Particularly we are convinced of the importance of monetary stability as an essential factor in the restoration of normal economic life in the world in which the maintenance of the gold standard in France and the United States will serve as a major influence.

It is our intent to continue to study methods for the maintenance of stability in international exchange. . . .

Generally my recorded opinion of Laval at the time was that he was an able French political leader. There could be no doubt as to his complete and almost blind devotion to French interests.

RENEWED SIGNS OF RECOVERY

By the latter part of October, 1931, because of the creation of the bankers' National Credit Association, and the publication of our other proposals, the country began to regain confidence that we could withstand the blows from abroad. Also, foreigners had lost their fears that the United States like Britain might go under financially. In the month of November, bank failures fell to about the normal pre-depression death rate of banks, as against $450,000,000 in October. The hoarding of currency dropped from the October level of $245,000,000 to practically nothing in November. The drain of "fear gold" to foreigners, amounting to $337,000,000 in October, changed to an inward flow of $89,000,000 in November. Industrial common stocks rose nearly 40 per cent. The price of wheat (helped by the Farm Board) rose nearly 50 per cent in a month.

Thus an acute crisis which was rapidly nearing panic had been averted. Again I began to hope that we had touched bottom and we would not need to ask Congress for very extensive financial legislation; also that the time had come when we could devote our energies to reforms and to other measures for the common good which the crisis had forced us to neglect.

CHAPTER 9

FOURTH PHASE OF THE DEPRESSION— NOVEMBER, 1931, TO JULY, 1932

By the end of November, 1931, however, our small burst of recuperation petered out, and all the ground we had gained—and more—was quickly lost. December opened under great economic strain and an opposition Congress faced us.

The whole economic situation in Europe proved more precarious in its foundations than even I had feared. If we could have had an accurate European balance sheet before us a year sooner, our course and our remedial measures would have been better. But we were defending ourselves in a dim light at best.

Soon the renewed blows on our economic system were grim enough, each harder than the one before. After a few weeks of enterprising courage the bankers' National Credit Association became ultraconservative, then fearful, and finally died. It had not exerted anything like its full possible strength. Its members—and the business world—threw up their hands and asked for governmental action.

EIGHTEEN POINTS OF A FEDERAL LEGISLATIVE PROGRAM

To meet this increasingly desperate situation, we expanded our program of economic defense and recovery measures, even further than at the Congressional meeting a month before. The following is the full program including secondary items, some of which were developed later in the session but are given here in full rather than in scattered parts.

1. Our tax receipts had fallen by more than one-half, and we were

faced with a $2,000,000,000 annual deficit. As the stability of the American government was the first necessity in the world, I proposed to balance the budget by drastic decreases and postponements of ordinary expenditures, and increased taxation.

2. In order that the country should be absolutely assured that the government was in position to meet any public necessity, I proposed for the emergency the establishment of a Reconstruction Finance Corporation, with a capital of $500,000,000 and authority to borrow up to $3,000,000,000 from either the Treasury or private sources. These resources were to be used for the following purposes:

(a) to establish and finance a system of agricultural credit banks that would make loans for crop and livestock production not to be had during the depression from existing banks;

(b) to make loans to the existing Farmers' Intermediate Credit Banks to enable them to finance the marketing of the crops;

(c) to make loans to building and loan associations, savings banks, insurance companies, and other real estate mortgage agencies so as to enable them to postpone foreclosures;

(d) to make loans to banks and financial institutions "which cannot otherwise secure credit where such advances will protect the credit structure and stimulate employment";

(e) to make loans to the railways to prevent receiverships;

(f) to finance exports that would aid the farmers and the unemployed;

(g) to finance modernization and construction of industrial plants and utilities so as to increase employment and plant efficiency;

(h) to make loans to closed banks upon their sound assets so as to enable them at least partially to pay out deposits to a multitude of families and small businesses who were in distress because their deposits were tied up pending liquidation or reorganization of these banks.

3. To liberalize during the emergency the eligibility requirements for discount of loans to member banks at the Federal Reserve Banks so as to widen the ability of banks to accommodate small or large business loans.

4. To make government bonds temporarily eligible for part coverage

of the currency, so as to compensate for our fluctuating gold supply and to prevent our being forced off the gold standard.

5. To authorize the Federal Reserve Banks to expand credit further by open market operations and lowered discount rates so as to counteract the credit stringencies caused by foreign withdrawals. While we knew that Reserve action had been futile in stopping booms, we hoped it might have some effect by expanding credit in depression.

6. Reform of the bankruptcy laws to facilitate reorganization of business concerns and settlement of overwhelming debts of individuals without destroying their business.

7. Reform in Stock Exchange and stock promotion practices.

8. Immediate reform of the banking system. I stated: "Our people have a right to a banking system in which their deposits shall be safeguarded," so that "the flow of credit be not subject to interruption."

9. Subscription by the government of further capital to the Federal Land Banks so as to permit expansion of their lending capacity by $1,000,000,000 with which to take over expiring farm mortgages, and relaxation of certain regulations in these banks in order to give more chance to farmers under mortgages.

10. Continuation of the Federal Farm Board stabilization of agricultural prices against panic selling and to make loans to farm cooperatives.

11. A system of Home Loan Discount Banks to protect home mortgages as the foundation for a national system of mortgage discount banks.

12. A continuation of our system of national, state, and local committees for family relief.

(a) An expanded public appeal for their support.

(b) An appropriation of 85,000,000 bushels of wheat and 500,000 bales of cotton from the Farm Board stocks to be distributed by the relief committees.

(c) In the early spring of 1932, when the resources of state and local committees for direct family relief were under strain, we secured an appropriation of $300,000,000 to aid the states, but contingent upon additions by the states, and to be expended through our committees.

(d) Appropriations of $600,000,000 to $700,000,000 for ordinary Federal public works (a direct charge on the Treasury).

(e) Authorization to the RFC to make loans up to $1,800,000,000 for 2 (g) above and to public bodies for "reproductive" public works, including slum clearance.

(f) Appropriation for the overhead expenses of our national unemployment organization.

13. Reorganization of the railways on a sound financial basis in the manner recommended by the Interstate Commerce Commission.

14. Authority to regulate interstate electric power rates and utility finance.

15. Ratification of the moratorium on intergovernmental debts.

16. Cooperation with other governments in promoting world recovery. This included the re-creation of the former World War Debt Commission to examine and report to Congress on the problems involved in these debts.

17. Appropriation for the expenses of the American delegation to the World Economic Conference to stabilize currency and lower trade barriers.

18. Authority to consolidate and abolish government bureaus and to make other administrative reforms in the interest of economy and efficiency.

I take up the details and troubles with each of these proposals in subsequent chapters.

THE DEMOCRATIC CONGRESS AND SOME PERSONALITIES

The start of the fourth and worst phase to date of the depression coincided with the convening of the Democratic-controlled 72nd Congress, December, 1931.

I had no reason to look to the new Congress with much enthusiasm or hope of friendly cooperation. In this session, we were dealing in reality with three elements: the normal practice of a political party seeking public office; a minority group intent, consciously and unconsciously, upon collectivism; and an overconservative group to whom our recommendations came as a shock.

In launching our program of action and reform, I said to Congress on December 8th:

We must put some steel beams in the foundations of our credit structure. It is our duty to apply the full strength of our government not only to the immediate phases but to provide security against the shocks and the weaknesses which have already been proven.

The new Senate comprised 48 Republicans, 47 Democrats, and 1 Farmer-Labor. But actually we had no more than 40 real Republicans, as Senators Borah, Norris, Cutting, and others of the left wing were against us.

Senator James Watson, Republican Senate leader, rejected my advice that the Democrats be allowed to organize the Senate and thereby convert their sabotage into responsibility. I felt that I could deal more constructively with the Democratic leaders if they held full responsibility in both houses, than with an opposition in the Senate conspiring in the cloakrooms to use every proposal of mine for demagoguery. Watson, of course, liked the extra importance of being majority leader, and the Republicans liked to hold committee chairmanships and the nicer offices in the Capitol.

The House had 219 Democrats, and of those quite a few were left-wingers. There were 214 Republicans, of whom 12, such as Fiorello La Guardia and Louis T. McFadden, were "Progressives." They almost invariably aided the opposition.

The Democrats organized the House with John N. Garner as Speaker and Henry T. Rainey, floor leader.

Garner [1] was a man of real statesmanship when he took off his political pistols. Philosophically he was a pragmatist, a bitter partisan and

---

[1] He served as Vice President with Roosevelt for eight years and had his awakening to the meaning of the New Deal only after five years, when he fell out with the President. In his authorized biography by Bascom Timmons, published in 1948, he says:

"I fought President Hoover with everything I had, under Marquis of Queensberry, London prize ring and catch-as-catch-can rules. But I always fought according to the rules. My judgment may have been frail as to the proper solution of the vexing problems but my course from 1931 to 1933, while I was Speaker, as in all my public career, put public welfare above partisan advantage. I thought my party had a better program for national recovery than Mr. Hoover and his party.

"I never reflected on the personal character or integrity of Herbert Hoover. I never doubted his probity or his patriotism. In many ways he was superbly equipped for the Presidency. If he had become President in 1921 or 1937 he might have ranked with the great Presidents. Today I think Herbert Hoover is the wisest statesman on world affairs in America. He may be on domestic affairs, too."

If Garner had a program he never disclosed it; certainly his interpretation of "catch as catch can" was made by himself. His main program of public welfare was to put the Republicans out.

adroit. His program of public welfare in this session was simple—get the Republicans out and the Democrats in. His mental orbit during this period was dominated by political tactics and strategy and his capacities in this field were of a high order. He was engagingly frank and honored his undertakings. The few times when I secured his agreement for certain action, his word was always good.

Rainey held honorary degrees from all the schools of demagoguery. He later proved to be an ardent collectivist of a muddled variety. His opposition, however, had a certain element of consistency as he was not only for overthrowing the Republican party but our economic and social system in general. He stopped at no misrepresentation, and no smear was too filthy for him to use.

Joseph T. Robinson, the Democratic Senate leader, was a man of considerable statesmanship, and at times he gave me cooperation. Had he not been under constant influence of malign politics, he would have gone down in history as a distinguished senator. He, however, was a senior of the old school of southern opposition.[2]

During the Congressional election, a year before, Senator Robinson repeatedly declared that his party had a complete program for economic recovery. And on December 5, 1931, before the session opened, Garner told the press: "The duty of the Democratic majority of the House is to offer such measures as we believe will best advance our country to prosperity and to enhance the comfort, security and contentment of our people." These were fine words, indeed.

But when I conferred with both of them, before introducing my program to the Congress, their actions belied those words.

I reviewed the gravity of the national situation and expressed my urgent desire to cooperate, adding that, if the Democrats had a constructive program, I would go the full length to support it. I asked for their program. They replied that it was my responsibility to propose a program and theirs to criticize it. The fact was, as shown by later experience, they had no program except to embarrass me and to assure the country that if I were thrown out, they could save the nation. They were

---

[2] Robinson later became the Senate majority leader for the New Deal. He had put through every Roosevelt collectivist measure for five years. Yet, before he died, he declared to friends that he had been misled.

very skillful in camouflaging their actions with loud oratory on human suffering.

The month before Congress met, I had interviews with more than 160 members of the Senate and House of both parties in an effort to secure expedition and unity of action.

On our side we had the advantage of the able and loyal men in the Cabinet and other leading positions in the administration and of many courageous men in Congress. I remember them with gratitude and with the fellowship that stems from principles held in common.

Senator Watson, as Republican leader of the Senate, was always a problem. His economic, social and political faith differed from mine, and he never fully buried his bitterness over my nomination. He had spasmodic loyalties and abilities. He was a cheerful soul, genial and at times adroit. When in 1929 the question of a Senate leader arose, some of the Senators consulted me. I suggested David Reed of Pennsylvania as a man of ability and integrity. Later they informed me that Borah had supported Watson for the position. This was unexplainable upon any philosophy except that of Puck.

Bertrand Snell, the Republican House leader, was sturdy, honest, and devoted. He was disposed to regard his opponents' tactics and smears with contempt which, however, allowed them to get away with character assassination. Their chief tactic was, of course, the constant parrot-call that I was the sole creator of the world depression.

In some despair at my personal failure to secure any assurance of cooperation from the Democratic side, I requested Congressmen Snell and Hawley and one or two other leading House Republicans to arrange a meeting of their own with Garner, Rainey, and other House Democratic leaders, and urge again that, in view of the perils confronting the country, we should handle all emergency measures in a completely nonpartisan manner. We on our side would join in any constructive program they might offer. Alternatively, if they would help work out our program, the Democrats would be given full credit, and they would be expected to introduce their share of the measures. Snell and Hawley reported that Garner and his fellows would agree to nothing. Rainey was especially bad, as Congressman Hawley confirmed in this note to me:

My dear Mr. President:

After a somewhat extended discussion of the situation in the country, Mr. Rainey stated that he would not sponsor the legislation as proposed by you nor would he urge the committees having jurisdiction of such legislation to consider and favorably report thereon. When I urged that the welfare of the country and its people required the prompt enactment of the remedial legislation as proposed by you, he gave as the reason for his refusal "We intend to beat him, Hoover." He repeated this in other words . . . [unprintable].

W. C. HAWLEY

No matter how much emotion a President may feel at all these aberrations of the democratic process, he cannot or, at least, should not display it lest he injure the process itself. There was a choice of two courses: The one was to battle publicly with the Democratic-controlled Congress; or to do one's best to cooperate, consult, explain, and implore, with the hope of getting somewhere.

I had felt deeply that no President should undermine the independence of legislative and judicial branches by seeking to discredit them. The constitutional division of powers is the bastion of our liberties and was not designed as a battleground to display the prowess of Presidents. They just have to work with the material that God—and the voters—have given them.

In these times of deepening depression I was crippled in another way from enlisting both Congressional and public support because fully to reveal the dangers that we were fighting off would have heightened the dangers themselves by the fanning of fear. With our weak banking system, such a full revelation might have stimulated public apprehension to the point of panic. Also, unless the President remains cheerful and optimistic he becomes a depressant. Congress and the press do not labor under such handicaps.

This being the last session before the Presidential election of 1932, it developed all that is worst in the democratic process. I am making no complaint. I accepted the job of my own free will.

THE DEMOCRATIC CONGRESS STARTS

In my message to Congress on December 8, 1931, I reviewed the situation with restraint because of the panicky feeling, saying in part:

The chief influence affecting the state of the Union during the past year has been the continued world-wide economic disturbance. Our national concern has been to meet the emergencies it has created for us and to lay the foundations for recovery. . . .

The economic depression has . . . deepened in every part of the world. . . . In many countries political instability, excessive armaments, debts, governmental expenditures, and taxes have resulted in revolutions, in unbalanced budgets and monetary collapse and financial panics, in dumping of goods upon world markets, and in diminished consumption of commodities.

Within two years there have been revolutions or acute social disorders in nineteen countries, embracing more than half the population of the world. Ten countries have been unable to meet their external obligations. In fourteen countries, embracing a quarter of the world's population, former monetary standards have been temporarily abandoned. In a number of countries there have been acute financial panics or compulsory restraints upon exchange and foreign trade. These disturbances have many roots in the dislocations from the World War. Every one of them has reacted upon us. They have sharply affected the markets and prices of our agricultural and industrial products. They have increased unemployment and greatly embarrassed our financial and credit system.

As our difficulties during the past year have plainly originated in large degree from these sources, any effort to bring about our own recuperation has dictated the necessity of cooperation by us with other nations in reasonable effort to restore world confidence and economic stability. . . .

. . . Cooperation . . . with foreign countries [upon the moratorium and Stand-still agreements] has contributed to localize and ameliorate a number of serious financial crises or moderate the pressures upon us and thus avert disasters which would have affected us. . . .

I retraced the domestic and foreign measures we had taken. I then made special proposals along the lines of those tentatively agreed upon at the White House conference of October 6th, related in the last chapter.

The Democratic leaders at once attacked my proposals, and denounced me as responsible for the depression. The nature of their future tactics immediately appeared. Their method was to sabotage and delay to as great an extent as possible, without lighting fires of public opposition.

One indication of the urgency was the failure of banks with deposits of over $400,000,000, during December and January.

In view of the gravity of the situation I urged Congress to remain in session over the Christmas holidays; but at the demand of the Democratic leaders it adjourned for about two weeks' vacation. The only legislation passed in December was a ratification of the moratorium on intergovernmental payments.

Congress having reconvened on January 4, 1932, and having shown little disposition for quick action, I followed up the December 8th message and again pointed out the gravity of the situation and urged speed in legislation, restating our program with additions. In this message I made a special appeal for nonpartisan action, saying:

At the convening of the Congress on December 7th I laid proposals before it . . . to unshackle the forces of recovery . . . I should be derelict in my duty if I did not at this time emphasize the paramount importance to the nation of constructive action . . . at the earliest possible moment. These recommendations have been largely developed in consultation with leading men of both parties, of agriculture, of labor, of banking and of industry. . . . They have no partisan character. We can and must replace the unjustifiable fear of the country by confidence.

During the following six months we were in constant battle against Democratic tactics of sabotage and delay which prolonged and deepened the depression.

CHAPTER 10

FOURTH PHASE OF THE DEPRESSION—
NOVEMBER, 1931, TO JULY, 1932 *(Cont'd)*

RECONSTRUCTION FINANCE CORPORATION

The first of the governmental props under the credit structure made necessary by our rotten banking system and pressures from abroad was the Reconstruction Finance Corporation.

In an effort to expedite the bill creating this Corporation, and to assure its non-partisan character, I sent for Democratic leaders Robinson and Garner and offered to accept their personal recommendations for one director each. The bill became law on January 22nd—nearly six weeks later than was at all necessary in view of its manifest urgency and of our conferences with the Congressional leaders, two months before the session.

Several of our proposals for this legislation were deleted or hamstrung. The security and other conditions for loans made were unnecessarily stringent. The securities required took no account of the fact that values were depressed below their true worth. (In the crisis in Detroit later on, this contributed to disaster.) The authority to make loans to industry for improvement of plants—one of my strongest and most urgent points—was eliminated. Certain types of loans to stimulate exports of agricultural commodities and to set up a series of agricultural banks to make loans for production purposes were deleted. Loans to enable closed banks to distribute the cash value of their assets were also deleted. Loans to public bodies which could have been used for reproductive public works were excluded. However, I determined to make the best of it and try to get it amended later. I issued the following statement upon the legislation to the press on January 22nd:

It brings into being a powerful organization with adequate resources, able to strengthen weaknesses that may develop in our credit, banking and railway structure, in order to permit business and industry to carry on normal activities free from the fear of unexpected shocks and retarding influences.

Its purpose is to stop deflation in agriculture and industry and thus to increase employment by the restoration of men to their normal jobs. It is not created for the aid of big industries or big banks. Such institutions are amply able to take care of themselves. It is created for the support of the smaller banks and financial institutions, and through rendering their resources liquid to give renewed support to business, industry, and agriculture. It should give opportunity to mobilize the gigantic strength of our country for recovery.

I appointed a bipartisan board with Eugene Meyer of the Federal Reserve Board as chairman. Mr. Meyer was a most able man with long experience. I appointed former Vice President Charles Dawes as president and administration head. The appointment of General Dawes gave great public confidence. Whether the RFC legislation was expedited by my prior promise to Robinson and Garner that they might each select a director, I do not know. They were, however, instantly ready with their two names. They selected Harvey C. Couch of Arkansas and Jesse Jones of Texas, who proved to be especially able directors. The other directors whom I appointed were Gardner Cowles, Sr., of Iowa, a Republican, and Wilson McCarthy of Utah, a Democrat. Ogden Mills, Under Secretary of the Treasury, was a director *ex officio*.

Originally, I expected Secretary Mellon to accept a directorship, but he urged that Mr. Mills take his place. Mr. Mellon, advancing in years and having served as Secretary of the Treasury longer than any other man, thought he would like to have some less strenuous appointment. As the Ambassadorship to Great Britain was then vacant, because of General Dawes' appointment to the RFC, I was glad to tender it to him. Ogden Mills replaced him early in 1932. The shift to Mills as Secretary was of great help, for he warmly supported my views on handling the depression. He had one of the finest intellects in the country, and was a man of the highest integrity and devotion to public interest.

Under the leadership of General Dawes, the RFC went to work vigorously to implement its curtailed powers. The bank failures measured in deposits were reduced during the following 6 months to a rate of about $10,000,000 a month (about normal mortality) as against a rate of about $200,000,000 a month prior to the creation of the corporation.

After the passage of the act, I took up the restoration of the powers which had been deleted. They were delayed for many months despite urging from me, and when the Congress, toward the end of the session, did take up these proposals, the opposition took a new tack. A series of amendments and expansions to our proposals were put before the House. The amendments were of two varieties: one being an authority to the RFC to make loans indiscriminately; the other, the addition of a huge pork barrel of "nonproductive" public works, which I describe later.

As to the loan maneuver, I said in part (July 11, 1932):

This expansion of authority of the Reconstruction Corporation would mean loans . . . for any conceivable purpose on any considerable security for anybody who wants money. It would place the government in private business in such fashion as to violate the very principle of public relations upon which we have builded our nation, and render insecure its very foundations. Such action would make the Reconstruction Corporation the greatest banking and money-lending institution of all history. It would constitute a gigantic centralization of banking and finance to which the American people have been properly opposed for the past one hundred years. The purpose of the expansion is no longer in the spirit of solving a great major emergency but to establish a privilege whether it serves a great national end or not. . . .

It would be necessary to set up a huge bureaucracy, to establish branches in every county and town in the United States. . . . Every political pressure would be assembled for particular persons. It would be within the power of these [RFC] agencies to dictate the welfare of millions of people, to discriminate between competitive business at will, and to deal favor and disaster amongst them. . . .

[The sole limitation under the amendment is that . . .] borrowers shall not have been able to obtain loans from private institutions upon acceptable terms. This at once throws upon the corporation all the doubtful loans in the United States. It would result in every financial institution calling upon their customers whom they regard as less adequately secured to discharge their loans and to demand the money from the government through the Reconstruction Corporation. The organization would be constantly subjected to conspiracies and raids of predatory interests, individuals and private corporations. Huge losses and great scandals must inevitably result. It would mean the squandering of hundreds of millions of public funds to be ultimately borne by the taxpayer.

. . . This proposal violates every sound principle of public finance and government. Never before has so dangerous a suggestion been seriously made to our country. Never before has so much power for evil been placed at the unlimited discretion of seven individuals (the Board of Directors).[1]

Finally, the Congress (July 16th) passed the additional authorities without this provision. They adopted the $1,800,000,000 for reproductive works, $300,000,000 for loans to states for relief, and authorized the Corporation to create the Agricultural Production Banks. They again refused to relax its earlier restrictions on loans and to give authority to make loans to industry for plant expansion. The authority to make loans to closed banks on their assets was stopped by Senator Glass. He informed me he was "for it but wanted to use it as a bait to pass the Banking Reform Bill." We never got it either way, and great suffering resulted from the freezing of small depositors' money.

Speaker Garner succeeded in inserting one terribly dangerous clause in the amended act which was ultimately to contribute to more disaster. He put in a provision requiring publication each month of the names of borrowers from the RFC and the amount borrowed. I objected that this would create fear that any institution borrowing was in difficulties and might cause a run upon any borrower bank or business. The Senate modified this to provide that the information be transmitted as a confidential communication to the clerks of the Senate and House. Senator Robinson informed me that he had an agreement with Garner that these communications would not be published, and he announced in the Senate wording to this effect.

[1] During the New Deal regime the RFC was expanded to include such very undesirable purposes. It finally blew up in a Senate investigation in 1951 where every evil that I had predicted was exposed!

Had it not been for Robinson's assurance, I would probably have had to veto the bill. In spite of such an assurance, however, Garner reversed this undertaking a few months later—and many runs on banks ensued.[2]

EXPANSION OF THE FEDERAL LAND BANKS

On January 23, 1932, Congress passed the authorization of increased capital for the Federal Land Banks. However, it rejected vital amendments to the old law which would have permitted much wider latitude to Land Banks in taking over farm mortgages from other institutions, and other provisions that would have secured better treatment for hard-pressed but deserving farmers—all of which would have prevented many foreclosures.

The Democratic majority delayed passing these latter portions of my recommendations for fourteen months—until March, 1933, just before I went out of office.

CREATION OF THE HOME LOAN BANKS

I have related in previous chapters the pressures which fell upon home owners during financial stress due to the inadequacies of our banking and mortgage lending machinery. I have mentioned my proposals for the creation of a national system of mortgage discount institutions, not only to prevent these stresses, but to make home mortgage money more readily available in normal times. All this seems dull economics, but the poignant American drama revolving around the loss of the old homestead had a million repetitions straight from life, not because of the designing villain but because of a fault in our financial system.

Had we been able to get a general mortgage discount institution established at the time I proposed, it would have saved thousands of homes, farms, and holdings of productive city real estate from foreclosure, and prevented many bank failures. And, above all, it would have promoted home ownership, and employment on home construction.

There was also another problem for the home owner. While in normal times he could easily borrow 50 per cent of the value of his

[2] After the New Deal came into power all my proposals were adopted.

property at reasonable rates, many new home seekers needed more than this, and so there had grown up a great business in second mortgages. These mortgages required, with various discounts and charges, from 8 to 25 per cent per annum and made home owning and construction too costly.

Since I could not get my larger plan through, I reduced it to the more limited project of the Home Loan Banks which had the wholehearted support of the savings banks and the building and loan associations, with their millions of hard-pressed members. I hoped that upon this foundation we could build the much needed larger structure.[3]

I announced to the press on November 13, 1931:

I shall propose to Congress the establishment of a system of Home Loan Discount Banks. . . .

For the present emergency purpose of relieving the financial strains upon sound building and loan associations, savings banks, deposit banks, and farm loan banks that have been giving credit through the medium of small mortgage loans upon urban and farm properties used for homes. Thereby to relieve pressures upon home and farm owners.

I described to the press the details of the proposal. In summary they were that the Federal government was to furnish the initial capital for this system to be repaid by a small percentage on loans and eventually to become, not a government institution, but a cooperative institution between the building and loan associations, the savings banks, and other home-loan agencies. The Home Loan Banks were to secure further capital by the issue of debentures.

I proposed to the chairman of the Congressional committees that the bill should authorize a special type of amortized home mortgage, where first mortgage loans would be based on 80 per cent of the valuation of the property in cases where borrowers were responsible people.

The security for the issue of debentures by the Home Loan Banks would have been ample under such provisions. There would be the property under the mortgage for 20 per cent less than its value, the guarantee of the discounter, and the capital of the Home Loan Banks.

[3] It has not been done yet, although it was recommended in 1949 by the Commission on Organization of the Executive Branch of the Government in order to relieve the Federal Government of many loan activities and for other purposes.

Early in January, 1932, the Banking and Currency Committee of the Senate formulated this bill, but with much more drastic provisions than I urged. Further hamstringing and delaying tactics began at once. For some unaccountable reason Senator Couzens, "the friend of the common man," became the mouthpiece for the opposition. The "common man" suffers much too much at the hands of some seekers for power and pomp. In Committee, Couzens proposed conditions surrounding loans which were so restrictive that the plan could not have functioned.

Early in February, I summoned the building and loan association leaders of the country to a conference at the White House. They agreed to wage a campaign of education—propaganda, if that word seems better—for the purpose of obtaining a proper law, promptly. They had a low opinion of Couzens' saintliness. At every meeting with Congressional leaders I urged the passage of the bill in its more liberal form. The insurance companies sent agents to lobby against it. We got our mangled bill reported out of committees—but got no further action.

In March I called upon Senator George Moses for aid. He was an adroit manager of legislation. He insisted on awaiting his chance, and I grew most impatient at his delays. However, on July 12th he arranged that Senator Watson should call up the bill. Senator Couzens promptly stabbed it by securing passage of amendments which, had they been finally incorporated, would have made the plan wholly inoperative. Senator Borah also tacked on an amendment authorizing a Treasury issue of one billion dollars fiat money, which, of course, had nothing to do with the Home Loan Banks. Senator Moses adroitly rid the bill of many of the obnoxious amendments, except Borah's. That the bill passed in the end was partly due to the fact that nobody liked Couzens.

Senator Couzens was a curiously perverse person, with alternating streaks of generosity and hatred and an instinct to be "agin" things. Although he called himself a "progressive," he was, without knowing it, a profound reactionary.

Our leaders tried to eliminate the Borah fiat money in the House. However, after it had been twice defeated in that body, Senator Glass sent me word not to worry, that at Borah's request he had drafted the text of that amendment and that Borah, not knowing anything about the technical aspects of the banking laws, would find that no consequential amount of fiat money could ever be issued under it.

The Act in final form limited the mortgages to be discounted to 50 per cent of the value of the property and eliminated all discount of delinquent mortgages. However, as the session was near to its end, I thought it better to take it in this crippled form, rather than run the risk of no bill at all. Although it authorized an appropriation to set up the banks, no definite appropriation had been voted. A resolution to appropriate funds, under the Senate rules, would need to go over a day unless unanimous consent could be obtained; and next day Congress was to adjourn. When it was proposed Senator Couzens promptly objected. But, when he was off guard, Senator Moses offered an authorization to the RFC to subscribe the capital as an amendment to a minor bill, which had been sent over from the House at the last moment. The amendment was carried, the conferees on this bill adopted it, and the Home Loan Banks were born.

The next day I signed the bill with the following statement:

I have today signed the Home Loan Bank Bill. This institution has been created on the general lines advocated by me in a statement to the press on November 13th last. . . . Its purpose is [to establish] . . . an institution for home owners somewhat similar to that performed in the commercial field by the Federal Reserve banks through their discount facilities.

There are to be eight to twelve such banks established in different parts of the country with a total capital of $125,000,000 to be initially subscribed by the Reconstruction Finance Corporation. Building and loan associations, savings banks, insurance companies, etc., are to be eligible for membership in the system. Member institutions are required to subscribe for stock of the Home Loan Banks and to absorb gradually the capital and they may borrow from the banks upon their notes to be secured by the collateral of sound home mortgages.

I noted that the Borah inflation amendment would not have much effect and continued:

I do not, therefore, feel that the amendment is such as would warrant refusal to approve the measure which means so much to hundreds of thousands of home owners, is such a contribution to their relief; such a contribution to establishment of home ownership; and such an aid to immediate increase of employment.

The bill had been tragically delayed for nine months, and its powers greatly attenuated. In the meantime many thousands of families had lost their homes. That was heartbreakingly unnecessary. Many mutual building and loan associations which might have been saved had collapsed. But, as one of the opposition expressed it, the service of the institution had been delayed so that no political benefits could come to my administration.

On August 6th, I announced the appointment of the directors of the Home Loan Banks [4] under the chairmanship of Franklin W. Fort. Fort, an able banker and a former Congressman, had the system set up and in action within thirty days.

SAVING THE GOLD STANDARD AND EXPANDING RESERVE BANK CREDIT

Our original program included temporarily enlarging the "eligibility" of securities for loans which could be borrowed upon from the Federal Reserve Banks together with an authority to them of further credit expansion. These matters had been considered and approved by the conference with Congressional leaders on October 6, 1931. The proposals were mainly to protect us against the effect of sudden withdrawal by foreigners of large deposits in the United States or from a "flight of capital" engendered by American citizens which might result in further gold exports. These possibilities carried the danger of shrinking credit and also of forcing us, like the British, off the gold standard. Secretary Mills and I had repeatedly urged Senator Glass and Congressman Steagall, Chairman of the House Committee concerned, to report the bill for this purpose out of their committees.

On February 7, 1932, Secretary Mills informed me that the gold situation had become critical, and that there was immediate danger of

---

[4] The succeeding administration partially removed the shackles on the Home Loan Banks to which I had objected. Nineteen years later, on Dec. 31, 1951, the eleven banks (two had been amalgamated) had a total of over 4,000 member institutions with aggregate assets of more than $15,000,000,000. During that period the banks had made loans of more than $3,000,000,000, all repaid except for a current outstanding balance. Under the provisions for the absorption of the capital by members, the government had been entirely paid off. As I had planned, it had become in effect a private institution.

not being able to meet foreign withdrawals and "earmarking" [5] which were then going on at the rate of $100,000,000 a week. He was greatly alarmed that we were within two or three weeks of being forced off the gold standard by inability to meet these gold demands.

Ours was a peculiar situation. The law required each Federal Reserve Bank to hold gold equal to not less than 40 per cent of the Federal Reserve notes in circulation and, further, to hold not less than 35 per cent in gold or other lawful money in reserve as against deposits in the Reserve Banks. Under the law, the remaining 60 per cent of currency backing and 65 per cent of deposits consisted mostly of "eligible" short-term commercial bills, in addition to gold or "other lawful money."

Because of the reduction of deposits in the commercial banks and thus of their ability to make loans, and the slackness in business, "eligible" commercial bills were insufficiently available for the 60 per cent end of the currency coverage; and gold had to make up the lack. So the gold reserve against the currency had been forced up from 40 to about 70 per cent. The increase in currency from hoarding of a billion dollars also had to be covered by gold reserves, which froze just so much more gold. Under all these pressures only about $300,000,000 of gold was left "free" for further foreign withdrawals. An investigation at this date revealed that foreigners, including the unpredictable French, still had demand deposits in our banks of about $1,000,000,000 which they could withdraw in gold at any moment.

In view of our legislative chaos and the abandonment of gold standards in the world, foreign owners of deposits in our banks were in the fear-mood and were making continued withdrawals or "earmarkings" which had the same effect. They were also engaging heavy shipments for the immediate future. Unless we relieved the situation, we should be compelled to refuse gold payments for export, which would be a public admission that the dollar was no longer convertible, and that we were off the gold standard.

At Secretary Mills's suggestion, I arranged a meeting of Governor Harrison of the New York Federal Reserve Bank, General Dawes, and Eugene Meyer, Governor of the Federal Reserve Board, at the White

---

[5] Earmarking was the action of foreigners who converted deposits into actual gold bullion, which was placed in storage at the Federal Reserve Banks.

House on February 8, 1932, to consider this matter. They all agreed that the situation was most critical.

The only solution was our earlier proposal of October 6, 1931, for expansion of the kinds of "eligible paper" by making government bonds available for the 60 per cent non-gold currency coverage. In normal times this would have been objectionable; but in the emergency it would have "freed" enough gold to allow the foreigners to take their gold away if they wanted to and still leave the 40 per cent gold coverage and other reserves. The gold standard thus would be safe.

The situation being so critical, I invited the Republican and Democratic majority leaders, the ranking members of the Senate Committee on Banking and Currency and administration officials to breakfast at the White House the next morning. At this meeting we revealed the dangers of the situation and strongly urged the agreement of the previous October for increasing eligible paper. We also again urged liberalized Reserve action, so as to permit the system to further expand credit to small business and, by open market operations, to fill the credit vacuums caused by gold and exchange withdrawals.

Secretary Mills, General Dawes, and Governor Meyer presented convincing arguments and were of great help. Finally Senator Glass retreated from his previous opposition and agreed, in response to my request, to introduce in his own name the necessary legislation. It was decided to emphasize matters relating to liberalizing the discount privilege and credit expansion proposals in order to avoid disclosure of the gold situation which might create more alarm both at home and abroad during the interval before the law was passed.

That afternoon I called in the House leaders and ranking members of the committees concerned and went over the situation with them. The fact that Senator Glass had agreed brought Mr. Steagall, the Democratic chairman of the House committee, and the other Democratic members around to our point of view. The Republican members supported me loyally. I suggested that Mr. Steagall introduce the bill in the House. It thus became known as the Glass-Steagall bill. It was passed without any debate as to the gold situation and became law on February 27th.

Thus we had secured three more items of the original program. However, they were delayed three months after they had been originally agreed to on October 6th (1931). And this delay prevented alleviation of much distress. I made a statement to the press in order to make clear the purpose of this legislation:

The bill should accomplish three major purposes.

First. In a sense this bill is a national defense measure. By freeing the vast amounts of gold in our Federal Reserve System (in excess of the gold reserve required by law), it so increases the already large available resources of the Federal Reserve Banks as to enable them beyond question to meet any conceivable demands that might be made on them at home or from abroad.

Second. It liberalizes existing provisions with regard to eligibility of collateral and thereby enables the Federal Reserve Banks to furnish accommodations to many banks on sound assets heretofore unavailable for rediscount purposes.

Third. The gradual credit contraction during the past eight months arising indirectly from causes originating in foreign countries and continued domestic deflation, but more directly from hoarding, has been unquestionably the major factor in depressing prices and delaying business recovery. . . .

I trust that our banks with the assurances and facilities now provided will reach out to aid business and industry in such fashion as to increase employment and aid agriculture.

EXPANDING FEDERAL RESERVE CREDIT

The third result of the Glass-Steagall Act was to enable the Federal Reserve System to embark, at the end of February, 1932, upon a much more extensive campaign of credit expansion through open market operations by purchase of government bonds, and later on to reduce the discount rate. The Board, under the leadership of Governor Meyer, initiated such a policy, and upon a large scale. About a billion dollars of "governments" were bought in the open market during the next four months, which in the usual ratios would have made available five to ten billions of dollars of credit to the ultimate borrower.

This action enabled us to defend any gap in the credit structure caused by foreign withdrawals of gold and exchange. Under non-boom conditions, however, the public was not disposed to take advantage of the increased credit. Again one part of the theory upon which the Reserve System was founded was tested—the idea that business could be activated during depression by Federal Reserve credit expansion and lower discount rates. Subsequent events showed it had little effect in that direction. Credit expansion certainly proved to be an effective method of promoting a speculative boom when people were optimistic. But when they were pessimistic, it had no effect whatsoever.

In the face of the prevailing jitters, a discussion of the danger to the gold standard through which we had successfully navigated was inadvisable for some time, even after the passing of the legislation.

But in the Presidential campaign eight months later at Des Moines, October 4, 1932, when all danger of public alarm over a gold crisis was passed, I described the situation. This address brought sharp repercussions, as will be shown later.

ATTEMPTS AT INFLATION OF THE CURRENCY

Added to the sabotage and delays of our constructive financial measures were the bills passed or introduced from the opposition side tinkering with the currency. The fears they created fed the fires of public discouragement. Senator Walsh, in January, 1932, introduced a fiat money bill into the Senate, with serious support. On March 29th a poll showed that the Patman bill for a soldiers' cash bonus of $2,300,000,000, to be paid with fiat money, would be passed by the House. On May 2nd the House passed the Goldsborough "rubber dollar" bill. In June, Borah's amendment to the Home Loan Bank bill, providing a billion dollars of fiat money, was passed against Republican opposition. Greenbacks were certainly exuding from the Democratic side with portents for the future.

STOPPING THE HOARDING

The hoarding of currency and coin was part of the whole fear complex. It had become widespread early in February, 1932. The total hoarding at this time amounted to more than one billion dollars, a considerable part in gold. This withdrawal of deposits was the natural result of the fear of the instability of the banks, but with this also went a fear of currency tinkering measures which had been introduced into Congress. This demand for currency from the banks restricted their ability to extend customer short-term commercial credit so vital to a healthy economy. I, therefore, organized a drive to educate the public against it. I received many counsels, including some from Democratic Senate leader Robinson, that to bring it out into the open would only stimulate more of it. However, I concluded it could not be worse.

At my request Colonel Frank Knox of Chicago undertook to direct the anti-hoarding campaign and did a good job. This educational work and other coincidental actions were successful. A considerable amount of currency returned to the banks, and we were not bothered with a dangerous increase in hoarding for another twelve months.

MRS. HOOVER AND THE EXECUTIVE COMMITTEE OF THE GIRL SCOUTS OF AMERICA

CHAPTER 11

FOURTH PHASE OF THE DEPRESSION— NOVEMBER, 1931, TO JULY, 1932 *(Cont'd)*

BANKING AND STOCK EXCHANGE REFORMS, AND THE WORLD ECONOMIC CONFERENCE

As thorough banking reform was one of the first necessities of the nation, I urged it incessantly during my whole four years.

In my first annual message to the Congress on December 3, 1929 (before the real crisis), I had urged that a joint commission be set up of representatives of the Congress, the administration, and the public, to study our whole financial system. Senator Carter Glass was the dominant Senate voice on banking, and he opposed this idea. The Senator was a cooperative man, except when he put on his political garments. He had an unparalleled linguistic capacity for vituperation, and at times indicated a conviction that few Republicans were better than inferior Democrats. That he had learned at his mother's knee from her bitter experience in Reconstruction days.

The reorganization which would have given the banking system the strength to withstand the terrific destruction of the depression should have been enacted before the shock came. But the public could not be sufficiently awakened to the necessity to overcome the banker opposition.

The failure to secure these reforms early in the depression was one of the reasons why we were compelled to put props under the structure to save it from collapse.

Although Senator Glass had rejected my idea of a joint investigation, six months after my recommendation, he did introduce a banking bill, and on May 30, 1930, the Senate Banking and Currency Committee announced that it hoped to have the bill ready for the next session.

I again urged reforms in my message of December, 1930. The Senate Committee, however, was not able to agree upon the bill as promised.

Therefore, in a public address at Indianapolis on June 15, 1931, I stressed the need for reform, saying:

The Federal Reserve System was inadequate to prevent a large diversion of capital and bank deposits from commercial and industrial business into wasteful speculation and stock promotion. It is obvious our banking system must be organized to give greater protection to depositors against failures. It is equally obvious that we must determine whether the facilities of our security and commodity exchanges are not being used to create illegitimate speculation and intensify depressions. . . .

On October 2, 1931, in an address to the American Bankers Association, I described in caustic terms the part which our banking system had played in credit inflation, its responsibility for booms and mad speculation, with the depressions and misery that inevitably followed. I appealed to the bankers to study the whole problem, to take part in reform, and to cure abuses.

In my message to the Congress on December 8, 1931, I returned again to the subject, saying:

Our people have a right to a banking system in which their deposits shall be safeguarded and the flow of credit less subject to storms. The need of a sounder system is plainly shown by the extent of bank failures. I recommend the prompt improvement of the banking laws. Changed financial conditions and commercial practices must be met. The Congress should investigate the need for separation between different kinds of banking; an enlargement of branch banking under proper restrictions; and the methods by which enlarged membership in the Federal Reserve System may be brought about.

On December 11, 1931, I again urged Congress, as the most important requirement of the day, to undertake "the revision of our banking laws so as to safeguard the depositors." Again I urged on January 4, 1932, as a cardinal part of our depression remedies, "revision of banking laws in order to better safeguard deposits."

By degrees we evolved a set of reform proposals which included advice sought from many practitioners and students of banking, and my own business experience. These I urged upon the Republican members of the Committees of Congress. They were:

To compel every commercial bank to join the Federal Reserve System.

To establish inspection of all commercial banks by the Federal Reserve System.

To attain gradual separation of promotion affiliates.

To further limit long-term credits from commercial banks. Or, alternatively, to separate savings and long-term-loan institutions from demand-deposit institutions. Or, as a further alternative, to create a national system of mortgage discount banks which would enable the commercial banks to rediscount their mortgage loans.

To establish state-wide branch banking by national banks under suitable regulations with provision that no new branches be established where there are adequate facilities, except by purchase of an existing bank.

Some, but not all, of these ideas came into being in later years.

The Senate Banking and Currency Committee then belatedly began in earnest the formulation of broad banking reform. I consulted with its members frequently, urging expedition.

On January 22, 1932, after three years of my urging, Senator Glass again reported his Banking Reform bill to the Senate, but five days later it was returned to the committee for revision and was again reported to the Senate on March 16th. It was wholly inadequate from my point of view, but better than nothing. It provided for revision of laws on group banking and promotion affiliates, for encouragement to branch banking, for insistence upon membership in the Reserve System, and for limits on loans for speculation. Public hearings were held, amidst a deluge of banking opposition. The bill was again sent back to the committee for revision, and again introduced to the Senate on April 9th. It was put on the calendar of privileged business on April 27th. The banking world particularly opposed the elimination of promotion affiliates, compulsory membership in the Federal Reserve System, the branch banking provisions and other leading features. The battle raged furiously through May; and on June 16th the Senate displaced the bill on the calendar.

After our defeat in the election, I returned to the charge in my fourth and final annual message to Congress on December 6, 1932:

The basis of every other and every further effort toward recovery is to reorganize at once our banking system. The shocks to our economic system have multiplied by the weakness of our financial system. I first called attention of the Congress in 1929 to this condition, and I have unceasingly recommended remedy since that time. The subject has been exhaustively investigated both by the committees of the Congress and the officers of the Federal Reserve System. . . .

The banking and financial system is presumed to serve in furnishing the essential lubricant to the wheels of industry, agriculture, and commerce, that is, credit. Its diversion from proper use, its improper use, or its insufficiency instantly brings hardship and dislocation in economic life. As a system our banking has failed to meet this great emergency. It can be said without question of doubt that our losses and distress have been greatly augmented by its wholly inadequate organization. Its inability as a system to respond to our needs is today a constant drain upon progress toward recovery. In this statement I am not referring to individual banks or bankers. Thousands of them have shown distinguished courage and ability. On the contrary, I am referring to the system itself, which is so organized, or so lacking in organization, that in an emergency its very mechanism jeopardizes or paralyzes the action of sound banks and its instability is responsible for periodic dangers to our whole economic system. . . .

The losses, suffering, and tragedies of our people are incalculable. Not alone do they lie in the losses of savings to millions of homes, injury by deprival of working capital to thousands of small businesses, but also, in the frantic pressure to recall loans to meet pressures of hoarding and in liquidation of failed banks, millions of other people have suffered in the loss of their homes and farms, businesses have been ruined, unemployment increased, and farmers' prices diminished.

That this failure to function is unnecessary and is the fault of our particular system is plainly indicated by the fact that in Great Britain, where the economic mechanism has suffered far greater shocks than our own, there has not been a single bank failure during the depression. Again in Canada, where the economic situation has been in large degree identical with our own, there have not been substantial bank failures.

. . . Methods of reform have been exhaustively examined. There is no reason now why solution should not be found at the present session of the

Congress. Inflation of currency or governmental conduct of banking can have no part in these reforms. The Government must abide within the field of constructive organization, regulation, and the enforcement of safe practices only.

On December 7th, I had an extended conference upon the bill with Senator Glass, Democratic Senate Leader Robinson, and Speaker Garner. On December 8th, the Glass bill was again given privileged position on the calendar. The fight, however, flared up, even though Senator Glass offered to compromise certain features. Democratic Senators Huey Long and Elmer Thomas started a filibuster against it. However, the bill was passed by the Senate on January 26, 1933, in a very mutilated form. But the Democratic leaders of the House refused to take action, on instructions from the President-elect.[1]

In a special message to the Congress on February 20, 1933, I made a final attempt to get even this bill through, saying in part:

The enactment by the House of the general principles embodied in the Glass Banking Bill which has already passed the Senate will greatly contribute to reestablish confidence. It is the first constructive step to a prerequisite of the functioning of the whole economic system.

REFORMING THE STOCK EXCHANGES (BY EXPOSURE)

A contributing factor to public fear was the continuous misuse of the New York and other stock exchanges. Early in the administration in 1929 I had tried to persuade the officials of the New York Stock Exchange to restrain the use of the Exchange for manipulation, destructive speculation and distribution of doubtful securities. Conscientious and leading members had informed me that the Exchange could do all this itself by changing its own rules. I had made no progress. They were in the "New Economic Era."

After the slump came, in October, 1929, the misuse of the machinery of the Exchange appeared in another sinister aspect. Insiders "sold short" and then by propaganda and manipulation which lowered stock prices caught investors who could no longer support loans they had obtained on stocks and were obliged to sell. The "shorts" bought them in.

---

[1] The Glass bill was passed promptly by the succeeding administration.

I deplored the idea of extending Federal power over organizations which had the power to remedy their own evils. The Stock Exchange properly conducted is a vital part of the free-enterprise system. In any event, the primary responsibility for initiation of official action lay on Governor Franklin Roosevelt of New York. That state had power to reform Exchange methods. Charles Evans Hughes, in the case of the dishonest management of the insurance companies, had not hesitated to clean them up in the public interest, and for the reputation of New York business.

In the summer and fall of 1931, during the European collapse, there were again systematic bear raids on the Exchange, and again I urged reforms on its directors. These actions appreciably deepened the depression.

In January and February, 1932, I twice again called Exchange directors to the White House and urged that they amend their rules so as to stop manipulation. I pointed out that new bear raids had again taken place in anticipation of every periodic crisis, and, in addition, there were other large pool operations against investors' interests, the information as to which was supplied me by responsible members of the Exchange. These responsible members formulated for me some curative amendments to their rules. The directors repeatedly promised they would adopt these amendments, but made only minor changes. I finally warned Richard Whitney and other directors that unless they took measures to clean their own house I would ask Congress to investigate the Stock Exchange with a view to Federal control legislation.

These discussions with Stock Exchange representatives having leaked out, I made a public statement on the 19th of February—in restrained terms—since I did not wish to add to public discouragement by denunciation, even though it would have been just:

There have been discussions, as is reported, between myself and other officials of the Administration with officials of the New York Stock Exchange. . . . I, and other Administration officials, again expressed our views to the managers of the Exchange that they should take adequate measures to protect investors from artificial depression of the price of securities for speculative profit. Individuals who use the facilities of the Exchange for such purposes are not contributing to recovery of the United States.

Despite these urgings I received still more depressing information that vicious pools were continuing in which corporation and even bank directors were manipulating their own stocks. I, therefore, called in Senator Frederic Walcott, strongest Republican member of the Senate Banking and Currency Committee, who, having been an honest investment banker, was familiar with Exchange practices, and Senator Peter Norbeck, chairman of the committee. Norbeck was a well-intentioned well-driller from South Dakota. I urged that the committee launch an investigation of practices of the Exchange, with a view to legislation and I gave them much information to start on. I was extremely loath to take this step, as we had enough burdens to carry, without all the discouraging filth such exposure entailed. But the truth could be brought out only under the compulsion which a Senate committee would exert. The Senate authorized the investigation on March 4, 1932. There was some doubt as to the constitutionality of Federal control of the stock exchanges but I hoped that at least, when we had exposed the situation, the Governor of New York would recognize his fundamental responsibility and act accordingly. That hope, however, proved to be little more than wishful thinking.

On April 2nd a group of New York bankers, headed by Thomas Lamont of Morgan & Company, protested my actions in a memorandum explaining the virtues of the Exchange. A few sentences from my reply are as follows:

My dear Mr. Lamont:

. . . Prices today [of securities] do not truly represent the values of American enterprise and property . . . [and the] pounding down of prices . . . by obvious manipulation of the market . . . is an injury to the country and to the investing public. . . .

. . . These operations destroy public confidence and induce a slowing down of business and a fall in prices.

. . . Men are not justified in deliberately making a profit from the losses of other people.

I recognize that these points of view are irreconcilable, but I hope you will agree with me that there is here an element of public interest.

Yours faithfully,

HERBERT HOOVER

In the meantime, a committee had been organized among New York bankers, chiefly through the efforts of Secretary Mills, to support the bond market, which was thoroughly demoralized. On April 3rd I received word from this committee that they could not get important financial houses to join them unless I agreed to call off the Senate investigation and halt my own activities in their direction. When I asked Secretary Mills if this were true, he made an unprintable reply amply in the negative.

It soon became evident that efforts were being made to smother the Senate inquiry. Republican Senate Leader Watson visited me with a strong appeal to quash this "dangerous activity." But Walcott's courage was equal to the mission. He undertook to build a fire under the Senate committee and finally got the inquiry under way. Quickly the committee exposed a rottenness far worse than even I had anticipated. Testimony confirmed to the public that directors of great corporations and banks had been manipulating and speculating in their own stocks. Huge pools had been organized for pushing stocks on to the public at prices far beyond their worth, and for manipulating prices upward and downward. Great figures in the industrial, financial, and political world had engaged in these operations. With the exposures over, such men as Albert Wiggin, chairman of the Chase National Bank, and Charles E. Mitchell,[2] chairman of the National City Bank of New York, resigned their positions. Among those brought before the committee to explain many very sorry things were Percy Rockefeller, John Raskob, chairman of the Democratic National Committee, Matthew Brush, Ben Smith, W. F. Kenny, M. J. Meehan, and others.

The shock to our people and their loss of confidence in the integrity of men high in business and finance was great indeed. Such exposures take no account of the thousands of honest, constructive men in the same walks of life.

To Senator Walcott and his Republican colleagues, we outlined our views of the character of the corrective legislation needed. I assumed that the Constitutional difficulty as to whether or not security trading was inter-state commerce could be overcome. I did not consider it neces-

---

[2] We subsequently obtained the indictment of Charles E. Mitchell of the National City Bank for malfeasance.

sary to set up a special commission of so-called administrative law, but to follow the British experience which had been reasonably successful over many years. Copies of the British laws adapted to our scene were furnished to the Senators. The ideas which we advanced were:

(a) A prospectus should be filed with the Department of Justice on every stock offering for interstate sale to the public, stating all the essential facts, including the direct and indirect beneficiaries.

(b) All promoters or other persons appearing upon the prospectus should be liable in damages to any persons injured through misstatement or incomplete disclosure, with the Department of Justice authorized to act in cases of malfeasance coming to their attention.

(c) Congress should enact definite statutory rules governing interstate purchase and sale of securities on the exchanges, again providing for damages to injured persons.

The essence of these proposals was to accomplish our ends through the courts.

The Senate committee had no time before the end of the 1932 session to formulate legislation; and, having lost the election, we could go no further with the matter.

The reaction from these exposures, of course, paved the way for drastic legislation in the Roosevelt administration. That legislation has perhaps hampered honest business. But when representative government becomes angered, it will burn down the barn to get a rat out of it.

Some statements having been made later in respect to the origin of the Senate inquiry, Senator Walcott wrote to me as follows:

I recall vividly the events which led up to our meetings at the White House, when you urged me, . . . to persuade the Banking and Currency Committee of the Senate to use every effort to determine the facts connected with . . . the New York Stock Exchange.

You explained very definitely to Senator Norbeck and me your reasons. . . . I then talked the matter over fully with several of the more active members of the Banking and Currency Committee, who were eager to get at the facts.

The situation was critical. You, as President, were urging haste and definite action. . . . Previous to these events, you had talked with me several times at the White House about the danger. . . . You gave me definite instructions to proceed without delay. . . . You were determined to get at some evil practices. . . .

. . . The complete study was made by public hearings and expert investigations, of the operations and ramifications of certain investment companies that were affiliates of some of the large national banks. . . .

You were backing courageously and without fear or favor all of these endeavors to get at the facts and correct the evils, and you, more than any one else, were responsible for the constructive reforms that were eventually adopted in connection with the correction of the abuses among the banks and bankers.

THE WORLD ECONOMIC CONFERENCE

When Premier Laval visited the United States in November, 1931, I proposed to him that at some appropriate time we should call a world economic conference to work out a plan for stabilizing currencies, curbing the growing barriers against international trade and removing a few other obstacles to recovery. He felt that the time was then not yet ripe for a successful conclusion of such a conference.

By the spring of 1932, the world-wide collapse of finance and gold convertibility of currencies, which began with the German crisis the year before, was turning into a violent trade war between nations. In this war, depreciated currencies, "managed" currencies, increasing tariffs, other restrictions on imports, quotas, and foreign exchange controls were the weapons. The results appeared everywhere in the creeping paralysis of exports and imports and the constant fall of commodity prices. Creditor-debtor relations, both domestic and foreign, were fast becoming intolerable.

It seemed to me that the time had arrived to revive the project of a world economic conference. Even an agreement to have such a conference and set a date would contribute to a revival of hope. On May 24th, I asked Secretary Stimson to discuss this project with Prime Minister MacDonald.

The British at first wished to include consideration of German reparations and war debts, but as we could not carry that with the Congress, they gave way. The Prime Minister finally approved, and in a few days the Conference was announced from London, to take place in the early winter of 1933 after the American elections were over.

In the meantime we, together with the principal nations, appointed technical delegates to prepare for the Conference. They at once began investigations and preliminary recommendations. As the whole of these problems rose with violence immediately after the election, I deal with them as part of the final phase of the depression.

The announcement of the Conference, however, did aid in restoring hope and confidence.

CHAPTER 12

FOURTH PHASE OF THE DEPRESSION— NOVEMBER, 1931, TO JULY, 1932 *(Cont'd)*

BALANCING THE BUDGET

Measures to balance the budget formed another major part of our program of economic defense and recovery.

During the first two fiscal years of my Administration ending June 30, 1929 and 1930, we had no budget trouble. In fact, we had a surplus of more than $700,000,000 for each year. But the depression began to eat into our revenues during the fiscal year ending June 30, 1931, and we had a deficit (omitting recoverable loans) of something more than $200,000,000. This in itself was not serious, but our major source of revenues, income taxes and corporation profits were going out from under us with appalling speed. In the fiscal year ending June 30, 1932, revenues dropped over $2,000,000,000, or more than 50 per cent of our total income.

National stability required that we balance the budget. To do this, we had to increase taxes on one hand and, on the other, to reduce drastically government expenditures. In reduction of expenditures we had to limit ourselves to ordinary government activities. At the same time, it was necessary to increase our extraordinary expenditures on unemployment, agricultural and financial relief. At once the Battle of the Budget with the Democratic-controlled Congress was on. I opened up the fight in my messages to Congress on December 8 and 9, 1931, saying:

The first requirement of confidence and of economic recovery is financial stability of the United States Government. . . . I must at this time call attention to the magnitude of the deficits which have developed and the resulting necessity for determined and courageous policies. These deficits arise in the main from the heavy decrease in tax receipts due to the depression and to the increase in expenditure on construction in aid to unemployment, aids to agriculture, and upon services to veterans. . . .

Several conclusions are inevitable. We must have insistent and determined reduction in Government expenses. We must face a temporary increase in taxes. . . .

The welfare of the country demands that the financial integrity of the Federal Government be maintained.

REDUCTION OF GOVERNMENT EXPENDITURES

In considering the actual budgetary problems the reader must bear in mind that reduction of expenditures may come in two ways: reduction of appropriations in response to Presidential recommendations and by the will of Congress; and changes in the laws which will allow reduction or postponement of established functions.

In my budget message of December 9, 1931, I called for a reduction of appropriations by $369,000,000 below the year before. I recommended legislation which, by relaxing certain requirements of law, would permit cuts of an additional $300,000,000.

Aside from Congress itself, I had the usual Presidential trouble with citizen pressure groups. These become violent, politically potent, and unreasonable especially in times of depression, but still more so when these pressures can be used as a political football.

On January 8, 1932, I asked our citizens publicly to cease their pressures on Congress, saying:

The flood of extravagant proposals . . . would imply an increase of government expenditure during the next five years of over forty billions of dollars or more than eight billions per annum. The great majority of these bills have been advanced by some organization or some sectional interest. . . . They . . . represent a spirit of spending in the country which must be abandoned . . . drastic economy requires sacrifice. . . .

Rigid economy is a real road to relief to home owners, farmers, workers, and every element of our population. . . .

Our first duty as a nation is to put our governmental house in order, national, state and local. With the return of prosperity the government can undertake constructive projects both of social character and in public improvement. We cannot squander ourselves into prosperity.

The Democrats promptly attacked my reduction proposals. On February 23rd, Speaker Garner asserted that any reorganization of laws was the exclusive function of Congress and he appointed a House Economy Committee to do the job. This body promptly went to sleep. On March 8th, I made an effort to awaken it with a public statement, but still it slept.

On April 4th, I urged that in view of the fact that four different Congressional committees claimed jurisdiction over these amendments, there should be set up a joint committee, representing the administration and the two Houses, to formulate an emergency program. Democratic Senate leader Robinson roundly denounced this plan. Then Garner's committee woke up and brightly demanded that the administration propose a detailed program of the legislation required to make the $369,000,000 functional reductions. All this was tiresome political horseplay which in Garner's view would give the administration the responsibility for all the heartaches and political aches.

But we accepted the challenge and even went beyond it, giving him all the details.

In a press statement to the country on April 15th, I said:

Sentiment has grown definitely in the last two weeks for the acceptance of a drastic . . . economy bill which will attack that quarter of expenditure which cannot be reached except by amendment and alteration of the existing laws. In other words, [it is] outside of the field that can be reached by appropriations. . . . The economies that can be reached in that direction are apparently close to $300,000,000, and that, added to the $369,000,000 already cut from the budget before it was sent to Congress . . . [will make] an aggregate from all of over $650,000,000. . . . That is the most drastic reduction of governmental expenses that has been undertaken by any government in any time in any one year.

The "economy" bill was finally passed by the House on May 3, 1932, with only $30,000,000 of our proposed $300,000,000 economies left in it. The total economies from this act and from reduction of appropriations were $150,000,000, instead of $669,000,000.

Because of private and public pressures and Congressional pork-barrel legislation, I was compelled to veto a multitude of special bills, including special pension bills, Indian claim bills, a veterans' bonus bill, and a bill for a huge fertilizer plant. The worst of these, however, was Speaker Garner's $2,300,000,000 pork-barrel bill to which I will refer again.

Aside from this battle to reduce "ordinary" expenditures, we were compelled to urge increased appropriations for relief, for public works in aid to the unemployed and for capital and loans for the RFC, the Farm Board, and other emergency credit institutions. Our Federal system of bookkeeping charged all capital subscriptions and loans to current expenses and wrote them off as such, irrespective of the certain recovery of them later. Had we set up the loans as a special fund our budget would have looked better—and that was done by the New Deal. I later give a detailed statement of expenses and revenues covering my whole administration.

INCREASING TAXES

The other side of the budgetary problem was to increase revenues. To balance the budget we were compelled to ask for an increase of $1,300,000,000 per annum in taxes in addition to our proposed savings of $670,000,000.

We made a special study of the whole incidence of such increases, and their economic and social effect. The Ways and Means Committee of the House, by majority Democratic, was led by a most able and considerate chairman, Charles R. Crisp. Secretary Mills and I had many conferences with him and furnished him a copy of my memorandum on the whole subject. This may have some interest to students and rather than interrupt the narrative, I give it in a footnote.[1]

---

[1] Prior to the World War of 1914 the tax burden had been so light that social and economic life was not much affected. But the burden after the war produced such effects no matter how it was applied. Moreover, the concept that taxes should never be used to produce economic and social effects, although constantly and violently stated, was mostly lip service. The tariff on imports had been used for this purpose since George Washington. The tax on margarine was another example.

. . . We must accept the fact that our tax burden would have social and economic consequences and must be applied, in some measure, in these lights.

Our major varieties of taxes are . . . import duties, excises on luxuries and non-

Whatever my views on the need for new taxes were, the Congress was naturally reluctant to increase them in face of a coming election. I, myself, was not ignorant of the liabilities in terms of votes. In this instance, I was reminded of one of our Congressmen who always made it a rule to vote for all appropriations and against all taxes. He held his seat for long years. But, it had to be done—votes or no votes.

Despite the urgent need of the country for prompt passage of the emergency legislation and balancing of the budget, Speaker Garner, on January 1, 1932, announced that the Ways and Means Committee would take up tariff legislation before taxes. This meant months of

---

essentials, and manufacturers' sale taxes. The other major sources are estate, income, corporation and capital gains taxes.

EXCISE TAXES

Taxes on luxuries and non-essentials obviously require little discussion. I consider we should increase . . . these taxes . . . I do not believe we should increase the excise taxes on necessities, as these fall "hidden" on the lower-income groups.

ESTATE TAXES

I believe that the estate tax, in moderation, is one of the most economically and socially desirable—or even necessary—of all taxes.

The American people have from the earliest moments been alive to the evils of inherited economic power. They had abolished primogeniture in the expectation that the division of fortunes between several heirs, and the frequent effect of "shirt-sleeves to shirt-sleeves," and the profligacy of heirs, would dissipate such power. But in time fortunes have become so large, and lawyers so cunning that they can freeze them into trusts extending over more than three generations.

Several millions of dollars is economic power and too often it falls into the hands of persons of little intention to use that power for public benefit either in expansion of enterprise and employment or for public services. It is the breeding ground of play boys and play girls of morally obnoxious and degenerating character.

I do not believe we should tax the moderate inheritances under, say, $100,000, for they are provision for dependents. And they are a stimulant to people to work and save.

The way to disperse dangerous or wasteful economic power is by the division of estates among a number of beneficiaries. Our Federal taxes are assessed against the estate instead of the beneficiary. My proposal is a graduated tax applied, not to the estate, but to the beneficiary, rising to a maximum of, say, 45 per cent, as against the present 23 per cent. Under this plan a fortune of $10,000,000 to one beneficiary would pay, say, 45 per cent, or $4,500,000, to the Government, while if it were divided among ten beneficiaries each of them would fall into a lower bracket of, say, 10 per cent, and thus the total tax would be $1,000,000 instead of $4,500,000. The Government would lose, but the country would gain greatly by the steady division of power.

INCOME TAXES

This is one of our main reliances. My general theory of income taxes is that they

delay. Moreover, it had no purpose but political agitation on a subject concerning which no legislation was possible at that time.

On February 12th, Chairman Crisp informed me that his committee could agree on some of our proposals to increase income, corporation, and estate taxes, but that there would need be a manufacturers' sales tax. I replied that I would agree—provided that there would be no tax on staple food and cheaper clothing.

A month later the committee reported the bill including part of our recommendations and containing a manufacturers' sales tax. The committee consisting of 15 Democrats and 10 Republicans had voted 24 to 1 in favor of the bill. Obviously there was partisanship on this tax issue.

It had been customary under both Democratic and Republican majorities of the House to consider tax legislation under a rule limiting

---

should start at fairly high minimums—$2,000 to $3,000 per annum—as the low-level incomes are paying a large part of the hidden taxes.

I think we ought to look into the British system of collecting the graduated taxes above this level at the source. It would probably save 10,000,000 income tax payers from having to make any returns to the Treasury.

I believe the Government income from the normal tax would be larger as many evasions would be impossible.

My view is that we should raise the upper brackets of the income tax to 45 per cent, as compared to the present 23 per cent, as an emergency matter and give a deduction for earned incomes as distinguished from incomes from rent, interest, etc.

CORPORATION TAXES

Taxes on the profits of corporations are a favorite with the public, who have little understanding that the larger corporations in the end always pass their taxes on in the price of goods and services, or that they undertake unjustified risks because when they lose then they deduct the losses from their profits. Nor does the public appreciate what a destructive tax it is on small business. I consider that a raise to about 15 per cent is as high as we could go and not produce these effects.

We have prepared for the House Committee a reform designed to aid the small businessman. It is based on the fact that at the beginning of all new production and distribution there must be "venture capital," for great risks must be taken in establishment of new inventions, new mines, and new businesses of all kinds. [The plan involved freedom of small business from double taxation, through both corporate and income taxes.]

CAPITAL GAINS TAXES

The capital gains tax was devised to take ill-gotten gains from the market speculator. This tax necessarily also allows the deduction of capital losses. The speculator's memory is better upon losses than profits. Also, he has a habit of taking any losses on stocks that he might have just before the end of the tax year and then after a little while promptly investing again in the same sort of security. I have been long convinced that over a period of years the net to the Treasury from him was less than nothing. I have already recommended that the Congress abolish or modify this tax.

debate. That had always been necessary, since every affected group in the country, if given time, would build up oppositions and no counter-organizations were possible. But Speaker Garner broke all precedent this time by ruling for unlimited debate. This was a good idea for politics prior to election.

From March 10th to March 25th the House debated the Crisp tax measure. Opposition developed at once from the manufacturers, who put on a high-pressure campaign. But the main opposition came from the Democratic side under the leadership of Republican Fiorello La Guardia. Notwithstanding that there was no tax on food and cheaper clothing, La Guardia demagogued it as "grinding the face of the poor," and "taking milk from babies and bread from mothers." [2]

I made an appeal to the public for support on March 15th. Nevertheless, the bill was defeated and sent back to committee. It was now four months since I urged Congress to do this most necessary job. After defeat of the bill, Garner made an eloquent speech demanding a balancing of the budget. That the House did not require four months to enact a major piece of legislation was evidenced by the passage of the Philippine Independence Bill in forty minutes under limited debate ruled by Speaker Garner.

On April 1st the House finally passed a wholly inadequate bill, and the struggle to balance the budget shifted to the Senate. On April 15th I appealed again to the country, and on April 27th I made a public address reviewing the whole subject of expenses and taxes.

Finally, on May 5th I sent a stiff message to Congress devoted solely to the necessity for balancing the budget as the next item on the recovery program. The major parts were:

I should not be discharging my Constitutional responsibility to give to the Congress information on the state of the Union and to recommend for its consideration such measures as may be necessary and expedient, if I did not report to the Congress the situation which has arisen in the country in large degree as the result of incidents of legislation during the past six weeks.

[2] Four years later La Guardia, as Mayor of New York, elected upon a platform of "protecting the poor," recommended and enacted a sales tax on some food and all clothing. In a dinner conversation with him after this, I chided him on his inconsistency. His reply was, "You're no politician."

The most essential factor to economic recovery today is the restoration of confidence. In spite of the unquestioned beneficial effect of the remedial measures already taken and the gradual improvement in fundamental conditions, fear and alarm prevail in the country because of events in Washington which have greatly disturbed the public mind.

The manner in which the House of Representatives rejected . . . the program unanimously reported by the Committee on Ways and Means; the character of the tax measures passed; the action of the House which would increase governmental expenditure by . . . enlarged expenditures in non-service-connected benefits from the Veterans' Bureau at the very time when the House was refusing to remedy abuse in these same services; the virtual destruction of the national economy program proposed by the executive . . . the passage of legislation by the House placing burdens of impossible execution upon the Federal Reserve System over the protest of the Federal Reserve Board; the threat of further legislation looking to uncontrolled inflation—have all resulted in diminishing public confidence and offsetting the constructive . . . efforts . . . undertaken earlier in the year for recovery of employment and agriculture.

. . . Nothing is more necessary at this time than balancing the budget. Nothing will put more heart into the country than prompt and courageous and united action. . . .

The details and requirements of the situation are now well known to the Congress and plainly require:

1. The prompt enactment of a revenue bill. . . .

2. A drastic program of economy which, including the savings already made in the Executive budget of $369,000,000, can be increased to exceed $700,000,000 per annum. . . .

. . . Uncertainty is disastrous. . . . I refuse to believe that the country is unable to reflect its will in legislation.

. . . If such a program should be agreed to by the leaders and members of both Houses it would go far to restore business, employment, and agriculture alike. It would have a most reassuring effect on the country.

On May 6th, after a storm of attack from the Democratic side, I issued a public statement supporting my message:

The issue before the country is the re-establishment of confidence and speed toward recovery by ending these delays in balancing the budget. . . . It is not a partisan issue. . . .

This is not a controversy between the President and Congress or its members. It is an issue of the people against delays and destructive legislation which impair the credit of the United States. It is also an issue between the people and the locust swarm of lobbyists who haunt the halls of Congress seeking selfish privilege for special groups and sections of the country, misleading members as to the real views of the people by showers of propaganda.

. . . This is a serious hour which demands [that] all elements of the government and the people rise with stern courage above partisanship to meet the needs of our national life.

The country as a whole supported the administration, but the Democratic leaders were set in their determination to delay recovery. The situation in the country became even more perilous. Finally, on May 31st I determined to address the Senate in person, not only on the budget but on other matters. It was a stiff address. Omitting the descriptive parts, I said:

An emergency has developed in the last few days which it is my duty to lay before the Senate.

The continued downward movement in the economic life of the country has been particularly accelerated during the past few days and it relates in part definitely to the financial program of the government. There can be no doubt that superimposed upon other causes the long-continued delays in the passage of legislation . . . have given rise to doubt and anxiety as to the ability of our government to meet its responsibilities. . . .

The immediate result has been to create an entirely unjustified run upon the American dollar from foreign countries [nearly $200,000,000 in May alone] and within the past few days, despite our national wealth and resources and our unparalleled gold reserves, our dollar stands at a serious discount in the markets of the world for the first time in half a century. This can be and must be immediately corrected or the reaction upon our economic situation will be such as to cause great losses to our people and will still further retard recovery. Nor is the confusion in public mind and the rising feeling of doubt and fear confined to foreign countries. It reflects itself directly in diminished economic activity and increased unemployment within our own borders and among our own citizens. . . .

. . . We must secure . . . quick and prompt national action, directed at one sole purpose, that is to unfetter the rehabilitation . . . of industry, agriculture and employment. The time has come when we must bring these dangers and degenerations to a halt by expeditious action.

In the stress of this emergency I have conferred with members of both parties of the Senate as to methods by which the strains and stresses could be overcome and the gigantic resources and energies of our people released from the fetters in which they are held. I have felt in the stress of this emergency a grave responsibility rests upon me not only to present the situation to the Senate but to make suggestions as to the basis of adjustment. . . .

I then traversed the whole of our proposals which I have previously described, and continued:

I am confident that if the Congress could find in these suggestions . . . a ground for adjustment of legislation . . . it would yield not only relief to the country but would reestablish that confidence which we so sorely need. . . . The inherent abilities of our people to meet their problems are being restrained by failure of the government to act. . . . Time is of the essence. Every day's delay makes new wounds and extends them. I come . . . in a sincere spirit of helpfulness. . . . In your hands at this moment is the answer to the question whether democracy has the capacity to act speedily enough to save itself in emergency. The nation urgently needs unity. It needs solidarity before the world in demonstrating that America has the courage to look its difficulties in the face and the capacity and resolution to meet them.

The following editorial comments from Democratic papers indicate public reactions:

Congress deserves what it has been given. It asked for all it has been given. Mr. Hoover's message is an unanswerable indictment. Bitter and savage as it is, in substance it is no more than a summary of the proceeding of Congress in the last two months. Any bare recital of those proceedings would inevitably give forth the bitter and savage tone of this presidential message. Congress has flagrantly and disgracefully deserted its own standards. . . . Congress has missed no opportunity to disembowel the policy of orthodox finance. [Baltimore *Sun.*]

A Democratic senator, Mr. Harrison, calls upon the President to bring order out of chaos. The budget is not balanced. Tax plans have gone astray. "If ever there was a time," he says, "when the President ought to speak out to his leaders in Congress, it is now." But the President has been speaking out to his leaders and appealing to his adversaries, vigorously and consistently since Congress convened five months ago. On the importance of Federal retrenchment and the necessity of balancing the budget he has spoken in no less than 21 messages, statements and addresses. . . . Responsibility for the chaos which now exists in Washington rests upon those members of Congress who have blocked the President at every turn and bolted their own party leadership. [*New York Times.*]

The Senate took on a burst of speed, and I was able to sign a tax bill on June 6th. The provisions included many of the points in my memorandum to Chairman Crisp, comprising increase in estate taxes, lifting the upper brackets to 45 per cent; increase of income tax up to 45 per cent in the higher brackets; increase of corporation taxes to about 14 per cent; gift taxes; increase of special excise taxes on various commodities, luxuries, services, admissions, stock transfers, checks, and a tax of one cent a gallon on gasoline; increase in postal rates.

The bill was intended to produce about $1,250,000,000 additional revenue. But these additions to our income had been delayed seven months and came too late to do any good during the fiscal year. Thereby our deficit looked worse than might otherwise have been the case.

Humor never dies in America. As a candidate for Vice President, John Garner, on October 17, 1932, said of us: "Their failure to balance the budget of a family of 120,000,000 people is at the very bottom of the economic troubles from which we are suffering."

CHAPTER 13

FOURTH PHASE OF THE DEPRESSION— NOVEMBER, 1931, TO JULY, 1932 *(Cont'd)*

UNEMPLOYMENT RELIEF MEASURES

I interrupt the narrative of the economic and political forces in this phase of the depression to give an account of our measures for relief of the unemployed during this, the deepest period of the depression.

I have already made clear our distinction between indirect and direct relief. Indirect relief, chiefly through construction work, now assumed two forms. The first, which we described as "nonproductive" public works, including roads, buildings, river and harbor improvements, involved a direct expenditure by the Federal Treasury and provided little subsequent employment. The cost of the second—"reproductive" works —was met either by private enterprise or by government loans when the works would repay the loans and furnish continued employment.

NONPRODUCTIVE PUBLIC WORKS

To indicate the size of our nonproductive public works, I may at once enumerate the expenditures in this indirect aid to employment, in four fiscal years ending at the dates listed:

June 30, 1930	$ 410,420,000
June 30, 1931	574,870,000
June 30, 1932	655,880,000
June 30, 1933	717,260,000
Total	$2,358,430,000

The total was greater than the expenditures of the whole thirty years of previous administrations. In addition, the expanded state and municipal construction induced by the administration amounted to at least $1,500,000,000 more than would have otherwise been the case.

Experience forced me to certain conclusions as to the use of nonproductive public works in relief of unemployment. In the 1922–1923 short depression, I had been greatly impressed with the effectiveness of public works for such relief and as a stabilizing device for planing out slumps after booms. However, from the experience in 1930–1933, I found many limitations upon the effectiveness of this device.

The first limitation was that the construction and capital goods' industries were the most sensitive to depression forces. They could mostly be postponed until another day. They could decrease by $8,000,000,000 per annum. To replace such volume with governmental public works would require that much of an increase in government expenses—or a rise of 400 per cent in the taxes of those times. Certainly such works as were possible proved to be no economic balance wheel in depressions.

The second limitation was that any particular nonproductive public works' project must be needed and useful either socially or economically. And there were only a few limited undertakings of this nature available.

The third limitation, from an employment point of view, was that the possible government works were not always near centers of unemployment.

The fourth limitation arose from the fact that, while theoretically government construction work involved the purchase of tools and machinery which would activate employment in the manufacturing centers, experience showed that when we were in a slump, a mass of such tools and machinery lay idle and available, so that little manufacture was actually stimulated.

The fifth limitation arose from the fact that with modern construction very little unskilled labor was needed, and the cost of supporting the family of a skilled laborer by payment of full wages ran into about $2,000 to $2,500 a year. Thus, to employ even half the unemployed would require $10,000,000,000 to $12,000,000,000 a year, and no such amounts of public works were available.

The sixth limitation was budgetary. How far should we incur deficits or borrow for such purposes? Would not the very existence of such large unbalance in government budgets depress employment?

In August, 1931, I published the results of a survey of employment in Federal nonproductive public works' activities, saying:

The number of persons directly or indirectly employed by the Federal Government in construction and maintenance of public works at the opening of the depression was 180,000. This time last year the number was increased to 430,000. The number was 760,000 on the first of August. That number will probably increase some in the autumn.

As unemployment was running more than twelve times this amount, it was obvious that nonproductive public works were no complete answer.

However, we had done such a good job of propaganda in our early hopes for the success of such methods, that there was popular pressure for more and more, finally in gigantic proportions. Two newspaper chains were advocating an appropriation of $5,000,000,000 per annum. Lest I be wrong in my conclusions, I appointed a committee of twelve leading citizens, representing the public, industry, and labor, in September, 1931, to consider the desirability of such nonproductive works as an aid to recovery. They strongly condemned any further expansion of such expenditures with this statement:

The proposals favoring a great public works program are usually discussed in terms . . . of three, five or seven billions to be raised by Federal bond issues. . . . The Committee is of the opinion that borrowing of large sums for public works emergency construction cannot be justified as a measure for the aiding in restoration of normal business activity. . . . Whatever may have been the causes of the present condition, the common sense remedy is to stop borrowing except to meet unavoidable deficits, balance the budget and live in our income. . . . In the long run the real problem of unemployment must be met by private business interests if it is to be permanent. Problems of unemployment cannot be solved by any magic of appropriation from the public treasury. . . . Hardships of the depression are in reality the readjustments being made in the endeavor to meet new and changing conditions. It does not appear reasonable to believe that a construction program financed by public funds in this country could greatly hasten or alter this process of economic adjustment, for fundamentally the general levels of commodity prices are international and alterations in them result from interchange of trade between countries. Experience of England and Germany substantiates this.

Despite all this experience and advice as to the ineffectiveness of non-productive public works, the agitation for their expansion continued. Huge appropriation bills had been introduced into Congress and were supported by a considerable section of the press—plus pork-barrel-seeking Congressmen.

There ensued a long battle. Speaker Garner championed a bill to provide straight nonproductive public works of $2,300,000,000 annually, in addition to the more than $600,000,000 we were already spending. His colleagues sent out to the local press of the country the amount each town and county would get from the barrel and, inspired by the vision of extensive appropriations for their districts, they pressed valiantly forward. It was good Democratic politics both from the point of view of proving me a heartless incompetent and the appeal to local greed.

On May 27, 1932, I commented on his proposals in a public statement:

I believe the American people will grasp the economic fact that such action would require appropriations to be made to the Federal departments, thus creating a deficit in the budget that could only be met with more taxes and more Federal bond issues. That makes balancing of the budget hopeless. The country also understands that an unbalanced budget means the loss of confidence of our own people and of other nations in the credit and stability of the government and that the consequences are national demoralization and the loss of ten times as many jobs as would be created by this program even if it could be physically put into action.

An examination of only one group of these proposals—that is, proposed authorizations for new post offices—shows a list of about 2,300 such buildings, at a total cost of about $1,500,000,000. The Post Office Department informs me that the interest and upkeep of these buildings would amount to $14,000,000 per annum, whereas the upkeep and rent of buildings at present in use is less than $3,000,000. Many of the other groups in this bill will no more stand the light of day than this example.

A total of over 3,500 projects of various kinds are proposed in this bill, scattered into every quarter of the United States. Many of these projects have heretofore been discredited by Congress because of useless extravagance involved. I do not believe that 20 per cent could be brought to the stage of employment for a year. I am advised by the engineers that the amount of labor required to complete a group of $400,000,000 of these works would amount to only 100,000 men for one year, because they are in large degree mechanical jobs.

This is not unemployment relief. It is the most gigantic pork barrel ever proposed to the American Congress. It is an unexampled raid on the public treasury.

Detailed lists of all these projects have been broadcast to every part of the country during the past twenty-four hours, to the cities, towns, villages and sections who would receive a portion of this pork barrel. It is apparently expected that the cupidity of these towns and sections will demand that their congressmen and senators vote for this bill or threaten to penalize them if they fail to join in this squandering of money.

I just do not believe that such lack of intelligence or cupidity exists amongst the people of our United States. . . . Our nation was not founded on the pork barrel, and it has not become great by political logrolling. I hope that those many members of Congress of both parties who I know will oppose this bill will receive the definite support of the people in their districts in resisting it.

PRIVATE REPRODUCTIVE WORKS

As I have shown, I undertook immediately after the crash in 1929 to organize cooperative action of industry in the expansion of construction. About one year later (October 6th) I stated:

The Department of Commerce reports to me that construction work by the railways and utilities in the last eight months amounts to about $4,500,-000,000 as compared with about $4,000,000,000 in the same period of the boom year of 1929, or an increase of about $500,000,000. In all previous depressions these works decreased, so that the gain is more than even the apparent figures.

Near the end of the year, in reporting to Congress upon this subject on December 2nd, I said:

The cooperation of public utilities, railways, and other large organizations has been generously given in construction and betterment work in anticipation of future need. The Department of Commerce advises me that, as a result, the volume of this type of construction work, which amounted to roughly $6,300,000,000 in 1929, instead of decreasing will show a total of about $7,000,000,000 for 1930.

This stimulation of private construction in the earlier stages of the depression was most fruitful of results, the increase above normal in the first two years being estimated at over $2,000,000,000.

However, the financial collapse of Europe in mid-1931 made it impossible for the industries to finance even normal expansion, and their financial abilities decreased rapidly under the strains of this European debacle.

I felt it was important to maintain the modernization and, in some cases, expansion of our industrial plants. Such action had three purposes: First, to provide more employment; second, with the growth of population, such expansion was necessary; and third, such work could well be done in time of depression and thus would tend to level off excessive pressures for construction when the demand for consumer goods was resumed. I had proposed authorities to the RFC to undertake loans for such purposes. This would have involved only the use of government credit, costing the government nothing.

At the same time, I had recommended an expansion of reproductive or "self-liquidating" public works by loans from the RFC. They comprised such works as toll bridges, power-producing dams, municipal waterworks and slum clearance. This was, I believe, the first proposal that the Federal Government aid in curing the slum evil. The revenues from such reproductive works would repay the government loans.

These authorities were refused in the original RFC law. I urged them repeatedly upon Committee members and, finally, in an address to the Senate on May 31st, I again urged "authority to the Reconstruction Corporation to increase the issues of its securities to the maximum of $3,000,000,000 in order that it may expand its services both in aid to employment and to agriculture on a wide scale."

We finally won our point for the reproductive public works and secured authority for loans of $1,500,000,000 from the RFC. Sadly enough, this authority was delayed six months and my proposal of loans to modernize and expand industrial plants was defeated.

However, the San Francisco Bay Bridge, the Los Angeles water supply from the Colorado River, the Jones Beach project in New York, the Mississippi River Bridge at New Orleans, and a hundred other reproductive works were the results. The government recovered their cost with interest.

In my message of December 6, 1932, on the state of the nation, I again went into these subjects, relating three constructive policies for future guidance which had evolved from all this experience.

The first was that nonproductive public works could not substantially ameliorate unemployment.[1]

The second was that loans should be made to industry so that it could take advantage of slack production to modernize plants and to expand them against the needs of a growing population. In any event, there is far more unemployment relief in this direction than in nonproductive public works.

The third great employment possibility was housing. The American people are always underhoused both in quantity and quality. There is never a time when homes are not wearing out. The country could always use economically 10,000,000 better homes, because the standard of living should always be advancing. It is the largest area of the construction industry. To provide easy finance and to give encouragement for better homes, my original proposed authority to liberalize discounting of loans by the Home Loan Banks would have done more good than billions of tax money. It offered the best single opportunity for aid to unemployment in the whole range of ideas. This proposal was held up by the Democratic opposition for nine months and even then came out greatly crippled.

DIRECT RELIEF OF DISTRESS

The impact of the European collapse greatly increased our unemployment and the need for direct relief to destitute families.

---

[1] The New Deal, in tackling this problem, of course threw our experience overboard. But they quickly found that no such enormous program of public works as they promised could be usefully and efficiently constructed. Therefore, to give employment under this heading they resorted to a gigantic festival of "boondoggling," the physical remains of which quickly disappeared. The distribution of these works in such manner as effectively to control the votes of congressmen became a public scandal.

I began to enlarge our organization to meet the increased load in August, 1931. Our departmental estimates of unemployed at this time had risen to about 8,000,000 which, after deducting the usual factors for between-jobbers and those not desiring work, and at the same time taking into consideration the number of workers per family and about 1,000,000 idle employees being provided for by employers, indicated possibly 3,000,000 families without breadwinners.

Colonel Woods, who had ably guided "The President's Committee for Unemployment Relief" since 1930, was compelled by ill health and overwork to resign in August, 1931. I persuaded Walter Gifford, president of the American Telephone & Telegraph Company, to take charge. We expanded the Committee to seventy members from all parts of the country, for a better check on municipal and state direct relief, and named it the President's Unemployment Relief Organization.

The surveys by this organization and the reports on the high state of public health proved that distress was being provided for. I, therefore, concluded that the responsibility for relief during the winter could again be carried by the relief system we had set up. Mr. Gifford appointed a staff of traveling inspectors to see that there was no failure. Under the chairmanship of Owen D. Young, we set up a nation-wide drive to aid the private relief agencies.

I opened the drive by an address on October 18th:

This broadcast tonight marks the beginning of the mobilization of the nation for a great undertaking to provide security for those of our citizens and their families who, through no fault of their own, face unemployment and privation during the coming winter. Its success depends upon the sympathetic and generous action of every man and woman in our country. No one with a spark of human sympathy can contemplate unmoved the possibilities of suffering that can crush many of our unfortunate fellow Americans if we fail them.

The depression has been deepened by events from abroad which are beyond the control either of our citizens or of our government.

I recounted the steps we had taken in organization, and continued:

This organized effort is our opportunity to express our sympathy, to lighten the burden of the heavy-laden, and to cast sunshine into the habitation of despair.

THE PRESIDENT'S ORGANIZATION ON UNEMPLOYMENT RELIEF
H. G. Lloyd, Philadelphia; Walter S. Gifford, New York; The President; Owen D. Young, New York; J. F. Lucey, Dallas; Samuel Mather, Cleveland; J. F. Bell, Minneapolis; Conrad H. Mann, Kansas City; Edward L. Ryerson, Chicago

MR. HOOVER AND THE HEADS OF THE NATIONAL ORGANIZATION
ON UNEMPLOYMENT (SEPTEMBER 24, 1931)

This task is not beyond the ability of these thousands of community organizations to solve. Each local organization from its experience last winter and summer has formulated careful plans and made estimates completely to meet the need of that community. I am confident that the generosity of each community will fully support these estimates. The sum of these budgets will meet the needs of the nation as a whole.

The possible misery of helpless people gives me more concern than any other trouble this depression has brought us. . . .

The success and character of a nation are to be judged by the ideals and the spirit of its people. Time and again the American people have demonstrated a spiritual quality, a capacity for unity of action, of generosity, a certainty of results in time of emergency that have made them great in the annals of the history of all nations. This is the time and this is the occasion when we must arouse that idealism, that spirit . . . that none who deserve shall suffer.

I would that I possessed the art of words to fix the real issue with which the troubled world is faced into the mind and heart of every American man and woman. Our country and the world are today involved in more than a financial crisis. We are faced with the primary question of human relations, which reaches to the very depth of organized society and to the very depth of human conscience. This civilization and this great complex, which we call American life, is builded and can alone survive upon the translation into individual action of that fundamental philosophy announced by the Savior nineteen centuries ago. Part of our national suffering today is from failure to observe these primary yet inexorable laws of human relationship. Modern society can not survive with the defense of Cain, "Am I my brother's keeper?"

That drive was successful, not alone in raising huge funds, but in awakening the national responsibility for being "my brother's keeper."

Late in October, 1931, to make doubly sure that distress was being taken care of, I again directed a renewed survey of the "direct relief" situation through the state committees and through the governors of the states. With one exception, the governors reported that with Federal indirect relief, and with appropriations in some cases by the state governments, the local committees could handle the problem. A still further check by the community chests in 227 larger cities reported their complete confidence that they could meet the emergency in these, the most difficult centers. As a still further check, I had a survey made by the

Federal Public Health Service. Surgeon General Cumming reported that the death rate was even lower than in the prosperous year of 1928. He showed that the most sensitive index of malnutrition—infant mortality—was at a lower rate than in any previous time. The explanation of this, no doubt, was that the local committees, organized and inspired by the fine women who did most of the work, were doing a better job of mutual help than ever before.

Of the governors reporting to Mr. Gifford, only Governor Pinchot of Pennsylvania—second richest state in the Union—refused to cooperate. His demand that the Federal government do the job, became the cry of all pseudo liberals. The Pennsylvania State Relief Committee, however, informed us they could get along without him.

Yet with the continuing degeneration of the situation (arising from the financial collapse in Europe), the reports of the committees and our governmental statistical agencies showed that the unemployed increased to about 10,140,000 as of January, 1932, or an increase of about 3,300,000 over the year before.

On January 2, 1932, after a renewed survey by the Public Health Service, I received from Surgeon General Cumming the report that:

Records . . . indicate that the mortality at the beginning of the winter of 1931–32 has continued on a very favorable level, the rate being only 10.7 per 1,000 as compared to 11.4, 12.0 and 13.2 in the last quarters of 1930, 1929 and 1928, respectively. . . .

Infant mortality . . . was definitely lower . . . the rate being 55.8 per thousand against 58.1. . . . This . . . showing has persisted during the last weeks of the year, the rate for the final quarter being 46.6 against an average of 56.9 for the corresponding period three years before the depression and against 51.9 for the same period of 1929, the lowest previous rate.

To reenforce our other measures, I secured from Congress the assignment for relief purposes of 85,000,000 bushels of wheat and 500,000 bales of cotton from the surplus held by the Farm Board. I arranged that the distribution should be made by the Red Cross through their chapters and our state and local relief committees. The Red Cross had the wheat milled into flour which provided the full bread supply for every family on relief for one year. The cotton provided over a dozen yards of cotton cloth to every family on relief.

In early March, 1932, I called a conference of Republican Senators Watson, Reed, Fess, Congressmen Snell and Hawley, together with Democratic Senators Robinson, Glass, and Congressmen Crisp and Steagall. These men represented the important Congressional committees concerned with relief and recovery. I stated that I wanted frank advice and I would make no public statement of their conclusions, so they could speak candidly. I presented certain questions to them:

1. Should we continue to administer direct relief through our organization of committees?

2. Should the Federal government take over the administration of and appropriate funds for direct doles?

3. Should the Federal government make grants to the states for our voluntary committee's support, conditional upon regular state and municipal participation also?

4. Should we expand appropriations from the Federal Treasury for public works beyond the programs I had proposed?

All those present favored continuing my committee organization. They opposed direct Federal government administration and doles. They agreed to grants-in-aid to the states if it became necessary. Except for Garner, they opposed expansion of nonproductive public works.

But the more politically-minded members of Congress, together with all the left-wing organizations in the country, were demanding that the Federal government take over relief entirely and give a dole. They could, however, cite no consequential failure of our voluntary committee system. The motive was political, and the fire was directed at stony-hearted Hoover.

On May 31, 1932, as a part of the RFC expansion bill, I proposed to the Congress that $300,000,000 be made available to the states to aid them in relief through our committee system. In presenting the matter, I said:

The sharp degeneration has its many reflexes in distress and hardship upon our people. I hold that the maintenance of the sense of individual and personal responsibility of men to their neighbors and the proper separation of functions of the Federal and local governments require the maintenance of the fundamental principle that the obligation of distress rests upon the individuals, upon the communities and upon the states. In order, however, that there may be no failure on the part of any state to meet its obligation in this direction I have, after consultation with some of the party leaders on both sides, favored authorization to the Reconstruction Finance Corporation to loan up to $300,000,000 to state governments where they are unable to finance themselves in provision of relief to distress.

I proposed that we set these amounts up in the form of loans as a restraint on state demands. At once we had a battle with the Democratic members of the House who wanted to base its distribution upon population rather than upon need. But on July 17th we snatched this measure from the pork barrel.

On July 5th, I asked Congress for an emergency appropriation of $120,000 to pay the clerical expenses of Mr. Gifford's organization so that he might carry on over the year. My message read:

The second Deficiency Bill just passed omitted an appropriation for continuance of the activities of the President's Organization on Unemployment Relief. I urgently request that Congress make a special appropriation of $120,000, to continue this work over the next fiscal year.

This organization, of which Mr. Walter S. Gifford is director, is composed of leading men and women throughout every state in the Union and has served to establish and coordinate state and local volunteer effort in relief of distress throughout the nation. . . .

[They are] . . . serving without pay or expense [to the Government]. It is non-partisan and representative of various economic and social groups. To function successfully it must have funds to employ a relatively small number of trained personnel, together with necessary office help.

The appropriation requested for continuance of this organization is infinitesimal in its ratio to the large resources which are put at the command of those in distress.

The Democratic leaders attacked the proposal and as a result it was not passed. I raised the money from private sources, one of them being my own pocket.

Another check-up by Surgeon General Cumming of the Federal Public Health Service in June, 1932, showed a further decrease in death and sickness rates, especially among infants. This not only proved that there was no widespread undernourishment, but also that the solicitude for those in difficulty by the 3,000 local volunteer committees of admirable men and women was having magnificent results. And the consequences in community cohesion were spiritual as well as physical.

With continued economic destruction from Europe and the obstruction in Congress, the depression reached a low point in July, 1932. The unemployed were estimated by our staff and the labor organizations at about 12,400,000, an increase of about 2,250,000 over the number in January, 1932. The number of persons receiving relief amounted to about 18,000,000. But our measures were effectively preventing any hunger or cold.

FOURTH PHASE OF THE DEPRESSION— NOVEMBER, 1931, TO JULY, 1932 *(Cont'd)*

AGRICULTURAL RELIEF

During my administration our agricultural relief policies included (a) higher tariffs; (b) loans to farm cooperatives from the Farm Board; (c) support of prices in wheat and cotton by the Farm Board; (d) loans by the RFC to stimulate farm exports; (e) loans from the RFC to the Intermediate Credit Banks to finance the marketing of crops; (f) expansion of the Federal Land Banks; (g) creation of the Agricultural Credit Banks to finance the farmers' production of ground crops and livestock; (h) provision of seed loans from the Department of Agriculture on easy terms; (i) especial emphasis on rural-area road building in our public works programs, by which we provided opportunities for wage employment of many farmers in the off-crop season.

Beyond these mostly emergency measures we developed a long-range program for the solution of the major difficulty in agriculture. During the war the government had called for the expansion of ground crops which resulted in plowing up much land of marginal productivity which had been mostly pastures. Since the war, we had still further mechanized farming, one consequence of which was to eliminate the animal consumers. In the meantime, foreign agriculture had recovered and our export markets reduced. We were, for these reasons, constantly overproducing. After the war the government had compensated manufacturers for their overexpansion of productive plants for war purposes. I had long held that there was similar responsibility to compensate the farmers. The difficulty was in finding a practical method for such a remedy.

After two years of investigation, experimentation, and a series of nation-wide conferences Secretary of Agriculture Arthur Hyde had devised a method of retirement of marginal agricultural land. The plan was that the government should lease the submarginal lands for twenty-one years—or for shorter periods in certain circumstances—and, by turning them into pasture or forest, take them out of the production of ground crops. Lease was preferable to purchase, because the owners retained their homes and some employment. Moreover, it would cost less, and with increased consumption from the growth of population, the government could eventually withdraw.

We proposed as a method of making leases that we ask for bids from farmers of the annual rental per acre they wanted for such lands. We would accept the lowest bids first until we had retired enough parcels. The lowest bids would obviously be on the least profitable lands. The Secretary had examined its application to several representative counties and found that the cost of retiring marginal war acreage would amount to a smaller sum annually than any other form of agricultural relief.

It was impossible to get sufficient Congressional support for its enactment in the 1931–1932 session, and we decided to offer the plan after the election. We introduced a plank in the Republican platform proposing the idea, and I supported it in the campaign. As we lost the election and our successor had advocated other ideas, there was little purpose in presenting it to the Congress. However, in order that the plan might be kept in public view, I incorporated it in a message to the Congress of February 20, 1933:

Pending the return of the great commercial countries to the gold standard and the consequent increase in world consumption and thus rise in world prices, it is essential temporarily to reduce farm production so as to remove the backbreaking surpluses of agricultural products and thus to raise agricultural income. The plan proposed by the Secretary of Agriculture some time since for temporary leasing of marginal lands is the least harmful and the most hopeful of all the plans which have been proposed. It has the merit of direct action in reducing supply to demand and thus unquestionably increasing prices; it would affect all farm products; give equal benefits to all farmers; is free of increased bureaucracy, very much less costly; and could be covered by a manufacturers' excise tax of probably 1 per cent to 2 per cent upon these commodities.

By our various activities, we had carried the farmers through a worldwide calamity with little dispossession from their farms, but with unquestioned tightening of their belts and some hardship. Certainly none of them went either hungry or cold, if our committees were told about it.

FOURTH PHASE OF THE DEPRESSION— NOVEMBER, 1931, TO JULY, 1932 *(Cont'd)*

CONSEQUENCES OF EIGHT MONTHS' OPPOSITION, DELAYS, AND REFUSAL OF NEEDED AUTHORITIES

One effect of the opposition from the Democratic-Progressive controlled Congress was to delay recovery until it would be too late to affect the forthcoming Presidential election. And it was disastrous to the country. It is worthwhile to review these tactics for the student of politics.

Promptly at the opening of the 1931–32 session, the opposition refused to enter into any program of cooperation, although several major measures had been agreed upon in the previous October 6th conference. The whole month of December was frittered away. The imperative items of RFC and Federal Land Bank legislation were not passed until the end of January, 1932, and then with serious deletions of needed authorities. I secured restoration of only part of these deleted powers in July, 1932. The Federal Reserve authorizations were delayed until mid-February. The creation of the Home Loan Banks was held up for nearly eight months and then passed in emaciated shape. The banking reforms, so essential to recovery, were delayed for over three years. The bankruptcy reform laws were delayed for two years and not fully completed until after the 1932 election. Balancing the budget was held up until June, 1932, and our proposed cuts in "ordinary" expenditures of $670,000,000 were reduced to $150,000,000. The regulation of electric power and a multitude of constructive secondary measures never got through.

Typical of the sabotage and obstruction tactics was Garner's placing of a tariff bill ahead of many of the reconstruction measures in the House, which resulted in great delays. Another instance was his almost unprecedented ruling that the practically unanimous Ways and Means committee revenue bill should be subjected to unlimited debate, which not only delayed but destroyed it. Still other instances were his preposterous pork-barrel and unlimited-loan bills. Still further instances were the veterans' bonus bills, and the fiat money bills.

During all this obstruction, our economic situation slipped lower and lower.

We reached our lowest point in the latter part of June or early July. By that time, the Democrats apparently felt that they had done enough damage to insure the election, and in the following month we got many of our measures through.

One could plot a curve of the ebb and flow of fear, which followed irresponsible congressional actions, by statistics of bank closings and the movement of gold.

The following table shows the RFC loans to banks, their failures and reopenings measured in deposits. (Closings are marked —, reopenings +.)

	Loans to Banks	Failures and Reopenings
December, 1931	. . . .	— $258,500,000
January, 1932..	. . . .	— 207,900,000
February	$ 45,000,000	— 42,500,000
March	127,000,000	+ 4,100,000
April	188,000,000	— 20,600,000
May	236,000,000	— 1,100,000
June	331,000,000	— 121,200,000
July	123,000,000	+ 21,200,000
August	105,000,000	+ 4,000,000
September	41,000,000	+ 600,000
October	31,000,000	+ 18,400,000
November	32,000,000	— 30,800,000
December	65,000,000	— 63,600,000
January, 1933..	64,000,000	— 120,000,000

The table shows the tragic results of delay in December and January. It shows that thereafter we had the bank failures practically whipped until June, when the climax of congressional obstruction plunged the country into despair. It also indicates the immediate restoration of public confidence when Congress adjourned in July.

The increase and decrease of fear are shown also by the gold export and import movement—a movement much greater than appears from this table of actual gold exports, because of the periodic engagements for future exports or earmarking and their later return to the banks (the plus sign signifies net imports—the minus sign, net exports of gold in millions of dollars):

	Exports	Imports
October, 1931..	− 337.7	
November		+ 89.4
December		+ 56.9
January, 1932..	− 73.0	
February	− 90.6	
March	− 24.7	
April	− 30.2	
May	− 195.5	
June	− 206.0	
July	− 3.4	
August		+ 6.1
September		+ 27.9
October		+ 20.6
November		+ 21.7
December		+ 100.9

Thus the great fears in October, 1931, were quieted in November and December by the creation of the bankers' National Credit Association and by our administrative proposals to the Congress. But with Congressional obstruction, fear rose to a maximum in June. Then with the adjournment and the effect of our measures, confidence began to return again.

WE WIN MOST OF THE BATTLE—WITH DELAYS

During the eight months of battle with Congress from December, 1931, to July, 1932, I had been badly battered about. Nevertheless, the accomplishments in terms of items of our program which passed were considerable. I summarize here the highlights of our successes and failures.

1. We created the Reconstruction Finance Corporation with $3,500,-000,000 resources:

(a) to support loans to building and loan associations, the Federal Farm Loan Banks, the Federal Intermediate Credit Banks, the insurance companies, railways, and banking institutions generally;

(b) to loan $1,500,000,000 for reproductive public works and slum clearance;

(c) to make loans encouraging export of agricultural products;

(d) to create the Agricultural Production Banks to fill the gap between the Intermediate Credit Banks and the Farm Loan Banks.

2. We secured an expansion of the Federal Land Bank resources to take up farm mortgages.

3. We secured seed loans for the farmers.

4. We secured the creation of the Home Loan Banks to relieve home owners from foreclosure.

5. We secured a change in the security coverage of the currency so as to protect the gold standard.

6. We liberalized the Federal Reserve credit expansion to meet shrinkage of credit by the withdrawals of gold and currency.

7. We secured authorization for the Federal Reserve Banks to make loans to small business.

8. We secured part of the reforms of the bankruptcy laws.

9. We maintained direct relief to the unemployed through our nonpolitical committee organization, with Federal aid only of 85,000,000 bushels of wheat and 500,000 bales of cotton from the Farm Board's surplus, and $300,000,000, to supplement state and local relief.

10. We secured $700,000,000 for nonproductive public works.

11. We secured the Federal Power Commission, but without any real powers.

12. We secured, in the last days of Congress, the color of authority to reorganize and consolidate the government bureaus (but it could not, under the law, be implemented until the next session).

13. We stopped billions in wasteful legislation by veto, reduced the ordinary expenses of the government by $150,000,000 per annum, and increased the revenues by $1,250,000,000, so that the budget was on the way to being balanced.

14. We secured ratification of the Intergovernmental Debt Moratorium.

15. We secured the calling of a World Economic Conference to lessen trade barriers and stabilize currencies.

Our defeats were:

(a) heartbreaking delays all along the line;

(b) overstringent requirements on RFC loans;

(c) refusal of authority to the RFC to make loans for industrial modernization;

(d) refusal of authority to the RFC for loans upon the assets of closed banks to relieve depositors;

(e) refusal to the Federal Farm Loan Banks of authorities which would have helped the farm mortgage situation;

(f) curtailment of the powers of the Home Loan Banks which would have relieved pressures on home owners;

(g) refusal of essential parts of our reforms of the bankruptcy laws;

(h) refusal of our railway reorganization proposals;

(i) refusal of authority to the Federal Power Commission to regulate interstate power rates;

(j) failure to pass the banking reform;

(k) the disastrous effect of repeated attempts to issue fiat money;

(l) refusal to revive the commission on war debts.[1]

During this period, we had also carried through many administrative measures in support of the situation, such as the standstill agreement; the National Credit Association; the relief of distress; the drives for relief funds; the support of employees by their employers; the agreed maintenance of wages in tune with the cost of living; the expansion of local public works and expansion of industrial construction; the Farm Board's support of farmers' prices, and a score of lesser actions.

RECOVERY BEGINS WITH THE ADJOURNMENT OF THE CONGRESS

With the adjournment of Congress in July, 1932, the whole country drew a sigh of relief. Confidence began to return. The net result of our battle was gain from an economic if not from a political point of view.

[1] An evidence that the failure to act upon these recommendations was purely political is the fact that, with few exceptions, they were passed in some form very early in the Roosevelt administration.

Up to date, we had warded off four paralysis-promising panics and now at last had turned the tide toward sound recovery.

But, slow and painful though progress was, popular government had functioned even against political sabotage. The fundamental moral strength of the system and of the people was greater than that of debilitating political tactics.

We went through the pit of the depression with the American financial Gibraltar paying every foreign demand, the dollar still ringing true on every counter of the world. Our cooperation with other nations in the moratorium on intergovernmental payments, the stand-still agreement, and the calling of the World Economic Conference, had contributed greatly to rebuilding confidence over the other parts of the world. The bottom of the depression abroad had also been reached in late June and July. Recovery was now on the way everywhere.

It is worth while to record here some independent views to the effect that recovery had begun at this time.

William Starr Myers, Professor of Politics of Princeton University, wrote in *The Guide,* November, 1939:

History now records that the Great Depression turned in late June or early July of 1932. Recovery began in all the other great commercial countries and continued upward for the next two years. President Hoover was the world leader who had contributed most to this victory over chaos. The battle against the depression had been won.

D. W. Ellsworth noted in the *Annalist,* February 21, 1936:

The bottom of depression was reached in 1932.

Leonard P. Ayres stated in *Economics of Recovery* (page 137):

The corner was turned in the country in the summer of 1932. . . . The most important factor in preventing our incipient recovery in 1932 . . . was political in nature.

Irving Fisher said in a speech before the American Economic Association, December 28, 1933:

We should have been further on the road toward recovery today had there been no election last year. Recovery started under Mr. Hoover but . . . a recession occurred because of fear over political uncertainties.

Even the New Deal Department of Commerce, in its *World Economic Review* for 1933, said:

The decline generally had been long and steep. . . . In the United States business improved substantially, from July until September, and held firm without much definite tendency either way in October and November. . . . The relatively long interval between the election and the inauguration of the new President proved unsettling to business and was a factor militating against further immediate improvement.

Kansas City Star, January 26, 1936:

The depression here, according to the League [of Nations] charts, reached its low point in June, 1932. Then there was an abrupt and important revival during the summer. In November began a deterioration.

Frank Kent wrote in the Baltimore *Sun,* March 9, 1936:

There is general agreement that the low point was reached in June, 1932, and all over the world recovery began at that time.

Walter Lippmann wrote in November, 1933:

There is very good statistical evidence which goes to prove . . . the world depression reached its low point in midsummer of 1932.

and in June, 1936,

The historians will . . . see that President Hoover, Secretary Mills and Governor Meyer had hold of the essence of the matter in the spring of 1932 when . . . they arrested the depression.

The National Industrial Conference Board, November 10, 1934:

The facts presented in the chart bring out clearly that the first steps toward recovery were taken in the year 1932.

Edmund Platt, former Vice Governor of the Federal Reserve Board, was reported in the *New York Times,* July 4, 1933, as saying:

If 1932 had not happened to be a Presidential year, the recovery begun then might have continued without any serious interruption.

The *New York Times* said on the different dates given:

(June 16, 1934) The change for the better in the last half of 1932 is beyond dispute. That this evident revival of confidence was suddenly reversed in February, 1933, is equally true.

(November 24, 1935) . . . the beginning of the turn must be assigned to 1932.

(November 26, 1935) We have already travelled far since the depression turned in 1932.

(January 2, 1936) Recovery . . . really began in 1932.

The Brookings Institution in 1937 reached much the same conclusions.

But proof of recovery was not only opinion; it was a statistical fact.

As I have already shown, the gold movement reversed itself, indicating international confidence in our emergence from the crisis. The net bank failures had changed into net openings.

The American Federation of Labor reported a decrease in unemployment of 800,000 persons—a reversal of the normal seasonal trend. The commercial indexes showed the following increases:

Car loadings	20 per cent
Electric power consumption	10 per cent
Dow-Jones industrial common stocks...	80 per cent

Our exports increased from $107,000,000 in June to $153,000,000 in October.

Various Federal Reserve Board indexes showed the following increases from late June to late September:

Prices of farm products.....	12 per cent
Industrial production.......	14 per cent
Production of iron and steel	20 per cent
Production of textiles.......	50 per cent
Factory pay rolls...........	10 per cent
Factory employment........	5 per cent
Freight-car loadings........	12 per cent
Bond prices..............	20 per cent
Common-stock prices.......	60 per cent

ACTION FROM THE ADJOURNMENT OF CONGRESS IN JULY UNTIL THE ELECTION IN NOVEMBER, 1932

To strengthen our recovery all along the line, we organized a Business and Industrial Committee in every Federal Reserve District under the direction of Secretary Mills and Henry Robinson.

On August 26, 1932, I addressed a conference of these district committees, saying in part:

We have asked you . . . to confer together and with the officials of the government agencies which are engaged in the problems of the depression. The purpose of the conference is to better organize private initiative and to coordinate it with governmental activities, so as to further aid in the progress of recovery of business, agriculture, and employment. . . . This is a meeting not to pass resolutions on economic questions but to give you the opportunity to organize for action. . . .

. . . We are convinced that we have overcome the major financial crisis— a crisis in severity unparalleled in the history of the world—and that with its relaxation confidence and hope have reappeared in the world. . . .

. . . It is not proposed that you attempt to settle here in a day great economic problems of the future. It is simply proposed that you organize for action in the problems immediately before us. . . .

We have a powerful governmental program in action for aid to recovery formulated and organized. . . . I am in hopes you will familiarize yourselves with its possibilities so as to coordinate your activities with it.

In the furtherance of business recovery it is clearly necessary that there be coordination of effort in hastening the return of unemployed to employment in their natural industries. . . .

. . . Agricultural relief is one of the primary foundations of all progress in our country, and upon it does the progress of your business depend. It is as much your problem as it is the problem of the farmer.

CHANGES IN THE ADMINISTRATION OF THE RFC

General Dawes had resigned as president of the RFC to devote himself to the difficulties of the Central Republic Bank & Trust Company of Chicago. General Dawes had not owned any interest in it since he became Vice President of the United States in 1924, but he felt a responsibility for it and believed that his prestige might pull it out of trouble.

I was anxious to secure a successor from the Democratic side, so that the Corporation should not be made a football in the forthcoming political campaign. First I urged Newton D. Baker, Mr. Wilson's Secretary of War, to undertake it. Although in our interview he had made no statement, I sensed that he was a candidate for the Democratic nomination for President. As President he would have been a blessing to the American people, for he was a man of greatest integrity, high ideals, large view of public affairs and a gentleman in every instinct. I had served with him during the war and had witnessed his fine administrative abilities, his high courage and urbanity in most difficult circumstances.

When Mr. Baker declined, I sent on July 26th for former Senator Atlee Pomerene of Ohio, who accepted the Chairmanship. As a Democratic Senator from that state he had enjoyed the respect of all parties. Charles A. Miller, a leading banker of Utica, New York, became President. At that time both Eugene Meyer, chairman of the Federal Reserve Board, and Secretary of the Treasury Mills found their *ex officio* service on the RFC Board, along with their other duties, too exacting and retired.

In addition to Messrs. Pomerene and Miller, the Board members were now Gardner Cowles, Sr., Jesse Jones, Harvey Couch, and Wilson McCarthy.

In order to avoid repetition I give the following table of the Corporation's activities over my entire administration. The outstanding loans at the end of my administration were as follows:

Banks and trust companies............	$ 672,467,000
Building and loan associations.........	63,100,000
Insurance companies	87,576,000
Mortgage loan companies............	109,904,000
Credit unions	439,000
Federal land banks..................	18,800,000
Joint-stock land banks...............	4,824,000
Agricultural credit corporations.........	2,201,000
Regional agricultural credit corporations	37,154,000
Livestock credit corporations..........	5,550,000
Railroads	296,251,000
Self-liquidating public works..........	18,664,000
Special agricultural credits...........	1,236,000
Relief payments to states	159,555,000
Total...................	$1,477,721,000[1]

In addition, some $200,000,000 of loans had been made and repaid. The Board had authorized further large "self-liquidating" loans for public works. As indicative of the widespread work of the Corporation, the report for the first six months showed loans to 4,158 institutions of one kind or another, of which 89 per cent were in towns of less than 100,000 population, situated in every state in the Union. The borrowers at that moment included 3,600 banks and trust companies (almost 20 per cent of the total of such companies), 418 building and loan associations, 63 insurance companies, 23 agricultural loan institutions, and 38 railroad companies.

SAVING THE BANKS OF CHICAGO

A typical incident during this period was the imminent closing of all the Chicago banks. It was also to bring down on us a storm of political wrath. On Saturday, June 25, 1932, I had gone to the Rapidan Camp for

[1] Many years after, Jesse Jones, who later became Chairman of the Board, informed me that the whole sum loaned at the end of my administration, except for certain relief advances to the states, had been recovered with an actual profit to the government after having paid full interest to the Treasury. After March 4, 1933, all the additional authorities that I had asked for and still more were granted at once to the New Deal. If we could have had the powers we originally asked for in December, 1931, we could have prevented much loss all over the country; we could have given more aid to employment and hastened recovery. Most important, we could have averted the Detroit debacle of February, 1933, which precipitated bank closures all over the state of Michigan. The difficulties in Cleveland followed in the train of Detroit.

a week-end respite from Washington heat. For the same reason, Secretary Mills was on Long Island and Chairman Meyer was in upstate New York. No director of the RFC was either in Washington or in New York City. During the week, scattered runs had begun on the Chicago banks. On Saturday morning these spread and increased in intensity, and great crowds gathered at the banks; the run was especially strong on the Dawes bank. The origins of this affair are still obscure, but subsequent investigation disclosed a systematic propaganda of alarm carried on by telephone.[2] On Saturday afternoon Melvin A. Traylor of the First National Bank of Chicago telephoned to me, recounting the disturbing situation. He said that, while his own bank could hold out for some time, the Dawes bank was the focal danger point; his institution would help the Dawes bank, but it could not carry the full load; and he appealed for substantial aid from the RFC. "If we do not get such support by Monday," he concluded in substance, "every Chicago bank —ours among them, of course—will have to close its doors."

I spent the rest of that day at the telephone, bringing the various financial agencies of the government into touch with one another. I directed the Federal Bank Examiner at Chicago to look into the situation and rush a report to Directors Jones and McCarthy of the RFC, who fortunately were in Chicago attending the Democratic National Convention. I asked them to drop everything else and find what this was all about and what could be done. They recommended an immediate minimum loan of $80,000,000 to the Dawes bank as the only means for averting a disastrous crash which would close not only the Chicago banks but also hundreds of their correspondent banks in the Middle West. The other directors of the RFC agreed by telephone, and the loan was made. It averted the threatened panic and saved hundreds of banks and their depositors.

In the subsequent Presidential campaign, the Democrats made much use of this loan, charging, of course, that we had spent a huge sum in fattening an eminent Republican while deserving Democrats ate husks. These insincere critics entirely ignored the fact that half the members of the Board of the RFC were Democrats of high standing; that the loan was made upon their unqualified recommendation; that these

[2] Some information uncovered later indicated that it was a Communist operation.

recommendations had also the support of Mr. Traylor, who at the moment was being mentioned as a possible Presidential candidate in the Democratic National Convention. The loan was later repaid in full with interest.

In a speech at St. Louis, given in my account of the Presidential campaign, I replied to the critics, and my remarks there throw some light on the strains and struggles of that hard period.

THE WORLD WAR DEBTS

During the summer of 1932 the question of readjustment of the war debts to the United States then under the moratorium began to loom up.

When I recommended to the Congress the ratification of the moratorium in December, 1931, I also raised the issue of further adjustment of the debts as an economic measure important to meet the continuing crisis, saying:

As we approach the new year it is clear that a number of the governments indebted to us will be unable to meet further payments to us in full pending recovery in their economic life. It is useless to blind ourselves to an obvious fact. Therefore it will be necessary in some cases to make still further temporary adjustments.

The Congress has shared with the Executive in the past the consideration of questions arising from these debts. I am sure that it will commend itself to the Congress, that the legislative branch of the Government should continue to share this responsibility. In order that we should be in position to deal with the situation, I recommended the re-creation of the World War Foreign Debt Commission, with authority to examine such problems as may arise in connection with these debts during the present economic emergency, and to report to the Congress its conclusions and recommendations.

However, the Democratic majority in the House objected, and Congress refused to authorize the revival of a World War Debt Commission, such as we had seven years before. The Congress not only refused but rapped my knuckles by including in their moratorium ratification, "It is hereby expressly declared to be against the policy of Congress that any of the indebtedness of foreign countries should in any manner be cancelled or *reduced*."

I opposed cancellation, but I was convinced that, unless we were prepared to reconsider an extension of the moratorium, or some reductions based upon capacity to pay, our debtors would all gang up on us and, with expressions of deep regret, repudiate their debts. It was obvious that the resumption of payments after the moratorium would cause the British, as well as several other nations, great temporary difficulties. On the other hand, the French needed no such relief, as they still had ample funds in American banks.

I tried very hard to impress on the Congressional leaders the danger that all these nations would combine in common cause and would claim moral justifications such as, "We spent our blood, you spent your money, we are unable to collect from Germany," etc. After such justification, no official in those countries could be reelected on a platform of payment resumption. The eminently proper course for us was to meet their justifiable needs during the depression and forestall any action which might incite repudiation.

We were quickly to see a movement in this direction by attempts to connect the German reparations with our debts. The German government, on November 19, 1931, in anticipation of the expiration of the moratorium, asked the Allies to send a committee to reinvestigate their capacity to pay reparations. On December 6th the Allies agreed to do so. On the 23rd this committee reported that Germany could not pay reparations for two years. A conference of Germany's reparation-holders was called for January 18, 1932, at Lausanne. They invited us to attend, but we had no claim to German reparations and, as our hands were tied by Congress, I declined.

The Lausanne Conference was postponed until June 15th. On July 8th it concluded with a reduction of German reparations from the hypothetical $30,000,000,000 to a total of about $700,000,000. However, it quickly developed that this settlement was only conditional. There was a secret gentlemen's agreement that it depended upon our canceling their debts to us. Being apprised of these facts, I instructed William R. Castle, Jr., Acting Secretary of State, to issue the following statement:

The American Government is pleased that in reaching an agreement on the question of reparations, the nations assembled at Lausanne have made a great step forward in stabilization of the economic situation in Europe.

On the question of war debts to the United States by European Governments there is no change in the attitude of the American Government which was clearly expressed in the President's statement concerning the proposed moratorium of intergovernmental debts on June 20th of last year.

Two days later, on July 11th, Neville Chamberlain, British Chancellor of the Exchequer, stated in the House of Commons that we had taken part in the Lausanne Conference and had presumably agreed with its decision. I immediately asked the State Department whether my instructions to keep our representatives from the conference had been violated. On July 12th our State Department secured a statement from Prime Minister MacDonald that we had taken no part at Lausanne, directly or indirectly. Secretary Stimson made a public statement to the same effect.

However, we were soon to see European debtors ganging up against us. On July 14th the British announced an agreement with France for a "solid front" on war debts. In answer to an inquiry from Senator Borah, I wrote the following letter:

My Dear Mr. Senator:

I have your inquiry this morning, through Secretary Stimson, as to the effect on the United States of recent agreements in Europe.

Our people are, of course, gratified at the settlement of the strictly European problem of reparations or any of the other political or economic questions that have impeded European recovery. Such action, together with the real progress in disarmament, will contribute greatly to world stability.

I wish to make it absolutely clear, however, that the United States has not been consulted regarding any of the agreements reported by the press to have been concluded recently at Lausanne and that of course it is not a party to, nor in any way committed to, any such agreements.

While I do not assume it to be the purpose of any of these agreements to effect combined action of our debtors, if it shall be so interpreted then I do not propose that the American people shall be pressed into any line of action or that our policies shall be in any way influenced by such a combination either open or implied.

Yours faithfully,

HERBERT HOOVER

Our debtors took open joint action in December, 1932.

In August, 1932, Mr. Fred C. Croxton, who had been Mr. Gifford's assistant, replaced him as chairman of the President's Unemployment Relief Organization. Mr. Croxton also administered the $300,000,000 fund which I had obtained from Congress through the RFC to aid the state committees in direct relief.

The distribution of that fund by months during my administration was as follows:

July, 1932 ...	$ 8,000,000
August	13,932,000
September ...	18,523,000
October	22,595,000
November ..	18,485,000
December ...	35,958,000
January, 1933	49,435,000
February	48,187,000

On September 15, 1932, I assembled the leaders of the "national drive" committee of the voluntary relief agencies at the White House to organize for the joint appeal of that autumn. Newton D. Baker had succeeded Owen D. Young as chairman of the appeal committee. I addressed them as follows:

For the third time representatives of the great voluntary relief agencies of this country are here assembled to consider with earnestness and sympathy what measures may be undertaken for the relief of those in distress among our people. . . .

Our tasks are definite.

The first is to see that no man, woman or child shall go hungry or unsheltered through the approaching winter.

The second is to see that our great benevolent agencies for character building, for hospitalization, for care of children and all their vast number of agencies of voluntary solicitude for the less fortunate are maintained in full strength.

The third is to maintain the bedrock principle of our liberties by the full mobilization of individual and local resources and responsibilities.

The fourth is that we may maintain the spiritual impulses in our people for generous giving and generous service—in the spirit that each is his brother's keeper. . . . A cold and distant charity which puts out its sympathy only through the tax collector yields a very meager dole of unloving and perfunctory relief.

With each succeeding winter in this period of great distress our problem has become larger and more difficult. Yet the American people have responded to meet it. . . .

That the American people have made a broad and courageous attack upon the consequences of our present unparalleled calamity is amply suggested by the state of public health in the Nation. . . .

I reviewed our great measures of indirect relief and continued:

. . . Let no man believe, because we have summoned the power of government to these ends, that it can replace your efforts. . . .

Your organizations have, therefore, a most difficult task. I am confident that you will succeed. Our people are the most generous of all peoples. Most of us started in life poor or with little. What we have is the result of our own toil in this land rich in resources and opportunity. Most of us have known the helping hand of others in some human service and some human kindness and today as never before do we owe repayment of that debt. I sometimes think of relief in terms of insurance. Over the years our people contribute to the aid of others. The unexpected time comes of their own need, and they draw from this common pool. There lies in this no loss of self-respect.

So long as the world stands, there will be human misfortune and human suffering from causes men cannot control. There will be nation-wide calamities the result of which may be that any one of us may be the giver and any one the receiver. . . .

On such occasions as these there is more to be done than merely giving. There is the helping hand that should go with giving. The friendly counsel, the aid to solution of family and individual problems, our outpourings of the human spirit beyond dollars alone. Many a family today is carrying a neighbor family over the trough of this depression not alone with material aid but with that encouragement which maintains courage and faith. . . .

This drive again obtained some hundreds of millions of dollars, either through the local committees or through the national funds.

With these various measures we were able to carry on the direct relief of those in distress until the end of my administration, March 4, 1933.

CHAPTER 17

FIFTH PHASE OF THE DEPRESSION—
SEPTEMBER, 1932, TO MARCH, 1933

I discuss the Presidential Campaign of 1932 in a later section of this volume rather than interrupt the economic narrative.

The fifth phase of the depression extended from the Maine election in September, 1932, to Franklin Roosevelt's inauguration on March 4, 1933, a period of four months.

After mid-July the whole world was on the march out of the depression. All nations with a free economy other than our own were rapidly recovering. With the ominous election returns from Maine on September 14th, the country began to realize that Roosevelt would win and there would be an abrupt change in policies. After that date the business world at once began to weigh the consequences of his policies. Whether his policies were justified or unjustified, they immediately caused our business world to stop, wait, and listen. The prices of commodities and securities immediately began to decline, and unemployment increased.

ATTEMPTS TO COOPERATE WITH ROOSEVELT
AFTER MY DEFEAT

Naturally, I had given some thought to the situation which would arise in the certainty of my defeat.

The four months' interregnum between election and inauguration (since shortened to two months) had always been a particularly difficult period, especially when there was a change of political parties, with all the overcharged campaign emotions.

However, there were outstanding problems in which I hoped the President-elect and I could cooperate, if the economic recovery of the nation were to be continued.

Aside from the vital recovery problems, we were faced with pressing matters in international relations. The Japanese invasion of Manchuria presented great difficulties; the moratorium on intergovernmental debts was expiring in December; the World Economic Conference was to assemble in January; we were in the midst of the World Disarmament Conference. None of these matters could be advanced unless the President-elect would cooperate during the interregnum. For on the foreign front my positive influence was ended, as no foreign government would come to an agreement with me unless they knew that Mr. Roosevelt approved it. As he had not criticized my foreign policies during the campaign, I naturally expected that we could cooperate in that field.

The Congress would meet in December and I also thought that he would naturally want to see legislation balancing the budget; reform in banking and bankruptcy; the enactment of the deleted authorities of the RFC, the Land Banks and the Home Loan Banks; reform of the Veterans' Administration and reorganization of the Federal Executive Branch. Indeed, if these matters were out of the way, such political liabilities as were in them would be on my back, and the new administration would have a propitious beginning. Obviously the Democratic-controlled Congress would not accept such recommendations from me unless the President-elect approved.

I determined to approach the President-elect at once, and made the first step while returning from Palo Alto, where I had gone to vote. In a short address to the train crowd at Glendale, California, on November 12, 1932, I said:

The majority of the people have decided to entrust the government to a new administration. The political campaign is over.

I asked for unity of national action in the constructive measures which have been initiated during the past three years for care of distress to protect the Nation from imminent dangers and to promote economic recovery. If we are to continue the recovery so evidently in progress during the past few months ... we must have continued unity in constructive action all along the economic front. I shall work for that unity during the remaining four months of this administration. Furthermore, it is our duty after the 4th of March to cooperate with our opponents in every sound measure for the restoration of prosperity. . . .

I must give in some detail the results of my efforts to cooperate with Mr. Roosevelt, particularly so that the causes of the bank panic four months later may be clear.

REFUSAL OF ROOSEVELT TO COOPERATE ON THE ECONOMIC CONFERENCE AND ON WAR DEBTS

One international problem boiled up two days after the election. The Secretary of State telegraphed me en route from California that our war debtors simultaneously had notified us of their intention to demand deferment of payments due on December 15th, at which time the moratorium would expire. They proposed an entire readjustment of the debts. This was in full accord with their Lausanne Agreement to act together on the question.

In view of the excitement this aroused, I resolved not to wait until my arrival in Washington, but to telegraph Mr. Roosevelt rather fully the background of this question and invite him to meet with me at the White House for purposes of unified action. This I did from Yuma, Arizona, on November 12th. After reciting the notice from the debtor countries and previous attitudes of the administration, I indicated a line I thought might be taken, saying: [1]

. . . I recommended to the Congress [in December, 1931] that a New Debt Commission be created to deal with situations that might arise owing to the temporary incapacity of any individual debtor to meet its obligations . . . during the period of world depression. Congress declined to accede to this . . . recommendation. . . .

The Debt Commission referred to was the joint Congressional-administration commission which had settled the debts some years before and I suggested that despite the former refusal, it might, with his cooperation, be revived.

[1] The full texts of the correspondence with the President-elect and public statements upon the problems which follow can be found in *The State Papers and Other Public Writings of Herbert Hoover*, ed. William Starr Myers, Vol. II.

Mr. Roosevelt on the 14th accepted my invitation to confer and concluded, "In the last analysis, the immediate question raised by the British, French, and other notes creates a responsibility which rests upon those now vested with executive and legislative authority."

I did not like the ring of this disavowal of any responsibility on his part, because the Democratic-controlled Congress would take no action without his approval. But we arranged to meet at the White House on November 22nd. He had expressed a wish to bring some adviser, and I thought it might be one of the senators, Glass, Hull, Swanson or Walsh, who were being discussed as members of his Cabinet and were familiar with these problems. He, however, brought Raymond Moley, who had been one of his aides.[2] Moley was an able man with a mind quick to grasp public problems.

Secretaries Stimson and Mills were present on our side. Of course, neither Roosevelt nor Moley could be familiar with the background of these complicated matters; worse still, they were obviously suspicious that we were trying to draw them into some sort of trap. Moley took charge of the conversation for Roosevelt. I, therefore, directed myself to primary educational work upon him, as he would influence the action of the President-elect.

We had prepared a factual statement as to the debts and our past policies which we presented to them. We also pointed out the importance of the World Economic Conference in ending the world-wide trade war, and of stabilization of currencies. We described the progress made in the Land Disarmament Conference in which we were participating.

I did my best to disabuse both of them of the idea that we might have any other purpose than cooperation for the good of the country. I pointed out the urgency of furthering the general world recovery which had started in July. Secretaries Stimson and Mills supported my suggestions in a lucid, broad-minded and friendly discussion of the problems.

Our concrete proposals were:

[2] Mr. Moley, after intimate association with Mr. Roosevelt, wrote the book *After Seven Years,* in which he exposed most of the fallacies of the New Deal from actual experience with it.

(a) That we should demand the December installments be paid (totaling about $150,000,000 altogether), in order to maintain the integrity of the obligations and to break down the organized collusive action of the European nations.

(b) That to indicate to these nations willingness to negotiate, I should recommend to the Congress, and that Roosevelt should express approval of, the revival of the former World War Debt Commission to negotiate questions remaining at issue after such payment.

(c) As the World War Debt Commission had been bipartisan, composed of three representatives each of the Senate, the House, and the President, we suggested that, if Congress agreed, I would appoint such Presidential members as Mr. Roosevelt approved, and that the Commission make no commitments until after his inauguration or, in any event, without his approval.

(d) As to the forthcoming World Economic Conference, we presented its importance and the steps already taken by our experts. We suggested that a Commission to revise the debts might have favorable influence upon the Economic Conference where agreement was vital on currency stabilization and trade barriers. Only thus could we end the world-wide trade war. We suggested that, without using the debts as a club, we had a right to some cooperation in return for debt favors granted, and that the settlement of the two problems of the Economic Conference and debts ought to proceed concurrently. We suggested that, for the Economic Conference, I should appoint a nonpartisan delegation to Mr. Roosevelt's satisfaction, and that, as there could be no conclusions prior to his inauguration, the Conference could proceed without delay.

Certainly Mills, Stimson, and I understood that they agreed to all our proposals. On these promises, I suggested that Roosevelt join me in a meeting with the Congressional leaders of both parties which I would call for the next day at the White House, where we would jointly urge the reactivation of a War Debt Commission. This would at once display our united front in the foreign field. Mr. Roosevelt stated he would rather not attend such a joint meeting but would communicate his approval to the Democratic leaders.

We suggested that after this White House meeting with the Congressmen we should draft a press statement upon the debt question to be issued in our joint names, stating our agreement as to what should be done. However, Roosevelt and Moley stated that they preferred that I alone should issue such a press statement after agreement with them as to its terms; and that Roosevelt should then issue an approving statement, the terms of which would also be jointly settled. It was agreed that Secretary Mills would meet with Roosevelt and Moley the next day to settle the texts.

When I met the Congressional leaders, I was astonished to find that Mr. Roosevelt had not communicated with the Democratic members. Nevertheless, I reviewed to the group the united demands the debtors had made, and their effect on our own and world economy. I urged that, unless we demonstrated a willingness to negotiate hardship situations, all European debtors would inevitably default the debts; that, once they defaulted, there could be no restoration, for no man could be elected to their parliaments on a platform of restoration. My arguments were of no avail, and the Democratic members informed me that they would oppose any reactivation of the Debt Commission.

Despite this rebuff, as Roosevelt had stated his agreement with us on the major lines of debt policy, we prepared a statement on the whole debt situation along the lines we had discussed with him. It was a full discussion of the question, mainly designed to clarify the Congressional and foreign minds. It recited the requests of the debtors that the debts be reviewed; the origins and obligations under the previous settlements; the fact that these could not be varied except by mutual consent; our policies of dealing with each debtor separately and separating questions of debt to us from enemy reparations; the basis of the moratorium; the fact that the settlements were unalterable except with the approval of Congress; the fact that I had the year before recommended reactivating the Debt Commission to consider situations arising out of the depression, but that the Congress had refused. The statement continued:

It is unthinkable that, within the comity of nations and the maintenance of international good-will, our people should refuse to consider the request of friendly people to discuss an important question in which they and we both have a vital interest, irrespective of what conclusions might arise from such a discussion. This is particularly true in a world greatly afflicted, where coöperation and good-will are essential to the welfare of all.

I believe, therefore, that Congress in view of the requests made by these governments should authorize the creation of an agency to exchange views with those governments, enlarging the field of discussion as above indicated and to report to Congress such recommendations as they deem desirable. Furthermore, such agency should be so constituted through complete or partial identity of membership with the delegations to the World Economic Conference. . . .

. . . Discussion [with our debtors] does not involve abandonment on our part of what we believe to be sound and right. On the other hand, a refusal to afford others the opportunity to present in conference their views and to hear ours upon a question in which we are both concerned, and an insistence upon dealing with our neighbors at arms' length, would be the negation of the very principles upon which rests the hope of rebuilding a new and better world from the shattered remnants of the old.

If our civilization is to be perpetuated, the great causes of world peace, world disarmament and world recovery must prevail. They cannot prevail until a path to their attainment is built upon honest friendship, mutual confidence, and proper coöperation among the nations.

These immense objectives upon which the future and welfare of all mankind depend must be ever in our thought in dealing with immediate and difficult problems. The solution of each one of these, upon the basis of an understanding reached after frank and fair discussion, in and of itself strengthens the foundation of the edifice of world progress we seek to erect; whereas our failure to approach difficulties and differences among nations in such a spirit serves but to undermine constructive effort. . . .

When Secretary Mills called upon Roosevelt next morning for the purpose of harmonizing the text of this press statement on the debt and Roosevelt's approving statement, he was informed by Moley that the President-elect would not be able to see him, but that we should issue our own statement and Roosevelt would comment upon it later. I accordingly issued to the press the above memorandum.

Mr. Roosevelt issued a statement on the 23rd which was not wholly cooperative, saying:

As to the debt payments due December 15th, I find no justification for modifying my statement to the President on November 14th when I pointed out that "the immediate questions raised by the British, French and other notes create a responsibility which rests upon those now vested with executive and legislative authority." . . .

I find myself in complete accord with four principles discussed in the conference between the President and myself yesterday and set forth in a statement which the President has issued today.

These debts were actual loans made under the distinct understanding and with the intention that they would be repaid.

In dealing with the debts each government has been and is to be considered individually, and all dealings with each government are independent of dealings with any other debtor government. In no case should we deal with the debtor governments collectively.

Debt settlements made in each case should take into consideration the capacity to pay of the individual nations.

The indebtedness of the various European nations to our government has no relation whatsoever to reparations payments made or owed to them.

Once these principles of the debt relationships are established and recognized, the methods by which contacts between our government and the debtor nations may be provided are matters of secondary importance. My view is that the most convenient and effective contacts can be made through the existing agencies and constituted channels of diplomatic intercourse.

No action by the Congress has limited or can limit the constitutional power of the President to carry on diplomatic contacts or conversations with foreign governments. The advantage of this method of maintaining contacts with foreign governments is that any one of the debtor nations may at any time bring to the attention of the Government of the United States new conditions and facts affecting any phase of its indebtedness.

It is equally true that existing debt agreements are unalterable save by Congressional action.

This statement was in general accord except for the suggestion that the reponsibility for action rested solely upon our administration and it also, in effect, rejected the reactivation of a Debt Commission. The suggestion that I should use my powers to negotiate through diplomatic channels was futile because no foreign power would seriously negotiate with a disappearing administration. Further, the Congress would take no action without his approval.

Roosevelt informed the reporters that "it was not his baby." The press was at once very critical of his attitude.

Said the Detroit *Free Press*:

It is highly unfortunate that Governor Roosevelt was unable to bring himself to meet the President half way. The refusal of the governor to cooperate actively with Mr. Hoover and his subsequent statement that the matter at issue was "not his baby," are indicative of the lack of largeness and vision more disquieting in a person about to become the Chief Executive of the nation. . . . Mr. Roosevelt had an opportunity unique in the history of the American presidency, and he failed to grasp it.

The *New York Herald Tribune* stated, November 24, 1932:

Americans are so accustomed to having Mr. Hoover do the right and courageous thing that his admirable statement on the debts will hardly occasion surprise. It covers a complex issue, endlessly bedeviled by national prejudices and selfishness, clearly, fairly, and with a minimum of words. . . .

It may be recalled that during the campaign there was heat and resentment in Democratic quarters when it was argued that a change of administration inevitably meant marking time for a number of months. Mr. Hoover has now done his utmost to prevent such a delay in respect to the debt issue. Mr. Roosevelt has felt unable to aid him. The delay must ensue.

The Baltimore *Sun* said (November 24) that the debts

may not be legally his baby until the fourth of March, but it seems to us that Mr. Roosevelt might wisely have given thought to the possibility that this baby, which is not now his, may soon develop into an unruly stepchild, permanently lodged under his roof, and disposed to play with matches.

However, I determined to insist upon payment of the December installments. The various governments were so informed, and also that if the payments were met, I would recommend negotiations to the Congress.

The principal debtors, with the exception of France, met the December 15th payments. The French raised a good deal of dust, but would have paid had it not been for an unfortunate press dispatch from Warm Springs which represented the President-elect as having said that he did not regard the payment of December 15th as a necessary condition for opening negotiations. The French press received this dispatch with elation and proceeded to eulogize Mr. Roosevelt as a great leader and to damn me a-plenty. The payment due from the French was about $50,000,000; they had more than $500,000,000 in New York banks at the time. Yet they declined to pay.

At this time, our domestic economic situation had begun to degenerate, and it would obviously strengthen matters if we could get the debt negotiations and the Economic Conference under way.

Believing that Mr. Roosevelt was misinformed and still hoping for cooperation, I sent him a telegram on December 17, 1932. Pointing out the impossibility of solutions without his cooperation and urging that we proceed with two measures, I emphasized that:

... as the economic situation in foreign countries is one of the dominant depressants of prices and employment in the United States it is urgent that the World Economic Conference should assemble at as early a date as possible. The United States should be represented by a strong and effective delegation. This delegation should be chosen at an early moment in order that it may give necessary consideration and familiarize itself with the problems, and secure that such investigation and study is made as will be necessary for its use at the conference. . . .

It is desirable that such delegation should include members of the Congress in order that such intricate facts and circumstances can be effectively presented to the Congress. . . .

If it were not for the urgency of the situation both at home and abroad and the possible great helpfulness to employment and agricultural prices and general restoration of confidence which could be brought about by successful issue of all these questions and the corresponding great dangers of inaction, it would be normal to allow the whole matter to rest until after the change of administration, but in the emergency such as exists at the moment I would be neglectful of my duty if I did not facilitate in every way the earliest possible dealing with these questions. It is obvious that no conclusions would be reached from such discussions prior to March 4th but a great deal of time could be saved if the machinery could be created at once by the appointment of the delegates as I have mentioned.

... I should be glad to know if you could join with me in the selection of such a delegation at the present time or if you feel that the whole matter should be deferred until after March 4th. I believe that there would be no difficulty in agreeing upon an adequate representation for the purpose. In such selection the first concern would be the selection of a chairman for the delegation.

The discussions and communications between myself and the President-elect had not been made public and I felt that without referring to them, I had a duty to report upon the status of the debt question and the Economic Conference to the Congress. Indeed, I had been besieged by Congressional members for such a statement. I complied in a special message on the 19th, urging again that we indicate the intention of the United States to deal with these questions and concluding:

... The situation is one of such urgency that we require national solidarity and national coöperation if we are to serve the welfare of the American people and indeed if we are to conquer the forces which today threaten the very foundations of civilization.

Mr. Roosevelt on the 19th replied to my telegram of the 17th, stating among other objections:

By reason of the fact that under the constitution I am unable to assume the authority in the matter of the agenda of the economic conference until after March fourth next, and by reason of the fact that there appears to be a divergence of opinion between us in respect to the scope of the conference, and further by reason of the fact that time is required to conduct conversations relating to debts and disarmaments, I must respectfully suggest that the appointment of the permanent delegates and the final determination of the program of the economic conference be held in abeyance until after March fourth. . . .

I feel that it would be both improper for me and inadvisable for you, however much I appreciate the courtesy of your suggestion, for me to take part in naming representatives. . . .

I think you will recognize that it would be unwise for me to accept an apparent joint responsibility with you when, as a matter of constitutional fact, I would be wholly lacking in any attendant authority.

Ordinarily I would have accepted this as ending any hope of coöperation, but our overall economic situation was continuing to degenerate. Also it seemed to me vital that we display a strong unity on the foreign front. As shown in these dispatches, I was not attempting to dictate policies but merely to set up machinery by which confidence could be sustained. Therefore, I addressed the President-elect again on December 20th, the essential paragraphs being:

> . . . In the face of . . . degenerating agricultural prices, [and] increasing unemployment . . . I am unwilling to admit that coöperation cannot be established between the outgoing and incoming administrations which will give earlier solution and recovery from these difficulties.
>
> *If you will review my previous communications and conversations I think you will agree that while outlining the nature of the problems my proposals to you have been directed to the setting up not of solutions but of the machinery through which . . . the ultimate solution of these questions can be expedited and coordinated to the end that many months of delay and increasing losses to our people may be avoided. . . .*
>
> With view to again making an effort to secure coöperation and that solidarity of national action which the situation needs, I would be glad if you could designate Mr. Owen D. Young, Colonel House, or any other men of your party possessed of your views and your confidence and at the same time familiar with these problems, to sit with the principal officers of this administration in endeavor to see what steps can be taken to avoid delays of precious time and inevitable losses that will ensue from such delays.

He replied on the 21st, again declining to cooperate on these lines, and said:

> . . . May I respectfully suggest that you proceed with the selection of your representatives to conduct the preliminary exploration necessary with individual debtor nations and representatives to discuss the agenda of the World Economic Conference, making it clear that none of these representatives is authorized to bind this government as to any ultimate policy. . . .

We already had technical commissions in action on the Economic Conference, and it was manifestly foolish to select further delegates for preliminary discussion unless the President-elect would participate. As the press was constantly carrying distorted and, at times, malicious stories from Albany as to these negotiations (which had been entirely confidential on my part) I issued the whole correspondence to the press on December 22, 1932, with the simple statement: "Governor Roosevelt considers that it is undesirable for him to assent to my suggestions for coöperative action on the foreign proposals outlined in my recent message to Congress. I will respect his wishes."

However, I continued to feel deeply that action through the World Economic Conference was essential, and that the foreign countries should know we wished to be cooperative. Therefore, on February 13th I presented some ideas for meeting the world situation in a public Lincoln Day address at New York. It was also intended as a revelation of the dangers which confronted us from what I now feared was Mr. Roosevelt's determination to abandon the convertible gold standard for "managed currency," despite the pledges he had given in the campaign.

This address in retrospect proved so accurate a summation of the world currency situation, the effect on us of abandonment of the gold standard, and our obligations in the matter, that I quote from it extensively: [3]

... The people determined this election. ... We accept and, as Americans, will continue wholeheartedly to do our part in promoting the well-being of our country. . . .

My purpose is . . . to discuss matters considering which there should be no partisanship.

Further steps toward economic recovery is the urgent problem before the entire world. . . .

. . . While we have many concerns in the domestic field we must realize that so long as we engage in the export and import of goods and in financial activities abroad our price levels and credit system, our employment, and above all our fears will be greatly affected by foreign influence. During the past two years the crash of one foreign nation after another under direct and indirect war inheritances has dominated our whole economic life. The time has now come when nations must accept, in self-interest no less than in altruism, the obligations to coöperate in achieving world stability so mankind may again resume the march of progress. Daily it becomes more certain that the next great constructive step in remedy of the illimitable human suffering from this depression lies in the international field. It is in that field where the tide of prices can be most surely and quickly turned and the tragic despair of unemployment, agriculture and business transformed to hope and confidence.

[3] The full text is given in *The State Papers and Other Writings of Herbert Hoover*, Vol. II, pp. 586–594.

Economic degeneration is always a series of vicious cycles of cause and effect. Whatever the causes may be, we must grasp these cycles at some segment and deal with them. . . .

I then described the steps of demoralization in international finance and its ultimate result in trade wars by manipulation of currencies:

. . . But a new phase is now developing among these nations that is the rapid degeneration into economic war which threatens to engulf the world. The imperative call to the world today is to prevent this war.

Ever since the storm began in Europe the United States has held stanchly to the gold standard. In the present setting of depreciated currencies and in the light of differences in costs of production our tariffs are below those of most countries; we have held free from quotas, preferences, discriminations among nations. We have thereby maintained one Gibraltar of stability in the world and contributed to check the movement of chaos.

We are ourselves now confronted with an unnatural movement of goods from the lowered costs and standards of countries of depreciated currencies, which daily increase our unemployment and our difficulties. We are confronted with discriminatory actions and barriers stifling our agricultural and other markets. We will be ourselves forced to defensive action to protect ourselves unless this mad race is stopped. We must not be the major victim of it all.

I then described the havoc of unstable currencies, and continued:

. . . Thus a mass of the gold dashing hither and yon from one nation to another, seeking maximum safety, has acted like a cannon loose on the deck of the world in a storm. . . .

Broadly, the solution lies in the reëstablishment of confidence. That confidence cannot be reëstablished by the abandonment of gold as a standard in the world. So far as the human race has yet developed and established its methods and systems of stable exchange, that solution can only be found now and found quickly through the reëstablishment of gold standards among important nations. The huge gold reserves of the world can be made to function in relation to currencies, standards of value, and exchange. And I say with emphasis that I am not proposing this as a favor to the United States. It is the need of the whole world. The United States is so situated that it can protect itself better than almost any country on earth.

Nor is it necessary from an international point of view that those nations who have been forced off the gold standard shall be again restored to former gold values. It will suffice if it only is fixed. From this source are the principal hopes for restoring world confidence and reversing the growing barriers to the movement of goods, and making possible the security in trade which will again revive a demand for such goods. To do this it is necessary to have strong and courageous action on the part of the leading commercial nations. If some sort of international financial action is necessary to enable central banks to coöperate for the purpose of stabilizing currencies, nations should have no hesitation in joining in such an operation under proper safeguards. If some part of the debt payments to us could be set aside for temporary use for this purpose, we should not hesitate to do so. At the same time the world should endeavor to find a place for silver, at least in enlarged subsidiary coinage.

If the major nations will enter the road leading to the early reëstablishment of the gold standard, then and then only can the abnormal barriers to trade, the quotas, preferences, discriminatory agreements, and tariffs which exceed the differences in costs of production between nations be removed, uniform trade privileges among all nations be reëstablished and the threat of economic war averted. A reasonable period of comparative stability in the world's currencies would repay the cost of such effort a hundred times over in the increase of consumption, the increase of employment, the lessening of the difficulties of debtors throughout the land, with the avoidance of millions of tragedies. The world would quickly see a renewed movement of goods and would have an immediate rise in prices everywhere, thereby bringing immediate relief to the whole economic system. . . .

The American people will soon be at the fork of three roads. The first is the highway of coöperation among nations, thereby to remove the obstructions to world consumption and rising prices. This road leads to real stability, to expanding standards of living, to a resumption of the march of progress by all peoples. It is today the immediate road to relief of agriculture and unemployment, not alone for us but the entire world.

The second road is to rely upon our high degree of national self-containment, to increase our tariffs, to create quotas and discriminations, and to engage in definite methods of curtailment of production of agricultural and other products and thus to secure a larger measure of economic isolation from world influences. It would be a long road of readjustments into unknown and uncertain fields. But it may be necessary if the first way out is closed to us. Some measures may be necessary pending cooperative conclusions with other nations.

The third road is that we inflate our currency, consequently abandon the gold standard, and with our depreciated currency attempt to enter a world economic war, with the certainty that it leads to complete destruction both at home and abroad.

The first road can only be undertaken by the coöperation among all important nations. Last April, in conjunction with the leaders of Europe, our government developed the idea of a World Economic Conference to deal with these questions. It is unfortunate that the delay of events in Europe and the election in the United States necessarily postponed the convening of that conference. It has been further delayed by the change of our administrations.

I then suggested that the war debts must be resettled on a basis of a reviewed capacity to pay, as a part of such stabilization:

. . . The full meed of prosperity among nations cannot be builded upon mutual impoverishment. It is to the interest of the world to join in bold and courageous action which will bring about economic peace. . . .

On our side this problem is not to be solved by partisan action but by national unity. Whatever our differences of view may be on domestic policies, the welfare of the American people rests upon solidarity before the world, not merely in resisting proposals which would weaken the United States and the world but solidarity in cooperation with other nations in strengthening the whole economic fabric of the world. These problems are not insoluble. There is a latent, earnest, and underlying purpose on the part of all nations to find their solution. Of our own determination there should be no question.

. . . The next forward step is as great as any in history. It is that we perpetuate the welfare of mankind through the immense objectives of world recovery and world peace.

Roosevelt's refusal to cooperate, in view of which negotiations and Congressional approval were impossible, prevented the re-erection of the War Debt Commission and postponed the World Economic Conference indefinitely. Apprehensions and fears over the country were greatly increased. In the end the Economic Conference failed. The debts were repudiated. But worse was to come immediately.

ATTEMPTS TO COOPERATE IN LEGISLATION

The President-elect and all the Democratic leaders had expended much oratory during the campaign in denouncing our expenditures and demanding a balanced budget. I consequently called a White House conference early in December, of Senator Robinson and Speaker Garner, with Secretary Mills. I proposed to them that it would be helpful if, in the short session of Congress, we carry out the disagreeable tasks of cutting expenditures and still further increasing taxes, as I had recommended in the last session. The revenues from the last tax bill were proving insufficient to balance the budget. Thus, Roosevelt could take charge with an unpopular job out of the way. They considered this action to be much in the nation's and Roosevelt's interest. It was agreed that my message of December 6th would urge the further reduction of expenditures and recommend the adoption of a manufacturers' sales tax. Such a levy, with a provision exempting all food and cheaper clothing, had been defeated by the Democratic leaders in the previous session despite the recommendations of their own controlled Ways and Means Committee. Now they undertook to support these measures. This support on Speaker Garner's part was an interesting comment on his earlier destruction of that tax bill. It at least implied that, being now free of the politics of an election, he became again the statesman he really was at heart. I urged this program in my state of the Union and budget messages. In addition to increased taxes, I advocated a $580,000,000 cut in "ordinary expenses."

The Democratic leaders temporarily secured approval from Roosevelt.[4] But we were quickly to come to grief. Three weeks later (Decem-

---

[4] Bascom N. Timmons writes in his authorized biography *Garner of Texas*:

"President Hoover, Speaker Garner, Secretary of the Treasury Ogden L. Mills and Senate Democratic Leader Joseph T. Robinson met at the White House and agreed upon a plan which they believed would alleviate conditions and, especially, would check bank failures.

"Key to the plan was new taxes to make up an indicated deficiency between income and outgo, and passage of the Glass bill. The Glass bill did not guarantee bank deposits but provided a liquidating corporation to speed up payment to depositors in closed banks. It also contained other far-reaching bank reforms.

"Garner, Robinson and other Democratic leaders conferred with Governor Roosevelt at Roosevelt's New York City home, 49 East Sixty-fifth Street, and discussed the plan. On leaving the Roosevelt home Garner and Robinson told newspapermen of the agree-

ber 28th), the President-elect announced from Albany that he was "amazed" and "horrified" that the Democratic leaders should support my proposals on the budget and taxes. Speaker Garner sent word to me that he, in turn, was "amazed" at Roosevelt's action. Roosevelt called another conference of these leaders on January 5th (1933), after which Garner reported to us that he could not keep his undertaking, and that the budget could not be balanced at this session. However, I returned to the subject in a special message to the Congress on January 17, 1933, in which I reviewed at length the whole program of increased revenues and reduced expenditures. Nothing happened.[5]

Two results came out of this episode. First, it served notice on the Democratic leaders in Congress and on us in the Administration that although he had not yet been inaugurated, the President-elect intended to dictate the conduct of Congress, despite his inconsistent refusal to make recommendations upon the War Debts and Economic Conference questions. Second, and more important, his failure to act on the budget under circumstances so favorable to the united action of both parties, and directly contrary to all the promises made in his campaign, greatly increased the epidemic of fears in the country.

VARIOUS REFORM MEASURES

The Democratic leaders, Robinson and Garner, also agreed with me at the early December conference that it would greatly aid the immediate situation and the new administration to get the banking

---

ment on the budget proposals, which paralleled their agreement with Hoover. Governor Roosevelt indicated to newspapermen he did not disapprove the plan.

"Garner called the proposed taxes 'sound but painful.' . . .

"Roosevelt a few days later told Garner he could not go along on the tax proposal. Garner went to Hoover and said:

" 'For the first time in my life I find myself unable to carry out an agreement. Governor Roosevelt is opposed to what we have planned, and it is a waste of time to try any legislation to which he will not agree.'

"Scores of banks closed their doors between election and inauguration. A nation gripped in gloom greeted inauguration day."

[5] After all this tumult, mine was the last attempt to balance the budget for twenty years. A new philosophy has superseded, that a deficit is a good thing, even in peace. It certainly makes life more easy and governing more popular for Presidents. But twenty years later the national debt had increased by more than $230,000,000,000, and the taxpayer had to suffer the consequences.

and bankruptcy reforms enacted by the Congress. I promised to include these measures in my message to the Congress, and did so. I repeated my urgings for these reforms in special messages of January 11th and February 20th. We secured part of the bankruptcy reforms.

In addition, just to keep the flag flying, I recommended to the short session on December 7th, and again on February 20th, the ratification of the St. Lawrence Waterway Treaty; our plan for retirement of marginal agricultural lands; the creation of a general mortgage discount system; extension of the powers of the RFC and Home Loan Banks; reform of the procedures in criminal cases; western range protection, and aid to child health.

REORGANIZATION OF EXECUTIVE DEPARTMENTS

On January 19, 1933, the Democratic majority of the House rejected my plan for the reorganization of government bureaus which I had sent under the limited authorities given in the last session. Not content with ignoring my proposals to increase the revenues, they also undertook to defeat my recommendations for decreased appropriations. The next day I made a public statement at a press conference, saying:

. . . I regret, of course, that the consolidation of 58 bureaus and commissions into a few divisions which I had directed by Executive Orders, has been nullified by the action of the House of Representatives. There was apparently no examination of the merits of the different Executive Orders by the House or the House committees. . . .

A White House statement on January 30, 1933, commenting on this situation, said:[6]

The Appropriation Bills for the next fiscal year for the State, Justice, Commerce, and Labor Departments—together with the independent offices bill—have now been reported out from the House Appropriations Committee. The President recommended total appropriations for these services of $1,058,741,556, including permanent appropriations amounting to $81,104,553, or $997,637,003, excluding permanent appropriations. The House Committee recommended $1,106,172,818 excluding permanent appropriations, or $128,-535,815 increase over the President's recommendations. To this should be

[6] *The State Papers and other Public Writings of Herbert Hoover*, p. 584.

added $1,268,480 for deferments which will be required in the fiscal year making a total increase for these services of $129,804,295.

Fighting to the end to keep down appropriations, on March 4, 1933, my last official act was to issue a statement upon a pocket veto of the independent offices appropriation bill, because it increased and did not reduce expenditures.

RELIEF

I have already related our measures to carry on the relief program until the change in administration. Despite the greatly increased load during the winter of 1932–1933, a survey of the work of the various relief agencies showed that, except for persons occasionally overlooked, there was neither hunger nor cold among the unemployed.

I had determined to ask Congress for larger sums to be given as grants-in-aid distributed through our committee system, since, obviously, the burden of the depression was weighing harder and harder upon the committees. Roosevelt, however, proposed to handle the problem by abolishing the committees and substituting direct Federal doles. It would have been impossible for my administration to force any bill that he did not approve through a hostile Congress.[7]

SELLING APPLES

One incident of these times has persisted as the eternal damnation of Hoover. Some Oregon or Washington apple growers' association shrewdly appraised the sympathy of the public for the unemployed. They set up a system of selling apples on the street corners in many cities, thus selling their crop and raising their prices. Many persons left their jobs for the more profitable one of selling apples. When any left-winger wishes to indulge in scathing oratory, he demands, "Do you want to return to selling apples?"

[7] For good or ill, the new administration wiped out all our system of nonpartisan committees and unpaid volunteer workers and substituted a Federal bureaucracy of its own political faith with a 200 per cent increase in cost, and great corruption.

CHAPTER 18

OMINOUS ECONOMIC SIGNS

The Presidential campaign had exposed many of Mr. Roosevelt's proposed economic policies and I discuss our debates in detail in the next section of this volume. But there were revealed several policies in particular which must be briefly mentioned here, as they profoundly affected the economic situation during the interregnum. With the election, business at once slowed down, for many reasons.

Roosevelt's attitude in the campaign was one of increasing antagonism toward business. He had said flatly that industry was overbuilt and expansion at an end. He had indicated that an era of government competition with business and government dictation to business was at hand. The conglomeration of men of declared radical and collectivist intentions who were his intimates and associates, and who were certain to occupy important positions in his administration, was in itself disturbing to the economic world. Thinking businessmen realized that the country had taken a sharp turn to the left.

Although Roosevelt had promised a reduction in national expenditures and a balanced budget, he had also promised expenditures for pressure groups which would prevent the balancing of any budget unless taxes were enormously increased. The bills introduced by Democratic leaders in the previous Congress were also ample confirmation that an era of great expenditures was at hand.

There were promised reductions in the tariff which naturally caused merchants and manufacturers to cancel orders and reduce stocks awaiting lower-priced imports and their effect on domestic prices.

Another disturbing factor was the fear of currency manipulation. There had long been a large element for "soft money," "fiat money" and "managed currency" in the Democratic party. Many such money bills had been fathered by important Democratic members of the previous Congress. The Democratic platform had straddled the issue of the gold standard by calling for "sound" money.

From this background and information in our hands, we had repeatedly charged during the campaign that if Roosevelt were elected there would be tampering with the gold standard or managed currency or fiat money issues. At Roosevelt's request, Senator Glass furiously denied it, and Roosevelt, himself, flatly denied it in a speech on November 4, 1932, citing the "covenant" on all issues, which stated that they were payable *in gold* of present weight and fineness. Nevertheless, tinkering with the currency was quickly to emerge.

The sum of all these matters was to turn the clock of recovery abruptly backward with the election. And failure to cooperate was to push it still further back.

What happened to the country by December 30th, less than four months after the Maine elections, is shown by the decreases in Federal Reserve and other economic indexes:

Farm prices............	14 per cent
Factory pay rolls........	7 per cent
Iron and steel production.	10 per cent
Textile production	10 per cent
Department store sales...	12 per cent
Corporate bonds	10 per cent
All common stocks......	18 per cent
Industrial common stocks	20 per cent

At approximately the date of election, the American Federation of Labor reported about 11,500,000 unemployed. By early January the number exceeded 13,000,000. One reason why unemployment rose so rapidly after the election was Mr. Roosevelt's promise of legislation by which the government would give all of the unemployed a job. This, together with other discouragements to employers, led them to abandon much of their support of idle employees and to reduce operations. At one time I had a list of some 500,000 employees who thus had been separated from support.

European countries were steadily making recovery, and no cause for the increased unemployment could be attributed to them. Whatever the cause, it was purely domestic.

DISASTERS FROM PUBLICATION OF RFC LOANS

A faggot on the fire at this time was the publication of RFC loans. A nervous public assumed that a bank, insurance company, or building and loan association was weak if it borrowed from the RFC. As I have stated, Speaker Garner's amendment to the law, passed over my protest in the previous July, required that these lists be communicated in strict confidence to the Clerks of the House and Senate. Their confidential character had been formally announced to the Senate by Senator Robinson, the Democratic leader.

The reports actually were held confidential until January 4, 1933. At this time, Garner put a resolution through the House making the loans public. The Democratic directors of the RFC; William Green of the American Federation of Labor; Democratic Governor Moore of New Jersey; and a host of others joined me in protesting vigorously. But all was in vain. Late in January the RFC Board sent me the first casualty list of sixty-two banks, totaling $70,000,000 of deposits, which had been compelled to close in consequence of runs started by the publication of their borrowing from the RFC.

On February 18, 1933, Senator Robinson, in an effort to make good his public assurance of the previous July, introduced a bill into the Senate to stop such publication; but in a few days he informed me that Roosevelt thought "everything should be public," and that effort died. Roosevelt was again running the government before being sworn in. By the end of February the RFC officials reported to me that banks with $200,000,000 deposits had runs for the same reason, and were compelled to close. (Soon after coming into office, however, Roosevelt stopped the publication of these loans.)

As the bank reopenings had exceeded failures during the four months of recovery from July to the election, we had reason to believe that the tide of bank failures was ended. But with the election in November the situation went into reverse. The rising fear is indicated by the failures measured in deposits:

1932–1933	Excess of closings over openings
November	$ 30,800,000
December	63,600,000
January	120,000,000
February	140,000,000

TINKERING WITH THE CURRENCY

The next blow to recovery came from a great fear that currency tinkering would be undertaken by the new Administration. A flood of rumors that the gold standard would be abandoned for some sort of "commodity dollar," "managed currency," or devaluation, by January became an actuality; the currency tinkerers emerged into the open like a flight of swallows before the spring.

On January 2nd, a group of thirty prominent economists having become greatly alarmed at these manifestations issued a public statement that "the gold standard of present weight and fineness should be unflinchingly maintained . . . agitation and experiments would impair confidence and retard recovery." That they should thus appear to doubt the President-elect's word, added to the fear.

On January 4th, Senators Connally, Wheeler, and Elmer Thomas made statements in the Senate in support of devaluation.

Roosevelt by this time had fallen into the hands of George F. Warren, a professor of agronomy at Cornell University. Warren had published a book reciting the effect on prices and world prosperity through the great flow of gold and silver during the period of Spanish Conquest and the gold and silver discoveries in the United States and Australia during the years 1849–1860. He contended that by devaluation a similar situation could be created. His academic guarantee was that devaluation would raise prices and wages. About this time a "business committee," with an imposing list of members under the leadership of Professor Warren, was formed to promote devaluation with assurances that it would raise the depressed prices. This committee included many of Roosevelt's supporters. Soon they began widespread propaganda under the title "Committee for the Nation."

There were not only rumors and statements by Roosevelt's friends of such manipulations; but to insiders there was positive knowledge. In the middle of January, Adolph Miller, a member of the Federal Reserve Board, informed me that the President-elect had suggested devaluation of the gold dollar in the presence of a number of bankers as a means of lifting prices.

By January 23rd the financial editor of the *New York Times* found it necessary to print a strong statement urging Roosevelt to reaffirm that there would be no tinkering with the gold standard and recalling President-elect Cleveland's statement in similar circumstances.[1]

On January 30th, Senator Elmer Thomas, one of Mr. Roosevelt's intimates, called attention in the Senate to a press statement that the President-elect had assured his advisers that he would sign a measure for "controlled currency inflation." The Senator added: "I am in favor of cheapening the buying power of the American dollar if this can be done; to the extent that the dollar is cheapened, to the same extent will commodity prices be increased."

On January 31st, Secretary Mills and I prepared a statement in refutation of the whole theory of devaluation, and Mr. Mills delivered it in a public address.

The same day Henry Wallace, who had been announced as a member of the new cabinet, declared: "The smart thing would be to go off the gold standard a little further than England has."

Also the same day, George L. Harrison, Governor of the Federal Reserve Bank of New York, issued a memorandum pointing out both the futility and the danger of devaluation and of any tinkering with the currency. The press commented widely on these devaluation statements. Roosevelt, when urged by the press, refused to make any comment. And the fire spread.

These burning flames of currency tinkering, the failure to balance the budget, defeat of banking reform, the collapse of our attempt at con-

[1] The *Times* said: "It is probable enough that the present spirit of hesitancy, not only in financial markets but in general trade, is more or less influenced by lack of such reassurance. . . . In numerous older similar occasions doubt and mistrust prevailed with exceedingly bad effect on financial sentiment, until the President-elect took matters into his own hands and publicly avowed his purposes. This was notably true in the pre-inauguration period of 1885 and 1893, at both of which junctures the maintenance of gold payments was being discussed uneasily and at both of which Mr. Cleveland stated so positively and so courageously his own views of the general problem as to remove at once all apprehension."

structive handling of the war debts, the postponement of the World Economic Conference, and the publication of RFC loans, all fired public fears to dangerous heat.

THE FLIGHT FROM THE DOLLAR

During the latter part of January, the consequences of these actions and rumors began to show up in a "flight from the dollar" by our citizens to points outside the United States. The volume was not wholly visible at the start. There was some small import of gold in January, but a large invisible flight was already in motion. "Smart" people were buying foreign exchange. They had only to buy pounds or francs, borrow money on them, and hold them until the dollar was devalued in order to reap the full amount of the devaluation. There was little risk, and the transactions required only small margins. Brokers reported to me that one gentleman had bought upwards of $10,000,000 worth of foreign currencies. The profits to the successful speculator were enormous—$1,000,000 invested in pounds sterling was worth $1,400,000 less than a year later.

Foreign banks and governments began turning their deposits in the United States into gold at the Federal Reserve Banks earmarked for future shipment which also obscured the real gold movement. This camouflaged flight increased in volume and speed.

The actual export of gold soon began and reached $160,000,000 in February and $122,000,000 in the first four days of March.

DOMESTIC HOARDING OF CURRENCY AND GOLD

Hoarding began in late January and grew by leaps. Many simply drew gold coin from the banks. "Knowing" persons bought gold bullion. One gentleman purchased several hundred thousand dollars' worth from the Alaska-Juneau mine. The buyers of foreign currencies were wiser than those of bullion or hoarders of gold coin, for the former reaped their harvest after devaluation, while the latter in the end had to surrender their gold to the Treasury. Still less knowing persons, on the basis of Roosevelt's Covenant speech, hoarded currency in the belief that the "covenant" assured its convertibility into gold.

During the entire year of 1932, the volume of currency in circulation had fluctuated about a base of $5,600,000,000. However, in the single month of February, 1933, there was an increase of $900,000,000—representing the withdrawals in cash by bank depositors. During the first four days of March, the circulation increased by more than $800,000,000.

The withdrawal of gold coin from the banks and the Treasury amounted to over $80,000,000 in the last ten days of February and over $200,000,000 in the first four days of March.

THE PANIC GROWS ACUTE AND I ATTEMPT AGAIN TO SECURE ROOSEVELT'S COOPERATION

Despite the evidence, I was reluctant to believe that Mr. Roosevelt would directly violate his own explicit word given three days before his election. Alternatively, if he did not intend to tinker with the currency, it seemed to me he would not want a panic of bank depositors to meet his inauguration. Moreover, he was advised by Senator Glass, his prospective Secretary of the Treasury, against such action.

I started trying to communicate with the President-elect over these dangers on the 6th of February. He had left on an ocean yachting trip with Vincent Astor on the 4th, and his aides repeatedly informed me that he would take up such matters only when he returned. In the meantime the fire of panic was spreading.

On February 13th, the *New York Times* again advocated assurances from the President-elect on maintaining the gold standard.

On the same day Bernard Baruch, who had supported Roosevelt, told a Senate committee that he regarded the country's condition as "the most serious in its history" and inflation as "the road to ruin." "The mere talk of inflation retards business. If you start talking about [devaluation] you would not have a nickel's worth of gold in the Reserve System day after tomorrow."

Melvin A. Traylor, an important Chicago banker who also had supported Mr. Roosevelt, told the Senate Committee, "Nothing but a declaration from Mr. Roosevelt that there will be no devaluation will save the situation from a general panic."

By this time, with all the fanning of fear, the country was off in a full cry of a general panic of bank depositors and a flight of capital to foreign countries. Large banking centers like Detroit and Cleveland were showing great stress.

Yet there was very little that an outgoing administration could do while handcuffed by a hostile Congress and an uncooperative President-elect. It was obvious that no encouraging statements or assurances from us, going out of office within a few days, carried any weight. Also, it was obvious that I could secure no remedies from the Congress without Roosevelt's explicit direction to the Democratic members.

As I have said, I had been trying daily for ten days to contact Roosevelt, without success. He returned on the 17th. That day, I at once sent him a longhand letter by a trusted messenger who delivered it into his hands in a few hours. It was unduly long, but I feared from the lack of understanding of such questions which he had displayed in our earlier interviews, and his two weeks' absence from the scene, that he did not fully grasp the situation:

My dear Mr. President-elect:

A most critical situation has arisen in the country of which I feel it is my duty to advise you confidentially. I am therefore taking this course of writing you myself and sending it to you through the Secret Service for your hand direct as obviously its misplacement would only feed the fire and increase the dangers.

The major difficulty is the state of the public mind, for there is a steadily degenerating confidence in the future which has reached the height of general alarm. I am convinced that a very early statement by you upon two or three policies of your Administration would serve greatly to restore confidence and cause a resumption of the march of recovery.

I then reviewed at length the situation which had developed.

I therefore return to my suggestion at the beginning as to the desirability of clarifying the public mind on certain essentials which will give renewed confidence. It is obvious that as you will shortly be in a position to make whatever policies you wish effective, you are the only one who can give these assurances. Both the nature of the cause of public alarm and experience give such an action the prospect of success in turning the tide. I do not refer to action on all the causes of alarm, but *it would steady the country greatly if there could be prompt assurance that there will be no tampering or inflation of the currency; that the budget will be unquestionably balanced, even if further taxation is necessary; that the Government credit will be maintained by refusal to exhaust it in the issue of securities. . . . It would be of further help if the leaders could be advised to cease publication of RFC business.*

I am taking the liberty of addressing you because both in my anxiety over the situation and my confidence from four years of experience that such tides as are now running can be moderated and the processes of regeneration which are also always running can be released. . . .

HERBERT HOOVER [2]

On February 18th, the press announced that Senator Glass had seen Mr. Roosevelt on his return, and had refused to accept the Secretaryship of the Treasury because the President-elect would not give him satisfactory assurances on maintaining the gold standard. Glass confirmed this to me.[3]

The next day the Baltimore *Sun* noted, "It is firmly believed in quarters close to both men that if satisfactory assurances had been given the Senator that the new administration under no circumstances would accept inflation as a policy his answer would have been different."

The *New York Times* said the Senator's refusal arose "from his uncertainty as to the degree the incoming administration will support his view on currency . . . and banking. It is not believed . . . Senator Glass received the assurances he required."

Similar dispatches appeared in the press all over the country and further inflamed the panic.

With little hope, I yet awaited anxiously every day a reply to my letter to Mr. Roosevelt or a reassuring statement.

In the meantime, the selection of William H. Woodin as Secretary of the Treasury had been announced. Secretary Mills at once urged him to secure a reassuring statement from Roosevelt on the currency. Woodin answered that no statement would be forthcoming.

On February 21st, Senator Simeon D. Fess made an appeal in the Senate:

There could be no statement issued that would have such an ameliorating effect and such a salubrious result as a statement from the incoming President that there will be no tampering with sound money in his administration.

[2] The full text may be found in Myers and Newton, *The Hoover Administration* (Charles Scribner's Sons), pp. 338–340.

[3] Moley's account of the matter appears on pp. 118–122 of his book, *After Seven Years.*

I had consulted our legal advisors as to the use of a certain unrepealed war power over bank withdrawals and foreign exchange. Most of them were in doubt on the ground that the lack of repeal was probably an oversight by the Congress, and under another law, all the war powers were apparently terminated by the peace. Secretary Mills and Senator Glass held that no certain power existed. There was danger that action under such doubtful authority would create a mass of legal conflicts in the country and would incur the refusal of the banks to comply.

I then developed the idea of my issuing an executive order under this power, provided Roosevelt would approve. My legal advisors agreed that, if he approved, it could be done because he could secure ratification in a few days from his overwhelming majority in the incoming Congress. Secretary Mills prepared a draft-order stopping payments from the banks to depositors except for necessities, and controlling foreign exchange so as to stop the flight of capital or speculation in exchange. This would have stopped the strain on the banks, kept them open for legitimate business and, in time, ended the panic when the public cooled off.

Mr. Mills pressed this idea upon Mr. Woodin, who reported to us that Roosevelt declined all our suggestions.

In the meantime, the press daily appealed to the President-elect for comment on the statements of Baruch, Traylor, Glass, and Fess. His refusal could have but one interpretation by knowing people.

The *New York Times* reported from London:

The judgment of financial circles here is that at no time in the recent economic history of America has there been greater need than at present for a flat declaration of monetary policy by the new American government. It is believed that if the inflation bogy is definitely laid by the new administration, the first long step toward restoring confidence will have been taken.

And from Paris:

The confusion of mind on Europe's markets concerning the future tendency of the dollar must be ascribed to lack of information regarding the definite intentions of the new American government. A declaration by Mr. Roosevelt declaring firm resolution to maintain a sound currency would

have an extremely reassuring effect. So would a plain statement on the
economic policy which he proposes to pursue.

Another brand on the fire of panic came from a well-meaning action
of the Federal Reserve Advisory Council. This committee of leading bankers, filled with anxiety, sent one of its number to Mr. Roosevelt on February 21st, asking him to make a public reaffirmation
of his election eve promise as to the gold standard. This member
reported his conclusion that devaluation was coming. I have no doubt
that at once most of these bankers ran to their telephones to call
their friends in every important city in the country and spread the
alarm. I knew two of them who did so.

On February 23rd, Roosevelt replied to my letter of the 17th saying
that mailing of his acknowledgment of my letter had been overlooked.
He offered no substantial aid. Six days had elapsed.

A statement from Roosevelt even at this date could probably have
stopped the panic. In any event, I could have stopped it if I had had
his support.

EFFORTS TO STEM THE BANK PANIC WITHOUT ROOSEVELT'S HELP

Despite Roosevelt's refusal to cooperate, we did not neglect any
possible means of stemming the tide.

Depositors' runs had closed perfectly solvent banks in Detroit, and
other closings followed in Cleveland. We made heroic efforts to save
these banks with alternate daily prospects of success and failure. With
RFC loans we could have prevented the debacle in Detroit, the chief
center of disturbance, if Senator Couzens had cooperated. But he was
threatening the RFC with dire vengeance if its Directors gave any
assistance.

Couzens claimed that loans could not, within the RFC law, be made
to the Union Guardian Trust Company, which was the key to the
situation, as the RFC directors admitted that the assets at their depressed
values did not warrant a sufficiently large loan to save the situation. I
urged that the low valuations were not true values and that the institution had certain assured earnings for the future which would, in time,
take up its deficit, but Couzens' threats caused the Board to delay action.

The Detroit issue was so great in its ramifications throughout Michigan and Ohio that I wanted to take the risk even if we lost a few millions.

Together with Secretary Mills and Under-Secretary Ballantine, I made great efforts to secure local support to that key bank which would make it eligible for RFC loans even on any definition of legal security. Henry Ford had $7,000,000 on deposit in this bank. I persuaded him to subordinate to the RFC loan any claim he might have on its assets. I secured an agreement from officials of the General Motors and Chrysler companies to deposit $1,000,000 each in the bank, subordinate to the loan. I then asked Couzens to the White House and proposed that he put up another $1,000,000, which would complete the job. He professed to be astonished and indignant. We parted with a remark from me: "If 800,000 small bank depositors in my home town could be saved by lending 3 per cent of my fortune, even if I lost, I would certainly do it." As Senator Vandenberg was a witness to this scene, it rankled in Couzens' mind until he died. The Detroit banks closed.[4]

On February 20th I received a call from Senator David Reed of Penn-

[4] After these events, Malcolm W. Bingay, editor of the Detroit *Free Press,* published various interviews with Senator Couzens upon his reasons for his attitude. These reasons were pure spite and vindictiveness toward certain men in Detroit.

On pp. 126–129 of *Detroit Is My Own Home Town* (Bobbs Merrill Co., Indianapolis, 1946), Bingay gives the following explanation of Couzens:

"On Sunday, February 12, 1933, there came rumors that the Union Guardian Trust Company was in difficulties and because of them the entire Guardian Detroit Union group would have to close their doors on Tuesday, following Lincoln's birthday, celebrated on Monday, to prevent panic.

"Here again stood forth stark raw drama with two old associates, now enemies, on opposite sides: Ford and Couzens.

"Edsel Ford, the son, was a director of the Guardian Detroit Union group. He and his father had poured millions into the institution time and again to save it—and had written them off as losses.

"Now the trust company needed something like $43,000,000 to save it from going under. Appeals had been made to the R.F.C. The members of the Reconstruction Finance Corporation stood ready, at Hoover's urging, to advance the money.

" 'Why should the R.F.C. bail out Ford?' he (Couzens) shouted.

"The old enmity toward the Detroit bankers as a group flamed anew. Couzens was gloating now in memory of the day when he was barred with his bank from the clearing house. He gave out interviews and statements claiming that the Detroit banks could not pay out, that they were hopelessly insolvent. He said that a loan of $43,000,000, or anything like it, was an outrage and that he would denounce it.

"President Hoover entered the controversy. He saw ruin ahead for the nation if Detroit toppled. He called Couzens to the White House and pleaded with him. . . .

"The Detroit banks paid out 100 per cent."

sylvania, who wished to take up matters with the Democratic Senators. At his request I gave him a note upon the urgency of action by Roosevelt which he wished to show his Democratic colleagues. The pertinent parts [5] were:

... The American people do not wait for a known business event; they act to protect themselves individually in advance.

The things they fear the most are inflation, an unbalanced budget, and governmental projects which will surtax the borrowing power of the Government . . . to stem the tide . . . assurance should be at once given by the new administration that they have rigidly opposed such policies. That is the only way to re-establish confidence. And therefore, my suggestion is that you should transmit to the Democratic leaders this fundamental necessity, that they may urge it upon the President-elect. . . .

... Unless this is done, they run a grave danger of precipitating a complete financial debacle. If it is precipitated, the responsibility lies squarely with them for they have had ample warning—unless, of course, such a debacle is part of the "new deal."

The Senator got nowhere in urging his colleagues to such action.

On the 21st of February Senator Fess asked if I would dictate a review for him of the causes and needs of the economic situation. The pertinent parts of my letter to him follow:

... *Today we are on the verge of financial panic and chaos. Fear for the policies of the new administration has gripped the country. People do not await events, they act. Hoarding of currency, and of gold, has risen to a point never before known; banks are suspending not only in isolated instances, but in one case in an entire state. . . .* It is this fear that now dominates the national situation. It is not lack of resources, currency, or credit.

After reviewing the course of events during the previous four months, the unwillingness of Roosevelt to cooperate with us in the foreign field, and the postponement of the World Economic Conference, I continued:

... There have been a multitude of speeches, bills and statements of Democratic members of Congress and others proposing inflation or tinkering with the currency. . . . The differences between Democratic leaders and the Presi-

[5] For the full text of this letter and the one following, see Myers and Newton, *The Hoover Administration*, pp. 351 ff.

HENRY FORD AND MR. HOOVER

dent-elect . . . caused them to reject the balancing of the budget. The publication by Democratic leaders of the House of the Reconstruction Corporation loans has caused runs on hundreds of banks, failures of many of them and hoarding on a wide scale.

There have been proposed in the Congress by Democratic leaders, and publicly even by the President-elect, projects involving Federal expenditures of tremendous dimensions. . . . The proposals of Speaker Garner that constitutional government should be abandoned because the Congress . . . is unable to face reduction of expenses, has started a chatter of dictatorship. The President-elect has done nothing publicly to disavow any of these proposals. . . .

There have been interminable delays and threatened defeat of the Glass Banking Bill, and the Bankruptcy Bill. . . .

In the interest of every man, woman and child, the President-elect has, during the past week, been urged by the saner leaders of his own party, such as Senator Glass and others, by myself and by Democratic bankers and economists whom he has called on for advice, to stop the conflagration before it becomes uncontrollable, by announcing firmly and at once that (a) the budget will be balanced even if it means increased taxation; (b) new projects will be so restricted that government bond issues will not in any way endanger stability of government finances; (c) there will be no inflation or tampering with the currency; to which some have added that as the Democratic party is coming in with an overwhelming majority in both houses, there can be no excuse for abandonment of Constitutional process.

The President-elect is the only man who has the power to give assurances which will stabilize the public mind, as he alone can execute them. Those assurances should have been given before now but must be given at once if the situation is to be greatly helped. . . .

The present administration is devoting its days and nights to put out the fires or to localize them. I have scrupulously refrained from criticism which is well merited, but have instead been giving repeated assurances to the country of our desire to co-operate and help the new administration.

What is needed, if the country is not to drift into great grief, is the immediate and emphatic restoration of confidence. . . .

The day will come when the Democratic party will endeavor to place the responsibility for the events of this . . . period on the Republican party. When that day comes I hope you will invite the attention of the American people to the actual truth.

TRYING OUT A BROKEN REED—PART TIME

The Federal Reserve Board was the primary agency of the government in matters of banking and currency. It was in a position to take some leadership, which might persuade Roosevelt or the Congress to undertake constructive action. The majority of the Board seemed paralyzed. The men on the Board who supported my proposals were Adolph Miller and Secretary Mills. Lacking any aid from Roosevelt, I decided, with the approval of Miller and Mills, to press the hesitant majority of the Board to some action.

In a note of February 22nd, I summarized the situation and concluded:

> ... I should like to be advised by the Board as to whether the Board considers that the situation is one that has reached a public danger and whether the Board considers the Federal Reserve system can protect the public interest, or whether the Board considers any measures should be undertaken at this juncture and especially what, if any, further authority should be obtained.

Mills and Miller urged that the Board suggest to Roosevelt his cooperation in using the old war powers that would control unnecessary withdrawals and foreign exchange, and publish their recommendations.

The Board replied on the 25th, minimizing the situation:

> ... While some of the recent developments are disturbing, and many proposals as to ways and means of dealing with them are being made, the Board feels it is essential in times like these that every suggestion be carefully weighed and considered from the point of view of whether it would be likely to bring even greater disturbance and make worse the situation that it is designed to correct. ...
>
> At the moment the Board does not desire to make any specific proposals for additional measures or authority but it will continue to give all aspects of the situation its most careful consideration.

As the Board would not follow Mills' and Miller's urging, I again formally addressed them. Mills aided in drafting the letter, hoping that with their influence Congress might act:

Gentlemen:

Since my letter of a few days ago the banking situation has obviously become one of even greater gravity. I naturally wish to be properly advised as to such measures as can be taken to prevent the hardships to millions of people which are now going on. Although the Board is not the technical adviser of the President, yet it appears to me that in the large sense it should be prepared to advise me as to the measures necessary for the protection of the banking and currency system in times of emergency. I would, therefore, be glad to know whether the Board considers it desirable:

(a) To establish some form of Federal guarantee of banking deposits; or

(b) To establish clearing house systems in the affected areas; or

(c) To allow the situation to drift along under the sporadic State and community solutions now in progress . . .

Very truly,

HERBERT HOOVER

The idea of bank guarantees put forward by Mills and myself provided for a temporary Federal guarantee of each bank depositor's account up to the value of the assets of the bank. If the assets were 100 per cent of the depositor's liability, the deposits would be guaranteed in full. If the assets were equal to 80 per cent of the deposits, then the depositor would be guaranteed that far, and his further claims suspended, pending reorganization of that bank. It was self-evident that 100 per cent assets existed in the great majority of banks and a quick inspection could establish the situation in the remainder. Indeed it was confirmed subsequently that only a small proportion of the banks measured in deposits were deficient of assets to meet their deposit liabilities. The plan would have kept all banks open and functioning.

In their meeting to consider this letter, the majority of the Board refused to support such a recommendation to the Congress. The essential sentences of the reply of the majority were:

March 2, 1933.

Dear Mr. President:

The Board has received and carefully considered your letter of February 28, 1933.

In response to your first inquiry, the Board has requested me to advise you that it is not at this time prepared to recommend any form of Federal guarantee of banking deposits. . . .

With respect to your second inquiry . . . in reference to the establishment of clearing house systems. . . .

We know that the question of issuing clearing house certificates has been or is being considered in the communities . . . but, for a number of reasons . . . [the Board] have not felt, up to this time, that it would be feasible or desirable for them to resort to such a device. . . .

Answering your third inquiry, . . . so far no additional measures or authority have developed in concrete form, which at the moment, the Board feels it would be justified in urging.

Miller called me again on March 2nd to urge the use of the old war powers to control the situation. I explained to him the attitude of Senator Glass and other legal advisors and the refusals of Mr. Roosevelt and Mr. Woodin. He wanted to try again to induce the Reserve Board members to use their influence with Woodin, Roosevelt or Congress, and at his request I gave him a note to lay before them at a meeting that evening, thinking that the Board's support might yet secure Roosevelt's approval to this plan:

Gentlemen:

I understand that the Board is meeting this evening to consider recommending to me the use of the emergency powers under Section 5 of the Enemy Trading Act as amended, *for the purpose of limiting the use of coin and currency to necessary purposes.* I shall be glad to have the advice of the Board. If it is the view of the Board that these powers should be exerted I would be glad to have your recommendation accompanied by a form of proclamation, as it would seem to me it should be issued by me before banking hours tomorrow morning.

I also take this occasion to acknowledge the receipt of your letter of February 28. I am familiar with the inherent dangers in any form of federal guarantee of banking deposits, but I am wondering whether or not the situation has reached the time when the Board should give further consideration to this possibility. . . .

The majority of the Board again declined to have any part in the proposed recommendations to Roosevelt or the Congress. I concluded it was indeed a weak reed for a nation to lean on in time of trouble.

CONTINUED URGING UPON ROOSEVELT TO COOPERATE

Meanwhile, I worked unceasingly in other directions to get Roosevelt to cooperate. At my suggestion Mr. Miller joined Secretary Mills in urging again through Mr. Woodin that Roosevelt make a statement on the gold standard, or in any event, give his support on the use of the executive order.

Upon Senator Reed's urging, I again invited Senators Robinson and Glass to the White House. I explained to them our proposals and suggested that they urge Roosevelt to approve of my using the old wartime powers, or to approve any other constructive step such as I had outlined to the Federal Reserve Board. The Senators informed me that nothing could be done without Roosevelt's approval, and that he would approve nothing. They professed to be very indignant at him.

Pressures from various quarters, including the majority of the Federal Reserve Board, were brought upon me to declare a national banking holiday until after the inauguration. I do not know whether this idea came from Roosevelt or not, but they were in communication with him. However, up to the day I left the White House, more than 80 per cent of the banks in the country, measured by deposits, were still meeting all depositors' demands. I, therefore, refused to declare a holiday but constantly proposed, up to the last moment of my Presidency (eleven P.M. of March 3rd), to put into effect the executive order controlling withdrawals and exchanges if Mr. Roosevelt would approve. That would have effectively prevented practically all the banks from closing and given time for the panic to subside. At this last moment I called Roosevelt on the telephone, and he, in the presence of Senator Glass, again declined.

Rixey Smith and Norman Beasley, on p. 83 of their authorized biography, *Carter Glass,* quote the Senator's confirmation of this telephone conversation. His account of his discussion with Roosevelt that night on the use of the old war powers is of interest. Roosevelt had stated that he intended to close all the banks.

"You will have no authority to do that, no authority to issue any such proclamation," protested Glass. . . .

"I will have that authority," argued Roosevelt. "Under the Enemy Trading

Act, passed during the World War and never rescinded by Congress. . . ."

"It is my understanding that President Hoover explored that avenue a year or two ago—and again during recent days," said Glass. "Likewise, it is my understanding that . . . it was highly questionable, though it has never been rescinded by Congress, the President has any such authority. Highly questionable because the likelihood is the Act was dead with the signing of the Peace Treaty, if not before."

"My advice is precisely the opposite."

"Then you've got some expedient advice," returned Glass. . . .

"Nevertheless," declared Roosevelt, "I am going to issue such a proclamation."

Glass left the Roosevelt suite that night, dreading what this portent of the future seemed to him to mean.

If Roosevelt's interpretation was correct, it was all the more reason for his joining with me in using it at once to save closing the banks.

To my astonishment, immediately after the inauguration Roosevelt announced that he had just discovered this old World War power and used it as authority not to keep the banks open but to close them.

Roosevelt did not need to *close* the banks—all he needed to do, until bank depositors got over their panic, was to restrict bank payments to necessary business and limit foreign exchange likewise. But closing the banks would be a sign the country was in the ditch. It was the American equivalent of the burning of the Reichstag to create "an emergency."

SOME REASONS WHY ROOSEVELT REFUSED TO COOPERATE

A statement of Rexford G. Tugwell (one of Roosevelt's close advisers) is worth repeating. James Rand, a responsible industrialist, ten days before the inauguration, had telephoned me this statement of Tugwell's as a warning. I confirmed his telephone message in the following letter, as I wanted it in the record:

My dear Mr. Rand:

I beg to acknowledge your telephone message . . .

"Professor Tugwell, adviser to Franklin D. Roosevelt, had lunch with me. He said they were fully aware of the bank situation and that it would undoubtedly collapse in a few days, which would place the responsibility in the lap of President Hoover. . . ."

When I consider this statement of Professor Tugwell's in connection with the recommendations we have made to the incoming administration, I can say emphatically that . . . [they] would project millions of people into hideous losses for a Roman holiday.

Yours faithfully,

Herbert Hoover

Some years afterwards, I asked Ray Moley why Roosevelt refused to cooperate with me in the banking crisis. He wrote to me:

I feel when you asked him on February 18th to cooperate in the banking situation that he either did not realize how serious the situation was or that he preferred to have conditions deteriorate and gain for himself the entire credit for the rescue operation. In any event, his actions during the period from February 18th to March 3d would conform to any such motive on his part.

A TOTALLY UNNECESSARY PANIC OF BANK DEPOSITORS

After the storm had blown over, institutions representing more than 98 per cent of deposits ultimately paid off their depositors. They should never have been closed. The 2 per cent of insolvent banks at depression values at the time of the panic could have recovered their position with the inevitable restoration of values and many of them did.

The whole panic was simply an induced hysteria among bank depositors.

It was the most senseless and easily prevented panic in all history.

We had successfully fought off four far greater crises during the three preceding years. We had no panic after the stock market collapsed in October, 1929. We had no panic when the financial crash of Europe culminated in the British collapse in September, 1931, nor when we were nearly forced off the gold standard in February, 1932, nor at the bottom of the depression in June, 1932, when our structure was greatly weakened by Congressional obstruction and foreign pressures. At any of these periods panic could have risen.

It is not difficult to explain why we had a panic of bank depositors during the few days before March 4, 1933. It was simply because the bank depositors were frightened. Their fright had mounted steadily for two months. What were they afraid of? Surely not an outgoing administration with but a few days to run. Certainly not of the foreign countries, for they were steadily recovering. It was fear of the incoming administration.

I may repeat that the event of March 3rd was a hysteria among bank depositors induced by Roosevelt's own conduct. Early in January he could have prevented it by ten words in reaffirmation of his promises, then only two months cold. Or by a little cooperation, he could have prevented even a temporary closing of the banks.

After discussing the Campaign of 1932, I resume description of the sixth phase of the depression. Huge unemployment continued for eight years after Roosevelt's inauguration until our manpower was absorbed by the Second World War.

The United States alone had deserted the world recovery which began in the previous July. We alone slipped backward. I will show that all other countries free of the New Deals or collectivism progressed uninterruptedly to full employment and prosperity within two years.

The Presidential Election of 1932

CHAPTER 19

THE BACKGROUND OF THE 1932 CAMPAIGN

In order not to interrupt the account of the depression, I have deferred discussion of the Presidential election of 1932 to this separate section. The details of political campaigns have little long-time historical interest. As this campaign, however, marked a turning point in the direction of American life, some record of the backgrounds and the debate is of value.

I had little hope of reelection in 1932 but it was incumbent on me to fight it out to the end. As I stated in the introduction, General Prosperity had been a great ally in the election of 1928 and General Depression was a major enemy in 1932. Especially was this true as the major strategy of the opposition was to attach to me, personally, the responsibility for the worldwide depression and its evils. The people were naturally greatly disturbed; many were suffering; and fear was a dominant emotion. In all this setting, demand for change in Administration was natural. And it was easily promoted by great promises on the part of the opposition.

Before I discuss the campaign itself, I must point out certain parts of the background of the previous four years, as they had a considerable influence on the vote and are essential to the political history of the times.

The over-all strategy of our political opponents during the period between their defeat in 1928 and their convention in 1932 was in some aspects new in American political life. It was simple enough. It has always been, and properly, the function of the opposition to criticize the administration. That is a necessary part of representative government. Nobody has a right to complain about it. But with the probability that I should be the Republican nominee again in 1932, it became the Democratic strategy to substitute attack on me personally for attacks on my policies or even on the Republican party.

With this strategy the Democratic leaders, after my election in 1928, promptly set in motion a continuous campaign of misrepresentation. It was financed by large funds and administered by a paid staff. The intervention of the radio in national life especially favored such a tactic.

John J. Raskob, a member of the Du Pont firm, was chairman of the Democratic National Committee during the 1928 campaign. He had been heralded in that campaign as bringing the efficiency and know-how of business to the management of politics. Apparently he felt the defeat of 1928 more deeply than would a practicing politician.

He and many others were devoted to Governor Smith and were determined to renominate him in 1932. Their ranks were strengthened by those who wanted to repeal the 18th Amendment, and Raskob was able to command large funds from his own and Governor Smith's ardent friends for these purposes.

FOUR YEARS OF PERSONAL ATTACK

Soon after my inauguration in 1929, Raskob and his associates selected two past masters of political attack to run the Democratic National Committee from Washington. They were Jouett Shouse, executive director, and Charles Michelson, publicity director, to whom they paid $20,000 each per annum plus expenses. Shouse over the years had shown a lively capacity for political opposition and Michelson came out of the smear departments of yellow journalism.

Michelson states [1] that Raskob assured him of $1,000,000 to conduct his operations. This promise was more than made good. The sworn statements to the Congress of the Democratic National Committee, together with their Senatorial and Congressional committees, show that after the 1928 election, and prior to their 1932 convention, they collected in cash, or subsequently cancelled, loans approximating $2,300,000. They were in debt when they came out of the 1928 campaign and

[1] Charles Michelson, *The Ghost Talks* (G. P. Putnam's Sons, New York, 1944), p. 15.

still in debt when they arrived at the 1932 convention, some minor part of their collections having been applied to reduce debts.

The magnitude of these between-campaign expenditures had never been equaled in American politics. Probably $800,000 to $1,000,000 was the extreme amount that had ever been spent between campaigns by a National Committee and the Congressional committees together—and this mostly to aid Senators and Congressmen in mid-term elections.

Among the contributors either in cash or in subsequently canceled loans in this period were: John J. Raskob, $462,000; W. F. and P. F. Kenny, $175,000; Herbert H. Lehman, $175,000; M. J. Meehan, $102,000; T. J. Mara (same address), $50,000; James A. Riordan, $50,000; T. F. Ryan, $50,000; B. M. Baruch, $50,000; Pierre du Pont, $31,000; Vincent Astor, $20,000. Other large donors in the 1928 campaign also contributed to Raskob after the 1928 election.

The same men had previously contributed the following amounts to Governor Smith's campaign of 1928: John J. Raskob, $110,000; W. F. Kenny, $125,000; Herbert H. Lehman and wife, $135,000; M. J. Meehan, $50,000; T. F. Ryan, $110,000; B. M. Baruch, $33,500; Pierre du Pont, $50,000; and Vincent Astor, $10,000. Certainly Governor Smith had the most loyal of friends.

Nor did the sums which they reported to the Congress represent all of their expenditure. The same group financed various anti-prohibition, free trade, professor committees and other organizations generally to carry on guerrilla warfare. These agencies were not required to report donations to the Congress. A modest estimate of them would be over $1,000,000 more.

From the office of Shouse and Michelson came a ceaseless torrent of ghost-written speeches supplied to Democratic Senators, Congressmen, and other party leaders. The attack included also a continuous flood of press releases and radio propaganda. The *Congressional Record* alone shows hundreds of such attacks. A President cannot with decency and with proper regard for the dignity of his office reply to such stuff. And in my case, some of the old-guard Republican leaders in the Senate and the House, who had been defeated in their Presidential ambitions in 1928, certainly did not exert themselves energetically in their traditional duty to counterattack and expose misrepresentations.

The attacks of the Raskob regime became so flagrant that even Democratic journalists protested. One of the most comprehensive of these protests was made by Frank Kent of the Baltimore *Sun,* in *Scribner's Magazine* of September, 1930, before I had been two years in the White House. He wrote:

The political agency in Washington that more than any other has helped to mold the public mind in regard to Mr. Hoover, magnifying his misfortunes, minimizing his achievements . . . [is] an illuminating illustration of the amazing power of unopposed propaganda in skillful hands. . . . The new Democratic publicity bureau . . . [under] Charley Michelson . . . was not in the least understood by the country as a whole . . . [It is] the most elaborate, expensive, efficient and effective political propaganda machine ever operated in the country by any party, organization, association or league. . . . Mr. Raskob, Chairman of the Democratic National Committee, . . . selected the astute, politically seasoned and personally popular Mr. Jouett Shouse of Kansas City to act as Executive Chairman . . . picked Mr. Michelson . . . of the New York *World* . . . a Democrat with a real capacity for mischief . . . [and] gave him a free hand. . . . The goal set for him was to "smear" Mr. Hoover and his administration. That is what he is there for and all he is there for . . . [and] paid $25,000 a year. . . . It has been his pleasant task to minimize every Hoover asset [and] . . . to obscure every Hoover virtue and achievement. . . . His game is to "plant" interviews, statements, and speeches with Democratic members of the Senate and House of sufficient standing and prominence to make what they say news. . . . [It is] priceless personal publicity for such men. . . . Speeches, interviews, articles, statements, he has written for them . . . have appeared as their own. . . . Every move Hoover has made is followed by the firing of a Michelson publicity barrage. . . . Editorials and news items have streamed through the mails to small papers hitting Hoover . . . in a hundred different ways.

A PHONY TEAPOT DOME

Many of the operations of Raskob, Shouse, and Michelson showed more subtlety than the direct attack stated by Mr. Kent. It is not worth while to record the full list of these actions. A few samples will suffice. A typical case was the publication, just prior to the 1930 Congressional election, of a series of articles by the New York *World,* with nationwide full-page advance advertisement and syndication. They charged us with great oil scandals—a "second Teapot Dome." It developed that *The World* had paid $12,000 through Michelson to a man named Kelley to prepare these articles. When Kelley agreed to take the money he was still an employee of the Department of the Interior, in charge of oil shale leases.

I at once directed the Attorney General to investigate the matter, and he reported:

Kelley has made an effort to give the public the impression that oil shale lands presently worth untold billions have been or are about to be lost to the Government. In his charges he uses such expressions as "oil shale worth forty billions" and "surrender of billions of dollars of oil lands." The facts are that oil shale has no substantial present commercial value; that the cost of mining the shale and extracting the oil greatly exceeds the value of the product. . . . While oil shale may have a potential value . . . the wild and reckless statements made in Kelley's charges respecting values reflect on the accuracy of all his statements.

The Geological Survey estimates a total of 8,257,791 acres of oil shale land in Wyoming, Utah, and Colorado, where the big shale deposits are found. Of that amount . . . during the present administration only 42,840 acres have been patented, and of that amount the patent of 23,057 acres was approved by Kelley himself. Patents on 15,778 acres were required to be issued as a result of the Krushnic decision by the Supreme Court. . . . The United States still owns 97 per cent of all its original oil shale lands. . . .

There is Kelley's charge that Assistant Secretary Finney wanted to destroy some papers relating to applications by claimants. . . . The papers in question never were destroyed and are in their proper places in the files. . . .

There stands out the fact that Kelley, when placed in charge of this oil shale matter in your Washington office, immediately got in touch with a newspaper, refrained from presenting any of his complaints to you, and sold his story to the press, and refused then to give to authorized public officials any statement of the matter. It is a just inference that his refusal to assist the Assistant Attorney General in his inquiry was merely to protect the news value of his proposed newspaper articles.

Despite all this *The World* persisted in distributing the lies. It was so wicked that I felt it necessary to issue a statement. After stating Secretary Wilbur's instant denial of the charges with proof of their falsity, I continued:

Yet despite all these opportunities to test the truth these agencies have persisted in broadcasting them for the last six weeks by every device of publicity. . . . It certainly does not represent the practice of better journalism. As a piece of politics it is . . . below the ideals of political partisanship. . . . But there is another and more important phase. I am interested and have a duty in the preserving and upbuilding of honest public service. . . . When reckless, baseless and infamous charges in the face of responsible denial are broadcast with no attempt at verification . . . the ultimate result can only be damage to public service as a whole . . . [and] damage to the whole faith of our people in men. . . . Men of a lifetime of distinction and probity . . . should not be subjected to infamous transactions of this character.

Later on, Secretary Wilbur compelled *The World* to make an abject apology. But this was in fine print, whereas the lie had been spread over the whole country by every ingenious method that money could pay for.[2]

I received a modicum of satisfaction because the exposure so discredited *The World* that it died soon after.

A PHONY SUGAR SCANDAL

A supposed sugar scandal was loudly announced in 1930 by Congressman John Garner, implying that I was associated with sugar lobbyists and beneficiaries of corruption. Investigation was made by a Senate committee. After days of dirt and publicity, Democratic Senator Walsh finally stated that there was not an atom of truth in it.

Another such example was an innuendo by Senator McKellar that I had misappropriated great sums from governmental relief appropriations during the Armistice. It happened that Senator Glass had been

[2] A biography of Joseph Pulitzer by J. W. Barrett, the last city editor of *The World*, published in 1941, is in reality a biography of that paper. In recounting this incident on pp. 420–425, he writes: "After talking with Herbert Pulitzer, Lippmann requested Kelley to come to New York at *The World*'s expense. Kelley unfolded his tale to Lippmann and Renaud." After some negotiations Kelley was paid "$12,000 for the articles, on condition that Kelley continue in the department until the articles were finished and then resign. . . . *The World* could have avoided the whole fiasco by following its rules of accuracy and fair play. It made no effort to obtain Secretary Wilbur's statement until after the series began. The most casual inquiry would have satisfied *The World* that there was nothing to back up Kelley's charges." Barrett seemed to believe the incident had some part in the death of *The World*.

Secretary of the Treasury at the time I was supposedly stealing one hundred million dollars. After the story had been blazoned across the country, Glass, in reply to a Republican Senator's demand, denied that it could be true. But this lie continued to spread for years.

An example of a more subtle attack was the faked hunger riot in Arkansas, which I have already described. It was planted in the press with great effectiveness and was designed to prove my hardheartedness.

SMEAR BOOKS

Another device was a flood of smear books. These cannot be attributed to Raskob's organization. Subsequent court proceedings showed that a down-and-out English literary beachcomber named Hamill was engaged by two men named Kenny and O'Brien, connected with Tammany Hall, to write the first of these books. It was purported to be a history of my life as an engineer. The partners apparently had difficulty in finding a publisher, for the book was issued by a Samuel Roth, alias William Faro, who had served several prison sentences for illegal publications. A quarrel sprang up among O'Brien, Hamill, and Roth over the matter. Hamill claimed that Kenny in giving him $1,700 had only made part payment for his services. O'Brien and Roth quarreled over the profits expected from selling half a million copies through the official Democratic organization. When this quarrel came before a New York judge, he threw out the whole case with a public excoriation. The quarrel thus came to the ears of one of my lawyer friends. My friend requested, from Hamill, the name of his lawyer, who would defend an action for criminal libel. Thereupon, Hamill took alarm and made under oath a complete written confession of the whole business, stating that he had fabricated every word of it. The Democratic National Committee did not circulate the book. However, Faro continued to push it. The Communists bought the remainder of the books and for years sold them in their bookstores. Finally the Communists brought out a cheap edition for wider circulation.

The Hamill book was the father of others. One came out under the assumed name of "John Knox." Another, repeating Hamill's, was written by Walter Liggett, a fellow traveler who was later murdered by gangsters in Minneapolis. As Liggett had no funds, somebody must have spent $2,000 or $3,000 for printing alone.

Another of the activities of some financed person was the persistent distributing of a photograph of a supposed sign, "No white men wanted," upon a Hoover ranch gate in California. This originated in 1928, and was denounced as a fake at the time by the county labor leaders; but for fifteen years afterwards some one continued to spread this photograph. Over the years, hardly a week passed by that some one did not write letters to me or Mrs. Hoover from all parts of the United States, either charging me with this action or asking that I deny it.

There were other blows below the belt during the campaign. A good example was the charge that I had prostituted the RFC to save the Dawes bank in Chicago. General Dawes had been president of the RFC before the loan. The loan had been made upon the recommendations of the Democratic directors of the RFC. The security was such that the government could lose no money; but, of far greater importance, it had stopped a panic in Chicago which would have closed all the banks. This attack became so violent an assault upon my personal honesty, that I was compelled to devote a large part of a speech in St. Louis to refuting it.

THE BONUS MARCH

Probably the greatest coup of all was the distortion of the story of the Bonus March on Washington in July, 1932. About 11,000 supposed veterans congregated in Washington to urge action by Congress to pay a deferred war bonus in cash instead of over a period of years.

The Democratic leaders did not organize the Bonus March nor conduct the ensuing riots. But the Democratic organization seized upon the incident with great avidity. Many Democratic speakers in the campaign of 1932 implied that I had murdered veterans on the streets of Washington.

The story was kept alive for twenty years. I, therefore, deal with it at greater length than would otherwise be warranted. As abundantly proved later on, the march was in considerable part organized and promoted by the Communists and included a large number of hoodlums and ex-convicts determined to raise a public disturbance. They were frequently addressed by Democratic Congressmen seeking to inflame them against me for my opposition to the bonus legislation. They were given financial support by some of the publishers of the sensational press. It was of interest to learn in after years from the Communist confessions that they also had put on a special battery of speakers to help Roosevelt in his campaign, by the use of the incident.

When it was evident that no legislation on the bonus would be passed by the Congress, I asked the chairmen of the Congressional committees to appropriate funds to buy tickets home for the legitimate veterans. This was done and some 6,000 availed themselves of its aid, leaving about 5,000 mixed hoodlums, ex-convicts, Communists, and a minority of veterans in Washington. Through government agencies we obtained the names of upwards of 2,000 of those remaining and found that fewer than a third of them had ever served in the armies, and that over 900 on the basis of this sampling were ex-convicts and Communists.

Some old buildings on Pennsylvania Avenue had been occupied by about 50 marchers. These buildings stood in the way of construction work going on as an aid to employment in Washington. On July 28th the Treasury officials, through the police, requested these marchers to move to other quarters. Whereupon more than 1,000 of the disturbers marched from camps outside of the city armed with clubs and made an organized attack upon the police. In the melee Police Commissioner Glassford failed to organize his men. Several were surrounded by the mob and beaten up; two policemen, beaten to the ground, fired to protect their lives and killed two marchers. Many policemen were injured.

In the midst of this riot the District Commissioners, upon Glassford's urging, appealed to me. They declared that they could not preserve order in the Capital, that the police were greatly outnumbered, and were being overwhelmed. With the same right of call on me as municipalities have on the governor of any state, they asked military assistance to restore order. At my direction to Secretary of War Hurley, General Douglas MacArthur was directed to take charge. General Eisenhower (then Colonel) was second in command. Without firing a shot or injuring a single person, they cleaned up the situation. Certain of my directions to the Secretary of War, however, were not carried out. Those directions limited action to seeing to it that the disturbing factions returned to their camps outside the business district. I did not wish them driven from their camps, as I proposed that the next day we would surround the camps and determine more accurately the number of Communists and ex-convicts among the marchers. Our military officers, however, having them on the move, pushed them outside the District of Columbia.

As this incident was made the base of a fabrication of smearing lies over years, I give the following official documents:

July 28th, 1932

THE PRESIDENT:

The Commissioners of the District of Columbia regret to inform you that during the past few hours, circumstances of a serious character have arisen in the District of Columbia which have been the cause of unlawful acts of large numbers of so-called "bonus marchers," who have been in Washington for some time past.

This morning, officials of the Treasury Department, seeking to clear certain areas within the Government triangle in which there were numbers of these bonus marchers, met with resistance. They called upon the Metropolitan Police Force for assistance and a serious riot occurred. Several members of the Metropolitan Police were injured, one reported seriously. The total number of bonus marchers greatly outnumbered the police; the situation is made more difficult by the fact that this area contains thousands of brickbats and these were used by the rioters in their attack upon the police.

In view of the above, it is the opinion of the Major and Superintendent of Police, in which the Commissioners concur, that it will be impossible for the Police Department to maintain law and order except by the free use of firearms which will make the situation a dangerous one; it is believed, however, that the presence of Federal troops in some number will obviate the seriousness of the situation and result in far less violence and bloodshed.

The Commissioners of the District of Columbia, therefore, request that they be given the assistance of Federal troops, in maintaining law and order in the District of Columbia.

Very truly yours,

L. H. REICHELDERFER, *President,*
Board of Commissioners of the District of Columbia

I reviewed the incidents at once to the press, saying in conclusion:

Congress made provision for the return home of the so-called bonus marchers who have for many weeks been given every opportunity of free assembly, free speech and free petition to the Congress. Some 6,000 took advantage of this arrangement and have returned to their homes. An examination of a large number of names discloses the fact that a considerable part of those remaining are not veterans: many are communists and persons with criminal records.

The veterans amongst these numbers are no doubt unaware of the character of their companions and are being led into violence which no government can tolerate.

I have asked the Attorney General to investigate the whole incident and to cooperate with the District civil authorities in such measures against leaders and rioters as may be necessary.

General MacArthur issued his own statement on September 28th, saying:

I sent word by General Glassford to the various camps that I was going to clear Government property and that I hoped that they would not be humiliated by being forced out. I hoped that they would take advantage of the time element and evacuate without trouble. We moved down Pennsylvania to the Avenue area. . . . That mob . . . was a bad looking mob. It was animated by the essence of revolution. The gentleness, the consideration, with which they had been treated had been mistaken for weakness and they had come to the conclusion, beyond the shadow of a doubt, that they were about to take over in some arbitrary way either the direct control of the Government or else to control it by indirect methods. It is my opinion that had the President not acted today, had he permitted this thing to go for 24 hours more, he would have been faced with a grave situation which would have caused a real battle. Had he let it go on another week I believe that the institutions of our Government would have been very severely threatened. I think it can be safely said that he had not only reached the end of an extraordinary patience but that he had gone to the very limit in his desire to avoid friction and trouble before he used force. Had he not used it at that time, I believe he would have been very derelict indeed in the judgment in which he was handling the safety of the country. This was the focus of the world today; and had he not acted with the force and vigor that he did, it would have been a very sad day for the country tomorrow. . . .

. . . After we cleared Pennsylvania Avenue, the insurrectionists fired their billets. . . . [This was] all done by the bonus marchers themselves; all done by the elements that were causing the trouble. I call them "insurrectionists." . . .

There were, in my opinion, few veteran soldiers in the group that we cleared out today; few indeed. I am not speaking by figures because I don't know how many there were; but if there was one man in ten in that group today who is a veteran it would surprise me.

. . . All of these moves of course had been at the solicitation of the District Commissioners, the District Government. They requested not only that those areas should be evacuated by the military, but . . . [the requests were made] . . . through General Glassford, speaking for Commissioner Reichelderfer and Commissioner Crosby. . . .

I have never seen greater relief on the part of the distressed populace than I saw today. I have released in my day more than one community which had been held in the grip of a foreign enemy. I have gone into villages that for three and one half years had been under the domination of the soldiers of a foreign nation. I know what gratitude means along that line. I have never seen, even in those days, such expression of gratitude as I heard from the crowds today. At least a dozen people told me, especially in the Negro section, that a regular system of tribute was being levied on them by this insurrectionist group; a reign of terror was being started which may have led to a system of Caponeism, and I believe later to insurgency and insurrection.

The President played it pretty fine in waiting to the last minute; but he didn't have much margin. . . . I have been in many riots but I think this is the first riot I ever was in or ever saw in which there was no real bloodshed. So far as I know there is no man on either side who has been seriously injured.

General Glassford, shortly afterwards, published a series of articles stating flatly that he had opposed calling out the troops, and that he could have handled the situation without them. The Attorney General, however, took sworn statements from the District Commissioners proving that Glassford had implored them to call for troops. Among the statements to the Attorney General was one from General MacArthur stating flatly that General Glassford had appealed to him directly for help and accompanied him throughout.

The misrepresentation of the bonus incident for political purposes surpassed any similar action in American history. Not only did Roosevelt use the incident in the 1932 campaign, but Democratic orators also continued to use it for twenty years after, despite all the refutations and proof to the contrary. I was portrayed as a murderer and an enemy of the veterans. A large part of the veterans believe to this day that men who served their country in war were shot down in the streets of Washington by the Regular Army at my orders—yet not a shot was fired or a person injured after the Federal government took charge.

And it was I who, as President, provided more for World War I veterans in need than any previous President, as I placed all needy and sick veterans on disability allowances.

The Roosevelt administration took a large part of it away from them. The following figures on the World War veterans' or dead veterans' dependents receiving regularly either pensions or disability allowances from the Federal government speak for themselves:

Hoover Administration		*Roosevelt Administration*	
1930	367,500	1934	462,900
1931	628,600	1935	473,500
1932	840,300	1936	479,000
1933	853,800		

That the Bonus March was largely organized and managed by Communists became clear with the passage of time, through disclosures by Congressional committees and repentant Communist leaders who participated in it. Benjamin Gitlow, who was a leader in the Communist party, later published a full account of the movement[3] in which he described the organization of the march and its direction in Washington by a Russian Communist agent from a safe hotel room, and the anger of the director when the attempt failed after the troops took charge without hurting a single veteran.

An acknowledged Communist who actually led in the march—John T. Pace—made a complete confession[4] which is worth partial repro-

[3] *The Whole of Their Lives* (Charles Scribner's Sons, New York, 1948).

[4] *Congressional Record*, Aug. 11, 1949.

Various other Communist participants have confessed, and the report of the House Committee on Un-American Activities of Aug. 23, 1949, brought out more detail upon the Communist inspiration and control of the Bonus March. In addition to Pace, Joseph Z. Cornfedder, a former Communist of the Central Committee of the Communist Party

duction as it shows the activities of the Communists in opposing my election in 1932. Pace stated:

I feel responsible in part for this often-repeated lie about President Hoover and General MacArthur. . . .

I led the left-wing or Communist section of the bonus march. I was ordered by my Red superiors to provoke riots. I was told to use every trick to bring about bloodshed in the hopes that President Hoover would be forced to call out the Army. The Communists didn't care how many veterans were killed. I was told Moscow had ordered riots and bloodshed in the hopes that this might set off the revolution. My Communist bosses were jumping for joy on July 28 when the Washington police killed one veteran. The Army was called out next day by President Hoover and didn't fire a shot or kill a man. General MacArthur put down a Moscow-directed revolution without bloodshed, and that's why the Communists hate him even today. . . .

But MacArthur did the job without firing a shot and acting under Mr. Hoover's instructions, prevented any violence.

. . . I was told . . . [after the riots] . . . to come to an address near Union Square (New York). It was a highly secret meeting and plenty of the big-shot Communists were there, including Browder, Foster, and Stachel.

Levine and I made reports on the bonus march and our work in Washington. Then a squat, dark-haired man was introduced to us as the "C. I. Rep" (Communist International representative). This man complimented me for my work. Speaking with a thick Russian accent, he said Moscow was pleased with my "working class leadership." He told me that Moscow wanted me to make a national tour speaking in every State to agitate against President Hoover and General MacArthur.

This Moscow agent said I was to refer to Mr. Hoover as "the murderer of American veterans" and to MacArthur as "the tool of the Fascists."

I knew that MacArthur's men didn't fire a shot, but I had at least one "commissar" with me during all my speaking tour to see that I followed instructions.

The "C. I. Rep" also told the party leaders to arrange my speaking tour under the auspices of the Workers' Ex-Servicemen's League, a Communist-front group.

---

at the time of the march, was examined. Also the party leadership and methods of organizing the veterans were further elaborated by Jacob Spolansky, a retired FBI agent, from personal experience at the time of the Bonus March, in *The Communist Trail in America* (The Macmillan Company, New York, 1951).

Communist leaders told me the smear campaign was successful. They were happy when the parlor pinks took up the smear against the two great Americans and even today the Reds boast that the propaganda drive of 1932 carried on by the Communists turned the Nation against Mr. Hoover.

On the basis of my personal experience, I want to repeat again and again that Mr. Hoover took the only step he could have taken to avert a bloody revolution right there in Washington.[5]

One of the cynical outcomes of the Raskob-Shouse-Michelson strategy was the defeat of Governor Smith in the Democratic Convention of 1932. His backers were not themselves left-wingers. In fact, they were most conservative types. But aided by the depression and suffering, they, without themselves realizing it then, succeeded in stimulating the radical movements and class feeling greatly beyond the natural tendencies in that direction usual in every depression.

When these men came to renominate Governor Smith in 1932, they found themselves overwhelmed by the Frankenstein they had created. The enlarged left-wing succeeded in nominating a leader of its own, Franklin Roosevelt. Governor Smith, by that time, had become a "reactionary."

This election of Presidents could have been somewhat cleaner.

[5] Despite repeated refutations, Mrs. Eleanor Roosevelt as late as July, 1949, repeated the Bonus March lie in *McCall's Magazine* of that date. When former Secretary of War Hurley demonstrated in the December issue that it was a lie, she made no adequate apology.

CHAPTER 20

THE CAMPAIGN DEBATE

During the campaign of 1932, I made only nine major political addresses: in Washington on August 11th, in Des Moines on October 4th, in Cleveland on October 13th, in Detroit on October 22nd, in Indianapolis on October 28th, in New York on October 31st, in St. Louis on November 4th, in St. Paul on November 5th, and in Salt Lake City on November 7th.[1] Except for "tank stops" I made no extemporaneous speeches.

The reason for this small number of addresses was my great burden not only of normal administration but of the depression. Moreover, I wrote my own speeches—and a proper presentation requires many days to prepare. I have never delivered a ghost-written public statement of importance. The proof lies in the preserved handwritten manuscripts of almost every draft. I did submit such drafts to my colleagues and did accept suggestions, but I entered them with my own hand.

On our side, in addition to my own debate, we were vigorously supported by speeches of Cabinet members—Ogden Mills, Arthur M. Hyde, William N. Doak, Ray Lyman Wilbur, Patrick J. Hurley, and Walter F. Brown—plus the many loyal Senators, Congressmen and citizens. These men carried on the fight night and day. Secretary Stimson, who had taken part in Republican political campaigns for many years past, felt that he must, as Secretary of State, be neutral. He was the first Cabinet leader in history to take that view. He confined himself to a mild nonpartisan speech on foreign relations.

[1] *Campaign Speeches of 1932 by President Hoover and Ex-President Coolidge.* Also, *The State Papers and Other Public Writings of Herbert Hoover,* edited by William Starr Myers (both published by Doubleday, Doran & Company, Inc., Garden City, New York).

Roosevelt's campaign has historical importance, because the new techniques which he introduced have affected all campaigns since. They mostly revolved around personal attacks. He delivered a multitude of ghost-written speeches, some written by irresponsible or ignorant men.

His friend, Judge Samuel I. Rosenman, organized early in the campaign what became widely known as the Brain Trust. The working force appeared to be Felix Frankfurter, professor of law at Harvard; Raymond Moley, professor of public law at Columbia; Adolf A. Berle, Jr., associate professor of corporation law at Columbia; Joseph D. McGoldrick, assistant professor of government at Columbia; Rexford Guy Tugwell, professor of economics at Columbia; and Thomas Corcoran, a sometime instructor at Harvard. Most significant of the group were Frankfurter and Tugwell, both devoted to "planned economy," the latter being the intellectual heir of Thorstein Veblen. One or two other professors, who were originally drawn into the Brain Trust, subsequently withdrew.

Nonacademic contributors to the Brain Trust included Louis Howe, Roosevelt's secretary; Hugh S. Johnson, an able but vituperative former army officer; Basil O'Connor, Roosevelt's law partner; Donald A. Richberg, a railroad labor lawyer; Harry Hopkins, a professional social worker; Charles W. Taussig, a molasses millionaire, and Senators T. J. Walsh, Elmer Thomas, and George Norris, three great masters of demagoguery.

It will appear later that this Brain Trust contained some men who were expert in semantics but grievously undernourished on truth.

Moley was an honest and convincing writer of speeches.[2] Hugh Johnson was, according to his account, a most influential speech writer.[3]

[2] Moley's book, *After Seven Years* (New York, 1939) is in considerable part devoted to showing how, when, and by whom Roosevelt's major speeches were ghost-written. He comments (p. 56) on "the dreadful feeling of responsibility" the writing of the speeches entailed. Roosevelt's mind "was neither exact nor orderly. . . . He knew this because he seldom trusted himself to say in public more than a few sentences extemporaneously, though I doubt that he would admit that he is often inaccurate in casual conversation. I labored with the tormenting knowledge that I could not afford to be wrong."

[3] Hugh S. Johnson also later wrote a book (*The Blue Eagle from Egg to Earth*, Garden City, New York, 1935) in which he described the ghost-writing process in great detail and with pride.

A considerable part of the conflict in ideas and misstatement of fact, and misrepresentation no doubt sprang from those ignorant of public experience and from a peculiar belief of some of them that intellectual honesty is not expected in political campaigns.

Roosevelt's speeches, except seven which are omitted, were arranged by Samuel Rosenman and published.[4]

In presenting the bare bones of the debate, it is necessary to omit repetitive paragraphs and the accompanying heat and eloquence on both sides—otherwise it would run into several volumes. I have, therefore, selected the paragraphs which present the essential point of view on major issues.

The campaign crystallized into about fourteen main topics:

1. Hoover's responsibility for the depression.
2. Hoover did nothing about it.
3. Extravagant Federal expenditures and taxes.
4. The gold standard and managed currency.
5. Tariff.
6. Agricultural policies.
7. Collectivist planned economy.
8. The Supreme Court.
9. Business regulation.
10. Government in competitive business.
11. Prohibition.
12. Labor and public works.
13. Foreign policy.
14. Relief of distress and humane services.

By the nature of things, we were somewhat on the defensive as to certain issues, especially in view of constant misrepresentation which could be met only by painstaking exposure and dreary recital of facts. We were, however, able to take the offensive, especially on currency, tariff, the Supreme Court, and collectivist planned economy.

Before discussing these various issues, I shall shortly dismiss the issues of foreign policy, relief of distress and humane services.

[4] *The Public Papers and Addresses of Franklin D. Roosevelt,* Vol. I, 1928–1932 (New York, 1938), pp. 647–860.

FOREIGN POLICY

Roosevelt made no reference to foreign policy except so far as tariff and private loans to foreigners related to it.[5] Nor did he raise any criticism of our national defense measures. I, however, presented our accomplishments and policies in these fields at length in addresses on August 11th, October 4th, 7th, 15th, 22nd, November 4th and 5th, and devoted almost the whole of my address of November 7th to these subjects.

RELIEF OF DISTRESS

Roosevelt made no mention or attack upon our measures of direct relief of distress. It is certain that if these measures had not been successful, every molehill would have become a mountain. He did complain of our public works program, about which he was badly misinformed.

OTHER HUMANE SERVICES

One constant refrain of the campaign which was hard to take with urbanity was the charge of neglect of humane services during my administration. It was, of course, good politics for an opponent to pound incessantly into the ears of millions of radio listeners, by direct statement and innuendo, the total heartlessness of his opponent.

Roosevelt's method is illustrated by his statement at Detroit on October 2, 1932:

> We cannot go back to the old prisons, for example, to the old systems of mere punishment under which a man out of prison was not fitted to live in our community alongside of us.

He overlooked the obvious fact that we in the Administration had enacted the greatest program of prison reform in all American history. He continued: "We cannot go back to children working in factories." Yet we had incessantly urged that the states adopt the Constitutional

---

[5] Raymond Moley in *Newsweek,* June 14, 1948, threw some light on this question: "It should be set down for the record that . . . F. D. R. deliberately declined, during the 1932 campaign, to take issue on foreign policy. When, that October, the question came up, I talked with F. D. R. about a speech on foreign policy. He said, 'Let's not say anything on foreign policy. Hoover's all right on that.' "

Amendment prohibiting child labor, and New York, under Governor Roosevelt, was one of the states refusing to take action.

In a radio address from Washington, I had said on September 29th:

. . . In this depression as never before the American people have responded with a high sense of responsibility to safeguard and protect the children not only as the humane necessity of the day but that there may be no danger for the future. . . . The continuous reports of the Public Health Service showing a less infant mortality, less infant disease than in prosperous times, can mark only one thing and that is the most extraordinary devotion to those who would be normally the most hard pressed. . . .

There is another opportunity growing out of these times to advance the cause of children. . . . That is the steady elimination of child labor. . . . it would not only help childhood, but would aid . . . adult breadwinners if more children were eliminated from those few industries where they are still employed. . . .

. . . We cannot afford to slacken one moment in the preparation of the new day of a generation of Americans stronger and better, not only physically and intellectually, but above all morally.

I referred to the White House Conference on Child Health and Protection and the "Children's Charter," given in September, 1932. In an address at Washington on October 24th, I again stated my long relations with health activities and my subsequent attempts to secure legislation for the rural county units in service of children:

. . . There is the well-being of the future generations of our children, the building up of safeguards around the home and the health of the parents and of the growing family . . . the treasures of childhood . . . the preservation of those precious exceptional children whose birth cannot be predicted of any class or moment and from whom comes the leadership of our democracy. . . .

At Indianapolis on October 28th, I continued my attack on these misrepresentations:

I now have before me other calumnies of the Democratic National Committee, circulated in the same fashion by instructions to their campaign speakers. These instructions bristle with such titles as these:

"How President Hoover has failed the children."

"His real interest in the Nation's children may be gained by his recorded effort to emasculate and disrupt the Children's Bureau. . . ."

Governor Roosevelt implies his indorsement of these calumnies by repeating their implications in his speeches when he speaks of what he calls "attempts that have been made to cut appropriations for child welfare."

And to Roosevelt's charge,

The United States Public Health Service states that over 6,000,000 of our public-school children have not enough to eat, many are fainting at their desks; they are the prey of disease . . .

I replied:

These things have importance only as indicating the desperate attempts to mislead the American voter. I am not required to defend my interest in children over the past score of years. But more to the point, I have a letter from the Chief of the United States Public Health Service declaring that no such statement as that quoted by Governor Roosevelt has ever been put out by that service. Further I have here an address, only a week old, by the President of the American Public Health Association, who is not a Government official, saying, "by and large, the health of the people are measured in sickness and death has never been better despite the depression." . . .

As to the Children's Bureau, . . . [during] the first year of my Administration, despite the hard times, I increased appropriations for the Children's Bureau from $320,000 to $368,000; in the second year I recommended appropriations of $399,000; and in the third year I recommended appropriations of $395,000, but the Democratic House of Representatives reduced this by $20,000. This scarcely looks like ruin of the Children's Bureau—on my part.

On October 13th, he said:

Attempts have been made to cut the appropriations for child welfare work. It seems to me that this is the last place in which we should seek to economize. I cannot agree . . . that this depression is not altogether a bad thing for our children.

You and I know the appalling fact that malnutrition is one of the saddest by-products of unemployment. The health of these children is being affected not only now but for all the rest of their lives.

The exact contrary was, of course, the truth.

The Bonus March provided another attack. There were many such misrepresentations, but these few are indicative of the methods. Some honest men must have believed them unreservedly.

Only once in the campaign did I protest at the charges that I neglected our people. I said at Fort Wayne, on October 5, 1932:

I wish to take the occasion . . . to say a word to . . . all the people of the great Midwest.

During my public life, I have believed that sportsmanship and statesmanship called for the elimination of harsh personalities between opponents. On this journey, however, I have received a multitude of reports as to the widespread personal misrepresentations which have been promulgated in the . . . past few weeks. I regret that the character of these personalities necessitates a direct word from me.

I shall say now the only harsh word that I have uttered in public office. I hope it will be the last I shall have to say. When you are told that the President of the United States, who by the most sacred trust of our Nation is the President of all the people, a man of your own blood and upbringing, has sat in the White House for the last three years of your misfortune without troubling to know your burdens, without heartaches over your miseries and casualties, without summoning every avenue of skillful assistance irrespective of party or view, without using every ounce of his strength and straining his every nerve to protect and help, without using every possible agency of democracy that would bring aid, without putting aside personal ambition and humbling his pride of opinion, if that would serve—then I say to you that such statements are deliberate, intolerable falsehoods.

Ever since I have left office my personal correspondence has been studded with touching man-to-man apologies from complete strangers, who said they had been misled, had taken part in these campaigns of lies, and wanted me to know they were sorry. Often they asked for a letter of forgiveness to ease their consciences.

This whole Democratic performance was far below the level of any previous campaign in modern times. Certainly it was below the character of the campaign with Governor Smith of four years before. My defeat would no doubt have taken place anyway. But it might have taken place without such defilement of American life.

CHAPTER 21

CHARGES OF RESPONSIBILITY FOR
THE DEPRESSION

One of Roosevelt's most effective campaign issues was of course the depression. His strategy was to allege that I had made the depression[1] and then done nothing about it. He stated six varieties of "proofs" and "causes" for which I was responsible: First, that the depression was entirely of domestic origin; Second, that I was personally responsible for the stock market boom and the orgy of speculation; Third, that as Secretary of Commerce I had caused the overbuilding of industry; Fourth, that as Secretary of Commerce I had been responsible for private loans to foreigners which by their default were a cause of the depression; Fifth, that the Smoot-Hawley Tariff had destroyed our foreign markets, drained the world of gold, made it impossible for foreigners to pay their debts, and started trade reprisals over the world; and Sixth,

---

[1] A curious commentary on all these statements of Roosevelt's appeared in an article by Mrs. Eleanor Roosevelt, which was published in her daily newspaper column, July 22, 1948: "If only we can avoid a repetition of the depression that culminated in Mr. Hoover's administration, we will be very fortunate. This depression, of course, had nothing to do with President Hoover's policies. . . ."

Arthur Krock, noting this statement, wrote the next day in the New York *Times*: "Considering the source and nature of this sentence, it must have astonished Herbert Hoover more than anything has in years. . . . In 1932 the current depression, its continuation and its causes was the principal issue. . . . Franklin Roosevelt and the Democratic orators referred to it as the 'Hoover Depression' and the people have been calling it that ever since. . . . What the Democratic candidate in 1932 said about President Hoover and his policies with respect to the causes of the depression . . . were the basis on which rested the popular judgment . . . and the electoral decision that turned Mr. Hoover out of office." After quoting Mrs. Roosevelt and referring to some subsequent events, he remarked: "These experiences could hardly have prepared the former President for a sweeping verdict of not guilty by this particular juror."

that by extravagance and reckless spending I had created a great Federal deficit which was strangling the country.

The miseries of the people and the wrongdoing of business (mostly exposed by my administration), with the help of innuendo and sly inference, furnished magnificent oratorical material for emotionalizing these issues.

In order that there may be no contention that this was not Mr. Roosevelt's prime campaign platform, I produce specimens from his flood of statements of this character. I do not include the chorus of other speakers; they took the tune from their candidate. I shall deal with his intellectual errors on the tariff and government expenditure in separate chapters.

ROOSEVELT CONTENDS I WAS RESPONSIBLE FOR THE STOCK MARKET BOOM OF 1928

In Columbus, Ohio, on August 20, 1932, Roosevelt said:

The Administration lined up with the stock market, and the warnings went unheeded. The President apparently forgot that in 1922 he himself had written as follows: "Thirty years ago our business community considered the cyclic financial panic inevitable. We know now that we have cured it through the Federal Reserve Board." And yet in 1929 he took the opposite course, nullifying the Board's effort. . . .

So I sum up the history of the present Administration in four sentences:

First, it encouraged speculation and overproduction, through its false economic policies.

Second, it attempted to minimize the crash and misled the people as to its gravity.

Third, it erroneously charged the cause to other Nations of the world.

And finally, it refused to recognize and correct the evils at home which had brought it forth; it delayed relief; it forgot reform.

So much for the dispassionate review of the facts of history. I have placed the blame. . . .

In Boston, October 31st, he said:

Instead of doing something during these six years, and especially the last year or two, he participated in encouraging speculation. . . .

And in Baltimore, on October 25th, he said:

The Horseman of Destruction in the Republican Administration gleefully gave encouragement to this speculation. . . . That is when we heard about the "chicken in every pot."

The White House and the Treasury Department issued statements that definitely encouraged and stimulated that speculative boom. . . .

ROOSEVELT CONTENDS THE DEPRESSION WAS WHOLLY OF DOMESTIC ORIGIN

In order to establish the depression as my sole responsibility, it was necessary for Mr. Roosevelt to insist that it was wholly of domestic origin, and that my statements to the contrary were misrepresentation. This was also a part of his contention that we had caused the world depression.

He said, at Columbus, Ohio, August 20, 1932:

Finally, when facts could no longer be ignored and excuses had to be found, Washington discovered that the depression came from abroad. In October of last year, the official policy came to us as follows: "The depression has been deepened by events from abroad which are beyond the control either of our citizens or our Government"—an excuse, note well, my friends, which the President still maintained in his acceptance speech last week. . . .

The records of the civilized Nations of the world prove two facts: first, that the economic structure of other Nations was affected by our own tide of speculation, and the curtailment of our lending helped to bring on their distress; second, *that the bubble burst first in the land of its origin—the United States.*

The major collapse in other countries followed. It was not simultaneous with ours. Moreover, further curtailment of our loans, plus the continual stagnation in trade caused by the Grundy tariff, has continued the depression throughout international affairs.[2]

He said at Sioux City, September 29th:

And so, summing up, this Grundy tariff has largely extinguished the export markets for our industrial and our farm surplus; it has prevented the payment of public and private debts to us and the interest thereon, increasing taxation to meet the expense of our Government, and finally it has driven our factories abroad.

[2] Italics supplied.

The process still goes on, my friends. Indeed, it may be only in its beginnings. The Grundy tariff still retains its grip on the throat of international commerce.

He said at Pittsburgh on October 19th:

I emphasize this history because our opponents have now become almost frantic in their insistence that this entire sequence of events originated abroad. I do not know where; they have never located "abroad," but I think it is somewhere near Abyssinia. . . . The "foreign cause" alibi is just like ascribing measles on our little boy to the spots on his chest, instead of to the contagious germ that he has picked up somewhere.

No, we need not look abroad. . . .

ROOSEVELT CONTENDS I OVERBUILT PRODUCTIVE INDUSTRY

Roosevelt had a muddled charge that I, when Secretary of Commerce, had somehow produced an overexpansion of American industry which, in his view, was one of the prime causes of the world disaster.

He said at Chicago, July 2, 1932:

In the years before 1929 we know that this country had completed a vast cycle of building and inflation; for ten years we expanded on the theory of repairing the wastes of the War, but actually expanding far beyond that, and also beyond our natural and normal growth. . . .

What was the result? Enormous corporate surpluses piled up—the most stupendous in history. Where, under the spell of delirious speculation, did those surpluses go? Let us talk economics that the figures prove and that we can understand. Why, they went chiefly in two directions: first, into new and unnecessary plants which now stand stark and idle; and second, into the call-money market of Wall Street, either directly by the corporations, or indirectly through the banks. Those are the facts. Why blink at them?

Then came the crash. You know the story. Surpluses invested in unnecessary plants became idle. . . .

He said at Columbus, Ohio, August 20th: "It was already obvious even to the Administration that the forced production of our industry was far too great for our domestic markets. . . ."

He said at San Francisco on September 23rd:

Our industrial plant is built; the problem just now is whether . . . it is not overbuilt. Our last frontier has long since been reached, and there is practically no more free land . . . We are now providing a drab living for our own people. . . .

Our task now is not discovery or exploitation of natural resources, or necessarily producing more goods. It is the soberer, less dramatic business of administering resources and plants already in hand, of adjusting production to consumption, of distributing wealth and products more equitably.[3]

He said at Albany, New York, on October 6th:

The theory upon which we have been proceeding for ten years is a shocking impossibility; it is that goods can be produced which cannot be bought.

ROOSEVELT CONTENDS I WAS RESPONSIBLE FOR
GIGANTIC LOSSES ON FOREIGN LOANS

In Roosevelt's mind the long-term private bond issues of foreign borrowers during the time I was Secretary of Commerce were in some way a cause of the depression. His involved argument of this part of my responsibility for the depression appears in his speech at Columbus on August 20, 1932:

The United States, which had already loaned fourteen billions abroad, was lending overseas at a rate of two billion dollars per year. Thus was produced, my friends, the crop of foreign bonds which American investors know to their cost today . . .

He said at Pittsburgh on October 19th:

Those famous loans to "backward and crippled countries," which he said would provide uninterrupted employment and uninterrupted industrial activity by expanding our export trade, no longer could be made.

Debtor Nations, no longer sustained by our improvident loans and no longer able to export goods, were drained of gold for debts and, one by one, were forced to abandon specie payments.

Finally, as a direct result of all these influences, our export markets dried up, our commodity prices slumped and our own domestic business itself

[3] I deal further with this address in Chapter 30.

declined at a more rapid rate than business in some of the backward and crippled countries.

He said at St. Louis on October 21st:

This is an unsavory chapter in American finance. These bonds in large part are the fruit of distressing policies pursued by the present Administration in Washington. None other, if you please, than the policy of lending to backward and crippled countries.

He said at Baltimore on October 25th:

The Horseman of Destruction came likewise from the false policy of lending money to backward and crippled countries. The Administration encouraged the policy that sought to open markets in foreign lands through the lending of American money to these countries. . . . It was utterly and entirely unsound, as I have demonstrated many times. It brought upon us a terrible retribution, and the record shows that this charge which I have made repeatedly in this campaign has never been answered.

MY REPLIES AS TO THE REAL CAUSES OF THE DEPRESSION

So much for the charges. We were to disprove these misrepresentations many times during the campaign.

In commenting on the charge that it was a "Hoover depression," I did not minimize the calamity that had befallen us, but gave facts to make clear the truth as to the forces in motion. I made reference to these questions in nearly every campaign speech, but I quote here only a few major statements. The answers to such misrepresentation unfortunately require more words than just calling it a dishonest statement.

In Washington on August 11, 1932, I said:

. . . The past three years have been a time of unparalleled economic calamity. They have been years of greater suffering and hardship than any which have come to the American people since the aftermath of the Civil War. As we look back over these troubled years we realize that we have passed through two stages of dislocation and stress.

Before the storm broke we were steadily gaining in prosperity. Our wounds from the war were rapidly healing. Advances in science and invention had opened vast vistas of new progress. Being prosperous, we became optimistic—all of us. From optimism some of us went to overexpansion in anticipation of the future, and from overexpansion to reckless speculation. In the soil poisoned by speculation grew those ugly weeds of waste, exploitation, and abuse of financial power. In this overproduction and speculative mania we marched with the rest of the world. Then three years ago came retribution by the inevitable world-wide slump in consumption of goods, in prices, and employment. At that juncture it was the normal penalty for a reckless boom such as we have witnessed a score of times in our history. Through such depressions we have always passed safely after a relatively short period of losses, of hardship and adjustment. We adopted policies in the Government which were fitting to the situation. Gradually the country began to right itself. Eighteen months ago there was a solid basis for hope that recovery was in sight.

Then there came to us a new calamity, a blow from abroad of such dangerous character as to strike at the very safety of the Republic. The countries of Europe proved unable to withstand the stress of the depression.

At Des Moines on October 4th, I reviewed the causes of the European collapse. And at Cleveland on October 15th, I directly answered Mr. Roosevelt's reiterated statements that I, or the Republican party, had brought the depression upon the American people:

Our opponents have been going up and down the land repeating the statement that the sole or major origins of this disruption and this world-wide hurricane came from the United States through the wild flotation of securities and the stock market speculation in New York three years ago, together with the passage of the Smoot-Hawley tariff bill, which took place 9 months after the storm broke. . . .

This thesis of the opposition as to the origin of our troubles is a wonderful explanation for political purposes. I would be glad, indeed, if all the enormous problems in the world could be simplified in such a fashion. If that were all that has been the matter with us, we could have recovered from this depression two years ago instead of fighting ever since that time against the most destructive forces which we have ever met in the whole history of the United States—and I am glad to say fighting victoriously.

Nowhere do I find the slightest reference in all the statements of the opposition party to the part played by the greatest war in history, the inheritances from it, the fears and panics and dreadful economic catastrophes which have developed from these causes in foreign countries, or the idea that they may have had the remotest thing to do with the calamity against which this administration is fighting day and night.

The leaders of the Democratic Party appear to be entirely in ignorance of the effect of the killing or incapacitating of 40,000,000 of the best youth of the earth, or of the stupendous cost of war—a sum of $300,000,000,000, or a sum nearly equal to the value of all the property in the United States, or the stupendous inheritance of debt, with its consequent burden of taxes on scores of nations, with their stifling effect upon recuperation of industry and commerce or paralyzing effect upon world commerce by the continued instability of currencies and budgets.

Democratic leaders have apparently not yet learned of the political instability that arose all over Europe from the harsh treaties which ended the war and the constant continuing political agitation and creation of fear which from time to time paralyzed confidence. They have apparently never heard of the continuing economic dislocation from the transfer on every frontier of great masses of people from their former economic setting.

They apparently have not heard of the continuing dislocation of the stream of economic life which has been caused by the carving of 12 new nations from 3 old empires. These nations have a rightful aspiration to build their own separate economic systems; they naturally have surrounded themselves with tariffs and other national protections and have thereby diverted the long-established currents of trade. I presume, however, that if our Democratic leaders should hear of these nine new tariff walls introduced into the world some 14 years ago they would lay them at the door of the Smoot-Hawley bill passed 12 years later.

They apparently have not heard of the increase of standing armies of the world from two to five million men, with consequent burdens upon the taxpayer and the constant threat to the peace of the world.

Democratic leaders apparently ignore the effect upon us of the revolution among 300,000,000 people in China or the agitations among 300,000,000 people in India, or the Bolshevist revolution among 160,000,000 people in Russia. They have ignored the effect of Russia's dumping into the world the commodities taken from its necessitous people in a desperate effort to secure money with which to carry on—shall I call—a new deal. . . .

The Democratic leaders apparently never heard that there followed revolutions in Spain and Portugal, Brazil, the Argentine, Chile, Peru, Ecuador, Siam, with attempts at revolution in a dozen other countries, resulting in their partial or practical repudiation of debt and the constant decrease in buying power for our goods.

They seem not to know that the further accumulation of all these causes and dislocations finally placed a strain upon the weakened economic systems of Europe until one by one they collapsed in failure of their gold standards and the partial or total repudiation of debts. They would hold the American people ignorant that every one of these nations in their financial crises imposed direct or indirect restrictions on the import of goods in order to reduce expenditures of their people. They call these "reprisals" against the Hawley-Smoot tariff bill.

They apparently have never heard of the succeeding jeopardy in which our nation was put through these destructions of world commerce, or the persistent dumping of securities into the American market from these panic-stricken countries; the gigantic drains upon our gold and exchange; or the consequent fear that swept over our people. . . .

Yet in the face of all these tremendous facts, our Democratic friends leave the impression with the American people that the prime cause of this disaster was the boom in flotations and stock prices and a small increase in American tariffs.

Such an impression is unquestionably sought by the Democratic candidate when he says:

"That bubble burst first in the land of its origin—the United States. The major collapse abroad followed. It was not simultaneous with ours."

. . . As to the accuracy of the statement . . . I may call your attention to a recent bulletin of the highly respected National Bureau of Economic Research, in which it is shown that this depression in the world began in 11 countries, having a population of 600,000,000 people, before it even appeared in our country, instead of the bubble having "first burst in the United States. . . ."

At St. Louis on November 4th I said:

. . . If the Democratic candidate actually wants to put the true causes of this situation before the American people, he should . . . disclose to the American people that the most tremendous fact in modern history was the Great War and its aftermath . . . the difficulties we are now struggling with . . . in the United States consist to a large degree of the tremendous increase in public debt, the foreign war debts and liquidation of war inflation, the necessity to maintain a larger army and navy to protect ourselves in a greatly disturbed world. This war having come on during a Democratic administration, and they having spent the money they should not have forgotten that the undertakings of that period are what create a multitude of the difficulties of this country today. They ought frankly to recognize the problem with which the American people are faced. They should not be appealing to discontent on a basis that ignores their full participation in the real causes.

I again reviewed the destruction in Europe, and the inevitable panic:

... He should recognize the fears which these events produced in our own citizens causing them to draw out $1,600,000,000 and put it into hoarding. . . .

Now all of this statement that I have given to you has importance in four respects: first, because it proves the falsity of the foundation of their campaign; second, because it shows their utter confusion of mind, and either their insincerity or their utter lack of grasp of the forces loose in the world, and consequently the danger of placing men who have such a lack of penetration into the control of the government of 120,000,000 American people; third, because the continuous broadcasting of misinformation . . . as to where this calamity came from . . . does not promise well for the government of these same 120,000,000 people. Fourth, because they should, as a responsible political party, cease to appeal to unthinking people for votes based upon their suffering by misleading them as to its causes.

At St. Paul on November 5th, I said:

Our opponents have endeavored to build a fantastic fiction as to the causes of these events in the last three years . . . and thus resort to the oldest trick of politics. . . . This incapacity to reach to the heart of things is a complete demonstration of their unfitness for the still gigantic task of leading the Nation back to . . . its forward march of progress.

I again reviewed the causes of the storm which struck us from abroad.

MY REPLY UPON THE ORGY OF SPECULATION

With regard to Mr. Roosevelt's statements that I was responsible for the orgy of speculation, I considered for some time whether I should expose the responsibility of the Federal Reserve Board policies from 1925 to 1928 of deliberate inflation under European influence, and my opposition to these policies. I concluded, however, that it would only result in further destruction of confidence and implied an attack on my predecessor in office.

I said at St. Louis on November 4th:

A circular placed in my hands since coming to this state, issued by the Democratic National Committee, says this depression was man-made, and that the man who made it was myself personally. . . .

. . . Despite overwhelming proof to the contrary but in order to make unceasing appeal to discontent, the present Democratic candidate and his corps of orators repeat [this] down to the last twenty-four hours. . . .

. . . In order to continue the false premise . . . he is now thrust back, as his sole remaining explanation, to the boom of 1928. He argues now that if there had never been a boom there never would have been a slump; and if there never had been a slump in the United States there would never have been a depression in the world.

. . . I beg to submit that some of the greatest leaders among the boom promoters of that period belonged to the Democratic Party, and the Democratic candidate himself assisted actually in promotions during that period which he now so warmly denounces. I do not criticize his acts. He was merely participating in the prevailing mood, like the former Democratic candidate who undertook the construction of the tallest building in the world at the same boom time. . . .

Many years ago the Democratic party undertook to remedy this whole question of booms and slumps by the creation of the Federal Reserve System. That was the new discovery of its founders and far from wanting the President to do this job they stipulated that this board should have these powers entirely independent of the President. . . .

It was indeed promised by Democratic leaders at the time the Federal Reserve System was created that they had found the solution to prevent booms, slumps, and panics. I could quote from a multitude of speeches at the time of the passage of the act and further from the assurance given in political campaigns as to this enormous accomplishment of their party.

I find in speeches of President Wilson, Secretary McAdoo, Senator Carter Glass, and other leaders of their party the recurrent idea that . . . the Federal Reserve System would prevent booms and consequently slumps and panics. A few of their expressions are of interest:

"We shall have no more financial panics."

"Panics are impossible."

"Business men can now proceed in perfect confidence that they will no longer put their property in peril."

"Now the business man may work out his destiny without living in terror of panic and hard times."

"Panics in the future are unthinkable."

"Never again can panic come to the American people."

The whole country went along for years with much confidence in these statements, and although no one can say with certainty it is likely that this confidence contributed to the building up of the boom which led to the crash. . . .

I could go further with this argument of futility by pointing out that the leading Democrats did not discover the Republican responsibility of this depression until it reached a vote getting state. Governor Smith two years ago implied that neither he nor any man takes the position of placing the responsibility for the business depression on the President or the Republican Party. And Governor Roosevelt, before he was nominated, made a characteristically vague statement of the same character.

Governor Roosevelt also in a recent speech in defending his boom argument said that when our boom collapsed all but 20 per cent of the people of the world were in a state of prosperity. If he will examine carefully a statement of the National Bureau of Economic Research, whose authority no one denies, he will find that the booms of the following nations had already collapsed: Germany, Australia, Japan, Mexico, Turkey, Rumania, Bolivia, Brazil, India, Poland and Bulgaria, embracing 600,000,000 people, and that coincidently thirteen other nations had been affected by those collapses—that is, the United States, the United Kingdom, Canada, Hungary, Italy, Argentina, South Africa, Czechoslovakia, Austria, Peru, Belgium, the Netherlands, and Spain—had begun to decline. If he will check up the portion of the world included in these nations, he will find he has been misinformed about 300 per cent.

MY REPLIES TO "OVERBUILT INDUSTRY"

Obviously, all our industrial capacity could not be used in time of depression. Mr. Roosevelt seized upon this temporary phenomenon as a *cause,* when in fact, it was simply a consequence. He went so far in this thesis in a speech in San Francisco (which I quote later on) as to assert that we needed no more plants and equipment.

I answered it in an address at New York on October 31st, saying:

...I do challenge the whole idea that we have ended the advance of America, that this country has reached the zenith of its power, the height of its development. That is the counsel of despair for the future of America. That is not the spirit by which we shall emerge from this depression. That is not the spirit that made this country. If it is true, every American must abandon the road of countless progress and unlimited opportunity. I deny that the promise of American life has been fulfilled, for that means we have begun the decline and fall. No nation can cease to move forward without degeneration of spirit.

. . . What Governor Roosevelt has overlooked is the fact that we are yet but on the frontiers of development of science, and of invention. . . . It would be the end of the American system.

. . . Progress . . . was not due to the opening up of new agricultural land; it was due to the scientific research, the opening of new invention, new flashes of light from the intelligence of our people. These brought the improvements in agriculture and in industry. There are a thousand inventions for comfort in the lockers of science and invention which have not yet come to light; all are but on their frontiers. As for myself I am confident that if we do not destroy this American system, if we continue to stimulate scientific research, if we continue to give it the impulse of initiative and enterprise, if we continue to build voluntary cooperative action . . . if we continue to build it into a system of free men, my children will enjoy the same opportunity that has come to me and to the whole 120,000,000 of my countrymen. I wish to see American government conducted in this faith and in this hope.[4]

MY REPLY TO ROOSEVELT'S FOREIGN BOND ISSUES ARGUMENT

Mr. Roosevelt had asserted that I was responsible for fourteen billion dollars of bad private bond issues for foreigners, which contributed to the depression.

There were at this time not 14 billions of private foreign bond issues. There were about 7 billions of these loans outstanding, of which only about 2 billions were in default.

I had repeatedly made public protest at the recklessness of some of these loans, and the regulatory measures I had set up in 1921 were publicly known. Particularly did we constantly warn against such loans

[4] In the six years after Roosevelt died the productivity of the United States increased about 100 per cent over 1929. It would not seem that we were much overbuilt.

SPEAKING AT SALT LAKE CITY

to Germany and former enemy countries as being second to reparations. The major losses arose from this quarter. Mr. Roosevelt never mentioned the kited German short-term bills and as they were still being held in our banks, I could not risk provoking a fear by using that piece of history to our credit.

I said in Indianapolis on October 28th:

... The Democratic candidate has had a great deal to say in endeavoring to establish the idea in the minds of the American people that I am responsible for bad loans by American bankers and investors in foreign countries. ...

The Governor has not stated to the American people my oft-repeated warnings that American loans made in foreign countries should be on sound security and confined to reproductive purposes.[5] ... In one of his addresses the Governor pretends not to be able to understand what a reproductive loan is and yet, as I will show you in a moment, he does know something about it. I will say at once that when we have surplus capital, properly secured loans for reproductive purposes abroad are an advantage to the American people. They furnish work to American labor in the manufacture of plants and equipments; they furnish continuing demand for American labor in supplies and replacements. The effect of such creative enterprise is to increase the standards of living amongst the people in those localities and enable them to buy more American products and furnish additional work for American labor.

I have no apologies to make for that statement. It is sound; it makes for the upbuilding of the world. ... If it be followed there will be no losses. In these statements the Governor entirely omits the conditions and warnings with which I have always pointedly surrounded the statements on this subject. Although no Federal official has the authority to control the security offered

[5] When Mr. Roosevelt used this smear again in 1936, I replied at Philadelphia, October 16th: "It is an economic fact that loans to foreigners must ultimately be transmitted to them in goods, services, or gold. Gold was not shipped. Therefore these private loans made employment of American workmen and American farmers in producing this amount of goods. In fact, those private loans contributed greatly to full employment in the United States during the whole decade of the twenties when unemployment existed in practically every other country in the world. President Roosevelt's statement is the more astonishing as he has himself advocated the loaning of money to foreigners, including Russia, with the excuse that they would create markets for products of American shops and farms. In later years he created the so-called Export Banks for this exact purpose. But in his case he has placed the risk on the taxpayer and not upon the private banker."

on these loans, none have defaulted where my proposed safeguards have been followed.

It is obvious from the Governor's many speeches that he now considers . . . the selling of foreign bonds in our country to be wicked and the cause of our calamities. One interesting part of all this tirade is that I have never been engaged in the selling of foreign bonds or foreign loans. The Governor has the advantage of me in experience in that particular. As late as 1928 the Governor was engaged in that business for profit and actively occupied in promoting such loans. At that time he was chairman of the organization committee of the Federal International Banking Company, a corporation organized for the selling of foreign securities and bonds to the American people. I have in my hand a prospectus of that Corporation in which the foreword, written by Mr. Roosevelt before he resigned this position to take the Governorship, reads as follows:

". . . The Federal International Banking Company will provide a new source of supply from which American demand for foreign investments may be satisfied. . . . It will put to sound protective uses a part of the surplus wealth of our Nation. . . . Its operations will be widely distributed in foreign countries and various industries."

It further states:

". . . that we must aid debtor nations to purchase our products, rehabilitate themselves, expand and develop, and earn money with which to liquidate their debts, that foreign loans should be facilitated to aid the export sale of American products."

Throughout the prospectus constant reference is made to the fact that it is organized under the law, and the impression is given that in consequence it has some sort of official blessing from the Federal Government.

. . . The Governor as a private promoter for profit during the boom of 1928 believed and practiced what the Governor, as Presidential candidate, now denounces as immoral and a cause of our calamities.

ROOSEVELT'S CONTENTION THAT WE FORCED OTHER NATIONS OFF THE GOLD STANDARD

Roosevelt said at Sioux City, Iowa, on September 29th:

Now, there was a secondary and perhaps even more disastrous effect of Grundyism. Billions of dollars of debts are due to this country from abroad. If the debtor nations cannot export goods, they must try to pay in gold. But we started such a drain on the gold reserves of the other nations as to force practically all of them off the gold standard. . . . Why, they just could not buy our goods with their money. These goods then were thrown back upon our markets and prices fell still more.

MY REPLY ON THE GOLD DRAIN

At Des Moines on October 4th I said:

An amazing statement was made a few days ago in this state that the passage of the tariff act of 1930 "started such a drain on the gold reserves of the principal commercial countries as to force practically all of them off the gold standard." The facts are that the tariff act was not passed until nearly one year after the depression began.

The earthquake started in Europe; the gold of Europe was not drained; it has increased in total every year since the passage of the act—and is right now $1,500,000,000 greater than when the act was passed, and the tariff is still on. It has been my daily task to analyze and know the forces which brought these calamities. I have had to look them in the face. They require far more penetration than such assertions as this indicate.

As this was repeated by Roosevelt, I was again compelled on October 15th to state:

. . . My opponent has said that it "Started such a drain on the gold reserves of the principal countries as to force practically all of them off the gold standard."

At Des Moines I defended the American people from this guilt. I pointed out that it happens there had been no drain of gold from Europe, which is the center of this disturbance, but on the contrary, that Europe's gold holdings have increased every year since the Smoot-Hawley tariff was passed.

. . . If it were not a matter of such utter gravity for the future of the United States, I should treat them not in a sense of seriousness but in a sense of humor. . . .

CHAPTER 22

THE "HOOVER DID NOTHING" ISSUE

Mr. Roosevelt not only advanced the thesis that I was responsible for the depression, but also insisted that I had done nothing about it. I give some samples of these frequent assertions:

He said at Chicago, July 2, 1932:

. . . For years Washington has alternated between putting its head in the sand and saying there is no large number of destitute people in our midst who need food and clothing, and then saying the States should take care of them, if they are. . . .

He said at Sioux City on September 29th:

. . . My friends, all that I can tell you is that with you I deplore, I regret the inexcusable, the reprehensible delay of Washington, not for months alone, but for years. . . .

He said at Albany, New York, on October 6th and 13th:

. . . This same leadership has been unable to do more than put temporary patches on a leaking roof without any attempt to put a new roof on our economic structure. . . .

. . . The Federal Government has a "continuous responsibility for human welfare, especially for the protection of children." That duty and responsibility the Federal Government should carry out promptly, fearlessly and generously.

It took the present Republican Administration in Washington almost three years to recognize this principle. I have recounted to you in other speeches, and it is a matter of general information, that for at least two years after the crash, the only efforts made by the national Administration to cope with the distress of unemployment, were to deny its existence.

He said, October 25th, at Baltimore:

The delay that they have practiced is the delay that they want you to adopt when they say, "Give us another term, and maybe we can do better. . . ."

He said on our actions in remedy:

. . . I want to say with all the emphasis that I can command, that this Administration did nothing and their leaders are, I am told, still doing nothing. . . .

The crash came in October, 1929. The President had at his disposal all the instrumentalities of the Government. From that day to December 31st of that year, he did absolutely nothing to remedy the situation. Not only did he do nothing, but he took the position that Congress could do nothing. . . .

He said in Boston on October 31st:

The present leadership in Washington stands convicted, not because it did not have the means to plan, but fundamentally because it did not have the will to do. . . .

. . . I have charged that he did nothing for a long time after the depression began. I repeat that charge. . . .

Instead of doing something during these six years, and especially the last year or two, he participated in encouraging speculation. . . . He failed to prepare action against the recurrence of a depression. On the contrary—the exact contrary—he intensified the forces that made for depressions by encouraging that speculation.

. . . Once more it is a leadership that is bankrupt, not only in ideals but in ideas. It sadly misconceives the good sense and the self-reliance of our people.

MY REPLY TO THE "DID NOTHING" STATEMENT

Simply to denounce all this as just misrepresentation, ignorance, and innuendo served no purpose. To answer required a slow unraveling of the truth—and not very romantic.

I first discussed our activities in an address in Washington on August 11th:

Our emergency measures of the last three years form a definite strategy . . . a continuous campaign waged against the forces of destruction on an ever widening or constantly shifting front.

Thus we have held that the Federal Government should in the presence of great national danger use its powers to give leadership to the initiative, the courage, and the fortitude of the people themselves; but it must insist upon individual, community, and state responsibility. . . . That where it becomes necessary to meet emergencies beyond the power of these agencies by the creation of new government instrumentalities, they should be of such character as not to supplant or weaken, but rather to supplement and strengthen, the initiative and enterprise of the people. . . .

We have not feared boldly to adopt unprecedented measures to meet the unprecedented violence of the storm. But, because we have kept ever before us these eternal principles of our Nation, the American Government in its ideals is the same as it was when the people gave the Presidency into my trust. We shall keep it so. We have resolutely rejected the temptation, under pressure of immediate events, to resort to those panaceas and short cuts which, even if temporarily successful, would ultimately undermine and weaken what has slowly been built and molded by experience and effort throughout these hundred and fifty years.

I then outlined our measures:

These programs, unparalleled in the history of depressions in any country and in any time, to care for distress, to provide employment, to aid agriculture, to maintain the financial stability of the country, to safeguard the savings of the people, to protect their homes, are not in the past tense—they are in action. . . .

And come what may, I shall maintain through all these measures the sanctity of the great principles under which the Republic over a period of 150 years has grown to be the greatest nation on earth.

I said at Des Moines, October 4th:

We have carried on an unceasing campaign to protect the Nation from that unhealing class bitterness which arises from strikes and lockouts and industrial conflict. We have accomplished this through the willing agreement of employer and labor which placed humanity before money through the sacrifice of profits and dividends before wages.

We have defended millions from the tragic result of droughts.

We have mobilized a vast expansion of public construction to make work for the unemployed.

We fought the battle to balance the Budget.

We have defended the country from being forced off the gold standard, with its crushing effect upon all who are in debt.

We have battled to provide a supply of credits to merchants and farmers and industries.

We have fought to retard falling prices.

We have struggled to save homes and farms from foreclosure of mortgages, battled to save millions of depositors and borrowers from the ruin caused by the failure of banks, fought to assure the safety of millions of policyholders from failure of their insurance companies and fought to save commerce and employment from the failure of railways.

We have fought to secure disarmament and maintain the peace of the world, fought for stability of other countries whose failure would inevitably injure us. And, above all, we have fought to preserve the safety, the principles and ideals of American life. We have builded the foundations of recovery. . . .

Many of these battles have had to be fought in silence, without the cheers of the limelight or the encouragement of public support, because the very disclosure of the forces opposed to us would have undermined the courage of the weak and induced panic in the timid, which would have destroyed the very basis of success.

Hideous misrepresentation and unjustified complaint had to be accepted in silence. It was as if a great battle in war should be fought without public knowledge of any incident except the stream of dead and wounded from the front. There has been much of tragedy, but there has been but little public evidence of the dangers and enormous risks from which a great national victory has been achieved.

I spoke at Detroit on October 22nd of the measures introduced:

I should like for a moment to review the whole program we proposed and have largely established to meet this emergency. Some of its effectiveness was lost by delays in placing these weapons in our hands, for in battle much depends upon being there on time. Some part of the losses, in failures, bankruptcies, falls in farm prices, increases in unemployment, was due to these delays. . . . *Much of it, and refusal to enact some measures, were the consequence of destructive Democratic opposition. . . .*

I then discussed in detail the measures which I have recounted in earlier chapters, and concluded:

It is now taken for granted that this Republican program has come of its natural self because in retrospect there is such universal recognition of its necessity. On the contrary, it has been wrought out of the fiery ordeal of hard and honest thought, the facing of the facts when loose-thinking or frightened men offered every temptation of specious panaceas. It was wrought against the heartbreaking obstructions and delays of the Democratic House.

. . . It is working every minute.

I stated at Indianapolis on October 28th:

The Governor of New York in a speech on October 25th stated:
"The crash came in October, 1929. The President had at his disposal all the instrumentalities of the Government. . . . He did absolutely nothing to remedy the situation. Not only did he do nothing, but he took the position that Congress could do nothing."
. . . It seems almost incredible that a man, a candidate for the Presidency of the United States, would broadcast such a violation of the truth. The front pages of every newspaper in the United States for the whole of those two years proclaimed the untruth of such statements. . . .

Again I reviewed the measures, step by step, beginning in 1929:

The Governor entirely ignores the most patent fact in the history of this depression—that, under the wise policies pursued, recovery of the United States from this first phase of the depression—that is, collapse from our own speculation and boom—began about a year after the crash, and continued definitely and positively until April, 1931, when the European crash took place.

And again the Governor, despite every proof, keeps reiterating the implication that measures taken by this administration have brought no fruitful result to the common man. He has been told . . . that the gigantic crisis which the United States faced was escaped by the narrowest margin, and that this was due to the unprecedented measures adopted by this administration. . . .

Why can [the Governor] not be frank enough to recognize the successful care of the distressed in the United States; that a vast amount of employment has been provided; that the savings of more than 95 per cent of the depositors in our banks have been held secure; that the 20,000,000 borrowers who otherwise would have been bankrupt by destructive pressures from forced selling of their assets in order to pay their debts have been protected; that the 70,000,000 life-insurance policies which represent the greatest act of self-denial of our people in provision for the future safety of their loved ones have been sustained in their validity; that foreclosure of hundreds of thousands of home and farm mortgages has been prevented?

He knows that the integrity of our currency has been sustained, that the credit of the Federal Government has been maintained, that credit and employment are being expanded every day.

The living proof of these measures, which were conceived from the human heart as well as the mind, can be found in the men and women in every city, every town, every township, and every block in this broad land, for they have been saved their jobs and secured from suffering.

I said at St. Louis on November 4th:

The whole campaign has many aspects parallel with a campaign which took place in a former depression, of which I will read you a short description from a journal published in Washington during that time. That journal said more than half a century ago—

"The circumstance on which the Democratic Party base their hope of success in the present campaign is unquestionably the hardness of the times. . . . Even the ravages of the grasshoppers, damages to the crops by drought in some sections and excessive moisture in others are to be traced by some mysterious process to the maladministration and extravagance of the Republican Party."

I summed up these monstrous campaign lies at St. Paul on November 5th, in a list of the twenty-one major measures taken by the Federal government and the crises they met. I then went on to summarize the deliberate sabotage by the Democratic Congress:

And now in contrast with this construction program of the Republican party I wish to develop for you the Democratic program to meet this depression as far as we have been able to find any definition to it. I would again call your attention to the fact that with the Democratic victory in Congressional elections of 1930 their leaders promised to produce a program which would redeem this country from the depression. No such program was produced, but. . . .

1. They passed the Collier Bill, providing for destruction of the Tariff Commission by reducing it again to a mere statistical body controlled by the Congress. . . .

2. They attempted to instruct me by legislation to call an international conference . . . by which the independence of the United States in control of its domestic policies was to be placed in the hands of an international body.

3. They passed an act instructing me to negotiate reciprocal tariffs, the result of which could only be . . . the reduction of farm tariffs in order to build up markets for other goods.

4. They passed an omnibus pension bill with unworthy payments as an indication of their economical temper.

5. They passed an inadequate patchwork revenue bill, the injustices of which to different industries and groups must yet be remedied.

6. They passed Indian claims bills to reopen settlements of 75 years ago in order to favor certain localities at the expense of the public Treasury.

7. They passed a bill instructing the Federal Reserve System and the Treasury to fix prices at averages prevailing during the years 1921 to 1929 by constantly shifting the volume of currency . . . thus creation of . . . a rubber dollar. This bill was stopped, but it has not been removed from their political calendar.

8. They defeated a large part of the national economy measure proposed by the Administration, by reduction of ordinary expenditures from $250,000,000 to less than $50,000,000. . . .

9. They passed the Garner-Rainey pork barrel bill increasing expenditures by $1,200,000,000 for unnecessary, non-productive public works, purely for the benefit of favored localities. We stopped this bill, but it is still on their political calendar.

10. They passed the cash prepayment of the bonus calling for immediate expenditure of $2,300,000,000 [in fiat paper money]. . . . We stopped this bill but it is still on their political calendar.

11. They passed the provision for the issuance of over $2,200,000,000 of greenback currency, a reversion to vicious practices already demonstrated in the last hundred years as the most destructive to labor, agriculture, and business. We stopped this bill and even as late as last night the Democratic candidate failed to frankly disavow it.

12. They passed the Rainey bill providing for direct personal banking for any conceivable purpose on every conceivable security to everyone who wants money, and thus the most destructive entry of the Government into private

business in a fashion that violates every principle of our Nation. I vetoed this bill—but Mr. Garner still advocates it and it has not been removed from their political promises.

13. They injected an expenditure of $322,000,000 for entirely unnecessary purposes in time of great emergency. . . .

14. The Congress passed [no] proper authority to the Executive for reorganization and elimination of useless Government commissions and bureaus. . . .

15. The Democratic candidate eloquently urges the balancing of the Budget, but nowhere disavows these gigantic raids on the Treasury, under which a Budget cannot be balanced.

Thus far is the program of the Democratic House under the leadership of Mr. Garner whose policies the Democratic party ratified by nominating him Vice President.

I then summarized Roosevelt's remedy for the depression:

16. The Democratic candidate adds to this program the proposal to plant a billion trees and thereby immediately employ a million men, but the Secretary of Agriculture has shown that the trees available to plant will give them a total less than three days' work.

17. The candidate promises to relieve agriculture with a 6-point program. . . . He disclosed no details of the plan except six methods by which he can escape from the promise.

18. The candidate has promised the immediate inauguration of a program of . . . public works, . . . to provide "employment for all surplus labor at all times." It would exceed in cost $9,000,000,000 a year. The works are unavailable, the cost would destroy the credit of the Government, deprive vast numbers of the men now working of their jobs and thus destroy the remedy itself. This fantasy is a cruel promise to these suffering men and women that they will be given jobs by the Government which no government could fulfill.

19. The Democratic Party makes its contribution to the emergency by proposing to reduce the tariff. . . . Their candidate states that he supports this promise 100 per cent. . . .

These are the only reliefs to this emergency that I can find in the whole Democratic program.

ATTACKS UPON OUR NEW CREDIT INSTITUTIONS

As a supplement to the "did nothing" argument, Roosevelt sought to minimize our measures to put props under our weak credit system.

Mr. Roosevelt either ignored or sneered at our measures to strengthen the financial structure.

He scarcely mentioned the Reconstruction Finance Corporation; our provisions for the farmers by granting large credits through the farm cooperatives; the enlarged resources of the Federal Land Banks; our Intermediate Credit Banks; our new system of Agricultural Production Banks. He deprecated the Home Loan Banks and the greatly expanded powers of the Federal Reserve System to assist business and agriculture.

He said at Albany on April 7th:

Closely associated with this . . . is the problem of keeping the home-owner and the farm-owner where he is, without being dispossessed through the foreclosure of his mortgage. . . . The two billion dollar fund which President Hoover and the Congress have put at the disposal of the big banks, the railroads and the corporations of the Nation is not for him.

He said at Topeka on September 14th:

In the first place, there is the necessity, as we all know, for the refinancing of farm mortgages in order to relieve the burden of excessive interest charges and the grim threat of foreclosure. Much was done in the last session of Congress to extend and liquefy and pass on to the Federal Government—the Nation—the burden of debt of railroads, banks, utilities and industry in general. Something in the nature of a gesture was made in the direction of financing urban homes. *But practically nothing was done toward removing the destructive menace of debt from farm homes.* . . .

He said at Sioux City, September 29th:

Today I read in the papers that *for the first time, so far as I know, the administration of President Hoover has discovered the fact that there is such a thing as a farm mortgage or a home mortgage.*

At Pittsburgh, October 19th, he said:

My program is opposed to, and aims to stop, the ruthless foreclosure of farm mortgages.

MY ANSWERS AS TO OUR CREDIT ACTIVITIES

I necessarily devoted a good deal of time in the campaign to clarifying the purposes and achievements of our credit operations.

At Washington on August 11th, I reviewed our actions in sustaining the credit structure, step by step.

As to mortgages on homes, I said at Cleveland, October 15th:

There is an agency of protection which we have created which has been near to my heart over many years. That has been the establishment of better opportunity for our people to purchase their own homes and to have a chance to keep them when they have undertaken this great step in life. In November of last year I propounded a plan for a national system of Home Loan Banks. These banks were for the purpose, with the temporary assistance of the Government, of mobilizing the resources of building loan, savings banks, and other institutions devoted to home ownership to enable them to borrow collectively on more favorable terms from the investor, and to assure to the borrower long-term payments at more reasonable rates. The literally thousands of heart-breaking instances of inability of working people to attain renewal of expiring mortgages on favorable terms, and the consequent loss of their homes, have been one of the tragedies of this depression. Had the Democratic House of Representatives acted upon this measure at the time of its recommendation, we would have saved hundreds of thousands of these tragedies.

I finally secured the passage of that bill through the Congress. Those banks will be operating by the end of this month. . . . It has already had one immensely beneficial effect, and there will be others. The anticipation of its aid has largely stopped foreclosing on homes, and with its operation it should afford every man, who wants to make a fight to hold on to his home, an opportunity to do so.

Speaking again on the mortgage question, I said as to the purposes of the RFC, the enlargement of Federal Reserve functions, the Farm Board, the Federal Land Banks, Home Loan Banks, etc., at Detroit on October 22nd:

Practically the only evidence of the attitude of the Democratic candidate upon this program is the sneer that it has been designed to help banks and corporations, that it has not helped the common man. He knows full well that the only purpose of helping an insurance company is to protect the policyholder. He knows full well that the only purpose in helping a bank is to protect the depositor and the borrower. He knows full well that the only purpose of helping a farm-mortgage company is to enable the farmer to hold his farm. He knows full well that the only purpose of helping the building and loan associations is to protect savings and homes. He knows full well that in sustaining the business man it maintains the worker in his job. He knows full well that in loans to the states it protects the families in distress.

Millions of men and women are employed today because there has been restored to their employer the ability to borrow the money to buy raw materials and pay labor and thus keep his job. If he be a farmer, it has restored his ability to secure credit upon which to produce his crops and livestock. If he be a home owner or a farm owner in jeopardy of foreclosure of his mortgage, it now gives him a chance. . . . If he be a merchant, it has stopped the calling of his loans and today enables him again to borrow to purchase his stock and thus start employment. If he be unemployed, it is making hundreds of thousand of jobs. If he be in distress it enables his state or city to secure the money which assures him that he will not suffer hunger and cold. Those who are in distress in this city are today receiving their bread and their rent from the result of these measures. But beyond this it is today creating new jobs and giving to the whole system a new breath of life. Nothing has ever been devised in our history which has done more for . . . the common run of men and women.

At Indianapolis, October 28th, I spoke again on these misrepresentations. I again showed the deliberate sabotage of these measures by the Democratic members of Congress, adding as to the Home Loan legislation:

Had that bill been passed when it was introduced, nearly a year ago, the suffering and losses of thousands of small-home owners in the United States would have been prevented. . . .

At St. Louis on November 4th, I said:

The Governor should recognize that unless we had taken other strong and unprecedented measures we could not have prevented the collapse of our insurance companies, our banks, the foreclosures on millions of homes and farms, the strangulation of credit which would have brought about almost total unemployment.[1]

---

[1] It is scarcely necessary to mention that after coming to the Presidency, almost the whole of Roosevelt's credit supports were built upon our measures—by adding to their authorities those which had been denied to my administration by the Democratic Congress.

RECOVERY FROM THE DEPRESSION WAS IN MOTION

The best answer to all this depression issue was our economic upswing from the bottom of the depression in July, 1932. Indeed our only hope of winning the campaign was a rapid economic upturn. Only that would carry complete public conviction as to the rightness of our policies. However, we needed another six months to prove it fully. I, of course, pointed repeatedly to the steady recovery that was already taking place at home and abroad.

At Des Moines on October 4th, I said:

Recovery began the moment when it was certain that these destructive measures of this Democratic-controlled House were stopped. Had their program passed, it would have been the end of recovery. If it ever passes, it will end hope of recovery. . . .

. . . The battle against depression is making progress. . . . We have forged new weapons, we have turned the tide from defense to attack. I shall continue the fight. . . .

The rills of credit are expanding. . . . Men are daily being reemployed. If we calculate the values of this year's agricultural products compared with the low points, the farmers as a whole are, despite the heartbreaking distress which still exists, a billion dollars better off.

At Detroit on October 22nd, I said:

. . . The measures and policies of the Republican administration are winning this major battle for recovery. They are taking care of distress in the meantime. . . . The tide has turned and the gigantic forces of depression are in retreat. Our measures and policies . . . have preserved the American people from certain chaos and have preserved a final fortress of stability in the world. Recovery would have been faster but for four months of paralysis during the [six] . . . months we were defeating proposals of the Democratic House of Representatives. . . .

Since it was known that the destructive proposals of the Democratic House were stopped, over $300,000,000 of gold has flowed into our country through restored confidence abroad; $250,000,000 of currency has returned from hoarding through restoration of confidence at home; the values of bonds have increased by 20 per cent, thus safeguarding every depositor in a savings bank and every policyholder in an insurance company. Manufacturing production has increased by 10 per cent. Some groups, such as textiles, have increased over 50 per cent in activity.

Contrary to the usual seasonal trend, building contracts have steadily increased. The Department of Commerce shows that over 180,000 workers returned to the manufacturing industry in August, 360,000 more in September, and there is evidence of even a still larger number in October. Car loadings have increased from 490,000 per week to 650,000 per week. . . . Exports and imports have increased nearly 23 per cent. Agricultural prices, always the last to move, have improved from their low points. . . . Bank failures have almost ceased; credit has begun to expand. Every week some improvement is recorded somewhere. . . . Improvement would have begun four months earlier but for the fear of the destructive Democratic program.

I reviewed further progress at Indianapolis on October 28th. At St. Louis on November 4th:

Since the adjournment of the Democratic House of Representatives last July down to the present moment, over 1,000,000 men have gone back to their normal jobs. They are going back at the rate of 500,000 a month unless they are intercepted by a change in policies.

. . . [The Democratic] leaders have taken no patriotic satisfaction in the fact that a million men have returned to work since the malign influence of the Democratic House and their allies was removed by adjournment of Congress, and the Republican measures and policies had an opportunity to work.

And at St. Paul on November 5th:

Over a million men have now returned to work in these four months.
. . . Certainly we are now gaining a half million a month.

Production of boots and shoes amounted to 34,000,000 pairs in October . . . higher than the same month of the previous year.

Hoarded currency continues to return; imports of gold withdrawn by frightened European holders have continued to increase; deposits of banks continue to show steady expansion. . . . They have increased by nearly a billion dollars. This is money being put to work and an evidence of renewed confidence.

A further indication . . . lies in the increased demand for electrical power, which has increased by over 8 per cent in the last four months. Every business index shows some progress somewhere in the nation.

However, the upturn was halted by the Maine elections at the end of September which, in effect, went against us. The fears of the business world at Roosevelt's announced policies started a downward movement for the next six weeks which greatly nullified our hopes of mitigating the political influence of the depression.

CHAPTER 23

THE FEDERAL EXPENSES AND TAX ISSUE

Roosevelt spent much time in severe criticism of our expenditures, taxes, and deficits. To grasp the significance of the "expenditures and taxes" aspect of the campaign the reader must have some understanding of the working of the Federal budget. Roosevelt in his discussions separated "ordinary" from "extraordinary" expenses. In the next section of this volume, I give a detailed statement of our annual expenditures and receipts on that basis.

Roosevelt asserted that our deficit was $5,000,000,000. Our apparent deficit for the whole four years was $3,447,000,000. But this included $2,459,000,000 of "extraordinary expenditures" for recoverable loans of the RFC and the various agricultural and home loan agencies. All of them were repaid subsequently. The burden on the taxpayer, or increase in the national debt, was less by this amount. Thus the net deficit was about $1,000,000,000, which represented the true increase of the national debt for my four years that would fall upon the taxpayer.

Even this whole deficit was due to the loss of revenue and not from increased expenditures. If revenues had remained at pre-depression levels, we would have had a surplus of more than $1,500,000,000, even after deducting all expenditures, including the recoverable loans.

Mr. Roosevelt ignored the fact that revenues had dropped by $2,000,000,000 a year, and that our increased "extraordinary" expenses were for relief, public works, and recoverable loans to support the distressed and bolster up the economic structure during the depression.

To a public unfamiliar with governmental accounts, it was difficult to demonstrate such misrepresentation adequately. The proof lay in later years. Despite an increase in taxes enacted during my last year, he had a deficit in his first four years of $13,078,000,000. Had he carried out his promise to reduce expenses 25 per cent (which gained him many votes), his total expenditures for these four years would have been $12,800,000,000 instead of the actual figure of $27,000,000,000. Never has a broken promise been so politically profitable and—so costly to the public.

Some specimens of his vigor in the good cause of reducing expenditures follow.

Mr. Roosevelt on July 30th repeated the Democratic platform with solemn assurances of his approval:

[I promise] an immediate and drastic reduction of governmental expenditures by abolishing useless commissions and offices . . . and eliminating extravagances . . . to accomplish a saving of not less than 25 per cent in the cost of Federal government. . . . Maintenance of national credit by a Federal budget annually balanced on the basis of accurate Executive estimates within revenues, raised by a system of taxation levied on the principle of ability to pay. . . .

Then he continued:

When the depression began, the administration, instead of reducing annual expenses to meet decreasing revenues, became sponsor for deficits which at the end of this fiscal year will have added $5,000,000,000 to the national debt.

To meet this staggering deficit, the administration has resorted to the type of inflation which has weakened public confidence in our government credit both at home and abroad.

High-sounding, newly invented phrases cannot sugar-coat the pill.

Let us have the courage to stop borrowing to meet continuing deficits. Stop the deficits. Let us have equal courage to reverse the policy of the Republican leaders.

He said at Sioux City on September 29th:

I accuse the present administration of being the greatest spending administration in peace times in all our history. . . .

And on my part I ask you very simply to assign to me the task of reducing the annual operating expenses of your national government.

He said at Pittsburgh on October 19th:

Our Federal extravagance and improvidence bear a double evil: first, our people and our business cannot carry these excessive burdens of taxation;

second, our credit structure is impaired by the unorthodox Federal financing made necessary by the unprecedented magnitude of these deficits. . . .

[The Administration] throws discretion to the winds, and is willing to make no sacrifice at all in spending; if it extends its taxing to the limit of the people's power to pay and continues to pile up deficits, then it is on the road to bankruptcy.

. . . Upon the financial stability of the United States government depends the stability of trade and employment, and of the entire banking, savings and insurance system of the nation.

To make things clear, to explain the exact nature of the present condition of the Federal pocketbook, I must go back to 1929.

Let me repeat those figures so that the whole country can get them clearly in mind. Leaving out "debt service charges" in both instances, the cost of carrying on the usual business of the United States was $2,187,000,000 in 1927, $3,168,000,000 in 1931—an increase in four years of one billion dollars!

That, my friends, is the story on the spending side of the ledger. But you and I know that there are always two sides—or ought to be—to a ledger that is supposed to balance. It is bad enough—that story of the spending side, and a billion dollar increase, that 50 per cent increase in four years! But it is less than half of the whole appalling story. . . .

. . . The plain precept of our party . . . is to reduce the cost of current Federal operations by 25 per cent. . . .

At St. Louis on October 21st, Roosevelt said:

I called attention in my address at Pittsburgh on Wednesday night to the great importance of Federal budget making as the foundation of the national credit. I pointed out that the Hoover administration had been responsible for deficit after deficit; that as one disastrous year succeeded another, no attempt was made to arrange the finances of the country so that at least the mounting loss of revenue might not be turned into a deficit for the next year. It is my pledge and promise that this dangerous kind of financing shall be stopped and that rigid governmental economy shall be enforced by a stern and unremitting administration policy of living within our income.

On July 2nd, accepting the nomination for the Presidency, Mr. Roosevelt said:

Just one word or two on taxes, the taxes that all of us pay toward the cost of government of all kinds.

I know something of taxes. For three long years I have been going up and down this country preaching that government—Federal and state and local—costs too much.

I propose to you, my friends, and through you, that government of all kinds, big and little, be made solvent and that the example be set by the President of the United States and his Cabinet.

He said at Pittsburgh on October 19th:

While the President claims that he did finally recommend new taxes, I fear this courage came two years too late and in far too scanty measure. . . . Perhaps it explains two complete concealments of deficits and the insufficiency of the action taken last winter. It is an error of weakness and an error which I assure you I will not make.

MY ANSWERS ON EXPENDITURES AND TAXES

At Washington on August 11th, I restated my actions on expenditures, balancing the budget, and reorganization of the government, all of which had appeared previously in a score of messages to Congress and public statements. I continued:

If we except those extraordinary expenditures imposed upon us by the depression, it will be found that the Federal government is operating for $200,000,000 less annually today than four years ago. The Congress rejected recommendations from the administration which would have saved an additional $150,000,000 this fiscal year. The opposition leadership insisted, as the price of vital reconstruction legislation and over my protest, upon adding $300,000,000 of costs to the taxpayer. . . . The opposition leadership in the House of Representatives in the last four months secured passage by the House of $3,000,000,000 in such raids. They have been stopped.

In Detroit on October 22nd, I said:

The Democratic candidate says that we have been extravagant, and in his various statements implies that we should make a defense of our policies. There will be no defense; none is needed. The ordinary expenses of the Federal government, except for relief purposes, have been reduced, while those of the government of New York State have been increased. Moreover, there will be proof that the Governor of New York, no doubt through ignorance of our fiscal system or through misinformation supplied to him, and totally ignoring the actions of the Democratic House of Representatives, has broadcast a misstatement of facts. . . . His conclusions are amazingly removed from the truth.

So few of the statements made by the Democratic candidate are in accordance with records of fact that it leaves me nonplused where to begin. It would take hours to dissect his each line and paragraph, so I must confine myself to a few representative misstatements.

. . . The Governor says he wants only to "compare the routine government outlay," "the ordinary costs of conducting government," and excludes all extraordinary items in his comparisons. On this basis, he says, we increased the routine ordinary cost of government by $1,000,000,000 between 1927 and 1931. . . .

The Governor states that . . . he will deduct from each of these comparative years what he calls "an exceptional item." . . .

The actual expenditures for 1927 were $3,585,000,000. For 1931 they were $4,220,000,000, or an increase of $635,000,000. Bear in mind the Governor says he wants to "compare the routine ordinary costs of conducting the government." He also says that he favors relief measures by the government. He then neglects to inform the country that the increased expenditures for 1931 over and above those for 1927 were almost wholly for relief of the depression. They include . . . emergency expenditures in relief of the depression of $815,000,000, and if we adopt the Governor's own definition of ordinary routine expenditures and deduct this sum, then the ordinary routine costs of government for 1931 were actually less than those of 1927—not one billion greater, as he states.

The year 1927 was an especially low year . . . and if the Governor wanted to be fair he could have adopted the [fiscal] year 1929, the last year before my Administration, in which you can be sure there was no waste under President Coolidge. . . . Had the Governor adopted that year with its total expenditures of $3,848,000,000 and deducted from 1931 the extraordinary expenditures due to relief, he would find there was an actual decrease in expenditures of upward of $300,000,000 in the ordinary conduct of government below the Coolidge level.

But of more importance, the Governor promises that he will reduce Federal expenditures a billion a year.

If the Governor means to reduce government expenditures $1,000,000,000 below "ordinary routine" costs of government, . . . then he must know the places where such reduction can be made.

To help him I may say that the "ordinary routine" expenditures for the current fiscal year are estimated at $3,647,000,000. Of these $1,980,000,000 are for public debt and certain trust and refund services to which the government is obligated, together with expenditures upon the Army and Navy. In the present disturbed state of the world we must not further reduce our defenses without a general agreement on reduction of arms. Thus, the Governor must find a cut of $1,000,000,000 out of the remaining $1,667,000,000 of "ordinary routine" government expenditures. Of this sum, $946,000,000 is for veterans and $216,000,000 for ordinary public works, while all other costs of government are about $505,000,000.

The last item includes the conduct of Congress, the judiciary, prisons, tax collection, accounting, foreign relations, public health, maintenance of lighthouses and airways, merchant marine, education, agriculture, various scientific bureaus, and a host of other critically important services. Assuming the wildest estimate, that these services could be reduced by one half, that half the lighthouses could be extinguished, half the Federal prisoners turned loose on the public, the Governor would still have to find $750,000,000 of economy. Even if he stopped all public works, he would finally have to take $500,000,000 off the $946,000,000 which the veterans receive. That would be a gross injustice. But that is where rash promises will inevitably lead.

After reviewing the actions of the Democratic Congress on economy,[1] I proceeded:

The Governor implies that . . . we have jeopardized the credit of the Federal government. The answer is . . . only ten days ago the Treasury sold $500,000,000 of notes at 3 per cent interest. That does not look like a discredited institution. . . .

The Governor's labored charge that . . . the facts were . . . concealed from the people is too silly to merit serious consideration. The actual Federal expenditures and receipts are issued to the public every day in the year at nine-thirty o'clock in the morning. . . .

Now I wish to turn for a moment to the specific Democratic program as shown by . . . actions in the House of Representatives. I have only to repeat and enumerate them. I hope by this time you are familiar with them. I can remember them by the dates when they were passed by the House of Representatives.

[1] See Chaps. 16, 18, 21.

March 4, 1932: The Gasque omnibus pension bill was passed by the House. As I have said, I vetoed it.

March 7, 1932: The revenue bill, introduced by the nonpartisan Ways and Means Committee, was torn to pieces on the floor of the Democratic House. It had to be sent back to committee, and an inadequate patchwork bill was substituted and passed. Long and harmful delays resulted. The injustices in that bill are yet to be remedied.

April 13, 1932: As I have said, I vetoed a bill passed by the Democratic House that would have set in train the opening of large Indian claims settled over seventy-five years ago. This was not in accordance with Democratic claims of economy.

May 3, 1932: The House committees and the Democratic House refused to pass the economies originally proposed by the administration from $250,000,-000 and reduced them to less than $50,000,000.

June 7, 1932: The Democratic Garner-Rainey bill was passed by the House, one section of which provided for increased expenditures by the taxpayer of $1,200,000,000. This was the pork-barrel bill. This bill did not get through the Senate because of public protest. The Democratic Vice-Presidential candidate still advocates it.

June 15, 1932: The Patman bill was passed by the Democratic House providing for the cash prepayment of adjusted-service certificates to veterans, requiring the immediate expenditure of $2,300,000,000.

June 15, 1932: The Democratic House passed a provision for the issuance of $2,300,000,000 of fiat money—a form of currency inflation best exemplified by the similar action by the German government in issuing paper marks in 1922. Had this measure ever become law, every farmer and every workman would be paying penalties for it today.

July 13, 1932: The House passed a bill injecting $322,000,000 of expenditures upon the taxpayer against my protests. These are by no means all the Democratic House did, but they indicate the controlling elements of that party.

I said at Indianapolis on October 28th:

We have listened to much prattle from the opposition about reducing government expenses. . . .

If I receive a mandate from the American people in this election, I shall be able not only to force upon this Democratic House real economies, but also be able to stop further raids by the Democratic party on the Treasury of the United States.

THE ISSUE ON EFFICIENT REORGANIZATION OF THE FEDERAL DEPARTMENTS

Mr. Roosevelt, ignoring the fact that the Democratic Congress had held up and finally defeated my proposals for reorganization of the Federal departments,[2] said on July 2nd in Chicago:

As an immediate program of action we must abolish useless offices. We must eliminate unnecessary functions of government—functions, in fact, that are not definitely essential to the continuance of government. We must merge, we must consolidate subdivisions of government, and, like the private citizen, give up luxuries which we can no longer afford.

At Sioux City on September 29th he said:

It is an administration that has piled bureau on bureau, commission on commission, and has failed to anticipate the dire needs and the reduced earning power of the people. Bureaus and bureaucrats, commissions and commissioners have been retained at the expense of the taxpayer.

At Pittsburgh on October 19th he said:

I have sought to make two things clear: first, that we can make savings by reorganization of existing departments, by eliminating functions, by abolishing many of those innumerable boards and those commissions which, over a long period of years, have grown up as a fungus growth on American government. These savings can properly be made to total many hundreds and thousands of dollars a year.

Roosevelt continued to talk on this issue in his October 25th, November 4th, and other speeches.

MY ANSWER ON REORGANIZATION OF THE DEPARTMENTS

Mr. Roosevelt's criticism of our failure to reduce bureaus and offices was complete misrepresentation as to the Congressional authority. A very limited authority, after two years of sabotage, had been granted to me in the last days of Congress in July, 1932, but was only operative while Congress was in session, and therefore could not even be proposed by me until December after this election was over. Moreover, it was the

[2] Three years later Roosevelt, asserting he had no authority, made exactly my proposals. Reorganization was not really undertaken until 1947–1948 by a Commission under my direction.

only particular ever stated by him as to his method of reducing government expenses 25 per cent (i.e., $1,000,000,000 per annum). The total savings by this route at the time could not possibly have exceeded one-fifth of this sum.

In Washington on August 11th I remarked:

I have repeatedly for seven years urged the Congress either themselves to abolish obsolete bureaus and commissions and to reorganize the whole government structure in the interest of economy, or to give someone the authority to do so. I have succeeded partially in securing authority, but I regret that no substantial act under it is to be effective until approved by the next Congress.

In Detroit on October 22nd:

The Governor points with satisfaction to the increase in expenditures of the Department of Commerce under my administration. He neglects to inform the American people that these increases were nearly all due to the transfer of bureaus to that Department with corresponding decrease in expenditures in other departments.

In Indianapolis on October 28th, I said:

The Democratic candidate has annexed, as if it were a new discovery, the recommendations which I made in 1922 and have continuously advocated ever since for the reorganization of the whole Federal administrative structure for the purpose of economy by the consolidation of bureaus and the elimination of useless boards and commissions. . . . If the Democratic candidate will read the law and inform himself fully upon the subject he must withdraw that statement.

CHAPTER 24

THE GOLD STANDARD AND MANAGED CURRENCY ISSUES

Both Secretary Mills and I were confidentially informed early in the campaign that some of Mr. Roosevelt's advisers proposed an abandonment of the gold standard or devaluation, and the substitution of a "managed currency" as an over-all method of raising prices and wages and providing a "scientific currency."

The Democratic platform, often repeated by Mr. Roosevelt, provided these weasel words:

A sound currency to be preserved at all hazards and an international monetary conference called on the invitation of our government to consider the rehabilitation of silver.

The omission of the word "gold" and the substitution of the weasel word "sound" was a compromise with the whole "soft money" history of the Democratic party. That history embraced proposals of greenbacks and "free silver"; the recent "rubber dollar"; and the fiat money legislation passed by the very last Democratic House in 1932. This in itself was a confirmation that tinkering with the currency was on the way again.

OUR POLICIES

Secretary Mills and I determined to smoke out in the campaign the whole devaluation-managed currency and fiat money issue. I launched our campaign on this issue at Des Moines on October 4th in a speech that began by describing our monetary policies and continued with the evidences of Democratic policies:

I wish to describe one of the battles we have fought to save this nation from a defeat that would have dragged farmers and city dwellers alike down to a common ruin. This battle was fought parallel with other battles on other fronts. Much of what I will tell you has been hitherto undisclosed. It had to be fought in silence, for it will be evident to you that had the whole of the forces in motion been made public at the time there would have been no hope of victory because of the panic through fear and destruction of confidence that very disclosure would have brought.

Happily we have won this battle. There is no longer any danger from disclosure.

When eighteen months ago the financial systems of Europe were no longer able to stand the strain of their war inheritances . . . an earthquake ran through forty nations. Financial panics; governments unable to meet their obligations; banks unable to pay their depositors; citizens, fearing inflation of currency, seeking to export their savings to foreign countries for safety; citizens of other nations demanding payment of their loans; financial and monetary systems either in collapse or remaining only in appearance. The shocks of this earthquake ran from Vienna to Berlin, from Berlin to London, from London to Asia and South America. From all those countries they came to this country to every city and farm in the United States.

First one and then another of these forty nations either abandoned payment in gold or their obligations to other countries. . . .

The shocks grew in violence and finally at the end of September a year ago the difficulties of Europe culminated with the suspension of gold payments by the Bank of England, followed by many other nations. . . .

The shocks which rocked these nations came from profound depths; their spread gave fearful blows to our own system, finally culminating in what, had they not been courageously met with unprecedented measures, would . . . have brought us to greater collapse than even other countries . . . made it impossible for American citizens to collect billions of the moneys due to us for goods which our citizens had sold abroad, or short-term loans they had made . . . At the same time citizens of those countries demanded payment from our citizens of the moneys due . . . and for securities they had sold in our country.

Before the end foreign countries drained us of nearly a billion dollars of gold and a vast amount of other exchange.

Then we had also to meet an attack upon our own flank by some of our own people, who, becoming infected with world fear and panic, withdrew

ON THE CAMPAIGN OF 1932

vast sums from our own banks and hoarded it from the use of our own people, to the amount of $1,500,000,000. . . . Even worse, many of our less patriotic citizens started to export their money to foreign countries out of fear. . . .

All this cataclysm did not develop at once; it came blow by blow; its effect upon us grew steadily, our difficulties mounted higher day by day.

This is no time to trace its effect stage by stage. . . . No statement of mine could portray the full measure of perils which threatened us.

Three of the great perils were invisible except to those who had the responsibility of dealing with the situation.

The first of these perils was the steady strangulation of credit through the removal of three billions of gold and currency by foreign drains and domestic hoarding from the channels of our commerce and business. And let me remind you that credit is the lifeblood of business, of prices, and of jobs.

Had the full consequences of this action been allowed to run their full extent, it would have resulted, under our system of currency and banking, in the deflation of credit anywhere from twenty to twenty-five billions, or the destruction of nearly half the immediate working capital of the country. There would have been . . . [a] call for payment of debt which would have brought about universal bankruptcy, because property could not be converted to cash, no matter what its value.

Another peril, which we escaped only by the most drastic action, was that of being forced off the gold standard. I would like to make clear to you what that would have meant had we failed in that sector of the battle. Going off the gold standard in the United States would have been a most crushing blow to most of those with savings and those who owed money, and it was these we were fighting to protect.

Going off the gold standard is no academic matter. By going off the gold standard, gold goes to a premium, and the currency dollar becomes depreciated. Largely as a result of fears generated by the experience after the Civil War and by the Democratic free-silver campaign in 1896 our people have long insisted upon writing a large part of their long-term debtor documents as payable in gold.

A considerable part of farm mortgages, most of our industrial and all of our government, most of our state and municipal bonds, and most other long-term obligations are written as payable in gold. . . .

I believe I can make clear why we were in danger of being forced off even with our theoretically large stocks of gold. I have told you of enormous sums of gold and exchange drained from us by foreigners (in excess of $1,000,-000,000). You will realize also that our citizens who hoard Federal Reserve and some other forms of currency are in effect hoarding gold, because under the law we must maintain 40 per cent gold reserve behind such currency. Owing to the lack in the Federal Reserve System of the kind of securities required by the law for the additional 60 per cent of coverage of the currency, the Reserve System was forced to increase the gold reserve up to 75 per cent. Thus with $1,500,000,000 of hoarded currency, there was in effect over $1,000,000,000 of gold hoarded by our own citizens.

These drains had at one moment reduced the amount of gold we could spare . . . where we could not hold to the gold standard [more than] two weeks longer because of inability to meet the demands of foreigners and our own citizens for gold.

In the midst of this hurricane the Republican administration kept a cool head and rejected every counsel of weakness and cowardice. Some urged . . . liquidation until we had found bottom. Some people talked of vast issues of paper money. Some talked of suspending payments of government issues. Some talked of setting up a Council of National Defense. Some talked foolishly of dictatorship. . . . Some assured me that no man could propose increased taxes in the United States to balance the budget in the midst of a depression and survive an election.

We determined that we should not enter the morass of using the printing press for currency or bonds. All human experience has demonstrated that that path once taken cannot be stopped, and that the moral integrity of the government would be sacrificed. . . .

We determined we would stand up like men, and render the credit of the United States government impregnable. . . .

We decided upon changes in the Federal Reserve System which would make our gold active in commercial use, and that we would keep the American dollar ringing true in every city in America and in the world; that we would expand credit to offset the contraction brought about by hoarding and foreign withdrawals. . . .

The . . . armies thus mobilized for this great battle turned the tide toward victory by July [1932]. The foreigners drew out most of their money, but finding that the American dollar rang honest on every counter, in new confidence they are sending it back. Since June $275,000,000 of gold has flowed back to us from abroad. Hoarders in our own country, finding our institutions safeguarded, have returned $250,000,000 to the useful channels of business. . . .

I have been talking of currency, of gold, of credit, of bonds, of banks, of insurance policies, of loans. Do not think these things have no human interpretation. The happiness of 120,000,000 people was at stake in the measure to enable the government to meet its debts and obligations, in saving the gold standard, in enabling 5,500 banks, insurance companies, building and loan associations, and a multitude of other institutions to pay their obligations and ease pressure upon their debtors. These institutions have been rendered safe and with them their 30,000,000 depositors, policyholders and borrowers. . . .

I wish I were able to translate what these perils, had they not been overcome, would have meant to each person in America. . . . Had we failed, disaster would have translated itself into despair in every home, every city, village and farm.

We won this great battle to protect our people at home. We held the Gibraltar of world stability. The world today has a chance. It is growing in strength. Let that man who complains that things could not be worse thank God for this victory.

DEMOCRATIC MONETARY POLICIES

After having thus laid down the Republican action and policies in currency matters, I went on to the attack. I reviewed the fiat money, inflation, and "rubber dollar" bills introduced or passed by the Democratic House.

At Detroit I said on October 22nd:

Recovery would have been faster but for four months of paralysis [by Congress] . . . while we were defeating proposals of the Democratic House of Representatives to increase governmental expenses by $3,500,000,000, *the issue of fiat money,* and other destructive legislation. . . . The Democratic House passed a provision for the issue of $2,300,000,000 of fiat money.

At Cleveland on October 15th, I again reviewed the currency tinkering of the Democratic House, and said:

If any of you will study what happened in Germany, or France, or Austria, or any other European country when they resorted to these measures in order to meet their immediate difficulties, you will find that the major hardship fell upon the working people. There was a time when the value of the German mark was five to the dollar. They tried this plan of relief [fiat money]. I have in my desk a five-million-mark note which before the entrance into these processes would have been worth one million dollars, and yet which I bought for actually one dollar. The effect of their experiment was a subtle and steady reduction of real wages, right and left.

We have fought a great battle to maintain the stability of the American dollar, the stability of its exchange, in order that we might protect the working people of he United States.

At Indianapolis on October 28th, I said:

One of the most important issues of this campaign arises from the fact that the Democratic candidate has not yet disavowed the bill passed . . . under the leadership of the Democratic candidate for Vice President to issue . . . greenback currency. . . . That is money purporting to come from the horn of plenty but with the death's head engraved upon it. Tampering with the currency has been a perennial policy of the Democratic Party. The Republican Party has had to repel that before now. In the absence of any declaration by the Democratic candidate on this subject for seven weeks of this campaign, no delayed promise now can effectually disavow that policy. The taint of it is firmly embedded in the Democratic Party. The dangers of it are embedded in this election. If you want to know what this "new deal" and this sort of money does to the people, ask any of your neighbors who have relatives in Europe, especially as to German marks.

In New York on October 31st, I again reviewed the actions of the Democratic House in respect to greenback money and tampering with the currency and continued:

No candidate and no speaker in this campaign has disavowed this action of the Democratic House. Fiat money is proposed by the Democratic party as a potent measure for relief from this depression.

The use of this expedient by nations in difficulty since the war in Europe has been one of the most tragic disasters to . . . the independence of man.

Ultimately, our speeches on the monetary issue were making such an impression that Mr. Roosevelt requested Senator Glass to reply. His speech was one of the most vituperative of his career—and that was something. Glass with his political clothes on was imperfect in his facts.

In this speech Glass said there never had been a crisis such as I described at Des Moines; that we never were in the slightest danger of going off the gold standard. He asserted that the Democratic platform meant the gold standard, and that, generally, a Democratic administration was a safe depositary for monetary powers. Glass himself had consented at a White House conference in the presence of many other men to father the Glass-Steagall bill, the very purpose of which was to prevent us from being forced off the gold standard. I considered this part of his speech needed correction. Senator James Watson, who was also present at that meeting, issued the following statement:

I notice by the press that Senator Glass has made the statement that he had no record of having been presented with the facts as to the gold crisis in the United States. . . . The Senator will perhaps remember the two-hour confidential conference of Senate leaders, including Senator Glass, called in February of last winter by the President, together with officials of the Treasury, the Federal Reserve System and the Reconstruction Finance Corporation. In that conference the President and these gentlemen urged the great gravity of the situation and the necessity for the immediate enactment of the legislation recommended by the President for extension of authority to the Federal Reserve System to enable them to prevent imminent jeopardy to the gold standard in the United States.

I well recall that it was pointed out by these officials that under the foreign drains of gold and the hoarding then current, together with the inflexibility of the Federal Reserve laws, and despite our nominal gold holdings, we had at that time only about $350,000,000 of free gold, and that losses to foreigners and hoarders were going on at a rate of $150,000,000 a week.

Although Senator Glass had been opposed to these proposed measures, in the face of the evidence presented he patriotically agreed to proceed with the increased authority asked for, and to introduce them in the Congress, where they were enacted and the dangers from this quarter were finally and completely averted.

ROOSEVELT PROMISES TO MAINTAIN THE EXISTING GOLD STANDARD

Secretary Mills effectively answered Senator Glass, also pointing out his participation in the legislation. Finally Roosevelt made the "Covenant speech" on the eve of the election. Its essential sentences were:

It is worthy of note that no adequate answer has been made to the magnificent philippic of Senator Glass the other night, in which he showed how unsound this assertion was. And I might add, *Senator Glass made a devastating challenge that no responsible government would have sold to the country securities payable in gold if it knew that the promise—yes, the covenant— embodied in these securities* was as dubious as the President of the United States claims it was.[1]

At St. Paul, Minnesota, on November 5th, I repeated my assertion as to the Democratic currency attitude and again related the currency tinkering measures of the last Congress.

Later in these Memoirs under the title "The Aftermath," I discuss Roosevelt's repudiation of the gold standard and the disasters which came from it, including the miseries of Senator Glass.

[1] This became known as the "Covenant speech." I have, in the previous section of this volume, pointed out that the covenant referred to was, "payable in gold of the present weight and fineness."

CHAPTER 25

THE TARIFF ISSUE

The tariff was yet another issue during the campaign on which we were able to wage effective battle.

Mr. Roosevelt, early in the campaign, made violent attacks on the Republican tariff.[1] I made many replies and corrected many misstatements.

He persisted throughout the campaign in calling the Smoot-Hawley Tariff the "Grundy" tariff. He used this expression more than thirty times. Senator Grundy was, at that time, the symbol of "reaction." As Senators Pittman, Walsh, and Hull were among Mr. Roosevelt's advisers on tariff speeches, he must have known better, for they were aware of Grundy's opposition to the bill and Grundy's speeches against it in the Senate. That Senator did not think the tariffs were not high enough, and he abhorred our flexible tariff.

Roosevelt attacked the tariff from three directions:

(a) That it had been a large factor in bringing about the depression (although enacted nine months after our stock market crash), as added proof of my responsibility for the crisis.

(b) That it caused a drain of European gold to the United States and thus forced European nations off the gold standard.

(c) That it had a direct disastrous effect on domestic life.

(d) By proposing to destroy the flexible tariff and to engage in reciprocal tariff agreements with other nations.

The tariff debate ran through a large part of the major speeches on

---

[1] After all this violent recrimination, Mr. Roosevelt, as President, increased the real tariff and trade barriers around the United States—all of which offers interesting reflection upon such subjects as abstract truth. I discuss this question fully in the next section of this volume.

both sides during the campaign. I give such extracts from Mr. Roosevelt's as will represent his position, and I quote from my replies. His addresses were a condensed attack and assertion which required the presentation of fact and argument at greater length. I was compelled to use more concrete evidence before the people than mere vituperative statements.

These answers paid off as the campaign went on, for the farmers and labor did not agree with the college professors who wrote Roosevelt's speeches. He then totally reversed himself, much to the consternation of the professors.

ROOSEVELT'S ORIGINAL IDEAS ON THE TARIFF

Mr. Roosevelt's attack on the tariff started with bitter and virulent terms. He said in Chicago on July 2nd:

A nation of 120,000,000 has been led by the Republican leaders to erect an impregnable barbed-wire entanglement around its borders through the instrumentality of tariffs which have isolated us from all other human beings in all the rest of the round world.

Go into the home of the business man. He knows what the tariff has done for him. Go into the home of the factory worker. He knows why goods do not move. Go into the home of the farmer. He knows how the tariff has helped to ruin him.

He said at Albany, in a radio address on July 30th:

We condemn . . . the Smoot-Hawley tariff.

And at Columbus, Ohio, August 20th, he called it,

The highest tariff in the history of the world.

He said at Columbus, Ohio, on August 20th:

We find a tariff that has cut off any chance of a foreign market for our products. . . .
Grundyism had its way.

He said at Topeka on September 14th, referring to "a ghastly fraud":

They destroyed the foreign markets for our exportable farm surplus beginning with the Fordney-McCumber Tariff and ending with the Grundy

Tariff, thus violating the simplest principle of international trade, and forcing the inevitable retaliation of foreign countries.

I cannot forbear at this point expressing my amazement . . . in the face of this retaliation—inevitable from the day the Grundy Tariff became law. . . .

The farmer asks the question: "How may we expect that our exports will be restored and some way provided by which our customers may pay for our surplus produce with goods which we farmers can use?" He reads the answer in the acceptance speech: "I am squarely for a protective tariff." . . .

This is unsound; it is unfair; it is unjust; it is not American! Industry can never prosper unless the agricultural market is restored and farm buying power returns.

He said at Seattle on September 20th:

That tariff, as you in the State of Washington well know, had the inevitable result of bringing about retaliations by the other nations of the world. Forty of them set up, just as you and I would have done, their own tariff defenses against us.

He said at Sioux City, Iowa, on September 29th:

The notorious and indefensible Grundy . . . tariff . . . a ghastly jest.

The destructive effect of the Grundy Tariff on export markets has not been confined to agriculture. It has ruined our export trade in industrial products as well. . . .

. . . An almost frantic movement toward self-contained nationalism began among other nations of the world. . . .

Now, there was a secondary and perhaps even more disastrous effect of Grundyism. Billions of dollars of debts are due to this country from abroad. If the debtor nations cannot export goods, they must try to pay in gold. But we started such a drain on the gold reserves of the other nations as to force practically all of them off the gold standard. What happened? The value of the money of each of these countries relative to the value of our dollar declined alarmingly and steadily. . . .

And so, summing up. . . .

The ink on the Hawley-Smoot-Grundy Tariff bill was hardly dry before foreign nations commenced their program of retaliation. Brick for brick, they built their walls against us. They learned the lesson from us. The villainy we taught them, they practiced on us. . . .

The Grundy Tariff still retains its grip on the throat of international commerce.

He said at Pittsburgh on October 19th:

Retaliation against his monstrous Grundy Tariff . . . against which the best economic and industrial thought in the country had stood in almost unanimous protest, and against which it once more protested within the past week . . . had already begun to strangle the world trade. . . .

He said at Baltimore on October 25th:

The Horseman of Destruction rode into every town and every country when the Grundy Tariff bill was passed and signed, for this Horseman was insatiable.

MY GENERAL ANSWERS ON THE TARIFF

I announced my position from Washington on August 11, 1932:

I am squarely for a protective tariff. The proposals of our opponents would place our farmers and workers in competition with peasant and sweated labor products. . . .

I am against their proposals to destroy the usefulness of the bipartisan Tariff Commission, the establishment of whose effective powers we secured during this administration twenty-five years after it was first advocated by President Theodore Roosevelt. That instrumentality enables us to correct any injustice and to readjust the rates of duty to shifting economic change, without constant tinkering and orgies of log-rolling in Congress. If our opponents will descend from vague generalizations to any particular schedule, if it be higher than necessary to protect our people or insufficient for their protection, it can be remedied by this bipartisan commission.

At Des Moines on October 4th, I took up the tariff in its relation to agricultural products:

The very basis of safety to American agriculture is the protective tariff on farm products.

The Republican party originated and proposes to maintain the protective tariff on agricultural products. . . . I propose to reserve this market to the American farmer.

Has the Democratic party . . . ever given one single evidence of protection of the home market to the American farmer from the products raised by peasant labor on cheap land abroad?

The Democratic party took the tariff off a large part of farm products in 1913. . . . A Republican Congress passed the emergency farm tariff in 1921 and a Democratic President vetoed it. The Democratic minority in the next Congress in 1921 voted against the revived emergency farm tariff. The Republican majority passed it, and the Republican President signed it.

The Democratic minority voted against the increase of agricultural tariffs in the Republican tariff of 1922. Most of the Democratic members of Congress voted against the increases in the tariff bill of 1930. . . . Their candidate states: "A wicked and exorbitant tariff"; "a ghastly jest" . . . This is a promise of reduction of farm tariffs. They will reduce agricultural tariffs if they come into power. Since when have our opponents become the friends of the farmer?

When you return to your homes you can compare prices with foreign countries and count up this proposed destruction at your own firesides. There are this minute 2,000,000 cattle in the northern states of Mexico seeking market. The price is about $2.50 per 100 pounds on the south bank of the Rio Grande. It is $4.50 on the north bank—and only the tariff wall between.

. . . Except for the guardianship of the tariff, butter could be imported for 25 per cent below your prices, pork products for 30 per cent below your prices, lamb and beef products from 30 to 50 per cent below your prices, flaxseed for 35 per cent below your prices, beans for 40 per cent below your prices, and wool 30 per cent below your prices. Both corn and wheat could be sold in New York from the Argentine at prices below yours at this moment were it not for the tariff. I suppose these are ghastly jests.

The removal of or reduction of the tariff on farm products means a flood of them into the United States from every direction, and either you would be forced to still further reduce your prices, or your products would rot on your farms. . . .

What the Democratic party proposes is to reduce your farm tariffs. Aside from ruin to agriculture, such an undertaking in the midst of this depression will disturb every possibility of recovery.

At Cleveland on October 15th, I said:

I stand on that principle of protection. Our opponents are opposed to that principle. [They propose] a tariff for revenue only. They propose to do this in the face of the fact that in the last year currencies of competing nations have depreciated by going off the gold standard and consequently wages have been lowered in thirty competing countries. This is a flat issue which every farmer and workman in the United States should consider from the point of view of his home and his living.

That it is the intention of the Democratic candidate to reduce the tariffs—on all commodities—must be clear from these typical expressions in respect to the present tariff used in this campaign: "wicked and exorbitant tariff," "its outrageous rates," "almost prohibitive tariffs," "the notorious and indefensible Hawley-Smoot Tariff," "the excessive rates of that bill must come down," "until the tariff is lowered," "our policy calls for lower tariffs."

Do you want to compete with laborers whose wages in their own money are only sufficient to buy from one-eighth to one-third of the amount of bread and butter which you can buy at the present rates of wages? That is a plain question. It does not require a great deal of ingenious argument to support its correct answer. It is true we have the most gigantic market in the world today, surrounded by nations clamoring to get in. But it has been my belief—and it is still my belief—that we should protect this market for our own labor; not surrender it to the labor of foreign countries as the Democratic party proposes to do.

I now come to the amazing statements that the tariff bill of 1930 has borne a major influence in this débâcle.

It requires a collection of dull facts to demonstrate the errors in these bald assertions by Democratic leaders.

At the beginning I may repeat that this tariff bill was not passed until nine months after the economic depression began in the United States. . . .

The Democratic party seldom mentions that 66 per cent of our imports are free of duty, but that is the fact. From half to two-thirds of the trade of the world is in nondutiable goods—that is, mostly raw materials; another part is in luxuries, upon which all nations collect tariffs for revenue; another part . . . is in competitive goods so far as the importing nation is concerned and therefore subject to protective tariffs.

The trade of the world has distressingly diminished under the impact of these successive dislocations abroad. But the decrease is almost exactly the same in the free goods everywhere as in the dutiable goods. . . . What was it that reduced the two-thirds of nondutiable goods?

If we explore a little further, we would find from the Tariff Commission that the total duties collected in a comparable year represent 16 per cent of the total imports, this being an increase from 13.8 per cent of the previous tariffs. In other words, the effect of the new tariff shows an increase of 2.2 per cent. This is the margin with which they say we have pulled down foreign governments, created tyrannies, financial shocks, and revolutions.

I may mention that upon the same basis the McKinley duties were 23 per cent; the Dingley duties were 25.8 per cent; the Payne-Aldrich duties were 19.3 per cent of the whole of our imports—all compared with the 16 per cent of the present tariff—and yet they produced in foreign countries no revolutions, no financial crises, and did not destroy the whole world, nor destroy American foreign trade.

And I may explore the facts still further. The five-year average of the import trade of the United States before the depression was about 12 per cent of the whole world import trade. Thus they would say that 2.2 per cent increase applied to one-eighth of the world's imports has produced this catastrophe.

I can explore this in still another direction. I remind you that we levy tariffs upon only one-third of our imports. I also remind you that the actual increases made in the Smoot-Hawley Act covered only one-quarter of the dutiable imports. I may also remind you that our import trade is only one-eighth of the import trade of the world. So they would have us believe this world catastrophe . . . happened because the United States increased tariffs on one-fourth of one-third of one-eighth of the world's imports. Thus we pulled down the world, so they tell us, by increases on less than 1 per cent of the goods being imported by the world.

At Cumberland, Maryland, I said on October 15th:

The people of Maryland had a large part in the passage of the first protective tariff in our country. On April 11, 1789, a group of manufacturing workers and others of Baltimore joined in a petition to President Washington and the first session of the First Congress. It was indeed the first petition filed with the Congress.

They prayed that the new government would render the country "independent in fact as well as in name" . . . by invoking upon all foreign articles which can be made in America such duties as would give a just and decided preference to their labors and thereby discontinue that trade which tended to so materially injure them."

President Washington responded to that petition and the first piece of legislation passed by the Congress and signed by the first President was a protective tariff.

I said at Charleston, West Virginia, on October 22nd:

In order to attack the tariff they have set up an ingenious hypothesis. . . .
I call your attention to the fact that 93 per cent of the market for the American workman is within the borders of the United States and 7 per cent outside the borders. They propose to place our 93 per cent at the disposal of all
countries in the world with the fantastic idea that the American farmer and
worker can increase his part of the 7 per cent by reducing his standards to
those of labor which can only buy one-third as much bread and butter.

And at St. Paul, Minnesota, on November 5th, I said:

In the face of these gigantic, appalling world-wide forces, our opponents
set up the Hawley-Smoot Tariff bill as the cause of all this world catastrophe. . . .

Suppose that we had never had the Hawley-Smoot Tariff bill. Do you
think for one moment that this crushing collapse in the structure of the
world, these revolutions, these perils to civilization would not have happened
and would not have reached the United States?

And yet, in order to make a political campaign by which they can play
upon discontent . . . they are compelled to set up this travesty of argument.
. . . They endeavor [by this appeal] to lead them away from discussion of
the actual measures which have been taken to meet the world situation, and
to follow a mirage of miscellaneous vague hopes.

THE FLEXIBLE TARIFF

Gradually the tariff discussion branched out into various side issues.

Mr. Roosevelt made numerous attacks on the provisions of the Smoot-
Hawley Act which established the flexible tariff under a bipartisan
commission. One attack was made at Sioux City on September 29th, and
another at Brooklyn [2] on November 4th, when he said:

During two long years, President Hoover's Tariff Commission has investigated the duties upon only seventy-three commodities—seventy-three out of
many thousands. And as a result eighteen schedules were reduced and
thirteen increased, . . . a careful estimate shows that at the present magnificent rate of progress President Hoover's tariff commission will complete
its examination of schedules and report upon them by the year 2005.

[2] This speech is suppressed in the authorized publication of the Roosevelt addresses.

My replies on the flexible tariff were made at Des Moines on October 4th, and in subsequent speeches. I said at Des Moines:

All tariff acts contain injustices and inequities. That is the case with the last tariff bill. Some people get too much and some too little. But those of you who have followed the accomplishments of this administration will recollect that I secured in the last tariff act, twenty-five years after it had originally been advocated by President Theodore Roosevelt, the adoption of effective flexible tariff provisions to be administered by a bipartisan body. That authority to a bipartisan Tariff Commission is based upon a definite principle of protection to our people and it is one of the most progressive acts which have been secured in the history of all legislation.

By maintaining that reform the country need no longer be faced with heartbreaking, logrolling selfishness and greed which come to the surface on every occasion when Congress revises the tariff.

This bipartisan Tariff Commission has now been engaged for over eighteen months in an effective revision of the tariff. It has heard every complaint. It has found that many rates were just, some were too high, and some too low. . . .

Our opponents opposed this reform in tariff legislation. . . . They promise in their platform to destroy it. The reasons for this action are obvious. The bipartisan Tariff Commission has proved a serious political embarrassment to them. Either House of Congress has the right to call upon the Tariff Commission for reconsideration of any schedule. Notwithstanding their outcries . . . after being in session for seven months, [the Democratic House] did not pass a single resolution requesting readjustment of a single commodity or a single schedule.

At Charleston, West Virginia, on October 22nd I said:

And now the Democratic party promises to destroy the effectiveness of the Tariff Commission. . . .

. . . To take that authority away means that the ability to change the tariff with changing tides of economic life is destroyed except by action of Congress, which in turn means the old scenes of logrolling, greed and compromise. . . .

At Indianapolis on October 28th I said:

In all this discussion about reducing tariffs it should be remembered that if any one of the rates or schedules of our tariff is too high, it has been open to our opponents during the whole of the last session of the House of Representatives to pass a simple resolution and thereby secure its review from the Tariff Commission. Did they do that? They did not.

At St. Louis on November 4th I said:

Now the tariff is composed of different schedules. If Governor Roosevelt is sufficiently informed on the tariff law to debate its merits, he must be sufficiently informed to say at once which schedules are too high. If he will do so we will at once have them examined by the Tariff Commission, as to the truth of his assertions, and we can give quick remedy.

At St. Paul, Minnesota, on November 5th I said:

In a speech last night the Democratic candidate stated that the Tariff Commission "during two long years, has investigated duties on only seventy-three commodities out of many thousands."

Again he has been misinformed and is broadcasting misinformation to the American people. The Tariff Commission has considered over two hundred and fifty items instead of the seventy-three he mentions. . . . But a greater misrepresentation lies in the fact . . . [that] its docket is practically clear. That means that this tribunal, which Governor Roosevelt says he will destroy has attended to practically every application presented by American citizens. . . .

THE "RECIPROCAL TARIFF"

Another branch of the tariff debate was the "reciprocal tariff."

Mr. Roosevelt, in many speeches, proposed this as a solution of all tariff ills.

He said at Topeka, Kansas, on September 14, 1932:

The Democratic tariff policy consists, in large measure, of negotiating agreements with individual countries permitting them to sell goods to us in return for which they will let us sell to them goods and crops which we produce. An effective application of this principle will restore the flow of international trade; and the first result of that flow will be to assist substantially the American farmer in disposing of this surplus.

He said at Seattle, on September 20th:

This principle of tariff by negotiation means to deal with each country concerned, on a basis of fair barter; if it has something we need, and we have something it needs, a tariff agreement can and should be made that is satisfactory to both countries. That, of course, avoids a violent and a general shake-up in business. It is a just method of dealing with our foreign customers. It keeps the general structure of international trade stable and sound. And it makes for world peace. It is practical. It is American! Let us lead the way!

I replied to the farmers at Des Moines on October 4th:

The Democratic Party proposes that they would enter into bargaining tariffs to secure special concessions from other countries. They represent this to be in the farmer's interest. But I may tell you here and now that the largest part of the whole world desires to make only one bargain with the United States. The bargain these countries wish to make is to lower our tariff on agricultural products in exchange for lowering their tariffs on our industrial goods.

I returned to this subject at Indianapolis on October 28th:

Beyond this the Democratic Party and their candidate propose to enter upon reciprocal tariffs. . . . It is a violation of a now firmly established principle of uniform and equal treatment of all nations without preferences, concessions, or discriminations. . . .

Though reciprocal tariffs are a violation of American principles, this Nation has fallen from grace and at times attempted to do this very thing. At one time twenty-two such treaties were negotiated for this purpose. Congress refused to confirm sixteen of them; two of the remaining failed of confirmation by other governments; and four others were so immaterial as not to excite notice. On another occasion Congress conferred on the Executive a limited authority to make such treaties, twenty-two of which were agreed upon, all of which were repealed by tariff acts. . . .

I spoke again on this subject on November 4th, at Springfield, Illinois, and at St. Louis.

ROOSEVELT RETREATS ON THE TARIFF ISSUE

As the debate proceeded, Mr. Roosevelt began to hedge until he came out for the Smoot-Hawley agricultural tariffs and finally for "protective tariffs on industrial goods."

He said at Sioux City, September 29th:

The Democratic leaders would put them as low as the preservation of the prosperity of American industry and American agriculture will permit. . . .

Of course, the *outrageously* excessive rates in that bill as it became law must come down. But we should not lower them beyond a reasonable point, a point indicated by common sense and facts. Such revision of the tariff will injure no legitimate interest. Labor need have no apprehensions concerning such a course.

He further modified his position at Baltimore on October 25th, repeating the Sioux City formula and adding:

My distinguished opponent is declaring in his speeches that I propose to injure or destroy the farmers' markets by reducing the tariff on products of the farm. That is silly. Of course I have made no such proposal. . . .

Of course outrageously excessive rates in that bill as it became law, must come down. But we should not lower them beyond a reasonable point indicated by common sense and facts.

The point indicated was that no tariff duty should be lowered to a point where our natural industries would be injured. . . .

Of course, it is absurd to talk of lowering tariff duties on farm products. I declared that all prosperity in the broader sense springs from the soil. . . . I know of no effective excessively high tariff duties on farm products. I do not intend that such duties shall be lowered.

He said at Boston on October 31st:

I favor—and do not let the false statements of my opponents deceive you—continued protection for American agriculture *as well as American industry.*[3]

[3] Raymond Moley (*After Seven Years,* pp. 47–49) discloses some high lights on this retreat. Of the writing for Mr. Roosevelt of the Sioux City speech he says: "Viewed in the light of hindsight, the most ominous of these battles during the campaign entered in the tariff issue, an apple of discord that had disrupted the Democratic party for a generation." He then describes the conflicts in the Brain Trust over the tariff with Senator Hull and others and continues:

"No speech in the campaign was such a headache as this [Sioux City]. . . .

"We showed Roosevelt the finished product. He rearranged it somewhat, made a few additions, and, when he had sent away the stenographer, smiled at me gayly. 'There! You see? It wasn't as hard as you thought it was going to be.'

"I allowed that I wouldn't have thought it would be hard at all had I known he was going to ignore the Hulls of the party, substantially, and merely throw them a couple of sops in the form of statements that some of the 'outrageously excessive' rates of the Hawley-Smoot tariff would have to come down.

"'But you don't understand,' he said. 'This speech is a compromise between the free traders and the protectionists.' . . .

"I reflected that it would take greater persuasive powers than even he possessed to sell this idea that the speech was a compromise to the low-tariff Democrats. I, for one,

MY COMMENT ON THE ROOSEVELT TARIFF RETREAT

At once, with Roosevelt's retreat at Sioux City, I began to inquire as to the real meaning of this hedging. I said at Indianapolis on October 28th:

The Democratic candidate from the day of his nomination iterates and reiterates that he proposes to reduce the tariff.

During the first seven weeks of this campaign he not only adopts their historic position and constantly repeats their platform but reenforces it by repeated statements.

Unquestionably my exposition has given their candidate great anxiety, because . . . he now announces within two weeks of the election that he does not propose to reduce tariffs on farm products.

This is the most startling shift in position by a Presidential candidate in the midst of a political campaign in all recent political history. What would Grover Cleveland or Samuel Tilden or Woodrow Wilson say to such a shift? Does the Governor realize that he has overnight thrown overboard the great historical position of his party? that he has rewritten the Democratic platform? . . .

---

could see in it only the clear inference that Roosevelt had reaffirmed Al Smith's abandonment of the historic Democratic position of tariff. . . .

"I was yet to learn the uses of self-deception.

"So, apparently, was Cordell Hull. Word drifted up from Tennessee later that he was profoundly grieved by Roosevelt's tariff stand. But the poor man did not learn what heartbreak could really be until after March 4th when he began to live with Roosevelt's tariff policies.

". . . Hoover demanded that Roosevelt specify what tariffs he felt were too high. So many hundreds of telegrams came in from farmers and processors asking whether the reference to 'outrageously excessive' rates in the Sioux City speech applied to the duties on this commodity or that, that Roosevelt himself decided to temper his statement on the Hawley-Smoot tariff. And so, in Baltimore, he turned his phrase around. *'I know of no effective, excessively high tariff duties on farm products. I do not intend that such duties shall be lowered,'* he said, rebutting the attack the Republicans were making throughout the West and Middle West.

"There was more word eating to come. Immediately, the barrage from the East and Northeast began. Did Roosevelt mean to suggest that the tariffs on manufactured articles were too high? In Boston, at almost the tail end of the campaign, the candidate manfully finished the job: 'I favor—and do not let the false statements of my opponents deceive you—continued protection for American agriculture as well as American industry.'

"So began seven years of evasion and cross-purposes on the tariff.

"But for the student of statesmanship the process was instructive."

I wish to extend this discussion a little further, that the Governor may explain himself on some more tariff questions. . . .

Perhaps the Governor and the whole Democratic party will now withdraw and apologize for the defamation to which I have been subjected for the last two years because I called a special session of the Congress and secured an increase in agricultural tariffs.

I myself am taking heart over this debate. If it could be continued long enough, I could drive him from every solitary position he has taken in this campaign. They are all equally untenable. Perhaps I could get him to declare himself upon other evasions and generalities. But even on the tariff he perhaps remembers the dreadful predicament of the chameleon on the Scotch plaid.

At Springfield, Illinois, November 4th, I said:

The Democratic candidate has made further statements as to which he can only confuse the public mind, and from which I do not believe American agriculture will secure much conviction. It is, of course, difficult for the Democratic party to maintain one theory on the tariff in the East and another in the West. But of one thing you can be sure, and that is that the party which placed the majority of farm products on the free list in the tariff bill which they imposed on the country in 1913, the party which voted against the emergency farm tariff in 1921, the party of the Democratic President who vetoed it, the party of the Democratic minority in the succeeding House which voted against the revival of the emergency tariff although it was forced through by a Republican majority and a Republican President, the party which voted against the increase in agricultural tariffs in the Republican tariff bill of 1922, and the party which voted against the increase in the Hawley-Smoot Tariff bill of 1930—the party whose platform the candidate who unceasingly has reaffirmed that platform and who denounced the Hawley-Smoot Tariff in unmeasured terms . . . and who has termed it frequently a ghastly joke, are scarcely the party and the candidate upon whom the Republican farmers of Illinois should depend for their protection. Certainly, whatever they may now say in words in the West, they depend upon their historical low-tariff policy to carry conviction in the East.

At St. Louis on the same day I said:

In the earlier part of this campaign the Democratic candidate held up the horrors of the Hawley-Smoot Tariff Act. . . . I established the complete absurdity of his tariff-bill argument, and the Governor has since, at Wheeling, Baltimore, and Boston, uttered confused changes in his tariff views. . . . If he will make his contradictory statements on the tariff consistent it will have the disastrous political effect of requiring the deletion, so my statisticians tell me, of over ten thousand eloquent words from what he has said upon this subject.

CHAPTER 26

AGRICULTURAL ISSUES

A great many words were expended in the campaign on agricultural discussion. I made major speeches to the farmers at Des Moines and Springfield. Mr. Roosevelt's major farm program was stated at Topeka.

On our side, I was opposed to all forms of regimented control of the farmer. In addition to several emergency measures we had established, I believed in the long-view remedy that we must systematically convert submarginal lands from ground crops into pastures. I believed the farmer had the same right to government aid in this relief measure as had been given to manufacturers in compensation for war expansion of plants. I had introduced a plank into the Republican platform proposing this plan. I argued that, with this aid and with tariff protection, our present liberation of credit, and the general recovery of the world, the farmer would be in good order.

Mr. Roosevelt's proposals for relief of farmers, with the segments of vituperation sifted out, were: (1) price fixing and control of production; (2) reduction of interest and relief of mortgage pressure; (3) reduction of the tariff on farm products; (4) reorganization of the Department of Agriculture, "looking toward the administrative machinery needed to build a program of *national planning*."

MR. ROOSEVELT'S PROPOSAL OF PRICE FIXING AND CONTROL OF PRODUCTION

At Topeka on September 14th, Mr. Roosevelt said, "I seek to give that portion of the crop consumed in the United States a benefit equivalent to a tariff sufficient to give you farmers an adequate price." He then stated the specifications of such a plan:

First: The plan must provide for the producer of staple surplus commodities, such as wheat, cotton, corn in the form of hogs, and tobacco, a tariff benefit over world prices which is equivalent to the benefit given by the tariff to industrial products. This differential benefit must be so applied that the increase in farm income, purchasing and debt-paying power will not stimulate further production.

Second: The plan must finance itself. Agriculture has at no time sought and does not now seek any such access to the public treasury as was provided by the futile and costly attempts at price stabilization by the Federal Farm Board. It seeks only equality of opportunity with tariff-protected industry.

Third: It must not make use of any mechanism which would cause our European customers to retaliate on the ground of dumping. It must be based upon making the tariff effective and direct in its operation.

Fourth: It must make use of existing agencies and so far as possible be decentralized in its administration so that the chief responsibility for its operation will rest with the locality rather than with newly created bureaucratic machinery in Washington.

Fifth: It must operate as nearly as possible on a cooperative basis, and its effect must be to enhance and strengthen the cooperative movement. It should, moreover, be constituted so that it can be withdrawn whenever the emergency has passed and normal foreign markets have been reestablished.

Sixth: The plan must be, in so far as possible, voluntary. I like the idea that the plan should not be put into operation unless it has the support of a reasonable majority of the producers of the exportable commodity to which it is to apply. It must be so organized that the benefits will go to the man who participates.

These, it seems to me, are the essential specifications of a workable plan. In determining the details necessary to the solution of so vast a problem it goes without saying that many minds must meet and many persons must work together.

This was a disguise for the "domestic allotment" plan, which had been proposed originally by General Hugh Johnson and supported by Henry Wallace, Sr., when Secretary of Agriculture, as the McNary-Haugen Bill.[1] It was a price-fixing scheme by which the American con-

[1] Herein lies one of the ironic humors in public life. Henry Wallace, Jr., who advised on this speech and who later became Secretary of Agriculture in the New Deal, at once on coming into office opposed this plan with precisely the arguments the Republicans had used against it. It was never put in action by the New Deal, and the killing of little pigs and restriction of acreage planted were substituted.

sumer was to pay a higher price for farm products, and the surplus to be exported at whatever lower price was necessary to get rid of it. To bring this about meant a gigantic governmental machine fixing prices and controlling distribution. It must lead ultimately to controlled production. It was obviously for this machinery that he proposed to expand the Department of Agriculture to "national planning." Governor Alfred E. Smith had openly and honestly supported this panacea by name in 1928, and it had cost him many votes among labor and business. Roosevelt avoided using the terms "domestic allotment" plan and "the McNary-Haugen bill," as those names were in disrepute.[2] He did attack the Republicans, however, for defeating the McNary-Haugen bill in the Coolidge administration. In any event, his plan and specifications were exactly the "domestic allotment" plan with reservations that allowed escape.

Mr. Roosevelt reaffirmed this plan of price fixing in various addresses. At Springfield, Illinois, on October 21, 1932, he said:

The three great steps which we must take are: First, the Federal Government owes it to agriculture to see that it gets a fair price for its products. That means that the prices of farm products must be raised above the present ruinously low levels to which they have fallen. . . . Pending the relief that will be afforded by properly adjusted tariff policy, measures must be taken to give the farmer immediate tariff benefit. This means in substance a practicable plan agreed to by agricultural leaders which will provide for the farmer a higher return for certain of his crops. I set forth these principles which such a plan must embody in my Topeka speech.

MY ANSWERS ON AGRICULTURE

In Washington, August 11th, I said:

No power on earth can restore prices except by restoration of general recovery and markets. Every measure we have taken looking to general recovery

[2] The deceit of this Topeka speech was ventilated later by one of its authors, Raymond Moley, who wrote in *After Seven Years,* pp. 44–45: "It laid down a set of specifications that forecast the New Deal's farm policy. More than any other single speech in the entire campaign, it captured the votes of the Middle Western farmers. Finally, it outlined the Domestic Allotment Plan without mentioning its name—outlined it so delicately that the urban voters, editors, and newspapermen accepted its broad propositions as generalities too vague to require examination. It won the Midwest without waking up the dogs of the East. And this speech was the direct product of more than twenty-five people!"

is of benefit to the farmer. There is no relief to the farmer by extending government bureaucracy to control his production and thus curtail his liberties, nor by subsidies that bring only more bureaucracy.

My major speech on agricultural policies was at Des Moines on October 4th, I said:

I wish to speak directly to those of my hearers who are farmers of what is on my mind, of what is in my heart, to tell you the conclusions I have reached from this bitter experience of the years in dealing with these problems which affect agriculture at home and their relations to foreign countries.

That agriculture is prostrate needs no proof. You have saved and economized and worked to reduce costs; but, with all this, yours is a story of distress and suffering.

What the farmer wants and needs is higher prices, and in the meantime to keep from being dispossessed from his farm, to have a fighting chance to keep his home. The pressing question is how these two things are to be attained. . . .

Every thinking citizen knows that . . . most of this distress . . . is due to the decreased demand for farm products by our millions of unemployed and by foreign countries. Every citizen knows that part of this unemployment is due to the inability of the farmer to buy the products of the factory. Every thinking citizen knows that the farmer, the worker, and the business man are in the same boat and must all come to shore together.

Every citizen . . . realizes that . . . we have been on this downward spiral of destructive forces. . . . If he has this vision, he today takes courage and hope because he . . . knows that these destructive forces have been stopped; that the spiral is moving upward. . . .

. . . The unprecedented instrumentalities and measures which we have put in motion, many of which are designed directly for agriculture—they are winning out. If we continue to fight along these lines we shall win.

I then described our experiments and our conclusions, together with those of farm leaders, for systematically converting submarginal land in ground crops back to pasture as provided in the Republican platform.

I then discussed the benefits to the farmer by the development of our waterways, the action we had taken in the drought of 1930, the need for reduced land taxes, and in description of our credit policies continued:

The very first necessity to . . . recovery in agriculture has been to keep open to the farmer the banking and other sources from which to make . . . loans for planting, harvesting, feeding livestock, and other production necessities. That has been accomplished indirectly . . . through the increased authority to the Federal Reserve System and its expansion of credits, and indirectly through the Reconstruction Corporation loans to your banks. It has been aided directly, through the Intermediate Credit banks and through the ten new Agricultural Credit institutions . . . now being erected in all parts of the country.

The mortgage situation—that is, long-term credits—is one of our most difficult problems. . . . In December we appropriated $125,000,000 directly to increase the capital of the Federal land banks, and we provided further capital through . . . the Reconstruction Corporation . . . to enable the Federal land banks to expand their activities and to give humane and constructive consideration to those indebted . . . who were in difficulties. . . .

. . . We have sought to further aid the whole mortgage situation by loans from the Reconstruction Corporation to banks, mortgage companies, and insurance companies to enable them to show consideration to their farmer borrowers. As a result of these actions hundreds of thousands of foreclosures have been prevented.

I outlined the delays of the Democratic Congress in effecting and deleting parts of these measures, and assured action to restore these parts if we carried the election.

Reviewing our efforts to rebuild international recovery and the purpose of the forthcoming World Economic Conference, I stated, "I shall send a representative of agriculture as a member of that world economic conference."

I then discussed a proposal to use a resettlement of war debts to open further markets for the farmer and again emphasized the importance of agricultural tariffs. I went on:

The government is giving aid by its vast constructive program for agriculture, for commerce, and for industry. . . . We are returning men to work. Every new man reemployed is a greater purchaser of farm products. . . . I come to you with no economic patent medicine especially compounded for farmers. I refuse to offer counterfeit currency or false hopes. I will not make any pledge to you which I cannot fulfill.

As I have stated before, in the shifting battle against depression, we shall

MR. AND MRS. HOOVER WITH GRANDCHILD
ATTENDING WASHINGTON'S CHURCH IN ALEXANDRIA

need to adopt new measures and new tactics as the battle moves on. The essential thing is that we should build soundly and solidly for the future. My solicitude and willingness to advance and protect the interests of agriculture is shown by the record. . . . It was in this industry that I was born.

At Springfield, Illinois, on November 4th, I amplified some of the proposals for agriculture which I had made at Des Moines and further amplified our plans for retirement of submarginal lands, and continued:

The Democratic candidate has developed one of the greatest mysteries of this whole compaign in his proposal for relief to agriculture. He has not been willing to state the method by which he proposes to secure the advance of agricultural prices. He has stated with great care six methods by which he can escape from any demand that he make good on his mysterious proposal.

And he could add two other doors of escape not mentioned—first, that it should be constitutional; and, second, that it should not violate the laws of practically every country in the world against the import of commodities produced as the result of subsidies. Under our law I closed the eighth door to New Zealand butter into the United States on one occasion because they were subsidizing production.

And on that same day, November 4th, at St. Louis, I said:

The people are still unable to find the method by which Roosevelt will execute his six-point program for farm relief. It is one of the great mysteries of this campaign.

THE FEDERAL FARM BOARD

Mr. Roosevelt was critical of all of our instrumentalities, and especially of the Federal Farm Board. At Topeka on September 14th he said:

The Farm Board began its stabilizing operations. This resulted in a tremendous undigested surplus overhanging the market; it put a millstone around the neck of the cooperatives. The effort resulted in squandering hundreds of millions of taxpayers' money. Farm Board speculative operations must and shall come to an end.[3]

He also charged that I had asked farmers to plow up every third row of cotton. I did not think the accusation was worth answering. The facts

[3] The irony of all this was that within a year Mr. Roosevelt adopted exactly these methods of price support.

were that a southern governors' conference had recommended plowing up every third row of cotton and had sent the recommendation to the Farm Board. One or two members of the Board publicly stated their agreement. The Board suggested that this was up to the governors.

MY REPLY ON THE FARM BOARD

At Des Moines on October 4th I said:

Those portions of the Board's activities which directed themselves to the support and expansion of cooperative marketing organizations have proved of great benefit to the farmer. Today over a million farm families participate in the benefits which flow from it. . . .

When the panic struck agricultural prices the Board determined that unless the markets were supported hundreds of thousands of farmers would be bankrupt by the sale of their products at less than the money they had already borrowed upon them, that a thousand country banks would likely be closed, and that a general panic was possible.

As a result of these emergency purchases the prices of farm commodities were temporarily held and their fall cushioned. The farmers secured hundreds of millions of dollars of income which they would not otherwise have received.

. . . I am convinced that the act should be revised in the interest of the farmer, in the light of our three years of experience.

At Springfield, Illinois, on November 4th I stated:

Hundreds of cooperative associations would have gone bankrupt in this depression except for the ability of the Farm Board to lend to them the necessary money to carry on their service. Today over 2,000,000 farm families, members of cooperatives, are receiving benefits solely because of consummation of this undertaking. . . .

Nowhere can I find that the Democratic candidate has agreed to continue these activities of the Farm Board.

The Democratic candidate does denounce the emergency purchases of farm products during the panic. The files of the Farm Board will show the insistent demand of farm organizations, both Democratic and Republican Senators and Congressmen, governors, bankers, and grain merchants for that emergency action to be taken. Some of the gentlemen who made these demands are the loudest critics of the Farm Board in this campaign.

I stated that this was an emergency action not to be carried on as a national policy.

At St. Paul on November 5th I said:

I have just heard of another of these actions [by the Democratic National Committee] which took place yesterday in the state of Ohio—the circulation of thousands of handbills stating that the Farm Board spends $5,000,000 annually in salaries and has a fund of $250,000 for traveling expenses. This statement is untrue. . . .

It states that Mr. Roosevelt will abolish the Farm Board. If true, that will be of interest to the 2,000,000 members of farm cooperatives in the United States.

. . . The administrative expenditures of the Board are less than $900,000 per annum, and I would call attention to the fact that the members of the Farm Board receive about $10,000 a year. The salaries referred to in this circular do not refer to the Farm Board. Many are exaggerated, and most of them are officials employed by farmer-owned, farmer-controlled, and farmer-managed cooperatives because they have sought for the highest skill in the marketing of their products. The Farm Board has no control of these salaries. They are paid at the will of the American farmer and his organizations.

But the point of most importance for me to make now is that this is typical of stories being spread through the nation with a view to misleading the people.

CHAPTER 27

LABOR, RELIEF, AND PUBLIC WORKS ISSUES

The questions of labor and public works for relief policies were inextricably mixed in the whole campaign debate.

Mr. Roosevelt's proposals on labor policies were largely indirect, such as blaming me for having created the depression, and having done nothing about it. In the campaign he gave no expression of his own views on labor organization or collective bargaining which I had advocated for many years.

On October 31st, at Boston, he said that I had

suggested an adequate system of public employment offices. But when Senator Wagner introduced a bill, President Hoover vetoed the measure that Secretary Herbert Hoover had sponsored.

It is quite true that I vetoed the Wagner bill, as it was an attempt by Tammany Hall and other city machines to obtain control of the Federal employment system.

As I have said, the direct relief of the unemployed was not injected as an issue into the campaign by Mr. Roosevelt. He, however, laid great emphasis upon increase of public works as the solution of unemployment. Some one of his Brain Trust placed in his mouth the misrepresentation that nothing of this sort was in progress.

He said in a radio address from Albany on October 13th:

From the long-range point of view it would be advisable for governments of all kinds to set up in times of prosperity what might be called a nest egg to be used for public works in times of depression.

. . . I have recounted to you in other speeches, and it is a matter of general information, that for at least two years after the crash the only efforts made by the national administration to cope with the distress of unemployment were to deny its existence.

He said at Boston on October 31st:

The country would be horrified if it knew how little construction work authorized by the last Congress and approved by the President has actually been undertaken on this date, the 31st of October. And I state to you the simple fact that much of the work for which Congress has given authority will not be under way and giving employment to people until some time next summer.

MY LABOR AND PUBLIC WORKS PROPOSALS

To show up this misrepresentation, I published the expenditures upon public construction during my administration in fiscal years:

1929	$356,500,000
1930	$410,400,000
1931	$574,870,000
1932	$655,880,000

This total of nearly $2,000,000,000 Federal public works was greater than the whole expenditure during the previous thirty years, including the Panama Canal. It accounted for a considerable part of the deficit.

I spoke briefly on these questions at Washington on August 11th. However, in a principal address at Cleveland on October 15th reviewing the whole of our relief measures and our labor policies, I said:

When I talk to you tonight about labor I speak not out of academic imaginings but from sharp personal experience. I have not only looked at these human problems from the fireside of one who has returned from a day's work with his own hands, but I know the problem that haunts the employer through the night, desperate to find the money with which to meet the week's pay roll. In public service during the years past I have had to look at these problems from the point of view of the national welfare as a whole.

RELIEF OF DISTRESS

My first concern in dealing with the problems of these times, while fighting to save our people from chaos and to restore order in our economic life, has been to avert hunger or cold among those upon whom these blows have fallen with heartbreaking severity—that is, the unemployed workers.

In the fall of 1930 I set up the President's Organization for Unemployment Relief with able leadership. Through cooperation of every state, town, and village the forces were organized. . . .

With these three years of unceasing effort in relief . . . we present to the world a record unparalleled in any other nation. That is a record expressed in technical terms yet interpretable in sheer human sympathy. That record is the information furnished to me constantly by the Surgeon General of the Public Health Service, which shows, down to this latest moment, that the adult mortality, infant mortality are at the lowest rate on record, and the general health of the American people is at a higher level today than ever before in the history of our country. . . . No such record could be established if the nation's unemployed were starving and without shelter.

UPHOLDING WAGES

In November, 1929, I assembled in Washington representatives of the leading employers, together with representatives of organized labor, . . . This has been the first time in history that the government has taken the leadership in securing an understanding between industry and labor of the complete mutuality of their interest in the face of national danger.

We worked out on that occasion many purposes.

The first was to uphold the standards of real wages. The second was to uphold the buying power of our working people until the cost of living had diminished. The third was to prevent that thing which had happened in every previous depression in our history, and that was an immediate attack upon wages as a basis of maintaining profits. This proposal had the sympathetic support of the employers of the country, and for nearly two years they maintained the standard of wages . . . in the face of disappearing profits. As the depression grew more severe there have been readjustments, but these readjustments have come about by agreement between employer and employee after profits were exhausted and the cost of living had been reduced with good will and little industrial conflict. As a result of these efforts we have had the astonishing spectacle of a country in which there have been less strikes and industrial conflicts, with all their bitterness, than ever in normal times.

Staggering Employment

The fourth of the undertakings made on this occasion was that the employers, faced with the necessity for reducing staffs, would stagger their employment—instead of discharging a portion of workers into complete disaster, they would spread the remaining employment over the whole of their employees. That has been done on a wide scale in the manufacturing industries, and millions have continued with some income who otherwise would have been destitute. . . .

Expanding Private Construction

The fifth of the undertakings made in 1929 was that manufacturers, railroads, and utilities would expand their construction of new equipment beyond their present needs in order to maintain employment to the utmost of their capacity. A vast sum of money was expended in these directions. . . .

. . . When history records this depression, it will record no brighter chapter in the whole history of the United States than the approach to this problem by both employers and leaders of labor in humanity and a sense of social responsibility. . . . If it had not been for these actions, this country would have been fired with the flames of bitterness and conflict between workers and employers; millions more would have been without jobs; wages would have been reduced far below their present levels.

Direct Public Works

Day before yesterday my opponent announced a plan "to set up in times of prosperity what might be called a nest egg to be used for public works in time of depression." . . .

He advances this apparently as a brand-new idea. Now it will doubtless surprise him to learn that the eggs not only have been laid but have hatched.

He either ignores or is ignorant of the fact that as far back as 1922, in our unemployment conference of that year under my chairmanship, we developed the idea of making use of public works to assist in the stabilization of employment in times of depression and laid the foundation for its operation.

Upon the breaking out of this depression in November three years ago, I announced that not only would the Federal government speed up its public works, but I requested the states and municipalities to do likewise.

WAGES

I have for many years advocated high wages as the economic basis for the country. That is the road to economical production and high consumption of products of the farm and factory.

In order to show you what the rates of wages are in the United States compared with other countries, I have this week secured through the Department of Commerce a calculation on a basis which I have used before for purposes of illustration. The actual wages in terms of the currencies of other countries are difficult to compare. We must find a common denominator.

If we say that 5 per cent of butter and 95 per cent of flour form the basis of that useful mixture called "bread and butter," then the weekly earnings in each country would buy at retail in those countries the following totals of this useful compound:

WEEKLY WAGES IF APPLIED TO THE PURCHASE OF "COMPOSITE POUNDS OF BREAD AND BUTTER" AS OF OCTOBER, 1932

	Railway Engineers	Carpenters	Electricians	Coal Miners	Weavers	Day Labor
United States......	1,069	1,064	1,300	734	565	393
United Kingdom ..	342	253	276	223	161	184
Germany	271	176	169	162	120	106
France	246	183	164	123	86	86
Belgium	288	228	240	180	199	160
Italy	275	118	149	70	67	85
Japan	131	86	90	57	31	55

Let no man say it could not be worse.

TEMPORARY PROHIBITION OF IMMIGRATION

. . . I have by administrative order practically prohibited all immigration from every quarter of the globe except the relatives of our residents. It has reduced the numbers of people coming into the United States seeking employment to less than those who are departing. . . . Had the net immigration taken place since the date of that order which took place in the two years previous, we would have had 400,000 jobs taken from our people or had just that many persons added to our unemployed. . . .

. . . *Emergency jobs have helped enormously, but the normal jobs are the permanent dependence of the worker. Emergency jobs will never heal the depression.*

I then reviewed the credit problem as related to labor and our measures in that direction.

. . . We created [these agencies] to preserve your savings deposits, your insurance policies; to protect you from foreclosure on your homes. We did it to hold for you the jobs you have and, finally, to recover the ground lost in the battle and restore the jobs which have been lost. It has been a battle with inevitable casualties, but that battle is now being won. . . . Normal jobs are coming back.

I should like to digress for a moment to a more personal matter. In my hand I have a copy of the instructions issued by the Democratic National Committee to their speakers. I find a paragraph referring to my "dark labor record." I am glad that is neither pink nor red. But they say: "First and indelible, his early record is clouded by his former partnerships which contracted cheap Chinese coolie labor in South African mines." It goes further with references to statements of Democratic leaders grieving over this coolie labor, and implies that I engaged in the slavery of human beings.

This calumny has been disproved and denounced time and again. Some of my friends have even gone to the extent of digging up the public records of twenty-eight years ago, which show that at the time Chinese labor was imported into South Africa I publicly protested on the ground that high-paid skilled labor would do the work more efficiently; and further, no South African concern with which I was ever connected ever employed a single Chinese laborer. But more important than this, I happen to have in the files in Washington, from the man who first penned those lies, a statement under oath, humbly and abjectly withdrawing them.

Such contemptible statements in a political campaign would be ignored were it not that they were issued by the authority of the Democratic National Committee, and they would be of no interest to the American people except that it is proposed that a political party shall be placed in power over one hundred and twenty millions of people on the basis of votes secured in this manner. . . .

In closing, let me carry these issues to a plane far above all personal considerations. . . .

To me a great historical truth has been revealed during this period of trial and stress. . . . Never during these trying weeks, months, and years has the soul of America yielded to the bitter sting of defeat. Bewilderment and dismay seized upon some of our people, but never did the spirit of America itself surrender. Never for an instant did the American people lose faith in the principles of their government, their institutions, their country, or their God. Had America not stood stanch in this world storm, had it surrendered, had our people lost faith, the tide of disintegration might now engulf us all. . . .

No one who has seen this battle as I have seen it, who has watched the bright fabric of recovery woven laboriously from day to day, with the stout efforts of American faith and confidence in its people, could harbor a doubt for the future of this nation.

If there shall be no retreat, if the attack shall continue as it is now organized, then this battle is won.

And in Detroit on October 22, 1932, I said:

I now wish to discuss a proposal of the Democratic candidate himself.

Early in September there appeared amongst the unemployed in some of our cities reproductions of a letter from Governor Roosevelt, which read:

"Mr. Lowe Shearon,

"358 Front Street,

"New York, N.Y.

"In accordance with your request I shall be glad to have you quote me as follows:

" 'I believe in the inherent right of every citizen to employment at a living wage and pledge my support to whatever measures I may deem necessary for inaugurating self-liquidating public works, such as utilization of our water resources, flood control and land reclamation, to provide employment for all surplus labor at all times.'

"Yours very sincerely,

"FRANKLIN D. ROOSEVELT"

There can be only one conclusion from this statement. It is a hope held out to the 10,000,000 men and women now unemployed that they will be given jobs by the government. It is a promise no government could fulfill. It is utterly wrong to delude suffering men and women with such assurances.

The most menacing condition in the world today is the lack of confidence and faith. It is a terrible thing to increase this undermining effect by holding out, for political purposes, promises to 10,000,000 men which cannot be kept and must end in leaving them disillusioned.

There are a score of reasons why this whole plan is fantastic. These 10,000,000 men, nor any appreciable fraction of them, cannot be provided with jobs in this fashion. The only way is by healing the wounds of the economic system to restore them to their normal jobs. . . .

But above all I ask you whether or not such frivolous promises and dreams should be held out to suffering unemployed people. Is this the new deal?

At Indianapolis on October 28th, and in New York on October 31st, I reviewed Roosevelt's sins of omission and commission on the issue of public works and stated that his promises in his letter to Shearon implied public works that would cost $9,000,000,000 a year.[1]

---

[1] A puzzling inconsistency in Mr. Roosevelt's position is given by Raymond Moley in *After Seven Years,* p. 173 n.: "Again and again, when we were formulating the plans for the campaign in 1932, Roosevelt had been urged by Tugwell and others to come out for a $5,000,000,000 public works program. He repeatedly shied away from the proposal. This seems to have been partly because, as Roosevelt explained, Hoover, despite all his preparations had not been able to find over $900,000,000 worth of 'good' and useful projects. . . . The $900,000,000 Hoover figure Roosevelt personally regarded as the probable outside limit of useful plans and projects."

CHAPTER 28

THE PROHIBITION ISSUE

Prohibition (the Eighteenth Amendment) was an important issue in the campaign.

We had done our best to enforce the Prohibition law. We enormously increased the jail population. We multiplied the fines, padlockings, and confiscations. Yet the illicit traffic increased. Even the original fanatically dry states of Ohio, Kansas, Iowa, and Alabama would not cooperate with the Federal administration in enforcement as the law anticipated.

As we approached the 1932 Presidential election the whole Prohibition question took on a new aspect. I, as party leader, had to abandon the Elihu Root formula and give advice to the party convention.

SENATOR BORAH ON PROHIBITION

On May 10, 1932, I invited Senator William E. Borah, the leader of the drys, to lunch. I told him that the Eighteenth Amendment and the Volstead Law could not be enforced and gave him detailed information as to state and local refusals to take their share of the load as the law implied. I stated that the whole liquor question should be returned to the states. They might, if they wished, reinstate Prohibition and enforce it in their own domains, as some of them had done before the Amendment. I said that the Amendment should be repealed.

To my great surprise Borah said that he agreed with me and would go along. We agreed that the Federal government should retain authority to protect any state from imports of alcoholic beverages if that state wished to be dry. He urged strongly that the Federal government reserve some power of review so as to compel the states to prevent the return of the old saloon with all its corruption. As a matter of fact, several plans of state control to prohibit the saloon were currently being discussed in the country.[1] I told him that I would go along on this proposal if he would support me in presenting it in the campaign, and if he could work out a constitutional formula.

THE REPUBLICAN PLANK ON PROHIBITION

After this agreement with Borah, I suggested that former Interior Secretary Garfield of Ohio be made chairman of the Resolutions Committee at the Republican Convention. I gave Mr. Garfield my ideas for the platform plank on prohibition, which he heartily approved, as follows:

An amendment should be promptly submitted that shall allow the states to deal with Prohibition as their citizens may determine but subject to the retained power of the Federal government to protect those states where Prohibition may exist. There should be a safeguard against the return of the saloon and its attendant abuses.

Mr. Garfield conferred with leaders of both the wet and the dry elements in the party. He reported that Senators Borah and Fess, on the dry side, and Reed and others on the wet side, would agree. I had little confidence in some two-man political agreements, and therefore suggested to Garfield that he arrange a joint meeting with Senators Borah and Fess, Secretaries Mills and Wilbur, and Postmaster General Brown, that they might, in one another's presence, agree upon the precise wording of the plank. I considered witnesses to Borah's attitude highly important and felt that the lawyers (the larger number) in the group should pass on its constitutionality. Mr. Garfield held the meeting and reported to me that they all agreed upon the proposed plank, including Borah.

When the Convention met on June 14, 1932, the Resolutions Committee, as expected, was divided—wet and dry. To get our idea accepted, Mr. Garfield finally allowed the drys to write a long preamble to our central idea and the wets to write a final paragraph to attach on the end. I was greatly distressed, as I was sure that this would be interpreted as a

[1] Several states subsequently adopted such plans.

straddle; but nothing could be done about it, as it already had been sent to the floor of the Convention. Secretary Mills called me up to say that it was the best they could do, that passage of the body of the resolution without the head and tail would hopelessly split the Convention. There followed a long debate on the floor between the opposing factions. I was listening to it over the radio when my private telephone rang and Mark Sullivan told me that Senator Borah wished to speak with me: Would I call him up? I did so at once. Borah said that he was listening to the debate and expressed great anxiety lest the plank might be defeated. I told him not to worry, that in the end it would be put through. Twenty-four hours later, Senator Borah made a public statement, denounced the platform plank, and declared that he would support no candidate on that basis. Certainly I had no support from him in the campaign.

In my acceptance address on August 11th I endeavored to present and clarify the issue:

Across the path of the nation's consideration of these vast problems of economic and social order, there has arisen a bitter controversy over the control of the liquor traffic. I have always sympathized with the high purpose of the Eighteenth Amendment, and I have used every power at my command to make it effective, over the entire country. I have hoped it was the final solution of the evils of the liquor traffic against which our people have striven for generations. It has succeeded in great measure in those many communities where the majority sentiment is favorable to it. But in other and increasing number of communities there is a majority sentiment unfavorable to it. Laws opposed by majority sentiment create resentment which undermines enforcement and in the end produces degeneration and crime.

We must recognize the difficulties which have developed in making the Eighteenth Amendment effective, and that grave abuses have grown up. In order to secure the enforcement of the Amendment under our dual form of government the constitutional provision called for concurrent action on the one hand by the state and local authorities and on the other by the Federal government. Its enforcement requires independent but coincident action of both agencies. An increasing number of states and municipalities are proving themselves unwilling to engage in such enforcement. Due to these forces there is in large sections an increasing illegal traffic in liquor. But worse than this there has been in those areas a spread of disrespect not only for this law but for all laws, grave dangers of practical nullification of the Constitution, a degeneration in municipal government, and an increase in subsidized crime and violence. I can not consent to the continuation of this regime. . . .

I refuse . . . on the one hand to return to the old saloon with its political and social corruption, or on the other to endure the bootlegger and the speakeasy with their abuses and crime. Either is intolerable. These are not the ways out.

The Republican platform recommends submission of the question to the states, that the people themselves may determine whether they desire a change. . . .

The Constitution gives the President no power or authority with respect to changes in the Constitution itself; nevertheless my countrymen have a right to know my conclusions upon this matter. They are clear and need not be misunderstood. . . .

It is my conviction that the nature of this change, and one upon which all reasonable people can find common ground, is that each state shall be given the right to deal with the problem as it may determine, but subject to absolute guarantees in the Constitution of the United States to protect each state from interference and invasion by its neighbors, and that in no part of the United States shall there be a return of the saloon system with its inevitable political and social corruption and its organized interference with other states.

THE DEMOCRATIC PLANK ON PROHIBITION

The Democratic Convention was also tangled over this issue. Its plank advocated repeal subject to control of interstate traffic by the Federal government to protect the states from the importation of intoxicating liquors in violation of their laws. At the same time they *urged* that the states prevent the return of the saloon. This idea of *urging* the states to prevent the saloon, instead of *requiring it,* was the only essential difference from the Republican formula—except that the Democratic plank was clear cut.

Mr. Roosevelt started by laying all the emphasis upon complete repeal, saying in Chicago on July 2nd:

I congratulate this Convention for having had the courage fearlessly to write into its declaration of principles what an overwhelming majority here assembled really thinks about the Eighteenth Amendment. This Convention wants repeal. . . . I am confident that the United States of America wants repeal.

After he had repeated this a few times he began to get storm signals from drys who were prepared to go along with him but who did not want the saloon. He began to tread water on this question.

At Sea Girt, New Jersey, on August 27th, after repeating the Democratic plank, he said:

Thus the Democratic platform expressly and unequivocally opposes the return of the saloon, and with equal emphasis it demands that there be Federal control of the liquor traffic to protect dry states.

Again at Pittsburgh, October 19th, he said:

At the same time I reiterate the simple language of the Democratic platform which in good faith opposes the return of the old-time saloon.

Subsequent events proved that there was not even an "urge" by the Roosevelt administration to prevent the return of the saloon.

CHAPTER 29

BUSINESS REGULATION ISSUES

The regulation of utility rates, security issues, banking, and railways all came up for discussion at one time or another. The opposition advanced the idea of regulations as if they were new in American life.

Their remarks were all accompanied by statements that I, in particular, had done nothing in this field. I was, by every implication, an agent of "Wall Street" and "big business."

I had myself developed the regulation of Alaskan fisheries, aviation, and radio. In repeated messages to Congress, I had advocated further laws expanding the regulation of banking, electric power, bankruptcy, and started the Senate investigation into stock exchanges with a view to regulation of security issues and trading. In an address in Washington on August 11, 1932, and before the American Bar Association on October 12th, I discussed the principles involved in expansion of regulatory powers. On the latter occasion I said:

Economic forces have spread business across state lines and have brought new strains upon our Federal system in its relationships with the state sovereignties. Laws that once were adequate to control private operations affecting the public interest proved unequal to these new conditions. . . . But for the success of regulation over interstate commerce . . . the development of our great system of economic production would have been delayed, individual rights would have been trampled down.

At Indianapolis on October 28th I said:

This depression has exposed many weaknesses in our economic system. It has shown much wrongdoing. There have been exploitation and abuse of financial power. These weaknesses must be corrected, and that wrongdoing must be punished.

At New York on October 31st I said:

I have already stated that democracy must remain master in its own house. I have stated that abuse and wrongdoing must be punished and controlled.
. . . Our American system demands economic justice as well as political and social justice; it is not a system of *laissez faire.*

In the ebb and flow of economic life our people in times of prosperity and ease naturally tend to neglect the vigilance over their rights.

It is men who do wrong, not our institutions. It is men who violate the laws and public rights. It is men, not institutions, who must be punished.

ELECTRIC POWER REGULATION

In an address on public utilities at Portland, Oregon, on September 21st, Mr. Roosevelt went into a long explanation of the relations between the government and utilities. He observed:

Since 1928 the distinguished gentleman who is running against me has done nothing to enforce the regulatory sections of the Federal Water Power Act. . . .

While President Hoover now urges Federal control no administration bill has been introduced in Congress in the past four years.

At one point he quoted a recommendation of mine, as Secretary of Commerce in 1925, before the great era of interconnection of power across state lines had taken place, in which I had opposed Federal regulation and supported state regulation. After the development of long distance transmission, I had advocated Federal regulation. From the beginning of my administration, I had urged it repeatedly to Congress. Roosevelt ignored the fact that I had succeeded in setting up the Federal Power Commission for these purposes but, despite several messages to the Congress, the Democratic majority had refused to give the Commission the authority I had recommended.

He cited the Insull crash in fraud without mentioning that we had Insull under indictment or that Insull had built his fantastic empire after I had urged regulation.

GOVERNMENT IN THE POWER BUSINESS

Mr. Roosevelt in his Portland address also edged into the socialistic area through government operation of electric power. He advocated the government's development of power for power purposes—as distinguished from the development of power as a by-product of dams for the multiple purpose of irrigation, flood control and improvement of navigation. The socialist content of the speech was:

I have strengthened the belief that I have had a long time . . . that the question of power, of electric development and distribution is primarily a national problem.

. . . State-owned or Federally owned power sites can and should and must properly be developed by the government itself. . . .

. . . The right of the Federal government and state governments to go further and to transmit and distribute . . . gives to the government that essential "birch rod" in the cupboard. My distinguished opponent is against giving the Federal government in any case the right to operate its own power business.

Roosevelt also pledged himself to Senator Norris to pass his Muscle Shoals bill, which I had vetoed. It would have put the government in competition with the people not only in the distribution of power but also in the manufacture and distribution of fertilizers.

MY ANSWERS ON POWER REGULATION

I said in Washington on August 11th:

I have repeatedly recommended the Federal regulation of interstate power. I shall persist in that. I have opposed the Federal government undertaking the operation of the power business. I shall continue that opposition.

I said at Indianapolis on October 28th:

I have repeatedly recommended Federal regulation of interstate power. I stated as early as seven years ago that "glass pockets are the safety of the industry as well as the public." I secured the creation of the independent Power Commission by the Congress two years ago. . . .

The Democratic candidate says he will preserve the great water powers for the people. That is already provided by the law since 1920, and it therefore presents no difficulty to vigorous campaign promises.

And in New York on October 31st I said:

Another proposal is that the government go into the power business. . . .
Three years ago, in view of the extension of the use of transmission of power over state borders and the difficulties of state regulatory bodies in the face of this interstate action, I recommended to the Congress that such interstate power should be placed under regulation by the Federal government in cooperation with the state authorities.

That recommendation was in accord with the principles of the Republican party over the last fifty years, to provide regulation where public interest had developed in tools of industry which was beyond control and regulation of the states.

I succeeded in creating an independent Power Commission to handle such matters, *but the Democratic House declined to approve the further powers to this commission necessary for such regulation.*

I have stated unceasingly that I am opposed to the Federal government going into the power business. I have insisted upon rigid regulation. The Democratic candidate has declared . . . he is prepared to put the Federal government into the power business. . . .

There are many localities where the Federal government is justified in the construction of great dams and reservoirs, where navigation, flood control, reclamation, and stream regulation are of dominant importance, and where they are beyond the capacity or purpose of private or local government capital to construct. In these cases, power is often a by-product and should be disposed of by contract or lease. But for the Federal government to deliberately go out to build up and expand such an occasion to be the major purpose of a power and manufacturing business is to break down the initiative and enterprise of the American people . . . it is the negation of the ideals upon which our civilization has been based.

The power problem is not to be solved by the Federal government going into the power business. The remedy for abuses in the conduct of that industry lies in regulation and not by the Federal government entering upon the business itself. I have recommended to the Congress on various occasions that action should be taken to establish Federal regulation of interstate power in cooperation with state authorities. . . . I hesitate to contemplate the future of our institutions, of our government, and of our country, if the preoccupation of its officials is to be no longer the promotion of justice and equal opportunity but is to be devoted to barter in the markets. That is not liberalism; it is degeneration.

From their utterances in this campaign and elsewhere we are justified in the conclusion that our opponents propose to put the Federal government in . . . business with all its . . . Federal bureaucracy, its tyranny over state and local governments, its undermining of state and local responsibilities and initiative.

BANKING REGULATION

Mr. Roosevelt had much to say at various times on banking wickedness and the need for regulation. He ignored the fact that the banks had been regulated for forty years, and that at every session of Congress, from the beginning of my administration, I had urged a revision of the banking laws and supported specific legislation which had been defeated by the Democratic Congress.[1]

SECURITIES REGULATION

Mr. Roosevelt, at Columbus on August 20th, delivered an address on the regulation of security issues. The paragraphs defamatory of my administration were based upon disclosures in the Senate investigation undertaken at my instance. His recommendations were "objectives," not methods. He, as usual, ignored the action I had already taken to bring about legislation.

Tired of Roosevelt's criticism of my administration because New York stock and bond promotion had not been controlled, I said at Indianapolis on October 28th:

The Governor does not inform the American people that . . . most of this takes place in New York State, which has . . . authority; and that the Governor has done nothing to reform that evil. . . . I recollect a Governor of New York who, believing wrong was being done to citizens of his own and other states on their life insurance, found a man in Charles Evans Hughes who cleaned it up once and for all.

RAILWAYS

Mr. Roosevelt delivered an address on the plight of the railways at Salt Lake City on September 17th.[2] His "New Deal" proposed nothing

[1] See Chapters 3 and 22.
[2] Years afterwards Ralph Budd, president of the Burlington Railroad, told me he had prepared this speech and had adopted the policies of my railroad committee, of which

new, merely stating the assumption that "we had done nothing." He made some six proposals, all of which were in operation during my administration.

I dismissed the issue at Indianapolis on October 28th, saying:

I have repeatedly recommended to the Congress a revision of our railway transportation laws in order that we might create greater stability and greater assurance of this vital service in our transportation. . . . I have supported the recommendations of the Interstate Commerce Commission, which are specific and not generalities. Our opponents have adopted my program in this matter during this campaign except certain glittering generalizations, as to which they do not inform us how they are to be accomplished, and upon which I enter a reservation.

---

he was a member. Moley (*After Seven Years*) confirms this, saying: "Berle and I [were] working with Will Woodin, Joseph B. Eastman of the Interstate Commerce Commission, Ralph Budd of the Burlington . . . on a draft of a railroad speech for Roosevelt."

CHAPTER 30

COLLECTIVISM BY "PLANNED ECONOMY"

All through the 1932 campaign, something was in the air far more sinister than even the miasmic climate of depression or a political campaign. I was convinced that Roosevelt and some members of his Brain Trust were proposing to introduce parts of the collectivism of Europe into the United States under their oft-repeated phrase "planned economy." That was an expression common to all collectivist systems. Paraded as liberalism, it had all the tactics and strategies of its European counterparts.

Their "economic planning" was not the long-established American process of revising our government problems by prior study of their solution. Their purposes were stated in various disguises of new meanings, hidden in old and well understood words and in terms of glorious objectives. They involved the pouring of a mixture of socialism and fascism into the American System.

The first evidence of these collectivist ideas appeared in the character and beliefs of Roosevelt's advisers and speech writers—Tugwell, Frankfurter, Wallace, Senators Norris of Nebraska and Thomas of Oklahoma, and others—whose long-standing declarations for years had been of the collectivist type.

Their influence appeared early in Roosevelt's campaign speeches. At Oglethorpe University on May 22, 1932, stripped of oratorical trimmings, he said:

We cannot review carefully the history of our industrial advance without being struck with its haphazardness, the gigantic waste with which it has been accomplished, the superfluous duplication of productive facilities, the continual scrapping of still useful equipment, the tremendous mortality in industrial and commercial undertakings, the thousands of dead-end trails into which enterprise has been lured, the profligate waste of natural resources. . . . Much of it, I believe, could have been prevented by greater foresight and by a larger measure of *social planning*. . . .

Of these other phases, that which seems most important to me in the long run is the problem of *controlling by adequate planning the creation and distribution of those products which our vast economic machine is capable of yielding*. . . .

It seems to me probable that our physical economic plant will not expand in the future at the same rate at which it has expanded in the past. We may build more factories, but the fact remains that we have enough now to supply all of our domestic needs, and more, if they are used. With these factories we can now make more shoes, more textiles, more steel, more radios, more automobiles, more of almost everything than we can use. . . .

Too many so-called leaders of the nation fail to see the forest because of the trees. Too many of them fail to recognize the vital necessity of planning for definite objectives. True leadership calls for the setting forth of the objectives and the rallying of public opinion in support of these objectives.

Evidence that the "New Deal" embraced such ideas cropped out in Roosevelt's speech of July 2, 1932, at Chicago:

In the years before 1929 we know that this country had completed a vast cycle of building and inflation; for ten years we expanded on the theory of repairing the wastes of the war, but actually expanding far beyond that, and also beyond our natural and normal growth. . . .

What was the result? Enormous corporate surpluses piled up—the most stupendous in history. Where . . . did those surpluses go? . . . They went . . . into new and unnecessary plants which now stand dark and idle.

Roosevelt said in a speech on October 6th:

We know that some measures of regularization and planning for balance among industries and for envisaging production as a national activity must be devised.

And at Albany on October 6th he implied controls of trade which would prevent international competition and would control domestic production, saying:

More realistic mutual arrangements for trade, substituted for the present system in which each nation attempts to exploit the markets of every other, giving nothing in return, will do more for the peace of the world and will contribute more to supplement the eventual reduction of armament burdens than any other policy which could be devised. At the same time it will make possible the approach to a national economic policy at home which will have as its central feature the fitting of production programs to the actual probabilities of consumption.

In an address to the Commonwealth Club in San Francisco on September 23rd, he boldly advanced the notion of complete government control of production and distribution, saying:

Our industrial plant is built; the problem just now is whether under existing conditions it is not overbuilt. Our last frontier has long since been reached, and there is practically no more free land. More than half of our people do not live on the farms or on lands and cannot derive a living by cultivating their own property. There is no safety valve in the form of a Western prairie to which those thrown out of work by the Eastern economic machines can go for a new start. We are not able to invite the immigration from Europe to share our endless plenty. We are now providing a drab living for our own people. . . .

Clearly, all this calls for a reappraisal of values. A mere builder of more industrial plants, a creator of more railroad systems, an organizer of more corporations, is as likely to be a danger as a help. The day of the great promoter or the financial Titan, to whom we granted anything if only he would build, or develop, is over. Our task now is not discovery or exploitation of natural resources, or necessarily producing more goods. It is the soberer, less dramatic business of administering resources and plants already in hand, of seeking to reestablish foreign markets for our surplus production, of meeting the problem of underconsumption, *of adjusting production to consumption, of distributing wealth and products more equitably, of adapting existing economic organizations to the service of the people. The day of enlightened administration has come.*

No such control of industry as this implied was possible without regimentation of the nation. I discuss this at greater length later on.

A further indication of the collectivist character of the New Deal emerged in an address at Topeka, Kansas, where Roosevelt proposed in disguised terms the old McNary-Haugen plan for agriculture. It was a price-fixing plan wholly impossible of consummation without control of what the farmer was to plant and market.

Still more evidence of these collectivist ideas was "managed currency." I have already outlined the course of that debate. Monetary manipulation placed the possible control of values, wages and prices in the hands of bureaucracy.

Another indication of collectivism could be found in Roosevelt's address at Portland, Oregon—not that part devoted to the regulation of interstate power rates, but those parts which plainly meant the government operation and competitive distribution of power.

TAMPERING WITH THE SUPREME COURT

Premonitory signs of tampering with the Supreme Court also began to appear in the campaign. At Baltimore on October 25th, Mr. Roosevelt said:

After March 4, 1929, the Republican party was in complete control of all branches of the government—Executive, Senate, and House, and I may add, for good measure, in order to make it complete, the Supreme Court as well.

This statement of his may have been evoked by one of mine made a few days before in Washington, on October 12th, when addressing the American Bar Association:

It is your task to prove again what none knows better than you, that the very citadel of the rights of the poor against the oppression of rulers and against the extortions of the rapacious is the judicial system of the country, and that the impregnable apex of that system is the Supreme Court of the United States. It is impregnable because its membership in successive generations down to this moment has comprised the highest character of our land who, preserving its great traditions, have armored it with the moral support of the people, and thus, without physical power or the need of it, is able to stand equal and alone against legislative encroachment upon the people's rights or executive usurpation of them and, more precious than either, against private injustice and the enactment of public laws in violation of the fundamental protections of the Constitution.

At Indianapolis on October 28th I called attention to Mr. Roosevelt's statement of October 25th, saying:

I invite your attention to that statement about the Supreme Court. *There are many things revealed by the campaign of our opponents which should give American citizens concern about the future. One of the gravest is the state of mind revealed by my opponent in that statement. He implies that it is the function of the party in power to control the Supreme Court.* For generations Republican and Democratic Presidents alike have made it their most sacred duty to respect and maintain the independence of America's greatest tribunal. President Taft appointed a Democrat as Chief Justice; President Harding nominated a Democratic Justice; my last appointment was a Democrat from New York State whose appointment was applauded by Republicans and Democrats alike the nation over. All appointees to the Supreme Court have been chosen solely on the basis of character and mental power. Not since the Civil War have the members of the court divided on political lines.

Aside from the fact that the charge that the Supreme Court has been controlled by any political party is an atrocious one, there is a deeper implication in that statement. Does it disclose the Democratic candidate's conception of the functions of the Supreme Court? Does he expect the Supreme Court to be subservient to him and his party? Does that statement express his intention by his appointments or otherwise to attempt to reduce that tribunal to an instrument of party policy and political action for sustaining such doctrines as he may bring with him? [1]

My countrymen, I repeat to you, the fundamental issue in this campaign, the decision that will fix the national direction for a hundred years to come, is whether we shall go on in fidelity to the American traditions or whether we shall turn to innovations, the spirit of which is disclosed to us by many sinister revelations and veiled promises.

In an address in New York on October 31st, I again called attention to Mr. Roosevelt's statement, saying:

I am not called upon to defend the Supreme Court of the United States from this slurring reflection. Fortunately that court has jealously maintained over the years its high standard of integrity, impartiality, and freedom from influence of either the Executive or Congress, so that the confidence of the people is sound and unshaken.

[1] Within two years Roosevelt was to attempt exactly that.

But is the Democratic candidate really proposing his conception of the relation of the Executive and the Supreme Court? If that is his idea, he is proposing the most revolutionary new deal . . . the most destructive undermining
of the very safeguard of our form of government yet proposed by a Presidential candidate.

And beyond all this was Mr. Roosevelt's incessant stirring of class
hate in the most classless people civilization had produced.

Another incident carried, to me, great conviction as to the collectivist
nature of the New Deal. On September 17, 1931, President Gerard
Swope of the General Electric Company in a public address had taken
the lead in a project for the reorganization of American industry. It
was called "economic planning." At that time I submitted the plan to
the Attorney General, with a note of my own, as follows:

This plan provides for the mobilization of each variety of industry and
business into trade associations, to be legalized by the government and
authorized to "stabilize prices and control distribution." There is no stabilization of prices without price fixing and control of distribution. This feature at
once becomes the organization of gigantic trusts such as have never been
dreamed of in the history of the world. This is the creation of a series of complete monopolies over the American people. It means the repeal of the entire
Sherman and Clayton Acts, and all other restrictions on combinations and
monopoly. In fact, if such a thing were ever done, it means the decay of American industry from the day this scheme is born, because one cannot stabilize
prices without restricting production and protecting obsolete plants and inferior
managements. It is the most gigantic proposal of monopoly ever made in
history.

The Attorney General replied that the plan was wholly unconstitutional.

Late in December, 1931, the United States Chamber of Commerce
had taken a step which struck me at the time as a bit humorous, coming
as it did from that citadel of economic freedom. It, however, was ultimately to have most serious consequences to the country. The Chamber
undertook a referendum of its members upon this scheme of "economic
planning." The referendum was favorable to the project, many of the
members having fretted greatly under the Anti-Trust laws. Upon

receiving this favorable referendum, Henry Harriman, president of the Chamber, called upon me and urged that I recommend the plan to the Congress. I informed him that if this plan were put into practice it would, through the creation of monopolies, drive the country into the Fascism of which it was mostly a pattern, or toward Socialism as the result of public exasperation.

Later, on September 23, 1932, during the campaign, Harriman again called upon me and urged that I give a public pledge to support the Chamber's recommendation. I refused. To me it violated the primary canons of human liberty. Harriman told me that Roosevelt had agreed to support the plan, and that if I would not make such a pledge a large number of highly placed business men would support my opponent, both financially and by their influence—which they did.

Mr. Roosevelt kept this pledge and the "NRA" was the resulting Frankenstein. I discuss this question further in the next section of this volume.

MY CHARGES OF COLLECTIVISM

I have no need to recite here my own concept of American life; I had often stated it over the years. I stated it in the campaign in the hope that the disguised collectivism would be understood. I directly pointed to those intentions on Roosevelt's part—or on the part of his ghost writers.

At Detroit on October 22nd, I said:

What you will determine on November 8th will be much more than a change of individuals, of even more importance than merely making a choice between the ways of coming out of this emergency. More than all that, it will determine the permanent course of the country.

The future of individuals is of no great importance in the life stream of the nation. . . . What is of vast importance is the measures and policies you adopt by your vote, and the men and forces who in front and behind the scenes will dominate our national life.

. . . Following will-o'-wisps is not progressive. That is not being liberal. Rather it is driving slowly to the tyranny which means the extinction under bureaucracy of liberty and hope and opportunity.

I spoke on the subject again shortly at Indianapolis on October 28th. I resolved finally to deal with the whole collectivist color of the New

Deal in an address at Madison Square Garden in New York on October 31st. My colleagues thought the subject too academic to impress a people who were largely unaccustomed to ideological discussion and would see little danger in Roosevelt's statements. But I felt that I must state my position and warn the people that the dangers from the New Dealers were more dangerous to free men than the depression itself. This address, in after years, has been more often reprinted and referred to in parts than any other of my campaign speeches. For these reasons I give extensive quotations:

This campaign is more than a contest between two men. It is more than a contest between two parties. It is a contest between two philosophies of government.

We are told by the opposition that we must have a change, that we must have a new deal. It is not the change that comes from normal development of national life to which I object, but the proposal to alter the whole foundations of our national life, which have been builded through generations of testing and struggle, and the principles upon which we have builded the nation. The expressions our opponents use must refer to important changes in our economic and social system and our system of government; otherwise they are nothing but vacuous words. And I realize that in this time of distress many of our people are asking whether our social and economic system is incapable of that great primary function of providing security and comfort of life to all of the firesides of our 25,000,000 homes in America, whether our social system provides for the fundamental development and progress of our people, whether our form of government is capable of originating and sustaining that security and progress.

This question is the basis upon which our opponents are appealing to the people in their fears and distress. They are proposing changes and so-called new deals which would destroy the very foundations of our American system.

Our people should consider the primary facts before they come to the judgment—not merely through political agitation, the glitter of promise, and the discouragement of temporary hardships—whether they will support changes which radically affect the whole system which has been builded up by a hundred and fifty years of the toil of our fathers. They should not approach the question in the despair with which our opponents would clothe it.

Our economic system has received abnormal shocks during the last three years, which temporarily dislocated its normal functioning. These shocks have in a large sense come from without our borders, but I say to you that our system of government has enabled us to take such strong action as to prevent the disaster which would otherwise have come to our nation. It has enabled us further to develop measures and programs which are now demonstrating their ability to bring about restoration and progress.

I then gave a short summary of the evidences of recovery.

We must go deeper than platitudes and emotional appeals of the public platform in the campaign, if we will penetrate to the full significance of the changes which our opponents are attempting to float upon the wave of distress and discontent from the difficulties we are passing through. We can find what our opponents would do after searching the record of their appeals to discontent, group and sectional interest. We must search for them in the legislative acts which they sponsored and passed in the Democratic-controlled House of Representatives in the last session of Congress. We must look into measures for which they voted and which were defeated. We must inquire whether or not the Presidential and Vice Presidential candidates have disavowed these acts. If they have not, we must conclude that they form a portion and are a substantial indication of the profound changes proposed. . . . And we must look still further than this as to what revolutionary changes have been proposed by the candidates themselves. . . .

We must look into the type of leaders who are campaigning for the Democratic ticket, whose philosophies have been well known all their lives, whose demands for a change in the American system are frank and forceful. I can respect the sincerity of these men in their desire to change our form of government and our social and economic system, though I shall do my best tonight to prove they are wrong.

I here gave a list including Senators Norris, Wheeler, Cutting, and Huey Long and the Brain Trust.

The seal of these men indicates that they have sure confidence that they will have voice in the administration of our government.

I may say at once that the changes proposed from all these Democratic principals and allies are of the most profound and penetrating character. If they are brought about, this will not be the America which we have known in the past.

The American System

Let us pause for a moment and examine the American system of government, of social and economic life, which it is now proposed that we should alter. Our system is the product of our race and of our experience in building a nation to heights unparalleled in the whole history of the world. It is a system peculiar to the American people. It differs essentially from all others in the world. It is an American system.

It is founded on the conception that only through ordered liberty, through freedom to the individual and equal opportunity to the individual will his initiative and enterprise be summoned to spur the march of progress.

It is by a society absolutely fluid in the movement of its human particles that our individualism departs from the individualism of Europe. We resent class distinction because there can be no rise for the individual through the frozen strata of classes. No stratification of classes can take place in a mass livened by the free rise of its particles. Thus in our ideals the able and ambitious are able to rise constantly from the bottom to leadership in the community.

The primary conception of this whole American system is not the regimentation of men but the cooperation of free men. . . .

It is founded on a peculiar conception of self-government designed to maintain this equal opportunity to the individual. Through decentralization it brings about and maintains these responsibilities.

The implacable march of scientific discovery with its train of new inventions presents every year new problems to government and new problems to the social order. Questions often arise whether, in the face of the growth of these new and gigantic tools, democracy can remain master in its own house, can preserve the fundamentals of our American system. I contend that it can; and I contend that this American system of ours has demonstrated its validity and superiority over any system yet invented by human mind.

It has demonstrated it in the face of the greatest test of our history—that is the emergency which we have faced in the last three years.

When the political and economic weakness of many nations of Europe, the result of the World War and its aftermath, finally culminated in collapse of their institutions, the delicate adjustments of our economic and social life received a shock unparalleled in our history. . . .

In spite of all these obstructions we did succeed. Our form of government did prove itself equal to the task. We saved this nation from a quarter of a century of chaos and degeneration, and we preserved the savings, the insurance policies, gave a fighting chance to men to hold their homes. We saved the integrity of our government and the honesty of the American dollar. And we installed measures which today are bringing back recovery. Employment, agriculture, business—all of these show the steady healing of our enormous wound.

I therefore contend that the problem of today is to continue these measures and policies to restore this American system to its normal functioning, to repair the wounds it has received, to correct the weaknesses and evils which would defeat that system. To enter upon a series of deep changes, to embark upon this inchoate new deal which has been propounded in this campaign would be to undermine and destroy our American system.

RESULTS OF THE AMERICAN SYSTEM

Before we enter upon such courses, I would like you to consider what the results of this American system have been during the last thirty years—that is, one single generation. . . . We have secured a lift in the standards of living and a diffusion of comfort and hope to men and women, the growth of equal opportunity, the widening of all opportunity, such as had never been seen in the history of the world. We should not tamper with it or destroy it; but on the contrary we should restore it and, by its gradual improvement and perfection, foster it into new performance for our country and for our children.

I then sketched the vast social and economic progress over this period.

We have more nearly met with a full hand the most sacred obligation of man, that is, the responsibility of a man to his neighbor. Support to our schools, hospitals, and institutions for the care of the afflicted surpassed in totals of billions the proportionate service in any period of history in any nation in the world.

Three years ago there came a break in this progress. A break of the same type we have met fifteen times in a century and yet we have overcome them. But eighteen months later came a further blow by shocks transmitted to us by the earthquakes of the collapse of nations throughout the world as the aftermath of the World War. . . .

But I ask you what has happened. This thirty years of incomparable im-

provement in the scale of living, the advance of comfort and intellectual life, inspiration, and ideals did not arise without right principles animating the American system which produced them. Shall that system be discarded because vote-seeking men appeal to distress and say that the machinery is all wrong and that it must be abandoned or tampered with? Is it not more sensible to realize the simple fact that some extraordinary force has been thrown into the mechanism, temporarily deranging its operation? Is it not wiser to believe that the difficulty is not with the principles upon which our American system is founded and designed through all these generations of inheritance? Should not our purpose be to restore the normal working of that system which has brought to us such immeasurable benefits, and not destroy it?

I then reviewed the evidences of collectivist intentions previously mentioned in this chapter and continued:

In order that we may get at the philosophical background of the mind which proposed profound change in our American system and a new deal, I would call your attention to an address delivered by the Democratic candidate in San Francisco on September 23rd:

"Our industrial plant is built. The problem just now is whether under existing conditions it is not overbuilt. Our last frontier has long since been reached. There is practically no more free land. There is no safety valve in the Western prairies where we can go for a new start. . . . The mere building of more industrial plants, the organization of more corporations is as likely to be as much a danger as a help. . . . Our task now is not the discovery of natural resources or necessarily the production of more goods, it is the sober, less dramatic business of administering the resources and plants already in hand . . . establishing markets for surplus production; of meeting the problem of underconsumption; distributing the wealth and products more equitably and adapting the economic organization to the service of the people."

I do challenge the whole idea that we have ended the advance of America, that this country has reached the zenith of its power, the height of its development. That is the counsel of despair for the future of America. That is not the spirit by which we shall emerge from this depression. That is not the spirit that made this country. If it is true, every American must abandon the road of countless progress and unlimited opportunity. I deny that the promise of American life has been fulfilled, for that means we have begun the decline and fall. No nation can cease to move forward without degeneration of spirit. . . .[2]

If these measures, these promises, which I have discussed; or these failures to disavow these projects; this attitude of mind, mean anything, they mean the enormous expansion of the Federal government; they mean the growth of bureaucracy such as we have never seen in our history. No man who has not occupied my position in Washington can fully realize the constant battle which must be carried on against incompetence, corruption, tyranny of government expanded into business activities. . . . These measures would transfer vast responsibilities to the Federal government from the states, the local governments, and the individuals. But that is not all; they would break down our form of government. Our legislative bodies cannot delegate their authority to any dictator, but without such delegation every member of these bodies is impelled in representation of the interest of his constituents constantly to seek privilege and demand service in the use of such agencies. Every time the Federal government extends its arm, 531 Senators and Congressmen become actual boards of directors of that business.

Capable men cannot be chosen by politics for all the various talents required. Even if they were supermen, if there were no politics in the selection of the Congress, if there were no constant pressure for this and for that, so large a number would be incapable as a board of directors of any institution. At once when these extensions take place by the Federal government, the authority and responsibility of state governments and institutions are undermined. Every enterprise of private business is at once halted to know what Federal action is going to be. It destroys initiative and courage. . . .

We have heard a great deal in this campaign about reactionaries, conservatives, progressives, liberals, and radicals. I have not yet heard an attempt by any one of the orators who mouth these phrases to define the principles upon which they base these classifications. *There is one thing I can say without any question of doubt—that is, that the spirit of liberalism is to create free men; it is not the regimentation of men. It is not the extension of bureaucracy. I have said in this city before now that you cannot extend the mastery of government over the daily life of a people without somewhere making it master of people's souls and thoughts. Expansion of government in business means that the government, in order to protect itself from the political consequences of its errors, is driven irresistibly without peace to greater and greater control*

[2] I may mention again that in the five years since Mr. Roosevelt's death the plant capacity and manufacturing production was doubled over even 1928.

of the nation's press and platform. Free speech does not live many hours after free industry and free commerce die. It is a false liberalism that interprets itself into government operation of business. Every step in that direction poisons the very roots of liberalism. It poisons political equality, free speech, free press, and equality of opportunity. It is the road not to liberty but to less liberty. True liberalism is found not in striving to spread bureaucracy, but in striving to set bounds to it. True liberalism seeks all legitimate freedom first in the confident belief that without such freedom the pursuit of other blessings is in vain. Liberalism is a force truly of the spirit proceeding from the deep realization that economic freedom cannot be sacrificed if political freedom is to be preserved.

Even if the government conduct of business could give us the maximum of efficiency instead of least efficiency, it would be purchased at the cost of freedom. It would increase rather than decrease abuse and corruption, stifle initiative and invention, undermine development of leadership, cripple mental and spiritual energies of our people, extinguish equality of opportunity, and dry up the spirit of liberty and progress. Men who are going about this country announcing that they are liberals because of their promises to extend the government in business are not liberals, they are reactionaries of the United States.

And I do not wish to be misquoted or misunderstood. I do not mean that our government is to part with one iota of its national resources without complete protection to the public interest. I have already stated that democracy must remain master in its own house. I have stated that abuse and wrongdoing must be punished and controlled. Nor do I wish to be misinterpreted as stating that the United States is a free-for-all and devil-take-the-hindermost society.

The very essence of equality of opportunity of our American system is that there shall be no monopoly or domination by any group or section in this country, whether it be business, sectional, or a group interest. On the contrary, our American system demands economic justice as well as political and social justice; it is not a system of *laissez faire*.

I am not setting up the contention that our American system is perfect. No human ideal has ever been perfectly attained, since humanity itself is not perfect. But the wisdom of our forefathers and the wisdom of the thirty men who have preceded me in this office hold to the conception that progress can be attained only as the sum of accomplishments of free individuals, and they have held unalterably to these principles.

In the ebb and flow of economic life our people in times of prosperity and ease naturally tend to neglect the vigilance over their rights. Moreover, wrongdoing is obscured by apparent success in enterprise. Then insidious diseases and wrongdoings grow apace. But we have in the past seen in times of distress and difficulty that wrongdoing and weakness come to the surface, and our people, in their endeavors to correct these wrongs, are tempted to extremes which may destroy rather than build.

It is men who do wrong, not our institutions. It is men who violate the laws and public rights. It is men, not institutions, who must be punished.

In my acceptance speech four years ago at Palo Alto I stated that—

"One of the oldest aspirations of the human race was the abolition of poverty. By poverty I mean the grinding by undernourishment, cold, ignorance, fear of old age of those who have the will to work."

I stated that—

"In America today we are nearer a final triumph over poverty than in any land. The poorhouse has vanished from among us; we have not reached that goal, but, given a chance to go forward, we shall, with the help of God, be in sight of the day when poverty will be banished from this nation."

Our Democratic friends have quoted this passage many times in this campaign. I do not withdraw a word of it. When I look about the world even in these times of trouble and distress I find it more true in this land than anywhere else under the traveling sun. I am not ashamed of it, because I am not ashamed of holding ideals and purposes for the progress of the American people. Are my Democratic opponents prepared to state that they do not stand for this ideal or this hope? For my part, I propose to continue to strive for it, and I hope to live to see it accomplished. . . .

My countrymen, the proposals of our opponents represent a profound change in American life—less in concrete proposal, bad as that may be, than by implication and by evasion. Dominantly in their spirit they represent a radical departure from the foundations of 150 years which have made this the greatest nation in the world. This election is not a mere shift from the ins to the outs. It means deciding the direction our nation will take over a century to come.

As we expected, we were defeated in the election.

CHAPTER 31

HOME AGAIN

Mrs. Hoover and I left the White House without regrets except that the job of recovery and some needed reforms were incomplete. We had no illusions that America would come to an end because we were going back home again. I had now been in almost full-time public service since 1914—nineteen years. And during that time we had not lived at home for a total of more than a few scattered months. The mental taste of one's own gadgets and gardens was good.

Democracy is not a polite employer. The only way out of elective office is to get sick or die or get kicked out. Otherwise one is subject to the charge of being a coward, afraid to face the electorate. When a President is out he carries no pension, privilege, nor pomp. He does not even carry away an honorary title, not even Governor, Judge, or Colonel. He is about the only retiring public official who is just Mister. He stands in line for a seat and for tickets just like other citizens.

When the British Prime Minister is defeated he may if he wishes receive a great title, he automatically draws a great pension, and everybody makes way for his Lordship.[1]

But the American method is better. It emphasizes the equalities of its democracy. And an ex-President is not devoid of honor or advantages. He is naturally recognized everywhere because his picture has appeared in every print every day for years. To his misfortune the pictures are mostly the flashlight sort with their mechanistic absence of flattery and implications of a prison personality. But recognition brings honor. The proof is that an ex-President is high in the seeking of autograph

[1] Some Prime Ministers delay this sign of retirement in order to hold position in the House of Commons, but most accept it—none fail on the pension.

hunters. And their appraisals of his relative importance are definite. One day a youngster demanded three autographs, which seemed to imply a generous compliment. I asked: "Why three?" "It takes two of yours to get one of Babe Ruth's."

The American treatment of an ex-President has other real advantages. He can just be himself. He can go and come without the restraint of representing a class or a symbol. Up to the time of this writing, I have traveled tens of thousands of miles alone or with Mrs. Hoover, have wandered in the slums of a score of cities, bought things in a thousand stores, visited hundreds of industrial works, been entertained in every sort of home from the roadside cottage to the greatest of establishments. And everywhere I received pleasant, often affectionate, greetings, never an offensive word—to my face.

It might be difficult for some families to adjust themselves to the abrupt drop from palace to cottage. And the White House is a palace more comfortable than that of most kings. Our family had long alternated between the luxury of great cities and the primitive living of world frontiers, so that this change was no bump. Indeed Mrs. Hoover and I found abundant compensations from being kicked out of a job after this nearly forty years of administrative responsibility and nineteen years of strenuous public service. There came a great sense of release. It was emancipation from a sort of peonage—a revolution back to personal freedom. It was a release not alone from political pressures but from the routines of twelve to fourteen hours of work seven days a week. Even mealtime had to be given over to the discussion of the problems of the day; the nights were haunted by the things that went wrong; the so-called vacations were tied to the telephone and telegraph or to the visitor who knew that now was the time to discuss his problem.

Therefore, for the first time in long memory, neither Mrs. Hoover nor I had to get up in the morning at the summons of a human or mechanical alarm clock with its shock into reality. Breakfast was to be had when we wanted it. We read the papers and listened to the radio after breakfast instead of between bites. We did it with complete detachment, for no longer did events so directly affect us as before. We looked over the hundreds of letters with the feeling that we did not have to answer them at all, or anyway not today. We could walk about and admire the neighbors' flower gardens and lay out our own. There were no scores of visitors to see at fifteen-minute intervals, most of whom wanted something for themselves that they ought not to have. Now we could choose our visitors without fear of injury to public or party interest. The many whom we met carried good cheer or useful conversation. There were no piles of documents to be signed before noon. There was no compulsion to make disagreeable decisions. We were not chained to the telephone bell nor were we the slaves of a host of secretaries. I was able to walk out the front door, get in an automobile without a chauffeur and just drive away anywhere—to see the country, to fish, or to visit. If it were not from a sense of service or ambition, there would be no recruits for public jobs at all. Men can make a living with far more satisfactions and many less wounds to the soul at other callings.

We received a hearty welcome home from the Governor of the state, the mayors, and a host of friends along the railway. At Palo Alto the students staged a vociferous reception. I found an accumulation of some twenty thousand letters, breathing devotion and loyalty; a third of them were hand-written on the blue-lined paper of lowly homes. We quickly organized a stenographic staff and gave to each of these letter-writers a signed acknowledgment of the friendship. It was a tiresome task, but it seemed to be the least one could do for so great an outpouring of affection.

In the years after leaving Washington, my various activities in many benevolent institutions, crusading against the New Deal[2] and advo-

[2] Any interested person can find ample demonstration of my occupation and views from the series of volumes of my public statements, published by a friend under the title "Addresses Upon the American Road."

Addresses Upon the American Road 1933–1938 (Charles Scribner's Sons, New York, 1938)

Further Addresses Upon the American Road 1938–1940 (Charles Scribner's Sons, New York, 1940)

Addresses Upon the American Road 1940–1941 (Charles Scribner's Sons, New York, 1941)

Addresses Upon the American Road 1941–1945 (D. Van Nostrand Co., Inc., New York, 1946)

Addresses Upon the American Road 1945–1948 (D. Van Nostrand Co., Inc., New York, 1949)

Addresses Upon the American Road 1948–1950 (Stanford University Press, Stanford University, California, 1951).

cating national policies, kept me constantly traveling. In 1934 Mrs. Hoover and I found that we must spend much of the time in the East and, therefore, we took an apartment in New York City where we spent a good part of the fall and winter months over many years.

New York is the place from where a large part of America's intellectual life is transmitted. Here centers the control of much of the magazine, the book, and the radio world. Some of its daily papers spread into every other newspaper office in the country. The control of many national charitable and educational institutions is centered here because of the closeness to "big money." A multitude of political, social, economic, and propaganda organizations spread out or infiltrate into the whole of American life from this great city. When one is interested also in the promulgation of ideas, it is more effective to be at the distributing point than at the receiving end.

In these settings and travelings about, I was able to observe the New Deal methods of "making America over" and their method of solving the depression with much detachment. In the next section I give a summary of the "aftermath" which amply confirmed all my warnings in the campaign.

The Aftermath

CHAPTER 32

THE AFTERMATH

THE GREAT DEPRESSION—SIXTH PHASE

In my last address a few weeks after the election of 1932 I said:

You will expect me to discuss the late election. Well, as nearly as I can learn we did not have enough votes on our side. . . . My country has given me the highest honor that comes to man. . . . That is a debt I can never repay.

Only a few rare souls in a century, to whose class I make no pretension, count much in the great flow of this Republic. The life stream of this nation is the generations of millions of human particles acting under impulses of advancing ideas and national ideals gathered from a thousand springs. These springs and rills have gathered into great streams which have nurtured and fertilized this great land over the centuries. Its dikes against dangerous floods are cemented with the blood of our fathers. Our children will strengthen the dikes, will create new channels, and the land will grow greater and richer with their lives.

We are but transitory officials in government whose duty is to keep the channels clear and to strengthen and extend their dikes. What counts toward the honor of public officials is that they sustain the national ideals upon which are patterned the design of these channels of progress and the construction of these dikes of safety. What is said in this or in that political campaign counts no more than the sound of the cheerful ripples or the angry whirls of the stream. *What matters is—that God help the man or the group who breaks down these dikes, who diverts these channels to selfish ends. These waters will drown him or them in a tragedy that will spread over a thousand years.*

My memoirs would be incomplete without an appraisal of the attempt to break down the dikes of American freedom—and its consequences.

The period from 1933 to 1941 may be viewed from two angles: first, as an attempt to revolutionize the American system of life, and second, as a mere continuation of the Great Depression into its sixth phase by inept economic action. It was, in fact, both—the first being largely the cause of the second. My interest in my country could not be ended by an election, especially as I knew the character and purposes of the men coming into power were not those of traditional America.

Demonstration of the rightness of the American manner of life, and the disaster to my countrymen following departure from it, requires an objective account of the social, economic, and governmental forces in action.

What had been, up to the election, an ideological debate was now transformed into a reality of national experience. In adopting the New Deal, most of the American people did not realize that they had departed from the road of free men. Our people had never been conscious of ideological systems. They had simply lived and breathed our own American manner of life. Moreover, they were little acquainted with the meaning of the abstract terms used in such philosophies. They did not believe that hideous dangers to their freedom lurked in generous-looking but distorted use of such phrases as "Liberalism," "New Deal," "Economic Planning," "Planned Economy," "Production for Use" and "Redistribution of Wealth." A people traditionally willing to "try anything once" welcomed such ideas—at first.

I shall prove that the penalty was nine years more of the Great Depression which ended in name only with the absorption of our man power and energies in war.

There should be lessons to free men in this experience.

Again in this section I have proceeded by topics rather than in chronological order. Topical treatment requires some retracing of events over short periods; yet, if the whole were put into chronological diary form, the particular movements which it is my object to trace would be utterly confused. Thus it is necessary to summarize briefly some of the incidents already mentioned in the previous chapters.

Again I have limited criticisms—aside from my own—to those by former colleagues or supporters of Roosevelt. My own observations occur only where it is necessary to indicate my views. Utterances of Roosevelt's former supporters should carry more conviction than those of his constant opponents.

No student will understand the vagaries and interplay of forces in the Roosevelt administration without first exploring the widely different character of the groups around him. He had been supported by the Democratic combination which had its origin in the Bryan campaign of 1896. Bryan had brought together old-line conservative Democrats (mostly Southerners), Northern radicals, and corrupt city machines. The binding tie of these groups over thirty years was one central theme —to get into office. But, in addition, Roosevelt had the support of a frustrated, suffering people who did not have the patience to fight through the inevitable economic penalties of a great war. This discontented group found a large leadership in the Intellectuals with a capital I, who had embraced some form or parts of collectivism.

The political exigencies of the new administration required that all these diverse groups be represented in its personnel. The interplay of the groups accounts for much of the inconsistency of ideological policies and the confusions in the administration.

Roosevelt himself leaned heavily to the "left"—"left of center," as he called it—and the left-wing group became the dominant force.

If we analyze the persons in the administration, the grouping becomes even clearer.

The old-line Democrats were represented in the Cabinet by such men as John N. Garner, Cordell Hull, James A. Farley, Homer Cummings, Claude Swanson, Daniel Roper, and George Dern who, if they really thought about it, believed in the American System and the nineteenth century interpretation of Liberalism. In addition, there were a group of really old-line Democrats who were genuinely desirous of promoting needed reforms. They were represented in policy-making positions by such men as Raymond Moley, Lewis Douglas, Joseph P. Kennedy, James Warburg, John W. Hanes, T. Jefferson Coolidge, and George Creel—all in second-string positions but of importance.[1]

---

[1] One of the New Deal phenomena has been the critical books written by representatives and important members of Roosevelt's staff, such as Garner, Hull, Farley, Creel,

Among the intellectuals who interpreted liberalism as a sort of collectivism were such representative minds as Madam Frances Perkins, Dean Acheson, Henry Morgenthau, Jr., Harold Ickes, Francis Biddle, Hugh Johnson, Frank Murphy, Henry A. Wallace, and Felix Frankfurter.[2]

To their reinforcement in the march on Washington came a host of dangerous men and women. Congressional committees later exposed several hundreds of them as fellow-travelers or members of Communist front organizations. Worse still was the later exposure that more than fifty men and women in important policy-making positions were members of the Communist party. Eight persons who had held important positions of trust were convicted as traitors or perjurers in relation to traitorous actions.

There were exposed, at one time or another, more than a thousand bad risks occupying important official positions in the Roosevelt administration. These groups exerted a decisive influence not only on domestic but also on foreign policies. These disclosures have shocked and shamed all real Americans. But shame is a minor result compared to the effect of their influence on and betrayal of America during the years.

Such was the New Deal's intellectual climate. The whole gamut, from the old-line Democrats to the traitors, called themselves "liberals."[3]

---

and Johnson. The books of all these men depict the Roosevelt policies and action bitterly.

[2] Hugh Johnson, an ardent member of the New Deal in its early years, said: "Even during the planning of the New Deal, there began to appear—faintly and little considered at first—pressures, and vetoes in advice, from a group then sometimes called 'The Harvard Crowd.' . . . Shortly after election there began to occur one of the cleverest infiltrations in the history of our Government. . . . [Frankfurter] is the *most influential single individual in the United States today.* His 'boys' have been insinuated into obscure but key positions in every vital department."

[3] George Creel, whose life job was studying character, who was one of Roosevelt's intimates over twenty years and, for four years prior to his disillusionment, was a part of Roosevelt's administration, writes in *Rebel at Large* (p. 370):

"Present-day 'liberalism,' as it has the impudence to call itself, is anti-American; for at its back, as cunning as secret, are men and women who give their allegiance to a foreign power. And what of their following? Dancing to the strings pulled by hidden hands is as motley a crew as ever gathered under one banner. Shoulder to shoulder with avowed Communists and subversive aliens stand the weird conglomeration known as 'fellow travelers,' made up of embittered failures, discredited politicians, crystalgazers, venal labor leaders, underpaid professors and overpaid actors, feminized

The left-wing New Dealers in time dominated particularly the policy-making positions in the Departments of State, Treasury, Agriculture, Interior, and Labor. They also controlled several regulatory commissions. In the foreign-affairs field, the common bond of the leftists was admiration of, or devotion to, Soviet Russia. But I am here concerned with domestic matters or such foreign action as directly affected our economic and social system.

During Roosevelt's first eight years the guiding phrases of the New Deal were not "Communism," "Socialism," and "Fascism," but "Planned Economy." This expression was an emanation from the caldrons of all three European collectivist forms. The phrase first popularized by Mussolini, and often mouthed by the Communists and the Socialists, was itself a typical collectivist torture of meaning. It was not a blueprint, but a disguise. It meant governmental execution and dictation. Ever since George Washington we have planned, with changing times, the necessary development of government within the limits of freedom. Our public schools, public works, safeguards to health, conservation, reclamation of the desert, creation of parks, highways, the beautification of cities, regulatory laws, and standards of conduct were proofs.

By a series of invasions of the judicial and legislative arms and the independence of the states, accompanied by such measures as managed currency, government operation of some industries and dictation to others, "Planned Economy" quickly developed as a centralization of power in the hands of the President, administered and perpetuated by an enormous Federal bureaucracy. It was an attempt to cross-breed Socialism, Fascism, and Free Enterprise.

The illusion of the advocates of this mixture was that they could have parts of economic collectivism and yet maintain representative govern-

---

preachers eager to gain an effect of virility, perennial sophomores, frustrated incompetents, idle wealth seeking protective coloration, motion-picture stars hopeful of a smoke screen to hide inanity and illiteracy, scatterbrains rejoicing in an emotional experience, and cowardly Esaus willing to trade freedom for a bogus security.

" 'Liberalism!' Not in all history has a word been so wrenched away from its true meaning and dragged through every gutter of defilement. Where once it stood for the dignity of man—the rescue of the spirit from the debasements of materialism—it now stands for the obliteration of individualism at the hands of a ruthless, all-powerful state, and shames human sympathy as a weakness even as it denies the practicability of ideals."

ment, the personal liberties, and the productivity of the nation. They were totalitarian "liberals." They believed that free initiative and creative individualism could survive without economic freedom. Their further illusion was that any economic system would work in a mixture of others. No greater illusions ever mesmerized the American people. The ultimate end would be to transform the people into a government of men and not of laws.

I believe that any objective student of social forces will agree that these men did their best to create a traditional "mass movement" to accomplish their aims. Such mass movements had been successful in the case of Russian Communism, German National Socialism, and Italian Fascism. All those movements sprang from the soil of postwar misery, the strivings for power, greed for the possessions of others, boredom with the routines of life, yearnings for adventure, or just frustration. These mass movements had many common characteristics. They exaggerated the miseries of the times. They condemned the existing economic and social systems as bankrupt. They cried, "Emergency! Emergency!" They promised Utopia. They envisaged a national devil. They stifled criticism with smearing and misrepresentation through the powerful agencies of government propaganda. They subjugated the legislative and judicial arms and purged their own party oppositions. They spent public moneys in subsidies to pressure groups. They distributed patronage to their adherents. They sought ceaselessly for more power.

The New Deal imitated all these methods, but it was successful in producing only a transitory rash of a "mass movement." It failed to produce the dynamism which had made such revolutions effective. The traditional American love of freedom and devotion to constitutional processes ultimately proved too deep for its schemes to work.[4]

It may be said at once that during the eight years under discussion

---

[4] H. G. Wells, one-half Socialist, one-half Communist, long an agitator of mass movements, visited Roosevelt several times at the White House. His summation (*Experiment in Autobiography,* pp. 681–682) is at least enlightening: "I do not say that the President has these revolutionary ideas in so elaborated and comprehensive a form as they have come to me; I do not think he has. I do not think he is consciously what I have called an Open Conspirator . . . But these ideas are sitting all around him now, and unless I misjudge him, they will presently possess him altogether. . . . My impression of both him and of Mrs. Roosevelt is that they are *unlimited* people . . . But as the vast problems about them expose and play themselves into their minds, the goal of the Open Con-

here the New Deal, despite its "Planned Economy" and its gadgets, the doubling of national expenditures, debt, and bureaucracy, totally failed to restore employment. During those eight years the numbers of persons unemployed and on relief proved each autumn to be about the same as they had been on the day Roosevelt was elected.

I will show that at the same time twelve great nations with free economy had, within two to three years, recovered from the world-wide depression and risen to levels of prosperity higher than even in the boom year of 1929.

During these eight years America continued to wallow in the Great Depression. In the end Roosevelt turned from the "New Deal" to international affairs and with the wrappings of war covered the utter debacle of "Planned Economy."

All of this will unfold as this narrative proceeds.

---

spiracy becomes plainer ahead. Franklin Roosevelt does not embody and represent that goal, but he represents the way thither. He is being the most effective transmitting instrument possible for the coming of the new world order. . . . He is continuously revolutionary in the new way . . ."

CHAPTER 33

BUILDING THE TROJAN HORSE
OF EMERGENCY

Every collectivist revolution rides in on a Trojan horse of "Emergency." It was a tactic of Lenin, Hitler, and Mussolini. In the collectivist sweep over a dozen minor countries of Europe, it was the cry of the men striving to get on horseback. And "Emergency" became the justification of the subsequent steps. This technique of creating emergency is the greatest achievement that demagoguery attains. The invasion of New Deal Collectivism was introduced by this same Trojan Horse.

I have outlined in previous chapters the cause and evolution of the wholly unnecessary panic of bank depositors which became Roosevelt's basis of emergency. He created it himself by refusing to cooperate. He continued to use that basis for every action and statement for years. In his authorized speeches and statements for 1933–1934[1] alone he justified action for more than two hundred Executive Orders with the word "emergency," and in his first two years he used the word more than four hundred times in public statements.

Roosevelt's assertions of his "emergency" became grotesque. Typical was a speech at Atlanta, Georgia, in December, 1935. In a nation-wide broadcast at St. Louis on December 16th,[2] I commented upon it. While some parts of it review the facts disclosed in the previous section of these memoirs, no attempt was ever made to refute this statement:

[1] *The Public Papers and Addresses of Franklin D. Roosevelt*, 1933 and 1934 volumes (Random House, New York, 1938).

[2] For the complete speech, see *Addresses upon the American Road* (1933–1938), pp. 87–100.

There has been no time in two generations when it is more needed that men stand up and discuss public questions. . . . The witchery of half truth fades only under the exposure of discussion. And there is only disaster in the dark alleys of inspired propaganda. There ideals and men are assassinated with poisonous whisperings. . . .

In speaking at Atlanta two weeks ago the President's first . . . defense for his gigantic spending, deficits, and debts was the assertion that "The mechanics of civilization came to a dead stop on March 3, 1933."

What happened on March 3, 1933, was an induced hysteria of bank depositors. The banking structure at large subsequently proved to be sound. That is scarcely a dead stop to civilization.

I have always believed that the newspapers are one of the mechanisms of civilization. They did not quit. At that time I saw no headlines that the farmers had ceased to till the fields. Most of you did not detect that the delivery of food to your doors had stopped. Railway managers apparently did not know that their trains had stalled. Somebody failed to inform us that the hum of our factories was silent. We still had to jump out of the way of the twenty-three million automobiles. Our churches, schools, and courts are a part of the mechanics of civilization. They did not close. And the Supreme Court seems to be functioning yet. If civilization came to a dead stop the press missed a great piece of news that day. . . .

The truth is that the world-wide depression was turned in June–July, 1932, all over the world. That was before the election of the New Deal. . . .

That turning was aided by the measures of our Republican government. These measures were within the Constitution of the United States. They were not that futile financial juggling which has violated economic law, morals, the Constitution, and the structure of American liberty. The turning was aided by the efforts of foreign governments. Every commercial country, including the United States, surged forward. Prices rose, employment increased, the whole agricultural, financial, and business structure grew in strength. After the election of the New Deal we began a retreat. Only in the United States was there an interruption. We were the strongest and should have led the van. And we lagged behind. . . . The other countries of the world went forward without interruption. They adopted no New Deal. Apparently those nations did not hear that the mechanics of civilization came to a dead stop on March 3, 1933.

It did not come to a stop even in the United States. It was meddled with. We have not got over it yet. But why did we have a panic of bank depositors in 1933? Because they were scared. We had no bank panic from the crash of the boom in 1929. We had no panic at the financial collapse in Europe in 1931. We had no panic at the most dangerous point in the depression when our banks were weakest in the spring of 1932. There was no panic before the election of November, 1932. When did they become frightened? They became scared a few weeks before the inauguration of the New Deal on March 4, 1933. . . .

. . . it gradually spread that the gold standard would be abandoned or that the currency would be tinkered with. . . . Shrewd speculators shipped their money abroad at fabulous profits. . . . The public in blind fear demanded gold and the "covenants" of the United States which called for gold. . . . The banking structure was not insolvent. After the banks were closed . . . [they in time, measured by deposits, were good for fully 99 per cent of their deposits]. . . . It was the most political and the most unnecessary bank panic in all our history. It could have been prevented. It could have been cured by simple cooperation. . . .

The breakdown in confidence which sounded the advent of the New Deal is of course a helpful statistical point when they want to show how good they have been to us.

CHAPTER 34

THE RECOGNITION OF RUSSIA AND THE WORLD ECONOMIC CONFERENCE IN 1933

In this analysis of the Roosevelt administration, I am not discussing his foreign policies in general. Two incidents during his first eight years, however, were destined to affect American social and economic life profoundly and are, therefore, incorporated here.

"Recognition" and thus the public condoning of Russia's unspeakable evils, had been refused by Presidents Wilson, Harding, Coolidge, and myself. The same opposition was also vigorously supported by five Secretaries of State, Lansing, Colby, Hughes, Kellogg, and Stimson. The reasons had been amply stated by Wilson's administration:

> The Bolsheviki . . . an inconsiderable minority of the people by force and cunning seized the powers and machinery of government [from the democratic state] and have continued to use them with savage oppression. . . . Their responsible statesmen . . . have declared . . . the very existence of Bolshevism . . . depends upon revolution in all other great countries including the United States. . . . The Third International, heavily subsidized by the Bolshevist Government from the public revenues of Russia, has for its openly avowed aim the promotion of revolution throughout the world. . . . There can be no confidence . . . if pledges are to be given with cynical repudiation . . . already in the mind of one of the parties. We cannot recognize . . . a government which is determined and bound to conspire against our institutions.[1]

[1] The Secretary of State, Bainbridge Colby, to the Italian Ambassador, Baron Avezzana, August 10, 1920.

The succeeding administrations reaffirmed this declaration. My own reasons, when President, for refusal of recognition can be stated in homely terms. If one of our neighbors is wicked in all his relations with the community we do not necessarily attack him. We even minister to him in sickness. But we do not establish his respectability in the community or offer him opportunities to extend his wickedness by asking him into our home.

At the time of recognition it was known to the entire world that more than five million people had been cruelly butchered in Russia. Millions were in Siberian slave camps. Bloody terror and murder of innocent people were rampant.

Although detailed knowledge as to Soviet aggressive intentions to destroy the free world and the determined immorality of their procedures was available from their own books, speeches, and actions, these were wholly ignored by Roosevelt.

There were two glaring examples of actual Soviet interference in the United States which were known to the President before the recognition. They were the Bonus March of 1932 and the flooding of the world with Soviet-printed counterfeit American money in 1933.

I have already described the activities of the Communists in the "marches" on Washington in 1932 and their attempts to provoke bloodshed.

The President-elect was informed by Secretary Mills of the Soviet's counterfeiting of American currency. He could also have read about it from statements in the press, from many European banks and from the denunciations of our own Federal Reserve Banks.

During my administration the Federal authorities, January 3, 1933, arrested a Russian named Dechow upon his arrival in the United States with a quantity of these counterfeits. The next day they arrested in Chicago a Russian Communist named V. G. Bartun for passing these bills. He was subsequently convicted on Dechow's evidence and sentenced to a long term in prison. On February 24th the *New York Times* carried a full exposure of the fact that the counterfeits were of Soviet government origin.[2]

[2] The *Times* was subsequently confirmed by Walter G. Krivitsky, a former Russian intelligence officer, in the *Saturday Evening Post* of Sept. 30, 1939. Krivitsky showed

Soon after his inauguration, Roosevelt began overtures to the Soviet government with a view to recognition. One of the placards which the New Dealers put up to prove they were "liberals" was "Recognition of Russia." Roosevelt used this poster to attract support of those elements in his campaign of 1932. He was also supported, of course, by the Communists and fellow traveler fifth columns which the Soviet government had already started as an underground "apparatus" in the United States. Secretary Hull, although he wrote various memoranda pointing out the dangers involved, finally swallowed Roosevelt's ideas that they could fend off these dangers by having the Russians sign a scrap of paper promising not to pursue their malevolent practices in the United States.[3] The recognition agreement (November 17, 1933) was well designed to pull wool over American eyes. It stated:

> The government of the Union of Soviet Socialist Republics [agree] . . . to refrain from interfering in any manner in the internal affairs of the United States . . . to refrain and to restrain all persons . . . under its direct or indirect control . . . from any act . . . liable in any way whatsoever to injure the tranquillity, prosperity, order or security . . . or any organization or propaganda . . . in any part of the United States, its territories or possessions. . . . or to permit the formation of any organization or group . . . which has as an aim the overthrow . . . of the political or social order . . . of the United States.

Also included in the agreement were assurances that Russia would pay its debts to the United States government and to private citizens. There were assurances of freedom of religion to the few American citizens in Russia, although the American people were given the impression it was religious freedom in Russia.[4]

Not an atom of these undertakings was ever carried out. At that very instant the Communists were organized in the United States to overthrow our government by violence and bloodshed. Within forty-eight

---

that in 1928 a Russian agent had procured the proper paper in the United States and $10,000,000 were printed by the Russian government's engraving establishment in that year. They swindled many people with them.

[3] Henry Morgenthau, Jr., "The Morgenthau Diaries," *Collier's*, Oct. 11, 1937, pp. 21 ff.

[4] James A. Farley, *Jim Farley's Story* (McGraw-Hill Book Co., New York, 1948), p. 44, gives sidelights on this part of the transaction.

hours, under Moscow leadership, the Communists began intensive violation of every word of the agreement, and over the years Communist organizations and Communist-front organizations bored into every vital organ in our country, including the government.[5]

THE WORLD ECONOMIC CONFERENCE

As previously mentioned, in May, 1932, I had arranged with Prime Minister Ramsay MacDonald, to convoke a world conference in January, 1933, for two major purposes—world currency stabilization and reduction of trade barriers such as quotas, cartels, preferential and excessive tariffs. The very announcement of the conference contributed to turning the tide of depression and gave new hope to a world in great economic disorder.

The proposals of the preliminary committee of experts, which included representatives of the different countries, added to the public hopes of a world-wide restoration of the gold standard and alleviation of trade barriers. As Mr. Roosevelt refused to cooperate with me, however, the conference had to be postponed until June, 1933.

In preparation for the Conference we had carried on (prior to the election) preliminary discussions with the representatives of foreign governments. We took the attitude that in the long run it was immaterial to different nations what number of grains of gold there were in the pound or franc or any other currency but it was important that the amount be fixed. After a period of readjustment, the prices of commodities in international commerce would revolve on the actual number of grains of gold in various currency units, not upon the name of the unit. There seemed to be a general willingness to agree upon this basis. Every nation involved considered the ending of currency wars to be the starting point of all programs in clearing trade barriers. All nations obviously expected the reestablishment of the gold standard

[5] Benjamin Gitlow, then a leader in the Communist party, but later on a repentant, wrote in 1938 (*The Whole of Their Lives,* pp. 264–265) not only that the Communist International the next day repudiated this agreement, but that Ambassador Litvinov, who had negotiated the agreement, forty-eight hours later informed a meeting of Communist leaders in New York, "It is a scrap of paper which will soon be forgotten in the realities of Soviet-American relations." Gitlow further states that the party line dictated from Moscow was to support Roosevelt in the campaigns from 1932 to 1938.

upon some basis. I had explained all this to Mr. Roosevelt in one of our preinauguration conferences.

Soon after his inauguration Mr. Roosevelt invited the prime ministers or special representatives of several countries to visit him in Washington. It was announced that preliminary conversations in the work of the conference on currency stabilization were the purpose of these meetings.

Following these conversations, joint statements were made by the President and each visitor in rapid succession, implying that they had all agreed upon the necessity for a return to the gold standard. Such statements were issued with Prime Ministers MacDonald of Britain (April 22nd), Herriot of France (April 28th), Bennett of Canada (April 29th), Jung of Italy (May 6th), Soong of China (May 18th), Ishii of Japan (May 27th). A passage from the statement made jointly with the Italian representative is: "We are in agreement that a fixed measure of exchange values must be reestablished in the world, and we believe that this measure must be gold."

On May 16, 1933, Roosevelt cabled to all nations participating in the World Economic Conference: "The world cannot await deliberations long drawn out. The Conference must establish order in place of the present chaos by a stabilization of currencies, by freeing the flow of world trade, and by international action to raise price levels." All of these preliminaries raised the Conference to an undertaking of great importance in the public mind.

Secretary of State Cordell Hull was made head of the American delegation to the Conference. Whatever the merits or demerits of free trade, it certainly can be said that Hull was a fanatic on this subject. He apparently believed that reduction of tariffs would cure all domestic and foreign ills, including chilblains. To him, this was the major purpose of the Conference.

What happened at the Conference is clear from both Hull's and Moley's memoirs.

Hull embarked with his great expectations as to tariffs. Roosevelt had promised him that, before his arrival in London, Congress would give him authority to settle a series of reciprocal tariff reductions with other nations at the Conference. Hull would thus have a great trading mart.

After he arrived in London, Roosevelt informed him that the legislative calendar was too full to present the matter. Poor Hull had written a great reciprocal tariff speech to open the Conference which he had submitted to the President by cable. But Roosevelt ordered large segments struck out. Hull complains that, in the meantime, the President was favoring provisions in the industrial and agricultural legislation which would greatly increase trade barriers. This was undoubtedly true, for the New Deal agricultural and industrial control measures and some direct legislation did greatly increase the actual tariffs.

In describing the Conference Hull writes:

The conference was not able to function with much definiteness or satisfaction. . . .

These contradictory views and attitudes characterizing the London Conference extended into the American delegation. . . . Few mistakes can be more unfortunate than for the official head of a delegation to a world conference not to have a chance to consult with the President on the selection of the entire personnel—or at least let the personnel have that distinct impression. Otherwise there is little sense of loyalty or teamwork on the part of some, and open defiance from others. This has been my experience. . . .

I left for London with the highest hopes, but arrived with empty hands.[6]

This amazing admission by Hull indicates that he was not even consulted by Roosevelt as to the members of his delegation—an experience which left him a sad and confused man. However, in his opening speech to the Conference on June 14, 1933, he retained a few brave remnants of his original effort, saying:

The success or failure of this Conference will mean the success or failure of statesmanship everywhere, and a failure at this crucial time would long be conspicuous in history.

Soon after the Conference was started, the President dispatched Assistant Secretary of State Raymond Moley to London, especially to undertake monetary stabilization. Moley, an intelligent man, has stated:

[6] *The Memoirs of Cordell Hull* (The Macmillan Company, New York, 1948), Vol. I, pp. 254, 255.

I had authority to negotiate a stabilization agreement and I also had Secretary Woodin's full confidence. I had—and have—documentary proof of this which has never been published.

... After I negotiated an agreement which was completely within my written instructions and which had the approval of Secretary Woodin, the President, for no good reason ever revealed, rejected it.[7]

Friction at once arose between Moley and Hull. Hull, in his *Memoirs*, has much to say about Moley. Moley, in his book, has much to say about Hull.

Then came (July 3rd) what was known as the "bombshell message" from Roosevelt upon stabilization. After a lecture on the beauties of a "managed" currency, he continued:

Our broad purpose is the permanent stabilization of every nation's currency. . . . When the world works out concerted policies in the majority of nations to produce balanced budgets and living within their means, then we can properly discuss a better distribution of the world's gold and silver supply to act as a reserve base of national currencies.

What some of this message meant is difficult to see, but certainly it was the negation of all his joint statements with the Prime Ministers. Hull describes Prime Minister MacDonald's reaction:

A few hours after [the message] arrived, Governor Cox, who I had arranged should see MacDonald every day, came rushing to my office. Very much wrought up, he said: "The British and other important countries are so aroused by the President's message that they have decided to call a meeting of the steering committee this afternoon, let it convene the conference in full session tomorrow, and then and there declare the conference adjourned indefinitely. In their resolution they will hang around the President's neck the sole responsibility for wrecking the conference." . . .

I was utterly astonished at MacDonald's bitter tone and sweeping condemnation. He boldly placed sole responsibility upon the American Government.[8]

Hull's conclusions as to this lost statesmanship require no addition from me:

[7] Letter of Feb. 1, 1948, to the Editor of the *New York Times.*
[8] *Memoirs*, Vol. I, pp. 262–263.

I believed then, and do still, that the collapse of the London Economic Conference had two tragic results. First, it greatly retarded the logical economic recovery of all nations. Secondly, it played into the hands of such dictator nations as Germany, Japan, and Italy. At that very time this trio was intently watching the course of action of the peace-seeking nations. At London the bitterest recrimination occurred among the United States, Britain, and France. The dictator nations occupied first-row seats at a spectacular battle. From then on they could proceed hopefully, on the military side, to rearm in comparative safety; on the economic side, to build their self-sufficiency walls in preparation for war. The conference was the first, and really the last, opportunity to check these movements toward conflict.[9]

Moley says of the "bombshell":

... This was not Franklin D. Roosevelt, private citizen, saying that two plus two made ten. . . . This was the President of the United States. . . .

At eight o'clock [on July 4] MacDonald telephoned and asked me to come again to Downing Street. . . . He turned a grief-stricken face to me as I came in and he cried out, "This doesn't sound like the man I spent so many hours with in Washington. This sounds like a different man. I don't understand." [10]

In describing the incident, James Warburg, a New Dealer and one of Roosevelt's financial advisers, who was with the American delegation, wrote later:

It is not difficult to see how the tone of this document shocked the representatives of the nations assembled in London perhaps even more than its content. As long as I live, I shall not forget the expression on Ramsay MacDonald's face when Governor Cox and I called upon him with this message, nor shall I forget the expression on the faces of the hundreds of delegates that crowded around the bulletin board at Kensington that day—nor the comments we had to listen to and read in the European press. . . .

One voice was lifted in a paean of praise: J. Maynard Keynes, the well-known English economist, proclaimed "Roosevelt magnificently right." [11]

Raymond Moley subsequently quipped: "Magnificently *left,* Keynes means."

[9] *Ibid.,* pp. 268–269.
[10] Raymond Moley, *After Seven Years,* pp. 256, 263.
[11] James P. Warburg, *The Money Muddle* (Alfred Knopf, New York, 1934), p. 119.

As a result of Roosevelt's torpedoing of the Conference, Warburg immediately resigned. His letter, dated July 6th, to Secretary Hull said in part:

I feel that I must ask you to accept my resignation as financial adviser of the American Delegation, on the very simple ground that we are entering upon waters for which I have no charts and in which I therefore feel myself an utterly incompetent pilot.

The London *Economist* of July 8, 1933, said:

Like King Charles II, the Economic Conference is taking an unconscionable time to die. . . .

. . . On Monday [July 3] the U. S. delegation in London issued a message from Mr. Roosevelt whose manner, no less than its matter, gave the Conference its *coup de grâce*. . . . not merely did the President loftily reject immediate exchange stabilization as one of "the old fetishes of so-called international bankers," not merely did he go out of his way to tilt at other countries' unbalanced Budgets, to the strange neglect of his own astronomical deficit; the implications of his message were that America . . . was determined to retain *ad infinitum* a "managed" dollar, whose exchange stability with other currencies would depend on the rest of the world keeping in step with the price level of the United States.

Moley [12] records:

On July 19th prices collapsed violently. For two days thereafter stocks and commodities crashed downward. The time of reckoning and readjustment had come at last.

Astonishingly enough, the President on July 26th cabled his congratulations on the success of the Conference to Prime Minister MacDonald.

He had not only destroyed the Conference and violated all his pledges to the foreign ministers, but also brought a great calamity on the whole world. For, by his actions, the world's greatest producer and the world's greatest market told other nations that it would carry on its economic war of currencies, repudiate its pledged word, break faith with any or all of them, and that it was none of their business.

[12] *After Seven Years,* p. 269.

CHAPTER 35

USURPATION OF POWER

COLLECTIVIZING THE LEGISLATIVE ARM

The first tenet of collectivism is the concentration of power.

Roosevelt's first step in this direction was the reduction of the legislative arm to a rubber stamp. During the first four years of his administration, bill after bill was drafted in the executive departments, sent to the Congress with "must" instruction, and passed without the members really knowing the content or purpose. We need introduce no evidence beyond that of Roosevelt's own supporters.

Governor Alfred E. Smith, who had been Mr. Roosevelt's political father, said on January 25, 1936:

In the name of Heaven, where is the independence of Congress? Why, they just laid right down. They are flatter on the Congressional floor than the rug under this table here.

They centered all their powers in the Executives, and that is the reason why you read in the newspapers reference to Congress as the rubber-stamp Congress.

We all know that the most important bills were drafted by the brain trusters and sent over to Congress and passed by Congress without consideration, without debate, and, without meaning any offense at all to my Democratic brethren in Congress, I think I can safely say without 90 per cent of them knowing what was in the bills. . . .[1]

Moley writes that no hearings were held by Rayburn's committee on the draft for the Securities Act of 1933: "The bill was hastily passed." [2]

[1] *New York Times,* Jan. 26, 1936.
[2] Raymond Moley, *After Seven Years,* p. 181.

George Creel, Roosevelt's intimate friend of twenty years, writes:

As time went on, the change in the President became increasingly apparent. Trial balloons were less frequent, and "must" bills were rushed up to the floor leaders in the Senate and House by messenger. Instead of attempting to placate opposition, he met it with resentment, and every Congressional debate on one of his proposals was regarded as an encroachment on the powers of the Executive.[3]

Arthur Krock, the Washington representative of the *New York Times* which supported Mr. Roosevelt, stated:[4]

From March, 1933, until last January, Mr. Roosevelt decided what *he* wanted to do legislatively, had a bill prepared to carry out the ideas, and sent it ready-made to Congress to sign on the dotted line. . . . Often his leaders introduced the measure without reading it. . . . Always the rank and file of Congress knew nothing of the bill's contents until they had read them in the newspapers. Sometimes they did not trouble to do that, voting "aye" on faith.

Stanley High, a one-time White House assistant to Mr. Roosevelt, says:

Thus Mr. Roosevelt has been and, apparently, proposes to continue to be his own legislature. There may be something to be said for this modification of our traditional practices. But there is no reason to ignore the fact that it is a modification.

. . . [The members of Congress'] readiness to swallow what the President had to offer was much more than a tribute to his hospitality. It was an indication of concern for their own political hides. If what they had to swallow sometimes looked and tasted like castor oil, there was no visible Black Shirt army to force it down their throats. But they took it, none-the-less and for much the same reason.[5]

The *Theses and Statutes of the Communist International* (Moscow, August 7, 1929), seems to have some analogies:

The central committee of the party must have its permanent representative in the parliamentary faction with the right of veto. *On all important politi-*

---

[3] George Creel, *Rebel at Large*, p. 290.
[4] *New York Times*, May 10, 1938.
[5] Stanley High, *Roosevelt—and Then?* (Harper & Brothers, New York), p. 85.

cal questions the parliamentary faction shall get preliminary instructions from the central committee of the party.

PACKING THE SUPREME COURT

The first requisite for continuing this collectivist action was the subjection of the Supreme Court. Limiting the independence of the judiciary was also the initial step undertaken by Lenin, Hitler, and Mussolini. I had prophesied in the campaign that this would come. Later on we will see Roosevelt's explosion after the judicial overthrow, in 1935 and 1936, of some of the important parts of Planned Economy such as the NRA, the AAA, the cotton, potato, and sugar controls, the oil and coal controls. While he delayed overt action against the Supreme Court until after the 1936 Presidential election, he none the less had already determined to bring it into subjection. The most complete disclosure of this determination prior to the election is given by George Creel, who was at that time a full member of the New Deal officialdom and an ardent supporter of Roosevelt, and also an occasional Washington correspondent for *Collier's*. He says:

Time after time, for example, he used my articles in *Collier's* to test out public opinion. Under such titles as "Roosevelt's Plans and Purposes" and "Looking Ahead with Roosevelt," he would outline the laws and policies that he had in mind, and then sit back to see what happened. Although every article was preceded by an editorial blurb that boasted of its authoritativeness, "due to Mr. Creel's long and close association with the President," it was still in his power to repudiate me if the reaction proved less than favorable.

Oftentimes he would actually dictate whole paragraphs, and have me read them back to him. . . .

I first became aware of his deep and even bitter feeling in August, 1935, when we were preparing the article entitled "Looking Ahead with Roosevelt." In June the Supreme Court had wiped out all of the codes set up under the NRA. . . . After considering NRA accomplishments in some detail, he set his jaw and dictated the following as his idea of how the article should start off:

". . . In the next few months, the Supreme Court will hand down fresh pronouncements with respect to New Deal laws, and it is possible the President will get another 'licking.' . . . then the President will have no other alternative than to go to the country with a Constitutional amendment that will lift the Dead Hand. . . ."

"Fire that," he said grimly, "as an opening gun."

Subsequently Roosevelt suggested another article. Creel reports:

We gave an afternoon and evening to its preparation. After summing up what he called "social gains," he switched to immediate and long-range objectives. . . . all, he pointed out, would have to run the gantlet of a hostile Supreme Court. . . .

And what if this proved ineffective? "Then," said the President, his face like a fist, "Congress can *enlarge* the Supreme Court, increasing the number of justices so as to permit the appointment of men in tune with the spirit of the age. . . ."

The article appeared in the December 26 [1936] issue of *Collier's*.[6]

After the 1936 election, the President brought his plan for remaking the judiciary into the open. He proposed various changes in the courts, but the kernel of his idea was:

When any judge . . . has heretofore or hereafter attained the age of seventy years and has held a commission or commissions as judge of any such court or courts at least ten years, continuously or otherwise, and within six months thereafter has neither resigned nor retired, the President, for each such judge who has not so resigned or retired, shall nominate, and by and with the advice and consent of the Senate, shall appoint one additional judge to the court to which the former is commissioned. Provided, that no additional judge shall be appointed hereunder if the judge who is of retirement age dies, resigns or retires prior to the nomination of such additional judge.[7]

As to what happened on that day, Vice President Garner said later:

The first time I ever heard of the bill, or that Joe Robinson or any of the others heard of it, was when the President and Homer Cummings (then Attorney General) read it to us in the President's office. It was all drawn to the last detail and ready for Congress. I loaded my automobile with senators and representatives and took them back to the Capitol. We were all so stunned we hardly spoke.[8]

[6] George Creel, *Rebel at Large*, pp. 290–294.
[7] *New York Times*, Feb. 6, 1937.
[8] Bascom N. Timmons, "John N. Garner's Story," Part II, *Collier's*, Feb. 28, 1948, p. 23.

At his press conference of February 12th, Roosevelt said:

As background, I think it might be useful to tell you that this particular message . . . dates back over a year and a half, a little over a year and a half in fact.

These proposals produced an immediate explosion, and Burton Wheeler, an erstwhile supporter of the President, led a long and bitter fight in the Senate against it. James Farley gives a glimpse of the pressures Roosevelt used in his effort to pass the bill:

"Are you entirely satisfied with the wisdom of your course?" I [Farley] asked pointedly. "Certainly," was his unhesitating answer. . . .

"First off," . . . [said] the President, "we must hold up judicial appointments in states where the delegation is not going along. We must make them promptly where they are with us. Where there is a division, we must give posts to those supporting us. Second, this must apply to other appointments as well as judicial appointments. I'll keep in close contact with the leaders." [9]

On February 5th I issued a press statement on the proposed court legislation in which I said:

Stripped of subsidiary matters, . . . the President's action amounts to this. The Supreme Court has proved many of the New Deal proposals unconstitutional. . . . It is now proposed to make changes by "packing" the Supreme Court. It has the implication of subordination of the court to the personal power of the Executive. Because all this reaches to the very depth of our form of government, it far transcends any questions of partisanship. [10]

On February 20th in a considered address on this question, broadcast from Chicago over a national radio network, I stated:

. . . I am speaking tonight not as a Republican; I am speaking as an American who has witnessed the decay and destruction of human liberty in many lands, who as President has witnessed the movement of these great floods which are testing the American levees built to protect free men. . . .

. . . [The] real issue is whether the President by the appointment of additional judges upon the Supreme Court shall revise the Constitution. . . .

This is no lawyers' dispute over legalisms. This is the people's problem. . . . It reaches to the very center of . . . [their] liberties. . . .

. . . Mr. Roosevelt demands the power to appoint a new justice parallel with

[9] James A. Farley, *Jim Farley's Story*, pp. 73–74.
[10] *Addresses upon the American Road* (1933–1938), p. 228.

every existing justice who is over seventy years of age. This means that two-thirds of the Court, or six of them, are to be given a sort of intellectual nurse, having half of the vote of each patient. . . .

. . . I wonder if those noble interpreters of human liberty, John Marshall and Oliver Wendell Holmes, would have served America as well in the last years of their lives had they possessed an intellectual nurse who also divided their vote.

But the President's proposal is far deeper and more far-reaching in purpose than these details. . . .

Mr. Roosevelt has sought many Acts of Congress which lead to increase in the personal power of the Executive. He has sought greatly to centralize the government. . . . The Supreme Court has found in fourteen of these laws which profoundly affect the public welfare that Mr. Roosevelt was within the Constitution in six cases and violated the Constitution in eight cases. In many of those decisions justices supposed to be of Mr. Roosevelt's realm of thought have concurred. Of eight important decisions adverse to Mr. Roosevelt's wishes four have been decided unanimously and of the six cases where the decisions were favorable three were unanimous. There can therefore be no real charge that the Court has not decided in accord with what the Constitution means. . . .

And what was the effect of these decisions which are now criticized? The unanimous decision on the NRA relieved the American people of a gigantic system of monopolies conducted by big business—a monopoly that even reached down to a jail sentence for pressing pants for less than the presidential approved price. Another of these acts was thrown out because it was based upon coercion of men to surrender their rights of freedom. And coercion is the antithesis of liberty. . . .

In the light of this background no one can conclude other than that the President seeks not to secure a Supreme Court that will find in accordance with the Constitution as it stands. He wants one that will revise the Constitution so it will mean what he wishes it to mean. . . .

. . . If a troop of "President's judges" can be sent into the halls of justice to capture political power, then his successor with the same device can also send a troop of new "President's judges" to capture some other power. That is not judicial process. That is force.

The Court and the Constitution thus become the tool of the Executive and not the sword of the people. . . .

In all the centuries of struggle for human freedom the independence of the judiciary from political domination has been the first battle against autocratic power.

In America we have builded over these two centuries certain sacred rights which are the very fibers of human freedom. . . . Upon them depends security from individual oppression. . . .

But these securities and these rights are no stronger than their safeguards. And of these safeguards none is so final and so imperative as the independence of the courts. It is here alone where the humblest citizen and the weakest minority have their only sanctuary. . . .

Self-government never dies from direct attack. No matter what his real intentions may be, no man will arise and say that he intends to suspend one atom of the rights guaranteed by the Constitution. Liberty dies from the encroachments and disregard of the safeguards of those rights. . . .

. . . Liberty is crumbling over two-thirds of the world. In less than a score of years the courts in a dozen nations have been made subjective to political power, and with this subjection the people's securities in those countries have gone out of the window. And, mark you this—in every instance the persuaders have professed to be acting for the people and in the name of progress. As we watch the parade of nations down that suicide road every American has cause to be anxious for our republic.

. . . We have already gone far on the road of personal government. The American people must halt when it is proposed to lay hands on the independence of the Supreme Court. That is the ultimate security of every cottage. It is the last safeguard of free men.[11]

Late in 1936 two writers, Pearson and Allen, in a book entitled *The Nine Old Men,* presented what were widely purported to be White House views. It also contained a story of my appointment of Chief Justice Hughes, according to which I offered him the appointment by telephone in the presence of Under Secretary J. P. Cotton, saying to Cotton that I hoped Hughes would decline. I learned that this statement had greatly pained the Chief Justice. I therefore wrote to him as follows:

New York City, February 19, 1937

My dear Mr. Chief Justice:

My attention has been called to the serializing of a . . . book on the Supreme Court in one of the newspapers here, in which a purported con-

[11] *Ibid.,* pp. 229–236.

versation of mine with Joe Cotton at the time of your appointment is related.

I scarcely need to say that no such conversation ever took place, and your own recollections will confirm mine that I never had any telephone conversations with you at all on the subject. I only write this so that you might file it away in your memoirs, although I think it is hardly necessary.

I am not capable of expressing my indignation at that book and its authors. . . .

Yours faithfully,

HERBERT HOOVER

In reply, the Chief Justice confirmed my statement and expressed his appreciation of having the record made.

On March 9, 1937, in a nation-wide "Fireside Chat," Roosevelt exerted all his charm on the American public in support of his judiciary bill. The technique was the same he always used, before and after: discrediting all opposition by subtle innuendos, never quoting directly, and always setting up a wicked straw man who was knocked down with a thunderous denunciation.

Senator Carter Glass, one of the President's makers and now an uneasy supporter, although ill and against his physician's advice, made a speech on March 29th, saying:

The proponents of the problem to which I shall address myself tonight have seemed fearful of a deliberate consideration of the proposal to pack the Supreme Court of the United States; they have defiantly avowed their purpose to take the discussion into every forum, with the unconcealed intention of bringing pressure to bear on Members of Congress to submit obediently to the frightful suggestion which has come to them from the White House. . . .

. . . There has been no such mandate from the people to rape the Supreme Court or to tamper with the Constitution. The Constitution belongs to the people. It . . . was ratified by the people as the Supreme Charter of their Government, to be respected and maintained with the help of God.

He ended with this reference to my statements in the campaign of 1932:

When once it was intimated by political adversaries that the Supreme Court might be tampered with, the insinuation was branded as a splenetic libel.

On June 14th, the Senate Committee on the Judiciary reported on the court-packing bill, with the unanimous recommendation that it be rejected by the Senate.

The report will stand as a great American historical document rising above petty questions of partisan politics, expounding the principles of a government by laws, not of men. In conclusion, the Committee stated, among other things:

It would subjugate the courts to the will of Congress and the President and thereby destroy the independence of the judiciary, the only certain shield of individual rights.

It contains the germ of a system of centralized administration of law. . . .

It points the way to the evasion of the Constitution. . . .

It stands now before the country, . . . a proposal that violates every sacred tradition of American democracy.

Its ultimate operation would be to make this Government one of men rather than one of law. . . .

It is a measure which should be so emphatically rejected that its parallel will never again be presented to the free representatives of the free people of America.

The Congressional battle continued until August 26th, when the bill was passed containing some unimportant provisions. Roosevelt issued a bitter denunciation.

Despite all this it cannot be denied that Roosevelt largely accomplished his purpose of destruction of the independence of the Supreme Court. Within four months after the attack the Court gave decisions upholding the validity of the minimum wage law of the State of Washington (March 29th); the Railway Labor Act (March 29th); the Wagner Labor Act (April 12th); the Social Security Act (May 24th). Some of these decisions were hardly consistent with the attitudes of some of the same judges in 1934–1936.

Roosevelt began to exult over this success in intimidating the Court even before the court-packing bill was defeated.

In his Introduction to the 1937 volume of his *Public Papers and Addresses* he says:

It was still the same Court with the same justices. No new appointments had been made. And yet beginning shortly after the message of February 5, 1937, what a change!

Along with all this cowing of the Court, Roosevelt, by appointment, succeeded in packing its membership.

Justice Van Devanter, one of the targets of the attack, resigned on May 18, 1937, and Justice Black, a rabid New Dealer and a reputed former member of the Ku Klux Klan, was appointed to his place. Justice Sutherland, another target, resigned on January 13, 1938, and New Dealer Justice Reed was appointed to his place. Constitutionalist Justice Cardozo died on December 1, 1938, and New Dealer Justice Frankfurter received his place. Later on, the resignation of Justice Brandeis and the death of Justice Butler gave opportunity for appointment of New Deal Justices Douglas and Murphy. For the first time in its history the Court was now dominated by one political and social philosophy, with a majority of a collectivist attitude of mind. To these six vacancies not a single Republican, nor a conservative Democrat, was appointed, although every President had hitherto sought to maintain a balance. Certainly these new appointments represented a minority group of the American people.

Another defection among Roosevelt's friends was that of Irvin S. Cobb, who had vigorously campaigned for him in 1932 and had directed some of his effective barbs of humor at me. In respect to the Court packing, Cobb said to a group in which I was present, subsequently sending it to me in writing:

Mr. Hoover. . . . Twice in bygone presidential campaigns I voted against you. The first time it was a party gesture, I being then, as now, a survivor of that well-nigh vanished species known as the Old Line Democrat. The second time it was a grievous error which I have since repented in sackcloth and ashes.

. . . Merely let me say to you, sir, that we are grateful because during your occupancy of the White House you never got the idea of burning down the temple of our fathers in order to destroy a few cockroaches in the basement.

THE PURGE

The "purge" of their own party members who protested was an essential tactic of Hitler, Stalin, and Mussolini. It was new in American life for a President to endeavor to estop conscientious opposition from members of his own party by opposing their reelection. A number of such Democratic Senators and Congressmen had joined the Republicans in decisive defeat of certain New Deal measures. Some of these Democratic "obstructionists" were coming up for election in November, 1938.

Edward J. Flynn, who succeeded James A. Farley as chairman of the Democratic National Committee, summarizes the purge as follows:

After the defeat of his Court program and to some extent because of the advice of Thomas G. Corcoran, the famous "purge" of Senators and Congressmen who had opposed him on the Court fight was started. As this program was developed, it was decided more or less to get rid of not only the members of the Senate and House who had opposed him in the Court battle, but also of those who had opposed him on legislation he had advocated in Congress.[12]

However, the story can be best told by the President's political manager, former Postmaster General Farley:

Late that January [1938] I got definite indication of what I had long feared—that the President's hate for members of the party who had opposed him on the Court fight . . . glowed as fierce as ever under the ashes of the past six months. . . .

My worst fears began to be realized at the White House conference the next day. From that time conferences were latticed with a pattern of purge talk. From the beginning I made it clear that I could not as Democratic chairman drop the reins of the party band wagon to whip the boys hitching a ride on the tail gate. . . .

In the next month he went over the whole political field as he prepared to distribute patronage rewards for "going along" and punishments for not "going along" to twenty-seven Senators and some three hundred Representatives. . . .

[12] *You're the Boss* (Viking Press, New York, 1947), p. 149.

. . . he paused at Gainesville, Georgia, to dedicate a public square named after him. He was introduced to a sizable crowd by Senator George. The President ignored the Senator but beamed over Governor Eurith D. Rivers.

The words the President spoke were not many but they were as heavy with ominous portent as the chains that Marley's ghost dragged to the bedside of Ebenezer Scrooge. . . . What was even more galling to southern members of Congress was the inference that those who had opposed him had been purchased by the vested interests. . . .

The next week the President . . . characterized the opposition as "an organized effort on the part of political or special interest groups" and then expressed personal disinclination to become a dictator. . . .

In a series of conferences in late April and May, the President reiterated his desire to defeat [Senators] Clark, McCarran, Smith, Adams, Tydings, Gillette, Van Nuys, George, and Lonergan. . . .

In the House the President was most anxious to defeat Smith of Virginia, O'Connor of New York, and Cox of Georgia. . . .

Early in July . . . the President delivered a "fireside" chat on one of Washington's warmest nights, but the speech had more than enough heat for Democrats, for he frankly acknowledged he was out to purge his party. . . .

. . . In Colorado, Adams was nominated without opposition. In Connecticut, Lonergan was renominated. . . . Of those marked for purging . . . Senators Gillette, Smith, Tydings, George, Van Nuys, Clark, McCarran, Adams, and Lonergan had all come through unscathed. Representative Smith won in Virginia and Representative Cox in Georgia.[13]

And there were members of his Cabinet whom he also wished to purge. Again we may refer to Mr. Farley's account:

I don't think the President ever forgave Garner. . . .

. . . I gathered that Homer's days [as Attorney General] were numbered. . . .

"What about Dan Roper?" he asked. "I am thoroughly dissatisfied with Dan but don't know how I can get rid of him. Maybe I could give him a diplomatic post of some kind." . . .

We talked of Frances Perkins and I got the impression that he would be pleased to have her resign.[14]

Later on he was to include two others of his Cabinet. Farley says:

[13] James A. Farley, *Jim Farley's Story*, pp. 120–146.
[14] *Ibid.*, pp. 84, 114–115.

Woodring's handwritten letter of resignation was never made public. Edison, who also was moved out for White House policy, had expected to go sooner or later and did not write a scorching letter.[15]

George Creel, Roosevelt's confidant at this time, later on said:

The tenacity of his resentments against all who dared to question his orders or infallibility was made manifest by the attempted "purge" of 1938. . . . He campaigned against the Democratic senators who had incurred his displeasure by voting against the Court bill. All were reelected; but instead of working any change in the President, defeat only heightened his implacability and strengthened his cold determination to crush all who conspired against the throne.[16]

POWER VIA BUREAUCRACY

There is no better pavement for the collectivist highway than more bureaucracy. It means favors; it means votes not only of the bureaucrats but of their relatives; it means centralization of government; it means personal power.

In the four years during my administration, of necessity we had to increase the functions of the government for aid to the unemployed, agriculture, and business; yet we had actually decreased the over-all number of government employees. Moreover, we had built up the merit system of selection until practically all possible officials were chosen under the bipartisan Civil Service Commission.

Someone must have misinformed Mr. Roosevelt, for he was more than bitter in his attacks upon my "bureaucracy" during the campaign of 1932. He reveled in this subject in speeches of May 22nd, July 30th, September 29th, and October 19th of that year. A few sentences are indicative:

I propose to analyze the enormous increase in the growth of what you and I call bureaucracy.

I accuse the present Administration of having piled bureau on bureau, commission on commission.

A complete realignment of the unprecedented bureaucracy that has assembled in Washington in the past four years [is necessary].

[15] *Ibid.*, p. 243.
[16] *Rebel at Large* (G. P. Putnam's Sons, New York, 1947), p. 295.

The official reports of the Civil Service Commission, while differing in detailed classification, give the totals of government civil employees and the percentage under the merit system. They were:

		Total Number	Percentage Chosen by Merit System
Coolidge	March 4, 1929	587,665	80
Hoover	March 4, 1933	566,986	81
Roosevelt	June 30, 1936	824,000	59
	June 30, 1940	1,002,820	55

Thus my administration had, in four years, decreased the number of employees by over 20,000. Roosevelt increased them in his first four years by about 258,000 and in eight years, by about 436,000.

The 19 per cent of non-Civil Service Commission appointees in my administration were almost wholly postmasters. However, I had established the rule that they also must pass the Civil Service merit examinations before I would propose them to Congress. Thus the change to a merit basis was almost complete.

Under the Civil Service laws the employees of all new agencies of the government, unless exempted, come automatically under the merit system of selection by the Commission. But in practically all important agencies created in the first four years of Roosevelt's Administration— some twenty-four in number—the employees were specifically exempted. These employees formed a huge army of political appointees. In the original establishment of the merit service law, authority was given to the President to "blanket" existing non-merit appointees into the Civil Service. Roosevelt periodically took advantage of this to fasten his political appointees permanently in the government without their having entered through the qualifying door of the bipartisan merit system. Even despite this, the statistical percentage of members of the Service gradually decreased.

Governor Alfred E. Smith, in an address of January 25, 1936, recalled the Democratic platform, and commented:

The next thing that is apparent to me is the vast building up of new branches of government, draining the resources of our people to pool and redistribute them, not by any process of law but by the whim of the bureaucratic autocracy. . . .

No bureaus were eliminated, but on the other hand the alphabet was exhausted in the creation of new departments and—this is sad news for the taxpayer—the cost, the ordinary cost, what we refer to as "housekeeping costs" over and above all emergencies, that ordinary housekeeping cost of government is greater today than it has ever been in any time in the history of the republic.

On numerous occasions, I commented on this. A few sentences from my speeches on October 5, 1935, and February 12, 1936, are indicative of my point of view. I said:

. . . The whole system of non-political appointments under the Civil Service which had been steadily built up by every administration for years has now been practically ignored. Almost this whole addition of 260,000 new people on the Federal payroll constitutes the most gigantic spoils raid in our history. Even Andrew Jackson appointed less than ten thousand.

Whenever you increase the numbers of political bureaucracy you not only have to pay them but they are veritable research laboratories for new inventions in spending money. Bureaucracy rushes headlong into visions of the millennium and sends the bill to the Treasury. And there are three implacable spirits in bureaucracy—self-perpetuation, expansion, and demand for more power. Moreover, they also serve to help win elections. . . .

Let us examine the record. The Coolidge officials under the Civil Service were about 75 per cent. The Hoover increase was to over 81 per cent. The Roosevelt decrease has been to 57 per cent. This is exhibit A of New Deal idealism.

All this sometimes reminds me of the small girl who said, "Mother, you know that beautiful jug that you said had been handed down to us from generation to generation?" Mother replied, "Yes, Ann, what of it?" And Ann answered solemnly, "This generation dropped it."

. . . Jackson also believed in "To the victors belong the spoils." [17]

Despite his actions to the contrary, Mr. Roosevelt professed great devotion to the merit system. He said on January 19, 1938:

In recognition of National Civil Service Week and the Fifty-fifth Anniversary of the enactment of the Federal Civil Service Act of 1883, I am glad

[17] *Addresses upon the American Road* (1933–1938), pp. 67, 121, 123.

to state once more my convictions with regard to the merit system for the federal government.

I have recommended and I support legislation for the extension of classified civil service upward, outward and downward. . . .

I conceive the establishment of a sound national personnel program to be one of the most important constructive steps in the improvement of government administration today.

The record seems to be exclusively downward.

REORGANIZATION OF THE EXECUTIVE BRANCH

President Taft had struggled to secure a more efficient organization of the executive branch of the government. Every President since Taft had appointed committees to study means and methods of accomplishing this. Every President had made recommendations to the Congress with little result in systematic organization.

I stated in a message to the Congress in 1931 that no reorganization of executive functions could take place unless authority could be given to the President to do the job, reserving to Congress the power to disapprove. Mr. Roosevelt repeated my proposals exactly, but without limiting the powers to executive functions, as I had done. Under his recommendations he could dominate the quasi-judicial commissions such as the Interstate Commerce Commission and the Federal Trade Commission.

These recommendations brought forth a storm of protest. It was not so much against reorganization of the executive branch as against Mr. Roosevelt's continued hunger for judicial power.

In March, 1938, a bill, amended to protect the quasi-judicial commissions from interference, passed the Senate by the narrow margin of 49 to 42.

In the President's drive for enactment by the House, he adopted an accustomed technique of setting up straw-men. He described the opposition's arguments as

silly nightmares conjured up at the instigation of those who would restore the government to those who owned it between 1921 and 1933, or of those who for one reason or another seek deliberately to wreck the present administration of the government of the United States.

These denials served only to increase suspicion that the bill, like the judiciary reorganization bill, aimed at still greater power for the President. The defeat of the measure in the House by 204 to 196 was due to Democratic votes, the Republicans being a minority.

In 1939 a bill giving authority for reorganization upon the same lines was passed; but it circumscribed with numerous restrictions and qualifications the powers of the President to abolish or move departments and agencies. However, nothing substantial happened to decrease the bureaucracy, as witness the record above.

POLITICAL USE OF RELIEF FUNDS

Having possession of billions for pump-priming, the New Dealers at once proceeded to a sideline of vote getting. Aubrey Williams, Harry Hopkins's deputy director, brazenly stated to a conference of WPA officials on June 27, 1938, "We've got to stick together; we've got to keep our friends in power."

Then came a long train of exposures of corruption. A Senate committee comprising four Democrats and one Republican, with Senator Sheppard of Texas as chairman, investigated relief actions in four states: Kentucky, Tennessee, Pennsylvania, and Ohio. They brought out fact after fact of misuse of funds. In one county in Pennsylvania more than $27,000,000 was expended prior to the election on highways alone. In Kentucky it was found that people on relief were required to change their registration from Republican to Democrat, and to sign up to support their candidates. The relief officials were required to subscribe to party funds. A political phenomenon was the discharge of many workers on relief immediately after the election.

The report of this committee to the Senate on January 3, 1939, stated in part:

The Committee believes that funds appropriated by the Congress for the relief of those in need and distress have in many instances been diverted from these purposes to political ends. The Committee condemns this conduct and recommends to the Senate that legislation be prepared to make impossible, so far as legislation can do, further offenses of this character.

The legislative program recommended by the committee indicates the kinds of abuse discovered. It included: (1) prohibition against political contributions by relief recipients; (2) requiring all Senatorial candidates to file accounts of receipts and expenditures for campaigns for nomination as well as election; (3) amendment of the Federal Corrupt Practices Act to prohibit a candidate's promising work, money, or other benefits in connection with public relief; (4) prevention of the "free mail" rule to put out purely political propaganda.[18]

Later Senator Rush Holt (Democrat) of West Virginia, a member of the committee, stated:

No amount of beautiful poetry or nice-sounding words can cover up or excuse the political usage of the WPA money as is shown by the facts.

This story of one county in my State is duplicated throughout the United States. In this one county the monthly payroll of bosses earning more than $1,000 each charged to project—not charged to administration—amounted to $20,380.[19]

ROOSEVELT'S OWN IDEAS OF PERSONAL POWER

In my account of the election of 1932, it is shown that Roosevelt was not backward in his forecasts of what was coming for the American people by way of revolution from American principles and traditions of free men. Some of them may well be recalled.

Stripped of oratorical trimmings, on May 22, 1932, he said:

That which seems more important to me in the long run is the problem of *controlling by adequate planning the creation and distribution of those products which our vast economic machine is capable of yielding.* . . .

It seems to me probable that our physical economic plant will not expand in the future at the same rate at which it has expanded in the past. We may build more factories, but the fact remains that we have enough now to supply all of our domestic needs, and more, if they are used.

He said in Detroit on October 2nd:

We know that some measures of regularization and planning for balance among industries and for envisioning production as a national activity must be devised.

We must set up some new objectives; we must have new kinds of management.

[18] *New York Times,* Jan. 4, 1939.
[19] *Congressional Record,* May 23, 1939, p. 5943.

And at Albany on October 6th Mr. Roosevelt implied such controls of trade as would prevent international competition and would regulate domestic production, saying:

More realistic mutual arrangements for trade, substituted for the present system, . . . will make possible the approach to a national economic policy at home which will have as its central feature the fitting of production programs to the actual probabilities of consumption.

In addition to his illuminating speeches during the campaign of 1932, statements from him during the first eight years are ample confirmation.

I omit his habitual defamation of the "Haves," "Plutocrats," "Economic Royalists," and his straw men set up to represent a non-existent economic system.

On June 24, 1933, he said:

Long before Inauguration Day I became convinced that individual effort and local effort and even disjointed Federal effort had failed and of necessity would fail and, therefore, that a rounded leadership by the Federal Government had become a necessity both of theory and of fact.

Again on January 4, 1935, he said:

The outlines of the new economic order, rising from the disintegration of the old, are apparent.

On January 3, 1936, he said:

In thirty-four months we have built up new instruments of public power. In the hands of a people's Government this power is wholesome and proper. · . . . [In wicked hands] such power would provide shackles for the liberties of the people.

He returned to this idea of instruments of power in a statement of January 20, 1937:

We are beginning to wipe out the line that divides the practical from the ideal; and in so doing we are fashioning an instrument of unimagined power for the establishment of a morally better world.

It may be remarked that the essence of representative government in this Republic is government by law. There is at least a tradition that no man shall possess the power to shackle the liberties of the people. It might be remarked further that the word "liberalism" comes from the word "liberty" and not from the word "shackles."

Through all these solemnly intoned pronouncements there ran the constant divergence between appearance and reality.[20]

There can be no dispute that Roosevelt was surrounded by many purposeful men who knew where they were going, who wrote his statements and, more important still, his legislative proposals and his executive "directives."

The economic views of the President's associates were no better stated than by Rexford Tugwell, who was indeed the ideologic philosopher of the Planners. He said:

It is . . . a logical impossibility to have a planned economy and to have business operating its industries, just as it is also impossible to have one within our present constitutional and statutory structure. Modifications in both, so serious as to mean destruction and rebeginning, are required.

In another place he said:

The challenge of Russia to America does not lie in the merits of the Soviet system, although they may prove to be considerable. The challenge lies rather in the idea of planning, of purposeful, intelligent control over economic affairs. This, it seems, we must accept as a guide to our economic life to replace *the decadent notions of laissez-faire philosophy.*[21]

On still another occasion he said:

Planning will become the function of the Federal Government—either that, or the Planning agency will supersede the Government, which is why, of course, such a scheme will be assimilated to the State.[22]

Roosevelt frequently denied any dictatorial tastes, but a small side evidence is indicative. That was the daily issuance of Executive Orders

[20] The historian, Charles A. Beard, wrote a book bitterly exposing the difference between appearances and realities in Roosevelt's foreign policies during the year 1941. Although a disappointed isolationist, and thus inspired in pointing out these enormous divergencies, Beard had been a New Dealer and had published a series of books eulogizing the New Deal without a single remark on the same extraordinary divergence in appearance and reality—and with much misrepresentation of its opponents.

[21] Rexford G. Tugwell and Howard C. Hill, *Our Economic Society and Its Problems.* (Harcourt, Brace & Co., New York, 1934). Italics mine.

[22] *American Economic Review,* March, 1932.

in peacetime. In his first term alone, he issued 1,486 such orders, as against an average of 166 for each previous four years of Presidents since George Washington. And that 143 years included four wars which necessitated more than the usual executive action. Such a quantity of orders constantly emphasized Congressional surrender of its responsibilities. Aside from legislation and administrative jobs, the mere formulation of these orders, which had the effect of law, gave vast opportunities to the "inner core."

Students who wish to arrive at the subcurrents around Roosevelt would do well to examine the platform of the Socialist party of 1932 and observe the uncanny fulfillment of its recommendations by Roosevelt's first administration. A student should also examine the many parallels of argument in Roosevelt's speeches of January 3, 1936, and June 27, 1936, with the program of the Communist International (Moscow), September 1, 1928. And all the New Deal acts should be contrasted with the Democratic platform of 1932, which Roosevelt endorsed "100 per cent."

CHAPTER 36

COLLECTIVISM COMES TO THE CURRENCY —AND ITS CONSEQUENCES

Although Roosevelt had denied any such intent during the campaign of 1932, he stepped as soon as possible into managed currency, the power to create fiat money, and the abandonment of the convertible gold standard just as I had forecast. In every case, that was the first step toward fascism, communism, socialism, statism, planned economy, or whatever other name collectivism happens to be using at the moment.

Currency convertible into gold of the legal specifications is a vital protection against economic manipulation by the government. As long as currencies are convertible, governments cannot easily tamper with the price of goods, and therefore the wage standards of the country. They cannot easily confiscate the savings of the people by manipulation of inflation and deflation. They cannot easily enter into currency expansion for government expenditures. Once free of convertible standards, the executives of every "managed-currency" country had gone on a spree of government spending, and the people thereby lost control of the public purse—their first defense against tyranny. With "managed currency," international exchange rates come under the control of the government. The consequence is currency war, as their manipulators in the end invariably seek to shift international prices to the supposed advantage of their own country.[1]

---

[1] Walter E. Spahr, professor of economics at New York University and executive vice president of the Economists' National Committee on Monetary Policy, has well said: "It seems reasonably clear that the peaks of attainment of individual freedom, of the competitive-economy–private-enterprise system, and of the widest use of the gold-coin standard were all reached at about the same time—roughly during most of the nine-

Uncertainty of values robs people of their power to test values and lessens their initiative. Depriving the people of confidence in their currency plants a fear in their hearts which causes them to hesitate in pursuing productive enterprises and renders them dependent upon the government. A convertible currency is the first economic bulwark of free men. Not only is this a question of economic freedom, but more deeply is it a question of morals. The moral issue lies in the sacredness of government assurances, promises, and guarantees.

Civilization moves forward on promises that are kept. It goes backward with every broken promise.

During my administration I refused to compromise with the principle of the convertible gold standard. Gold at $20.67 an ounce—23.22 grains to the dollar—was the relative measuring stick of our wages, our services, our pensions, our debts, and our assets. In a world of abandoned standards and fluctuating currencies, the transactions, the faith, and the

---

teenth century and up to the disruptions caused by the First World War. Since then, governments have become increasingly dictatorial. Individual freedom has suffered a sharp setback throughout the world."

Our greatest authority on money, Professor Edwin W. Kemmerer, wrote in *Gold and the Gold Standard* (McGraw-Hill Book Co., New York, 1944), p. 178:

"The first merit of the gold standard . . . is its *simplicity*. . . .

"Closely related to this merit of simplicity, is a second, that of *possessing the confidence of the public*. . . .

". . . 'We have gold,' says an old proverb, 'because we cannot trust Governments.'

"This distrust of government and politics in American monetary affairs has been deep and widespread for many years, and for very good reasons. Our record in this field has been bad. . . . Witness the blundering way in which our Congress handled American bimetallism from 1791 to the Civil War, Jackson's war with the Second United States Bank, and our subsequent sad experiences with the bank notes of the wildcat banks. Witness our 17 years' experience with inconvertible greenbacks from 1862 to 1879, our unfortunate silver legislation of 1878 and 1890, and the absurd and highly expensive silver policies of Franklin D. Roosevelt's administrations. Witness, further, the petition signed by 85 members of Congress in 1933 to President Roosevelt, asking him to appoint Father Coughlin as economic adviser to the United States delegates at the World Monetary and Economic Conference in London, and the subsequent jettisoning of that Conference by the President in the interest of the ill-fated Warren gold purchase plan. Witness the Thomas amendment of 1933, with its numerous monetary heresies, including the revival of long-discredited greenbackism.

"With a record like this behind them, is it surprising that the American people have more confidence in a fundamentally automatic monetary system, that functions for the most part in accordance with nature's economic laws, than in highly managed systems that function chiefly according to the laws and judgment of politically conditioned men?"

confidence of the whole earth was thus able to rest upon the American dollar. What stability there was in international trade resulted from this Gibraltar's clinging to its convertible gold standard.

A prime requisite of world recovery was the maintenance and strengthening of this fortress of financial integrity. But, beyond all that, it was the protection of the citizen's primary freedom from money peonage and the disguised seizure of his assets without compensation by his government.

I have already recorded our charges in this matter in the campaign of 1932 and Senator Glass's attack on me for suggesting that Roosevelt intended to manipulate the currency.

I may well recall here that in this attack Glass exhibited a sadly failing memory of the circumstances of our successful battle against being pushed off the gold standard in the winter of 1932. We easily proved that Glass himself had taken part in our preventive measures by the documentation and legislation in that battle.

Despite Glass and his oratory, we drove Roosevelt to his "Covenant" speech of November 4, 1932, which can well be repeated here:

> It is worthy of note that no adequate answer has been made to the magnificent philippic of Senator Glass the other night, in which he showed how unsound this assertion [Roosevelt's intention to abandon the gold standard] . . . was. And I might add, *Senator Glass made a devastating challenge that no responsible government would have sold to the country securities payable in gold if it knew that the promise—yes, the covenant—embodied in these securities* was as dubious as the President of the United States claims it was.[2]

This speech is omitted from the volumes of Roosevelt's speeches authorized and edited by him. It can be found in the *New York Times* of November 5, 1932.

After this speech, prior to the abandonment of the gold standard, Roosevelt approved an issue of $800,000,000 in securities of the United

---

[2] The italics are mine. The "covenant" was the printed statement on all government bonds, "The principal and interest hereof are payable in United States gold coin of the present standard of value," and on gold certificates, "Redeemable in gold at the United States Treasury."

States government payable in "United States coin of present value." How he reconciled this action with his intent to destroy 49 per cent of their value has never been disclosed.

ABANDONMENT OF THE GOLD STANDARD

The march toward "managed currency" came quickly in legislation following Roosevelt's inauguration. It is desirable here to review briefly these acts.

The Emergency Banking Act of March, 1933, not only reaffirmed the doubtful World War I act of October 6, 1917, in the use of which Roosevelt had refused to support me. It gave the President in a national emergency—as to the existence of which he was made sole judge—authority to assume complete control over all "transactions in foreign exchange" and "transfers of credit between, or payments by, banking institutions."

On April 5, 1933, the President issued an Executive Order requiring all persons to deliver all gold coin, gold certificates, and bullion to the banks in exchange for currency, the banks to deliver the gold to the Federal Reserve. He set up fines of up to $10,000 and imprisonment as a penalty. He claimed as authority both the Trading with the Enemy Act of 1917 and the Emergency Banking Act. It can be said at once that the Congress did not know they were giving away any such authority. Even a dummy Congress would at least have raised some protest had it known it in time. However, the thing having been done, the rubber-stamp Congress specifically condoned the action ten months later by Section 13 of the Gold Reserve Act of January 30, 1934. The amount of gold in the banks and the Treasury at that time was over $4,000,000,000. The actual amount of gold scraped up from personal holdings proved to be under $400,000,000—a trivial return for such a gross governmental violation of pledged word and personal liberty.

One of the poignant episodes in the course of these currency actions was the scathing denunciation of them by Senator Glass as a betrayal of the promises he had been given in return for his agreement to attack my administration during the 1932 campaign. When Roosevelt abandoned the gold standard Senator Glass, on April 27, 1933, attacked the President in one of his most bitter statements on the floor of the Senate:

I reproached the then President of the United States [Hoover] and the Secretary of the Treasury for saying that this country was within two weeks of going off the gold standard. . . . Franklin D. Roosevelt, now President of the United States . . . said the speech was to him an inspiration. . . . He textually commended the speech which so bitterly criticized his political adversary. . . .

England went off the gold standard because she was compelled to do so, not by choice. . . .

Why are we going off the gold standard? With nearly 40 per cent of the entire gold supplies of the world, why are we going off the gold standard? With all the earmarked gold, with all the securities of ours that they hold, foreign governments could withdraw in total less than $700,000,000 of our gold, which would leave us an ample fund of gold, in the extremest case to maintain gold payments both abroad and at home.

To me, the suggestion that we may devalue the gold dollar 50 per cent means national repudiation. To me it means dishonor; in my conception of it, it is immoral.

All the legalistic arguments which the lawyers of the Senate, men of eminent ability and refinement, may make here, or have made here, have not dislodged from my mind the irrevocable conviction that it is immoral, and that it means not only a contravention of my party's platform in that respect, but of the promises of party spokesmen during the campaign. . . .

. . . there was never any necessity for a gold embargo. There is no necessity for making statutory criminals of citizens of the United States who may please to take property in the shape of gold or currency out of banks and use it for their own purposes as they may please. . . .

If there were need to go off the gold standard, very well, I would say let us go off the gold standard; but there has been no need for that.

Later on Senator Glass sent me, through Ogden Mills, a verbal apology for his address during the campaign and word that he had made it at Roosevelt's request and upon a solemn assurance that there would be no tinkering with the gold standard. Mr. Mills suggested he write me a note, but he never did. However, he did show me good will by warning me of a harmful and wicked action directed against me.[3]

Ernest K. Lindley, a columnist supporter of the Roosevelt adminis-

[3] Norman Beasley, *Politics Has No Morals* (Charles Scribner's Sons, New York, 1949), pp. 101–103.

trations, provides an interesting description of Roosevelt's intellectual processes:

Mr. Roosevelt at no time said that by *sound money* he meant the *existing gold content of the dollar.* . . . The conservatives naturally assumed he meant a dollar of the existing gold content, and Mr. Roosevelt undoubtedly was glad to have them think so without completely quashing the hopes of the inflationists of various schools.[4]

That hardly corresponds with the promises to Senator Glass or the "Covenant" speech of November 4, 1932.

DEVALUATION

The second great shift into managed currency was the Thomas amendment to the Agricultural Adjustment Act of May 12, 1933, which authorized the President (a) to direct the Secretary of the Treasury to enter agreements with the Federal Reserve Banks for them to conduct "open market operations" in purchase of government bonds to the additional holding of $3,000,000,000; (b) to issue $3,000,000,000 of unsecured currency which should be legal tender; (c) to fix the weight of gold in the dollar at not less than 50 per cent or more than 60 per cent below present rate; (d) to fix the weight of silver in the dollar; (e) to determine the ratio of gold and silver; (f) to adopt unlimited coinage of silver; (g) to adopt unlimited issuance of silver certificates; (h) to set different prices for domestic and foreign silver.

Congress thus gave to the President legal authority over money as absolute as that of Tiberius Caesar or Henry VIII, Stalin or Hitler. It consummated the dreams and promises of every American tinkerer with the currency since the foundation of the Republic.

As to the "Thomas amendment," Raymond Moley records for April 18, 1933:

That night there was scheduled a conference at the White House for discussion of the coming meetings with MacDonald and the other British representatives who were on the Atlantic en route to Washington. We joined the President promptly after dinner—Secretary Hull, Secretary

---

[4] Ernest K. Lindley, *The Roosevelt Revolution: First Phase* (Viking Press, New York, 1933), pp. 37–38. Italics mine.

Woodin, Senator Pittman, Herbert Feis, James Warburg, Budget Director Douglas, Bill Bullitt, and myself. But we never did get down to the business for which we'd gathered because, as we filed into the room, Roosevelt handed me the copy of the amendment Thomas had given him. . . .

At that moment hell broke loose in the room. Douglas, Warburg, and Feis were so horrified that they began to scold Mr. Roosevelt as though he were a perverse and particularly backward schoolboy.[5]

The sinister character of this action so much inspired and welcomed by the President has no better illustration than Senator Elmer Thomas' own exposition of the amendment in the Senate on April 24th, when he said, among other things:

Mr. President, it will be my task to show that if the Amendment shall prevail it has potentialities as follows: It may transfer from one class to another class in these United States value to the extent of almost $200,000,000,000. This value will be transferred first from those who own the bank deposits; secondly, this value will be transferred from those who own bonds and fixed investments. If the Amendment carries and the powers are exercised in a reasonable degree, it must transfer that $200,000,000,000 in the hands of persons who now have it, who did not buy it, who did not earn it, who do not deserve it, who must not retain it, back to the other side, the debtor class of the Republic, the people who owe the mass debts of the nation.

This would have been a transfer of the savings by self-denial of the thrifty to the have-nots with vengeance attached.

All of which was reminiscent of William Jennings Bryan's "Cross of Gold" speech, which had won for him the nomination of the Democratic party for President thirty-seven years before, in 1896.

Senator Thomas was obviously ignorant of the fact that a large part of the debts which he wished to transfer from the "haves" to the "have-nots" were owed by governments (national, state, and local) to 100,-000,000 holders of insurance policies, 50,000,000 savings-bank depositors, and other small creditors. The latter included tens of millions of prudent persons with ordinary bank deposits, together with 12,000,000 members of building and loan associations. Furthermore, more than $10,000,000,000 of such debts were owed to educational, hospital, and

[5] Raymond Moley, *After Seven Years*, p. 159.

other public-endowed institutions. Another effect was to lessen the debts of large corporations, to the benefit of their stockholders. These debts also lay behind the savings of millions of people. This was robbing the "Common Man" for the privileged "haves."

Moley further records that after the passage of the Thomas amendment Lewis Douglas, Director of the Budget, said, "Well, this is the end of Western civilization." The disaster was not quite that bad, but its repercussions have been bad enough.

A further step in managed currency was the Congressional Public Resolution No. 10, of June 5, 1933, by which any of the actions of the President altering the obligations of *private* and *public* contracts were given force of law, no matter whether those contracts were entered into before or after the actions of the President. It resembled an *ex post facto* law. It provided for abrogation of the gold clause in all government and private contracts and substituted inflated paper money for their discharge.[6]

The President, having abandoned the gold standard and obtained the authority of the Thomas amendment, went into action. In the fall of 1933, farm prices had been dropping rapidly and unemployment was increasing. Since September the price of wheat had dropped by 25 per cent and unemployment, according to the American Federation of Labor figures, was greater than when Roosevelt was elected.

On October 22nd the President made an optimistic "fireside" chat entitled, "We Are on Our Way." He announced the devaluation of the dollar as the remedy, and affirmed his intention to see that this was carried out. His important sentences were:

It becomes increasingly important to develop and apply the further measures . . . to control the gold value of our own dollar. . . .

I am authorizing the Reconstruction Finance Corporation to buy gold newly mined in the United States at prices to be determined from time to time. . . . Whenever necessary to the end in view, we shall also buy or sell gold in the world market. . . .

This is a policy and not an expedient.

It is not to be used merely to offset a temporary fall in prices. We are thus *continuing to move toward a managed currency.*

[6] Moley, *After Seven Years,* p. 160.

The authority of the RFC to buy gold can be questioned, but we will let that pass. We may give the inside story in Secretary of the Treasury Morgenthau's own words:

But a more basic program to meet the commodity price situation was the attempt to raise the price of gold by government purchase of gold at high prices. This program was based on the theory of Professor George Warren of Cornell that if the price of gold were to increase, commodity prices would rise again. . . .

. . . I had a telephone installed in the Cabinet room to keep track of the purchases. F. D. R. was in a grand humor.

"I have had shackles on my hands for months now," he said, "and I feel for the first time as though I had thrown them off."

Every morning Jesse Jones and I would meet with George Warren in the President's bedroom to set the price of gold for the day. Franklin Roosevelt would lie comfortably on his old-fashioned three-quarter mahogany bed. . . .

The actual price [of gold] on any given day made little difference. Our object was simply to keep the trend gradually upward, hoping that commodity prices would follow. One day, when I must have come in more than usually worried about the state of the world, we were planning an increase from 19 to 22 cents. Roosevelt took one look at me and suggested a rise of 21 cents.

"It's a lucky number," the President said with a laugh, "because it's three times seven." I noted in my diary at the time: "If anybody ever knew how we really set the gold price through a combination of lucky numbers, etc., I think they would really be frightened." . . .

But he rather enjoyed the shock his policy gave to the international bankers. Montagu Norman of the Bank of England, whom F. D. R. called "old pink whiskers," wailed across the ocean: "This is the most terrible thing that has happened. The whole world will be put into bankruptcy." . . . The President and I looked at each other, picturing foreign bankers with every one of their hairs standing on end with horror. I began to laugh. F. D. R. roared.[7]

This method of devaluing the currency of the American people by steadily increasing the buying price of gold continued from October,

[7] "The Morgenthau Diaries, V—The Paradox of Poverty and Plenty," *Collier's*, Oct. 25, 1947.

1933, through January, 1934. The general philosophy seemed to be that if the number of inches in the yardstick were lessened then there would be more cloth in the bolt. Instead of confidence and stability, it produced wide fluctuations and chaos. Concerning the month of December, James P. Warburg, one of Mr. Roosevelt's assistants at the time, states:

J. Maynard Keynes, who had earlier pronounced Roosevelt "magnificently right," came out with a stinging criticism.

Keynes, upon whom Fisher and Warren leaned heavily for support, described the "gyrations of the dollar" under the Government's manipulation as "more like a gold standard on the booze" than an ideally managed currency.

And, horror of horrors for Warren, he characterized as "foolish" the idea "that there is a mathematical relation between the price of gold and the price of other things." [8]

On January 30, 1934, the rubber-stamp Congress passed the "Gold Reserve Act" already referred to. The next day an Executive Order fixed the gold dollar at 15 5/21 grains of gold, nine-tenths fine; that is, a price of $35 per ounce of fine gold. The Treasury was to purchase all gold offered at this price, both domestic and foreign, and to sell at this price to foreigners only. The "profit" from the devaluation by the increase in paper money value of gold in government hands was about $2,000,000,000. Of this, $1,800,000,000 became a fund for the stabilization of foreign exchange, and $200,000,000 was used to retire some outstanding Treasury currency. Roosevelt abolished gold coins but maintained silver coins.

A passage in Senator Glass's authorized biography throws light on this transaction:

One night, on summons, Glass went to the White House.

The President disclosed he was planning to capture the gold stocks owned by the Federal Reserve Banks. He explained by buying these gold stocks at the then price of $20.50 an ounce for gold, and immediately revaluing the gold at $35 an ounce, the Treasury would have a "profit" of $2,800,000,000; or, as he said, "nearly $3,000,000,000."

[8] James P. Warburg, *The Money Muddle* (Alfred A. Knopf, New York, 1934), p. 159.

Glass was shocked. For a moment he said nothing, scarce believing his ears, then protested:

"That isn't a 'profit,' as you call it—it is nothing but a bookkeeping mark-up. Furthermore, that gold you are proposing to confiscate belongs to the Federal Reserve Banks, and the Treasury of the United States has never invested a penny in it. You are proposing to appropriate something that does not belong to the Government, and something that has never belonged to the Government."

"The Treasury will pay the Federal Reserve Board for the gold at its present market value," returned Roosevelt.

"And confiscate the difference, setting up a fictitious 'profit' on a fictitious price?"

. . . Roosevelt . . . inquired:

"What do you think of it?"

"I think it is worse than anything Ali Baba's forty thieves ever perpetrated," angrily snapped the Virginian.[9]

As a result of Roosevelt's manipulations, what the status of gold is to our American currency and governmental obligations is not clear, even to this day. The so-called gold reserve for the currency consists of gold certificates issued by the Secretary of the Treasury to the Federal Reserve Banks. These are not certificates of specific dollars in terms of gold or subject to demand by the Reserve Banks. They cannot secure possession of the gold. James Warburg describes all this:

It is just as if I said:

"You put four dozen eggs in my warehouse and I will give you a receipt for eggs. Not four dozen eggs. Just eggs."

That is not all. Under the terms of this "gold certificate" the Secretary of the Treasury, in his sole discretion, determines whether the Federal Reserve Banks may get any gold at all for their certificates.

So it is not even a receipt for just eggs. It is for eggs—maybe.[10]

On February 18, 1935, the Supreme Court upheld the gold legislation in respect to private contracts but declared it unconstitutional as to government obligations. The Court, however, observed that no damages could be recovered, on the ground that holders of such obligations

[9] Smith and Beasley, *Carter Glass,* pp. 358–359.
[10] Warburg, *The Money Muddle,* p. 184.

were not damaged. This was an extraordinary assertion for if the purchasing power of the citizens' money were to be diminished by 40 per cent, they certainly had lost something on their holdings of government gold-convertible obligations.

SILVER REALIZES BRYAN'S DREAM—AND MORE

On June 15, 1934, Roosevelt sent a long message to Congress asking for a further extension of the powers to devalue the gold dollar. One of the incongruous conflicts of intellectual understanding was his expressed determination to make the currency inconvertible into gold, but at the same time make it convertible into silver.

Congress passed a further act promoting silver on June 19, 1934. The act provided for enlarging the silver base to 25 per cent of the value of the metallic reserves. The Secretary of the Treasury was authorized to purchase silver until the ratio of gold value to silver value in the reserves reached 3 to 1.

Six weeks before this act, May 3, 1934, Roosevelt gave an address at a memorial to William Jennings Bryan. He did not mention the 16 silver to 1 gold ratio which was the impassioned demand in Bryan's "Cross of Gold" speech. However, one of the New Deal objects of gold devaluation and monetization of silver was apparently to reach for the Bryan formula of a Utopia that would transfer wealth from the "haves" to the "have-nots," increase wages, and generally do good.

During the thirty-seven years after Bryan announced the "Cross of Gold" the American people had rejected this idea by holding to a convertible gold currency. In this period we had made more progress in the standard of living and increased comfort than in the whole of the previous hundred years.

But the administration certainly failed to find salvation on the renewed Bryan route. At the time of his agitation in 1896, the price ratio of gold to silver was about 30 to 1. Instead of reducing gold to a ratio of 16 to 1, Roosevelt's devaluation increased the ratio from 50 to 1 to a ratio of 80 to 1. Gold was $20.67 per ounce and foreign silver about 40 cents per ounce prior to these acts, and gold was $35 an ounce and silver 40 cents an ounce after them. It certainly did not produce Bryan's millennium.

One purpose of all this hubbub about silver was to satisfy the eighteen silver senators, who obtained a higher price for domestic silver on the specious argument that they were increasing employment in silver mines.

As a matter of fact, most domestic silver then and since has come as a by-product, and production increases or decreases without much regard to the price of silver. The total number of workmen in predominantly silver mines that might have been affected was less than 2,000. The domestic premium cost the government more than $12,000,000 a year, and $6,000 per man per annum was a high price for providing these 2,000 jobs. Moreover, some of them would have kept their jobs at the foreign price of silver.

During Roosevelt's first eight years, we spent more than $1,000,-000,000 buying foreign silver and burying it at West Point.

One tragic effect of this policy of unlimited silver purchases was to drain China and India and Mexico of silver and thus force them to abandon their silver standard, to the demoralization of their economies.

Director of the Budget Lewis Douglas resigned in August, 1934, and later wrote:

> The Government, by its fiscal policies, has deliberately laid the base for another inflation on a scale so gigantic that the bubble of the 1920's may finally seem small by comparison. We are now evidently going to have bigger and more painful inflation under Government sponsorship and induced by direct Government action. The New Deal is only the former "New Era" dressed up in different clothes. When the next bubble bursts, let it not be forgotten that the responsibility lies directly at the door of the present Administration.[11]

SOME SUBSEQUENT ECONOMIC HISTORY OF DEVALUATION

The subsequent economic history of Roosevelt's repudiation of the "covenant" has some interest. His belief that prices and wages would rise with devaluation was, as I have said, the same illusion that by reducing the yard to 21.2 inches from 36 inches, there would be more cloth in the bolt. It did not have this effect.

Dr. Rufus S. Tucker, after examining the data from many sources,

[11] Lewis W. Douglas, "Blowing the Bubble!" *Atlantic Monthly,* Jan., 1936, pp. 40–41.

concludes [12] that there was no appreciable relation between currency devaluation and recovery.

An inquiry by a competent group of economists under Dr. Edwin W. Kemmerer demonstrated that prices and wages did not rise appreciably in the United States from devaluation.

However, there were four other immediate consequences of great importance arising from managed currency and devaluation.

SHIFTS IN PROPERTY OWNERSHIP

Although it has not been investigated statistically, Senator Elmer Thomas *et al.* did, I believe, make some shift from the "haves" to the "have-nots" by a shift in relative value of prior-lien security holders (who were the debtors) over to the equity holders. I was a trustee of a number of charitable trusts. I would not previously have dreamed of approving speculation by such institutions through investing in common stocks. A month after the Thomas amendment and Roosevelt's declaration, I felt compelled to advise these institutions that their only possible protection lay in converting bonds into common stocks. The financial position of those institutions which followed this advice was greatly improved. Since then most charitable trusts have steadily converted their bonds into common stock. The whole of these transactions is a commentary upon confidence in bonds after 1933.

RELATIVE VALUE OF OUR CURRENCY TO FOREIGN CURRENCIES

Another effect of devaluation was the change in the position of our money relative to that of foreign countries. That was immediate, positive, and disastrous. The foreigners could pay their debts to the United States with 49 per cent less gold than before. Likewise they could buy the same amount of goods from the United States with 49 per cent less gold than before. Also, they could buy American securities and other property for 49 per cent less gold than before—and they did. Contrariwise, American buyers of foreign goods had to pay more gold for them than before—and therefore bought less of them. The immediate effect was a vast increase in the movement of gold into the United States.

---

[12] *The Annalist,* Aug. 21, 1936.

GOLD MOVEMENT TO THE UNITED STATES

Roosevelt always seemed to be in a general fog about gold movements. In the campaign of 1932, he said:

Debtor nations, no longer sustained by our improvident loans and no longer able to export goods, were drained of gold for debts and, one by one, were forced to abandon specie payments.[13]

This was an absolute prevarication, as I pointed out in a campaign address:

The gold of Europe was not drained; it has increased in total every year . . . and is right now $1,500,000,000 greater. . . .[14]

The actual gold holdings in the United States were $3,854,000,000 on January 1, 1929, and $4,226,000,000 on January 1, 1933—an increase of only $372,000,000.

But Roosevelt's devaluation did cause a flood of gold from the world into the United States. During the first eight years of his administration we were flooded with more than $15,000,000,000 of foreign gold, for reasons I have stated above. It represented foreigners' purchases of our goods or assets at a 49 per cent discount. We put the gold in the ground at Fort Knox where it brought no interest or returns—and we paid interest or dividends on the foreigners' investment.

SUBSIDIZING SPECULATORS

There was still another by-product of devaluation. Shrewd American speculators either deduced from the attitudes of Roosevelt and his associates that it was coming or had inside information. They bought huge amounts of foreign currencies before devaluation and sold them afterwards at huge profits and little risk. Some of the men close to Roosevelt's campaign did beautifully in this pasture.

Hugh Johnson, one of Roosevelt's greatest supporters in the campaign of 1932 and a subsequent high official in the New Deal, ultimately recanted. On the devaluation, he said:

[13] *The Public Papers and Addresses of Franklin D. Roosevelt,* Vol. I, 1928–1932 (Random House, New York, 1938), p. 802.

[14] For full text, see (Herbert Hoover's) *Campaign Speeches of 1932,* p. 37.

Some siren had slipped in and sold the Administration the age-old fallacy that if it would tinker with the currency "just-a-leetle," it could blow value back into deflated assets, and by "controlled" monetary inflation relieve the burden of all debt.

. . . It did not work as planned, "to restore prices to the 1926 level." That failure was important but not fatal. The fatal thing was that a pledge had been dishonored; that the priceless ingredient of the whole New Deal formula—*integrity,* which makes *confidence*—had been adulterated.[15]

There can never be justification of a devaluation of currency except in national bankruptcy or national debt too great for the country to bear. No such situation existed in 1933.

DEVALUATION INCREASED THE TARIFFS

In the 1932 campaign, the Democrats had made a great issue out of the disasters they predicted would flow from the modest increases in the Smoot-Hawley Tariff (mostly agricultural products). The fact was that 65 per cent of imported goods under that tariff were free of duty, and that legislation increased the tariffs on the 35 per cent dutiable goods by somewhere about 10 per cent. But the greatest tariff boost in all our history came from Roosevelt's devaluation.

The result of devaluation was equivalent to increasing the American tariffs by 49 per cent. And this applied to goods hitherto free of duty (65 per cent) as well as to dutiable goods. The cause of this was that the devaluation did not raise prices in the United States, but raised the price of foreign currencies to American buyers. For instance, one Dutch guilder could be bought for 40 cents prior to devaluation. A few months afterwards, it cost 67 cents. The prices of foreign goods were not sensibly affected. Therefore, an American merchant importing foreign goods had to pay about 50 per cent more for them. The effect was the same as if a universal tariff of 50 per cent had been imposed. This increased charge applied also to purchases of foreign services such as shipping and insurance.

The whole operation made a mockery of all the Roosevelt reduction-of-tariff promises.

On March 22, 1934, the President recommended authority to con-

[15] "Think Fast, Captain," *Saturday Evening Post,* Oct. 26, 1935, p. 5.

summate Reciprocal Trade agreements. This was his supposed compliance with campaign promises to reduce tariffs. The act was passed on June 12th, authorizing agreements to reduce American tariffs up to 50 per cent. Agreements were concluded with several countries from which it was claimed we received reciprocal advantages. The overriding fact was that having effectively increased the tariffs by about 50 per cent through devaluation of the dollar, the end result kept the tariffs about the same as the Smoot-Hawley level, and the reciprocal tariffs did not affect the new wall of 50 per cent around the 65 per cent of our duty-free imports.

Aside from these indirect increases in tariffs, Roosevelt in his various activities imposed special tariffs on such extensive imports as crude oil, gasoline, lubricating oils, coal, coke, lumber, copper, and whale oil which had previously been on the free list.

The actual result of these special increases was later shown by the Department of Commerce to have lifted the average portion of imports subject to tariff to 41.4 per cent from 33.2 per cent during the Hoover Administration.

This does not take into account the indirect tariffs through devaluation either on dutiable or on free imports. We can also examine from actual experience the effect of the Roosevelt policies of devaluation and supposed lowering of the tariffs. If we compare the four years from 1927 through 1930—a period prior to depression influences and prior to all the tariff action—with the four years from 1935 through 1938, after all Mr. Roosevelt's and Mr. Hull's tariff tinkering, we find that both our imports and our exports decreased instead of increased.

	Exports Per Capita	Imports Per Capita
1927–1930	$38.23	$32.05
1935–1938	20.99	17.94

Thus the heated promises in the campaign of 1932 to increase foreign trade by reciprocal trade and reduced tariffs were not fulfilled. In fact, Roosevelt's actions greatly destroyed our foreign trade.

It might be added, Secretary Hull's great theme that his reciprocal tariffs would produce peace in the world also did not work.

Indeed by this currency tinkering the United States government repudiated its pledged word, the Democratic party repudiated platform pledges, the President of the United States repudiated his public assurances.

Should Mr. Roosevelt meet Senator Smoot in the next world, his first act should be an apology.

CHAPTER 37

FASCISM COMES TO AGRICULTURE

Along with currency manipulation, the New Deal introduced to Americans the spectacle of Fascist dictation to business, labor and agriculture.

Fascism came to agriculture by way of the Agricultural Adjustment Act of March 12, 1933, sent by the President to Congress as a "must" and passed with little real debate.

This act and supplemental acts, in their consequences of control of products and markets, set up an uncanny Americanized parallel with the agricultural regime of Mussolini and Hitler. In short summary, it provided: [1]

(a) That wheat, cotton, corn, rice, tobacco, hogs, and dairy products were basic farm products. Later on, potatoes, cattle, peanuts, and grain sorghums and sugar were added to the basic commodities. (These 12 basic products comprised about 80 per cent of all farm produce.)

(b) An authority "to provide for reduction in the acreage or reduction in the production for market, or both, of any basic agricultural commodity, through agreements with producers or by other voluntary methods, and to provide for rental or benefit payments in connection therewith."

(c) A "processing tax" upon processors of farm products with which to pay these benefits, the tax to be rebated on exports.

(d) The establishment of a "parity price" for certain agricultural

[1] It is of passing interest that this was not the "domestic allotment" plan proposed by Roosevelt in the 1932 campaign. It also violated several of the six conditions with which he surrounded it. In March, 1933, Henry A. Wallace, Secretary of Agriculture, denounced that plan as unworkable, although his father, Henry C. Wallace, in the Harding administration had been its great advocate.

commodities on a level with their purchasing power in terms of articles the farmer purchased during the period (except tobacco) from August, 1909, to July, 1914.

(e) Authority to the Secretary of Agriculture to enter legally into marketing agreements with producers and processors, the anti-trust laws being suspended. Handlers were required to take out a license from the Secretary of Agriculture on pain of a fine or impressment with revocation.

(f) To dispose of cotton already accumulated by the Federal Farm Board on loan or purchase, options were given to the producer to purchase it over a period, provided he reduced his acreage by 30 per cent.

Mr. Roosevelt said that only farmers "who *agreed voluntarily*" to "adjust" their production would receive benefit payments. As a matter of fact, by bureaucratic action there was little voluntary about it. The first step of coercion was to require every farmer, in order to get the subsidy on one basic commodity, to sign an agreement to accept government dictation on all basic products. If the farmer preferred to forfeit benefits, and thus retain his independence, he soon found himself in trouble marketing his crops.

Every county was equipped with county boards to inspect and deliver benefits. These boards acted directly under the administration in Washington. The political implications were enormous.

Gradually Roosevelt further stepped up the coercive character of controls. The presumed "voluntary" agreement, with all its coercive attachments, did not satisfy the New Deal fascist instinct.

On October 6, 1933, by Executive Order, the President created the Commodity Credit Corporation. It was a Delaware state-registered corporation, ultimately possessing $3,000,000,000 of funds financed by the RFC and the Treasury. The set-up was not authorized by Congress until two years later. The original purpose of this corporation was to make direct loans to farmers on their commodities. These loans were to be fixed at amounts which would support "parity prices" irrespective of the market prices, and without recourse on the borrower. That is, the farmer had a "put" on the government. The corporation made many million individual loans on "basic commodities." But there were coercions in all this, for loans were available only to farmers who "signed up" on all their crops. It was the pure religion of a coercive "Planned Economy."

But coercion was to go still further.

By the Sugar Control Act of May 9, 1934, further compulsion was imposed on all those farmers. A processing tax was placed on sugar, and quotas were imposed on imports and on the acreage of sugar cane and beets a farmer could plant, with penalties for violation. Subsidies were paid on the reduced acreage. At the same time the tariff on sugar was reduced. Aside from dictation, one effect in the long run would be the substitution of foreign sugars for American production.

The Tobacco Control Act of June 28, 1934, was another step in coercion, as it set up quotas on imports and on national, county, and individual farm tobacco production, with a tax of $33\frac{1}{3}$ per cent on production in excess of allotments.

The Cotton Control Act of April 21, 1934, was still another step in coercion. Maximum quotas on production for the nation, the states, the counties, and the individual farmers were dictated, and a tax of up to 50 per cent of the market value, or a minimum of five cents per pound, was levied on cotton produced by any farmer in excess of his allotment. The farmers could be jailed or fined for violations.

On April 8, 1935, Congress passed an act authorizing loans to finance, in whole or in part, purchases of farm lands by tenants. It became a great bulwark for distribution of patronage by the Democratic National Committee.

A compulsory Potato Control Act was passed on August 24, 1935. Quotas were established on imports, and on production by each state and each individual farmer. A tax was imposed of $\frac{3}{4}$ cent per pound on all potatoes, but rebated to farmers who complied with their quotas. A complicated system was established in the effort to head off fraud.

On August 24, 1935, at the insistence of Roosevelt, the AAA was greatly expanded and amended by the Congress. In addition to "benefits" for reducing production, authority was given to "remove from the channels of trade" basic commodities that endangered the "parity prices." Authority was given to store such commodities on the farms and elsewhere—the "ever-normal granary" of Secretary Wallace. A complicated scheme of voting, with a bare majority of the farmers actually voting, was binding on all. With Wallace's committees in every county, and agents in every township, who could withhold benefits and loans, the necessary "majority" was inevitable for this "democratic process." There was something reminiscent of the Soviet conduct of "elections" in all this.[2]

The Supreme Court on January 6, 1936, declared the AAA unconstitutional. The Court held that the act was essentially one regulating agricultural production, which was not interstate commerce, and that the processing tax was a subterfuge and was not really for the purpose of revenue. The Court declared the Bankhead Cotton Act unconstitutional at the same time. The Potato Act was repealed February 10, 1936, in consequence of these decisions.

While these acts were in force, Secretary of Agriculture Wallace performed diligently in his realm of economy of scarcity for the world and the American people. His success is shown by the Department of Agriculture *Year Book* as follows:

	1932	1934
Acres of 40 crops harvested	363,606,000	295,933,000
Acres of 17 principal crops	344,486,000	276,070,000
Pigs saved	82,526,000	56,766,000
Cattle, Dec. 31	70,280,000	68,846,000
Hogs, Dec. 31	62,127,000	39,066,000

All of which planned scarcity did not seem to be the remedy for the one-third *undernourished* in Mr. Roosevelt's slogan, "One-third of the nation is ill-housed, ill-clad and *ill-nourished*."

One of the "planned economy" solutions for agriculture was the construction of "subsistence homesteads," authorized as public works on July 21, 1933. The scheme was to build part-time farming communities near the industrial centers or to establish new industries in these "subsistence homestead" centers.

These ideas, however, went much further. Resettlement of the agricultural population generally was undertaken with divided tracts of land equipped with buildings and livestock. The settlers were attracted by loans of 100 per cent without personal obligation. These ideas were

[2] See W. L. White, *Land of Milk and Honey* (Harcourt, Brace & Co., New York, 1949), pp. 110–121.

further expanded to build "green-belt suburbs" to cities. The devious alphabetical path of these organizations was first "the Selective Homesteads" under Secretary of the Interior Ickes. On April 30, 1935, by Executive Order, these were absorbed into a new agency called Resettlement Administration under Rexford Tugwell. On January 1, 1937, the ideas were expanded, and the name was changed to Farm Security Administration. On August 14, 1946, the whole was reconstituted as the Farmers' Home Administration. The record of this organization and its predecessors showed over $2,000,000,000 expended in "loans," and a deficiency in bad loans and interest paid by the government in the vicinity of $500,000,000.[3] The changes in names enabled the burying of much odious history. Periodic Congressional investigations showed such items as 16,000 employees in the "Farmers' Home Administration," $35,000,000 expenses to administer old loans, and new loans of $90,000,000 annually.

As to results, for instance, the "resettlement" of thirteen families at Sioux Falls cost $20,520 per family. The resettlement of two hundred textile families at Hightstown, New Jersey, cost $7,850 per family. The resettlement of two hundred and fifty families from cities to "Westmoreland Homesteads" in Pennsylvania cost $5,390 per family. R. A. Faul resigned from managing one of these "cooperative" farms at Tempe, Arizona, saying, "The only difference between this cooperative farm and Russia is that the Government here is paid its share in cash instead of in kind."

Nearly all these ventures finally blew up in a mess of scandals.

On the assumption that one-third of American families were undernourished and ill housed (which was and is statistically false), the families in distress saved by these agencies were fewer than one in a thousand. The photographs in the press were, however, convincing of great humanitarianism. While these affairs contained large lumps of pure socialism, I am inclined to classify this agency under the heading of "vote fly paper." They involved a paid government agent and a paid farmers' advisory committee in most rural counties, whose persuasive powers were very great.

[3] See the 1947 report on this organization by the Commission on Organization of the Executive Branch of the Government.

There is irony even in economics. During 1931–1932, when for months hardly a single order for the export of wheat and cotton had come to the United States from Europe as a result of their financial collapse, I had directed the Farm Board to make loans on farm products and to purchase the unmarketable surpluses of wheat and cotton to the extent of their authority and resources. These surpluses we later mostly distributed to the unemployment relief committees by authority of Congress. In the campaign of 1932 Mr. Roosevelt referred to this on September 14th, saying:

The Farm Board began its stabilizing operations. This resulted in a tremendous undigested surplus overhanging the market; it put a millstone around the neck of the cooperatives. The effort resulted in squandering hundreds of millions of the taxpayers' money. Farm Board speculative operations must and shall come to an end.

A note from *The Morgenthau Diaries* adds the humor:

We experimented with propping up prices through government lending. . . .

. . . On the night of October 16th, as I was spending a quiet evening at home, the telephone rang. It was the President.

"We have got to do something about the price of wheat," he said, strain and weariness apparent in his tone. "I can't take it any longer. . . . Can't you buy 25,000,000 bushels for Harry Hopkins and see if you can't put the price up?"

Henry Wallace, I knew, had the machinery for buying; and, if Hopkins would agree to take it off my hands for relief distribution, I would be certain not to get stuck with loads of surplus wheat.

I started in on the buying game first thing in the morning. Wheat was perched precariously at 64⅞ when I placed the first order for 1,000,000 bushels. By the end of the day we had worked it up 10 cents.

"Squeeze the life out of the shorts," F. D. R. said to me, with the old fight in his voice, "and put the price up just as far as you can." [4]

Governor Alfred E. Smith, speaking on January 25, 1936, repeated the Democratic platform plank of 1932:

We condemn the extravagance of the Farm Board, its disastrous action which made the government a speculator in farm products, and the unsound

[4] *Collier's,* Oct. 25, 1947.

policy of restricting agricultural products to the demands of domestic markets.

He added:

Listen, and I will let you in on something. This has not leaked out, so kind of keep it to yourself until you get the news.

On the first of February we are going to own 4,500,000 bales of cotton. The cost is $270,000,000.

And we have been such brilliant speculators that we are paying thirteen cents a pound for it when you add storage and carrying charges, and it can be bought in any one of the ten cotton markets in the South today for eleven dollars and fifty cents a bale. Some speculators!

I had many personal contacts during this period with the moral effects of the New Deal at the farm level, as Mrs. Hoover and I did much motoring over the country, covering some twenty states. On these journeys we made it a practice to stop in auto camps with all their opportunity to talk with the folks. The farmers related astonishing stories of their experiences.

In confirmation of many of these stories, a friend in Pennsylvania had requested me, when in the neighborhood, to visit a large cotton ranch in the San Joaquin valley for which he was executor, and advise him of my impressions of the management. The intelligent manager was immersed in the planned economy program to destroy some 800 acres of his growing cotton out of some 3,000 total. He explained to me that he had about 800 acres of poor growth, and that the bonus payable was more profitable than the growing of it to harvest. On the other hand, should he destroy his good cotton, he would make less than under the government loan scheme. On his asking my advice, I stated that good citizens did not take advantage of the government by picking their worst crops, and that his boss would not like him to do so, no matter how evil the government's practices.

A few months later the manager called upon me. I asked what had happened about the cotton. He said:

I was sitting on the porch one afternoon when Secretary Wallace's County Committee came up the front walk. The Chairman called out to me, "Here comes the Wall Street money. Have you any poor cotton?" I replied that I had 800 acres that was pretty poor. He said, "Which quarter sections are they?" I told him. He filled out a written order to plow them under and directions how to get the money. We are about $12,000 better off than if we had grown it.

One evening when I was stopping at my son Allan's ranch, one of the foremen came in and said he had a check from the government for reduction of two hundred pigs which did not exist. I asked him to explain. He said the pig destruction payments were based on a three-year average; that he had owned a hog farm up the valley two years before but had sold it, and that this was his payment for his proportion of the three-year average.

One night Allan called me on the telephone saying that he had two news reporters in his ranchhouse; that during the day Secretary of Agriculture Wallace in Washington had informed the press "off the record" that the former President's son Allan, as the largest owner of the Kern County Land Company, was one of the largest recipients of federal subsidies for curtailing crops; that the subsidies were over $20,000 per annum; that no doubt the press could expose the fact by demanding the facts from Allan. The law prohibited the disclosure by government officials of individual subsidies. I asked Allan if he owned any shares at all in the Kern County Land Company. He said he owned a few shares. He said he had bought them because that company controlled his water, and thus he had obtained a right to see the company's annual statements. It seemed to me a pretty immoral attempt to smear me over the shoulders of a decent boy. I asked him what proportion of the government subsidy given to the Kern County Land Company his shares would entitle him to receive. He replied that it would be about two dollars, but added that he was taking no subsidies, and that Wallace's farm regimentation was depriving him of the opportunity to buy feeder cattle and calves, which affected his operations. I suggested that he explain how Wallace had mistaken $2 for $20,000 and then charge the Secretary with unconstitutionally robbing him of his honest earnings, violating the law as to disclosure, and trying to smear me over his shoulder. Allan did so in language that echoed all over the country. The New Deal left him alone thereafter.

There were some objectives and procedures in these agricultural policies from which I did not dissent. But the regimentation, coercion, and personal, autocratic government, despite all the clatter about "voluntary agreements" and "democratic action," were as wide a departure from a society of American free men as those of the fascist regimes of Italy and Germany. And they were wholly unnecessary and ineffectual as a remedy of our farm problems.

On January 16, 1936, in an address on the agricultural policies of the New Deal at Lincoln, Nebraska, over a national hook-up, I stated some of the difficulties of debate:

I have recently debated various realities of the New Deal at Oakland, New York, and St. Louis. I propose now to explore it further, particularly its agricultural policies and their effect on the whole people.

The New Deal has developed a new technique in debate. They set up a glorious ideal to which we all agree unanimously. Then they drive somewhere else or into the ditch. When we protest they blackguard us for opposing the glorious ideal. And they announce that all protesters are the tools of Satan or Wall Street. When we summon common sense and facts they weep aloud over their martyrdom for the ideal.

The New Deal explanations of their agricultural policies exceed thirty million words. You will not expect me to turn the light into every dark corner in thirty minutes. Some of the rugged prima donnas who have directed these policies have resigned and said worse things than I would say. One quality of the old Regulated Individualists was team work.

Right at the outset let us get some things perfectly clear. There is an agricultural problem. It concerns the entire nation. It concerns the happiness of 7,000,000 homes. Our country will not have reached either full moral or economic stature until confidence and hope shine in these homes. The problem is still unsolved.

Aside from its flagrant flouting of the Constitution the New Deal farm method had within it destruction both to the farmers and to the nation. A new program is necessary. . . .

I shall debate the subject in five directions.

Part One will be the reasons why the farm question is of national interest. I hope this part will be emphatic.

Part Two is a few words upon the causes of the farmers' troubles. I hope this part will not wholly spoil the stock in trade of many politicians, for they have to live also.

Part Three is what the New Deal is doing to the farmer as a citizen, along with all other citizens. These are the things to avoid in the future. I hope this part will not be too sad.

Part Four is what the New Deal has done to the farmer in his farming business. This is also sad.

Part Five consists of some discussion of a new program. It may shock those who believe in doing nothing for human ills. It may shock those who believe that all healing medicine comes off the collectivist brew.

In all parts there are remarks on what the New Deal has been doing to the whole structure of human liberty and American institutions in the guise of farm relief.

Each part has unpleasant features to somebody. . . . But truth always wins at last—if the nation survives in the meantime.[5]

On February 29, 1936, a new Agricultural Act was passed to eliminate the problem of constitutionality. The legalistic theory of "soil conservation" was set up. This act had as its stated purpose: (a) to preserve and improve soil fertility; (b) to conserve national land resources; (c) to protect rivers and harbors against soil erosion; (d) to restore the purchasing power of net income per person on farms to equality with the purchasing power of the net income per person not on farms, such as existed from August, 1909, to July, 1914—"parity."

By authorities granted and by withholding payments or making "benefit" payments for "conservation" and loans at Secretary of Agriculture Wallace's discretion, the coercive power of the government was reestablished as fully as before: (1) to limit the production of farm products; (2) to establish prices; (3) to control planting and, at the discretion of the Secretary of Agriculture, almost all of the farmers' activities.

On June 3, 1937, Congress further revised and expanded the February act. Except for the change in names and terms, the coercive methods of the AAA of 1933 were continued.

[5] The full text may be found in *Addresses upon the American Road* (1933–1938), pp. 101–113.

But a year after the new act of 1936, the canny farmer increased his cultivated acreage by about 45,000,000 acres, and yet at the same time drew the benefits for reduction.

On September 1, 1937, a Sugar Control Act was passed to replace the one declared unconstitutional in January, 1936. The economic consequences were the same as before.

A revision of the control of agricultural production and prices was again undertaken in an act of February 6, 1938. This new AAA was based upon soil conservation and the regulation of commerce in specified major agricultural products. Although these devices were simply disguises for something else, they served to get by the more compliant (by now beaten down and packed) Supreme Court.

The same "voluntary" signing up by farmers was required as under the original plan; that is, if the farmer received any benefits on one commodity, or for soil conservation, or commodity or marketing loans, he had to obey the stipulations on all other basic products, and if he did not sign up, he was subjected to many embarrassments and difficulties in marketing his crops. This and a new Sugar Control Act were again as purely fascist as any action of Mussolini or Hitler.

The economic failure of all these fascist-colored agricultural measures can best be shown by the index of farm prices for the four years prior to the world depression of 1929 in a free economy compared with Roosevelt's second-term farm dictatorship. They were as follows, if we take the year 1940 as 100:

PRIOR TO THE DEPRESSION		ROOSEVELT ADMINISTRATION	
1925	156	1937	122
1926	146	1938	97
1927	141	1939	95
1928	149	1940	100

(Source: Department of Agriculture)

There were no subsidies paid the farmer in the first period given, and obviously he was far better off under a free economy than under all these subsidies and coercions.

The total direct costs of these operations to the taxpayers, including the losses of the Commodity Credit Corporation and direct payments to producers, during eight years, were as follows:[6]

1933	$ 73,000,000	1937	$ 922,000,000
1934	364,000,000	1938	804,000,000
1935	881,000,000	1939	1,159,000,000
1936	825,000,000	1940	1,491,000,000

[6] Compiled from the Budget reports.

CHAPTER 38

FASCISM COMES TO BUSINESS— WITH DIRE CONSEQUENCES

Among the early Roosevelt fascist measures was the National Industrial Recovery Act (NRA) of June 16, 1933. The origins of this scheme are worth repeating. These ideas were first suggested by Gerard Swope (of the General Electric Company) at a meeting of the electrical industry in the winter of 1932. Following this, they were adopted by the United States Chamber of Commerce. During the campaign of 1932, Henry I. Harriman, president of that body, urged that I agree to support these proposals, informing me that Mr. Roosevelt had agreed to do so. I tried to show him that this stuff was sheer fascism; that it was merely a remaking of Mussolini's "corporate state" and refused to agree to any of it. He informed me that in view of my attitude, the business world would support Roosevelt with money and influence. That, for the most part, proved true.

In my philosophy the anti-trust acts had emancipated and protected the American people (common man, if you will) from the vicious growth of *laissez-faire* economics inherited from Europe. By maintaining competition, our industries were forced into channels of constantly improving methods and plants and constantly lowering prices with the increasing consumption of goods. European industry with its uncontrolled *laissez-faire* had grown into a maze of cartels, trusts and trade restraints the result of which was to stagnate improvements in favor of price and distribution controls.

Now with the NRA, Roosevelt shackled his common man to unrestrained monopolies. The act, as drafted by the administration, was passed by rubber-stamp methods on May 27, 1933. The President made a flat statement that its purpose was to repeal the anti-trust acts as follows:

One of the greatest restrictions upon such cooperative efforts [of industry and business] up to this time has been our anti-trust laws . . . "with the authority and under the guidance of the Government private industries are permitted to make agreements and codes insuring fair competition." . . .

History probably will record the National Industrial Recovery Act as the most important and far-reaching legislation ever enacted by the American Congress.

I was of the same opinion as expressed in this last sentence, but from the opposite point of view.

The act was divided into several titles, of which we are here concerned with Title I.

This title authorized the President to establish code agencies, to appoint employees without Civil Service requirements, to fix their compensations and delegate his powers to them. It authorized the President to approve codes "of fair competition" proposed by industrial or trade groups or associations, or to set them up on his own motion. Any violation of the codes was to be deemed a violation of the laws against unfair competition and subject to fine and imprisonment as a misdemeanor. As a further penalty, he was authorized to license businesses and to deprive individual concerns of their license to do business, with fines and penalties. Every code was to include the right of employees to bargain collectively through their own representatives and the provision for compliance by employers with maximum hours, minimum wages, and other conditions of employment approved by the President.

The text of the act stated that the codes were not to promote nor permit monopolies or monopolistic practices.

This was sheer window dressing. As a matter of fact, the codes were the very essence of monopoly because they provided for fixing prices and wages, and for control of production and distribution practically by the trades themselves. Some chambers of commerce rejoiced at the effective freedom from the anti-trust acts.

On June 16th, the President, by Executive Order, appointed Leon

Henderson economist and General Hugh S. Johnson administrator. Henderson was one of the inner core of "planned economy" advocates, and his left-wing activities were collectivism itself. Johnson was a regular army officer who later turned columnist. He possessed a minimum knowledge of economics, but very great powers of vituperation. According to Moley's and Johnson's own statements, he had written several of Roosevelt's speeches in the campaign of 1932. As administrator, he produced a blue eagle insigne to be displayed by every home and business establishment. No one was to do business with a non-holder of the Blue Eagle. "Compliance Boards" were established in industries and counties to coerce the people, and machinery was erected for prosecution of code violators. The whole of this added up to complete coercion.

Johnson certainly produced headlines and public entertainment. President Roosevelt had said: "Those who cooperate in this program must know each other at a glance by the bright badge of the Blue Eagle."

Johnson proclaimed, "May Almighty God have mercy on anyone who attempts to trifle with that bird."

Great parades were staged throughout the country. For instance, 250,000 participants in New York and 35,000 in Cleveland proclaimed the end of the depression. The radio and the press ceaselessly clattered with the great discovery of economic salvation.

Much ado was made by Roosevelt about the child labor prohibition introduced into the codes. Yet as Governor of New York, he had refused to support ratification of the Republican Constitutional Amendment to end this evil.

The President on March 14, 1934, reenforced the National Recovery Administration by issuing an Executive Order requiring all suppliers of the government or contractors to the government, to sign up under the NRA codes. Again, on August 14, 1933, Herbert L. Petty, secretary of the Federal Radio Commission, addressed a circular to all licensed radio stations in the United States, opening: "It is the patriotic, if not the bounden legal duty of all licensees of radio broadcasting stations to deny their facilities to advertisers who are disposed to defy, ignore or modify the codes established by the NRA."

At the level of the people, the NRA was one of the greatest trials that could come to their primary freedoms. I saw many instances of this.

One night to avoid the heat, Mrs. Hoover and I were motoring home from fishing on the Rogue River. We stopped about midnight at the only hot-dog stand still open in a northern California village. We were waited on by a wholesome woman who, after she had served us, blurted out: "You are Mr. Hoover! I am in great trouble. Would you tell me what to do?"

She poured out a torrent of words to the effect that she and her husband had kept their place for ten years; they had worked very hard, for they must, by rotation, keep open eighteen hours a day to catch enough of the motor and truck traffic day and night to make a living; they had bought a small farm from their savings and had paid 60 per cent of the cost; rent from a tenant paid just enough to cover the taxes and interest; in another six years they hoped to have it completely paid for and go there to live; a frail old relative—nearly eighty—had come to them destitute; they had taken her in and given her lodging, food, and $2 a week pin money to putter around and help with the work, what little she could.

Now the NRA Compliance Board, upon which sat one of their competitors, had ordered them to keep open only twelve hours a day and pay a minimum wage of $11 per week to the old lady. They had explained and explained that it meant ruin, but the Board was adamant and had given them until the next day at noon to comply or be closed up. What could they do? About this time the husband came in. He was a husky-looking Vermonter. His immediate contribution to the conversation was: "Do I have any *rights*? Hasn't an *American* some *rights*?"

The whole Bill of Rights rose in my mind. I asked if he had ever heard if it. He hesitated, and I surmised he was wondering if it was some other bill to pay. I told him to go to the high-school library in the morning, get a copy of the Constitution of the United States, and read the first ten Amendments, which were the Bill of Rights. He would find that the spirit of six of these rights had been violated by the Compliance Board, although some sharp lawyers might deny it. I wrote out a list of the violations. I told him to go before the Board, read them the Bill of Rights, tell them in no uncertain tones where they were violating the Constitution, and then defy their orders. He was to report to me what happened, and I would advise the next step. I had in mind a generous lawyer in the county seat near by who I knew would handle the case for the glory of it. However, a few days later I received a letter from the woman: "We did just what you told us. When my husband finished defying them with that Bill of Rights, I told them where they got off. They haven't dared do anything to us since." It was this sense of the inalienable rights in the heart of most Americans that would save America yet.

Another instance among many was a woman who owned a small filling station where she did all the work. On my pulling up for gas she looked at me and broke out: "You are Mr. Hoover! What are these New Dealers doing to us? Haven't I any rights any more? I voted for Roosevelt, and this is what I get." She showed me an order from the local NRA enforcement officer telling her to reduce the price of gas 2 cents a gallon, and to do it at once or be closed up. She explained that she made about $4 a day and had three children to support, and that this order did not leave her enough to buy food for the children. I told her that they had no right in morals or law to issue such an order. I gave her the name of a leading lawyer friend in San Francisco, who would charge her nothing, and told her to refer them to this lawyer if they molested her again, and defy them. This she did; the NRA wanted no such test case in the hands of such a lawyer, and she did not hear from them any more. The lawyer was greatly disappointed. Going by some weeks later, I stopped for gas again, and she made me a present of a cactus in a pot. The symbolism was a little mixed as to persons. She volunteered she would vote the Republican ticket until she died.

As literally hundreds of appeals from such injustices came to me, I established a system of volunteer lawyers—old friends—who would advise. In no case did the authorities persevere against a threat of exposure.

All this was "planned economy" in action at the "grass roots." Soon dissent began to appear. Professor William F. Ogburn of the University of Chicago, a high official of NRA, quit with the statement that it was a futility. A small tailor, Jack Magid, in New Jersey filled the headlines for a few days because he was arrested for pressing clothes at five cents less per suit than the code called for. Public indignation got the man out of his cell.

During the progress of the NRA Senator Glass expressed himself in a letter to Hugh Johnson, who had objected to the Senator's criticism:

... Gentlemen who persist in questioning the motives of others; who vituperate respectable citizens as Tories and accuse them of a lack of patriotism merely because they disagree with the extraordinary methods being pursued in Washington; who revile persons who have spirit enough to protest against tyranny and to resent threats of reprisal and resist the destruction of their business under a system of unprecedented experimentation—gentlemen who pursue this course without the sanction of law and, as some think, far beyond the intent of Congress, should not be supersensitive when other persons and newspapers assume the role of critic.[1]

Glass did not state his opinions on the NRA to Johnson alone. He wrote to a newspaper columnist who had protested his criticisms:

... I have come to the conclusion that the nation is in a state of hysteria and that there are few men of discernment and courage left. . . .

... the methods employed have been brutal and absolutely in contravention of every guaranty of the Constitution and of the whole spirit of sane civilization. The government itself has resorted to blackmail, boycott and to a species of threats that will forever mark a black page in the history of the country.

... Unless I am frightfully mistaken in my conception of things, I shall always be glad of having voted against the wretched law.[2]

And all was not well within the NRA. Many Senators began to criticize the whole setup and proposed an independent investigation. Roosevelt named Clarence Darrow, a noted left-wing criminal lawyer, to head a committee which, to the surprise of everyone, brought in a report in May, 1934, castigating the whole business with such words as "monopolistic," "grotesque," "ghastly," "oppressive," "savage," "fictitious." Johnson denounced the report but resigned on September 24, 1934, and Roosevelt appointed a board to administer the show.

Another witness from the inside who ultimately brought the NRA into the court of public opinion was George Creel, at one time a great

---

[1] Rixey Smith and Norman Beasley, *Carter Glass*, p. 362.
[2] *Ibid.*, p. 364.

Roosevelt supporter and for a period the head of the NRA west-coast division. In his repentant memoirs he recounts two visits to Washington at that time:

A visit with the President did nothing to allay my fears or clear up my confusions. . . . Instead of being alarmed by the spirit of improvisation, he seemed delighted by it, whooping on the improvisers with the excitement of one riding to hounds. . . .

Before long . . . all but the cockeyed could see that the NRA was headed hell-bent for a bust. Going back to Washington was like a journey into bedlam, for all touch with the sane and simple had been lost. Each visit found scores of new agencies, boards, and commissions, headed by campus experts and pink-pill theorists; and the spread of the bureaucratic mania had the sweep of a pestilence. Instead of holding to a comparatively small number of basic codes, the administration went crazy, and soon some six hundred were in active operation with more in process of preparation. As one instance out of scores, the manufacturers of egg beaters and bird cages were not put under the Wire Code, but had separate codes of their own. . . .

Creel writes of a subsequent visit to Washington:

I had thought that Southern California was the world's closest approach to bedlam and babel, but Washington made the Epics, the Utopians, and the Townsendites seem staid and conservative. Under Coolidge and Hoover the White House had held the solemn hush of a mortuary establishment, but now it lacked nothing but a merry-go-round and a roller coaster to be a Coney Island. High-domed "planners," home-grown economists, overnight sociologists, magic-money nuts, social workers, and campus experts elbowed and shouted, and even the minstrel touch was provided by Tommy Corcoran's accordion and George Allen's anecdotes.[3]

Governor Alfred E. Smith, the political maker of Roosevelt, quoted on January 25, 1936, from the Democratic platform of 1932 and then observed, of the NRA: "A vast octopus set up by government that wound its arms around all the business of the country, paralyzed big business and choked little business to death." [4]

Charles F. Roos was the director of research in the NRA. Later, in a detailed book on economic planning, he concluded:

[3] George Creel, *Rebel at Large,* pp. 275–277, 289.
[4] *New York Times,* Jan. 26, 1936.

Economic planning, even of a mild "fixing" type, must remain impracticable. . . . The choicest gains go to the groups exhibiting the greatest political power. Competition, with all its imperfections, is greatly to be preferred. To entrust the economic order to such "planners" would be rash indeed; there would be a greater chance that they would reduce it to chaos than that a baby handed a watch and hammer would smash the watch.[5]

Despite the rising tide of failure and opposition, Roosevelt continued his enthusiasm over the success of NRA. On January 4, 1935, in his annual message to Congress, he said:

The purpose of the . . . Act to provide work for more people succeeded in a substantial manner . . . and the Act has . . . greatly improved working conditions in industry.

On February 20th he recommended to the Congress the extension of the NRA authority, which was about to expire. He wanted laws making codes even more compulsory, saying:

Voluntary submission of codes should be encouraged but at the same time, if an industry fails voluntarily to agree within itself, unquestioned power must rest in the Government.

I had kept still during this hysteria until the people could learn something from experience. Public resistance was growing. Finally, on May 15, 1935, I issued a blast against the whole works:

. . . the one right answer by the House of Representatives to the Senate's action . . . is to abolish . . . [the NRA] entirely. . . .
This whole idea of ruling business through code authorities with delegated powers of law is un-American in principle and a proved failure in practice. The codes are retarding recovery. They are a cloak for conspiracy against the public interest. They are and will continue to be a weapon of bureaucracy, a device for intimidation of decent citizens.
. . . I suggest that the only substitute for an action that rests on definite and proved economic error is to abandon it. We cannot build a Nation's economy on a fundamental error. . . .
The multitude of code administrators, agents or committees has spread into every hamlet, and, whether authorized or not, they have engaged in

[5] Charles Frederick Roos, *NRA Economic Planning* (Cowles Commission for Research in Economics Monograph, No. 2, Principia Press, Bloomington, Ind., 1937).

the coercion and intimidation of presumably free citizens. People have been sent to jail, but far more have been threatened with jail. Direct and indirect boycotts have been organized by the bureaucracy itself. Many are being used today. Claiming to cure immoral business practices, the codes have increased them a thousandfold. . . . They have . . . deprived the public of the benefits of fair competition.

This whole NRA scheme has saddled the American people with the worst era of monopolies we have ever experienced. However monopoly is defined, its objective is to fix prices or to limit production or to stifle competition. . . . These have been the very aim of certain business elements ever since Queen Elizabeth. Most of the 700 NRA codes effect those very purposes.

Exactly such schemes to avoid competition in business were rejected by my Administration. . . .

NRA codes have been crushing the life out of small business, and they are crushing the life out of the very heart of the local community body. . . .

The codes are preventing new enterprises. In this they deprive America's youth of the opportunity and the liberty to start and build their independence. . . .

The whole concept of NRA is rooted in a regimented "economy of scarcity"—an idea that increased costs, restricted production and hampered enterprise will enrich a Nation. That notion may enrich a few individuals and help a few businesses, but it will impoverish the nation. . . .

If . . . we subtract the persons temporarily employed by the coded industries as the direct result of the enormous Government expenditures, we find that the numbers being employed are not materially greater than when it was enacted. NRA's pretended promises to labor . . . have only promoted conflict without establishing real rights. . . .

Some business interests already have established advantages out of the codes, and therefore seek the perpetuation of NRA. Even these interests should recognize that in the end they . . . will become either the pawns of a bureaucracy that they do not want or the instruments of a bureaucracy the American people do not want.[6]

The Supreme Court on May 27, 1935, unanimously decided that Title I of the National Industrial Recovery Act was an unconstitutional attempt to use the interstate commerce power to fix prices, etc., and that it was an invalid delegation of legislative power to the President. In delivering the decision, Chief Justice Hughes said:

[6] *Addresses upon the American Road* (1933–1938), pp. 45–47.

Congress cannot delegate legislative power to the President to exercise an unfettered discretion to make whatever laws he thinks may be needed or advisable. . . .

If the commerce clause were construed to reach all enterprises and transactions which could be said to have an indirect effect upon interstate commerce, this Federal Authority would embrace practically all the activities of the people and the authority of the State over its domestic concerns would exist only by sufferance of the Federal Government.

Justice Cardozo's concurring decision pointed out that this might be in violation of the commerce power, but, in addition, "This is delegation running riot!"

The President, at his press conference, fell into a great rage over the decision. He said: "The implications are more important than any made during my lifetime or yours and probably since the Dred Scott decision. . . . It belonged to the horse and buggy stage of the Constitution." Instead of business' taking the nose dive he prophesied, however, it at once began to pick up.

It was here that the idea of subjugating the Supreme Court began to take form in his mind. But he kept quiet on the subject until after the 1936 elections.

DICTATION IN THE OIL INDUSTRY

At the urging of my administration, the major oil-producing states had set up conservation controls to prevent the huge waste of gas pressures from newly discovered oil pools. As the gas pressures were vital to the life of the fields, the possible total production was thus decreased. The resultant flush-flow floods of oil periodically demoralized the industry. I had urged the oil states to enter upon an interstate compact to assure coordination of their efforts through the Constitutional provision for such action. My proposals were defeated by the oil producers. The economic planners, with the aid of the oil industry, neatly turned our recommendation into Federal control by securing legislation through Section 9 of the NRA (June 16, 1933) which provided for prohibition in interstate commerce of oil in excess of amounts set by the state conservation boards and applying Federal codes and licenses to the industry.

On July 11th the President issued an Executive Order placing the act in force, and on August 28, 1933, by an Executive Order, he appointed Secretary Ickes as "Oil Administrator." The codes established gave complete control of production, imports, exports, wages, and prices to the Federal Government. Here again was complete fascism.

On January 7, 1935, the Supreme Court declared the petroleum provisions of Section 9 of the NRA unconstitutional, and with the declaration of the unconstitutionality of the NRA itself, some five months later, the Administrator's code powers crashed; but Ickes kept the title and the staff.

On August 9, 1935, Oklahoma, Texas, California, New Mexico, Arkansas, Colorado, Illinois, Kansas, and Michigan signed a compact jointly to conserve oil and gas, and thus reserved the powers of government to the states. The oil industry had seen enough of the economic planners and preferred local government. It was glad now to follow my recommendation of 1931.

DICTATION IN THE COAL INDUSTRY

The Bituminous Coal Conservation Act (Guffey bill) was passed on August 30, 1935, creating the National Bituminous Coal Commission with power to make rules and regulations. The code provided (a) immunity from anti-trust acts in marketing coal; (b) minimum and maximum prices; (c) prohibition of certain "unfair practices"; (d) a coal labor board; (e) obligatory collective bargaining by representatives of the workers' own choosing; (f) agreement by merely two-thirds of industry on wages and hours to be binding. The act provided a 15 per cent tax on all coal producers with a rebate of 90 per cent to operators who became members of a code to be promulgated by the Commission. Wages, production, and prices were promptly fixed or dictated. Again, here was pure fascism.

On May 18, 1936, the Supreme Court declared the Coal Conservation Act of 1935 to be unconstitutional, again declaring that wage and price fixing was an unwarranted delegation of legislative power, a violation of "due process" and not interstate commerce.

With the confidence that he would discipline the Supreme Court,

Roosevelt on May 25, 1936, proposed the reenactment of coal controls. The new law was passed by the Congress on April 26, 1937.

It was in many particulars similar to the Act of 1935, with attachments. It again created a National Bituminous Coal Commission of seven members, with the following powers of purest fascism: (a) the findings of fact by the Commission to be binding upon the courts; (b) authorization of a code under which production, minimum and maximum prices, and various marketing prices were regulated; (c) "voluntary" joining of the code, but the imposition of a tax of 1 cent per ton on coal mined and 19½ per cent on sales of all coal to be rebated to "members" only.

Under New Deal domination, the Supreme Court, reversing itself, declared this act constitutional on May 20, 1940.

The whole works was later abolished by the Congress.

DICTATION TO THE RAILROADS

On September 17th in the campaign of 1932 Roosevelt made a speech concerning the plight of the railroads, which he deemed to be my fault. He gave no credit to our revision of the bankruptcy acts which provided for orderly reorganization of overcapitalized and bankrupt companies. He gave little credit to our Reconstruction Finance Corporation, which was busy in aid to their rehabilitation from the depression. He promised the railroads great things.

On May 4, 1933, he recommended emergency railroad legislation. The bill drafted by the administration was passed as a "must" on June 16th, setting up a Federal Coordinator of Transportation. The Coordinator was to divide the railways into three groups—eastern, southern, and western—with a coordinating committee over each group. The committees were to suppress unnecessary services and pool terminals, and promote financial reorganization of the companies. The Coordinator was authorized to issue and enforce orders to produce these results but not to reduce the number of employees below that of May, 1933. Freedom from the anti-trust laws was granted. There were fines up to $20,000 for each violation of orders. The whole was the usual nebular set-up of "planned economy" without prescribed standards of conduct —but plenty of coercion.

That this did not help the railroads is shown by the following table,[7] which lists the number of miles in receivership or trusteeship, with its percentage to total railroad mileage:

Year Ended Dec. 31	Miles in Receivership or Trusteeship	Percentage to Total Railroad Mileage
(Hoover)		
1929	5,703 miles	2.19
1931	12,970	4.99
1932	22,545	8.71
(Roosevelt)		
1933	41,698	16.24
1935	68,345	26.87
1937	75,118	29.71
1938	76,938	30.80
1939	77,414	30.99

The "coordination" finally died.

[7] Calendar years. Source: Interstate Commerce Commission Reports.

CHAPTER 39

FASCISM COMES TO LABOR—
WITH CONSEQUENCES

Section 7a of the NRA (June 16, 1933) provided for the inclusion in all codes of a provision requiring collective bargaining through representatives of labor's own choosing, the establishment of minimum hours, minimum wages and conditions of labor. If no voluntary code could be agreed upon, the President was authorized to prescribe one. Roosevelt by Executive Order, on June 30, 1933, established the National Labor Relations Board to administer it. The board died when Title I of NRA was declared unconstitutional in May, 1935.

On July 5, 1935, the so-called Wagner Act (a) created the National Labor Relations Board of three members with authority to make rules and regulations; (b) confirmed the right of labor to bargain collectively through representatives of their own choosing; (c) provided for elections in which workers were to choose representatives; (d) provided for the prosecution of unfair practices through the courts, where the findings of fact by the Board were to be binding; (e) established regulations as to "unfair practices."

The right of collective bargaining by representatives of labor's own choosing had been long since expressed in the anti-injunction law enacted in my administration. But there were great evils in this legislation and its administration.

The worst evil was the failure of Congress to set proper standards of unfair practice. Furthermore, in violation of the whole spirit of American justice, the Board was judge, jury, and prosecutor. There was no effective appeal from its decisions. It issued a multitude of regulations, many beyond any authority of the Congress, even including a limitation on what the employer could discuss with his employees. Parts of these regulations were later declared unconstitutional.

The Board appointed by Roosevelt presents a prime exhibit of the collectivist character of his officials and also of the collectivist character of the regime. Its membership warrants a few paragraphs.

A committee of the House of Representatives reported the results of an exhaustive investigation of the National Labor Relations Board in December, 1940. The majority of the committee, including Democratic members, found:

1. The existence of a large group among the Board's personnel motivated by the social concept of an employer-employee relationship based upon class conflict rather than cooperative enterprise;

2. A complete lack of loyalty and belief in democratic institutions and processes, demonstrated at times by an open or half-concealed allegiance to alien and subversive doctrines and by affiliation with or sympathy for un-American organizations advocating the overthrow of our political and economic system; at others, by a bold defiance of the will of the people of the United States;

3. A flagrant disregard of constitutional rights and procedures as demonstrated by the invention of nonstatutory remedies, the use of economic pressure devices and the abuse of administrative discretion;

4. The interpretation of this law by certain members of the Board and its staff as an affirmative mandate to use the power of their official position and prestige as a stimulus to drive employees to accept and join forms of organization not of their own choice, thereby actually depriving the workers themselves of their statutory right of self-organization.

The Congressional committee then made a statement as to the character of the principal officials. They found the chairman, Joseph Warren Madden, was of extreme leftist beliefs and had appointed like-minded persons to the staff. They reported that Edwin S. Smith, a Board member, Nathan Witt, secretary, Abraham Wirin, senior attorney, David Saposs, chief economist, Alger Hiss, counsel, Fred Krivonos, special examiner, Grant Camon, field examiner, Regional Directors Edwin Eliot and Aaron Warner, together with a number of minor officials, were associated with the Communist-front organizations. (Some of them were later exposed as actual members of the Communist party.)

The administration of the act with this set-up was naturally even worse than the law itself. The Board proceeded to an orgy of dictation in industrial labor relations. Communist-controlled unions were favored and aided in expansion. The development of left-wing labor unions under the Board was to become a powerful stimulus to collectivism and even communism. In 1935 John L. Lewis launched an expansion of industrial unions as opposed to the craft unions of the American Federation of Labor. This subsequently became known as the Congress of Industrial Organizations (CIO). Lewis was neither a Socialist nor a Communist, but he associated himself with such men as Harry Bridges, Ben Gold, Lee Pressman, and other proved members of the Communist party.

Lewis was in need of skilled organizers. At once the leaders of the former Communist Trade Union Unity League, which took instructions from Moscow, stepped in and undertook much of the work. For the first time we saw labor leadership actually in the hands of the Communist party.[1] The expanded CIO was considerably staffed and controlled by both Socialists and Communists. The leftist leanings of the whole movement were greatly encouraged both by Roosevelt and by the members of the Labor Relations Board, to the detriment of the basically non-Communist, non-Socialist American Federation of Labor. In 1940

[1] Benjamin Gitlow, in *The Whole of Their Lives* (Charles Scribner's Sons, New York, 1948), p. 285, has pointed out that the Communists' control of the CIO will be difficult to eradicate:

". . . Getting control of the unions is . . . the number one task of the Communist party. By getting control of the unions, the communists mean getting control of the unions in the decisive, the basic industries of the land, the industries upon which the economic life of the country depends.

"Through the organization of the C.I.O., the communists achieved this objective. A campaign may succeed within the C.I.O. to eliminate known communists from positions and membership in C.I.O. unions. The government, through its special agencies and by enactment of legislation, may take upon itself the power to cleanse the unions of communism as a step towards security and the preservation of the state. But both courses will fail to dislodge the communists from the foothold they have gained in the C.I.O. unions. The bulk of the communist membership and their followers will remain in the unions, as will a considerable number of trade union officials who carry out Party orders. The Party has anticipated both the move by the C.I.O. officially, and by the government, by having its forces in the C.I.O. unions just melt into the membership where they now operate as trade unionists and not as communists. When the occasion arises the closed buds will suddenly burst open and the communists will appear once more in full bloom."

John L. Lewis and the United Mine Workers withdrew from the CIO, and the names of Lee Pressman, Harry Bridges, Ben Gold, Irving Potash, John Santo, Harold Christoffel, James Matles, and Jules Emspach, some of them Communists and all certainly leftists, became more prominent in its ranks. There was another important contributing factor to this movement. By the recognition of Russia in 1933, our doors had been opened to Communist infiltration to the extent that many labor unions became Communist-controlled.

The Communist character of the CIO quickly emerged into the daylight by a series of Communist-ordered "sit-down" strikes in Michigan during the summer of 1936 in which they held possession of industrial plants for weeks. By late 1936, neither Governor Murphy nor President Roosevelt had made protest, although it was patently a violation of Constitutional rights. Senator Byrnes and Vice President Garner denounced them furiously and supported resolutions against them in the Senate.

The Board so favored the Communist-infected CIO unions that the American Federation of Labor protested violently. Their Convention in October, 1937, passed the following resolution:

The National Labor Relations Board has, together with and through a number of its Regional Boards, repeatedly denied employees the right of designating the bargaining unit, and has thereby denied employees the right of selecting representatives of their own choosing. . . . [It] has attempted to destroy the validity of contracts entered into between legitimate organizations and their employees—in some instances with full knowledge of the facts involved, and in others without any apparent effort to ascertain the facts.

William Green, president of the A. F. of L., said on August 20, 1938, at the Massachusetts State Federation of Labor convention:

My arm will be palsied and my tongue will be silenced before I will ever compromise with a seceding movement or a common foe. . . . We will mobilize all our political and economic strength in an uncompromising fight until this Board is driven from power. . . . The Board is a travesty on justice.

Again, Green said:

The National Labor Relations Board has failed to administer the National Labor Relations Act successfully. This is not a charge. It is a fact. . . .

The Board has exceeded its public purpose and has vitiated the objectives of the act in these major respects:

(1) Through arbitrary determination of appropriate collective-bargaining units in representation cases, the Board has imposed upon workers, regardless of their wishes, the type of organization it favored.

(2) By administrative fiat, in direct conflict with the act, the Board has set aside legally valid and binding contracts entered into in good faith between bona fide unions and employers.

(3) In a large number of instances, the Board's agents have shown gross favoritism and bias in the handling of cases, furthering one union against another and one form of organization against another.[2]

Donald Richberg, a prominent lawyer for the labor unions, was influential in the formulation of this Wagner legislation and at one time was general counsel for the Labor Board. In later years he was to say:[3]

The abuses of this labor power by many labor leaders in recent years, the recklessness with which the entire public interest has been sacrificed, even in time of war, to advance the private interests of well-organized minorities, have made it plain that the dominance of the general welfare must be reestablished by law.

George Creel, Roosevelt's twenty-year intimate friend, says:

How else can the labor troubles of today be seen except as the direct result of Franklin Roosevelt's determination to continue in office at whatever cost? Packed boards and biased executive orders made a joke of collective bargaining and destroyed the health of the labor movement by the creation of "political company unions," dependent on White House favor and awarded privileges in return for support. Today, by the gilding process of time, these privileges have taken on the color of inalienable rights.[4]

Senator Edward R. Burke, Democrat of Nebraska, said in an address on May 18, 1938:

Fear of the inquisitorial activities of this agency [NLRB] has spread like a blight over management, workers, and investors of capital. The Administration of the National Labor Relations Act has been such as to snuff out the

---

[2] William Green, "Labor Board *vs.* Labor Act," *Fortune*, Feb., 1939, p. 79.
[3] *New York Times,* May 11, 1948.
[4] George Creel, *Rebel at Large,* p. 337.

fires of industry and send millions of workers into the line of the unemployed.

An example of coercion is cited by Samuel Pettengill, former Democratic Congressman, who said:

In August, 1939, NLRB entered into an arrangement with the Reconstruction Finance Corporation. Under it NLRB was to notify RFC of any American business against which a "charge" had been made, or was about to be made [*sic*] that it had been guilty of an unfair labor practice. If the concern had arranged for a loan from the RFC, the latter was to withhold all disbursements to the borrower. We are told that Secretary Perkins' Wage and Hour Division made similar arrangements with the RFC, and that an effort was made to induce the Treasury to do the same with reference to public building construction.

Two points should be stressed. It has never been the rule that a penalty could be imposed upon an American before he was found guilty of an offense. In the horse and buggy days, a citizen had first to be found guilty before suffering a penalty. He was entitled to a fair trial before judgment, and judgment before jail.

That is old stuff today. The New Deal injustice is to shut off credit the instant anyone is "charged" with violating the law, or even when he is "about to be charged." The assumption now is that the citizen is guilty first and innocent only if he can prove it.[5]

Few people contested the right of labor to bargain collectively for representatives of its own choosing, but the entire absence of fair play and of any semblance of judicial spirit along with the Communist infiltration made the career of this legislation one of the most regrettable in all the history of American freedoms. Out of it all came the stirring of class warfare in the most classless country in the world.

Alfred E. Smith, Roosevelt's political creator, in a published address on January 25, 1936, said:

What are these dangers that I see? The first is the arraignment of class against class. It has been freely predicted that if we were ever to have civil strife again in this country it would come from the demagogues who would incite one class of our people against the other.

[5] Samuel B. Pettengill, *Smoke-Screen* (Southern Publishers, Kingsport, Tenn., 1940).

Certainly these New Deal acts did not bring industrial peace. The increase in industrial conflict is shown in the Department of Labor record of man days lost in labor conflicts:

Under Hoover		*Under Roosevelt*		*Under Roosevelt*	
1929	9,975,213	1933	16,872,128	1937	28,424,857
1930	2,730,368	1934	19,591,949	1938	9,148,273
1931	6,386,183	1935	15,456,337	1939	17,812,219
1932	6,462,973	1936	13,901,956	1940	6,700,872
Totals	25,554,737		65,822,370		62,086,221

Ordinarily, labor clashes are at their maximum in the descending stages of depression in the effort to prevent wage reductions; and, had there been recovery such as Roosevelt from time to time claimed, these clashes should have diminished.

Out of all this came a new political force which was to be a powerful support to Roosevelt. In aid to him the CIO organized a definite political agency—the Political Action Committee, to a considerable degree dominated by Socialists under Hillman and Communists under Lee Pressman. For years their smearing propaganda was poured upon me as the principal symbol of economic wickedness.

CHAPTER 40

INTRODUCTION TO SOCIALISM THROUGH ELECTRICAL POWER

A good example of how the New Deal pattern of collectivism applied to a specific industry occurred in the field of electric power. As later reported by George Creel and others of the New Deal inner circle, Mr. Roosevelt had great dreams of the Federal government's taking over the electrical power services of the country. He gave assurances of "public power" in the campaign in 1932. George Creel says, "It was one of the President's enthusiasms in the early days of the New Deal, and he talked long and largely of 'not just one TVA, but eight, ten, even a dozen.'"[1]

On July 15, 1934, the President established the National Power Policy Committee to develop plans for national electrification under the chairmanship of Secretary Harold Ickes. As a matter of fact the United States, under private enterprise, had developed the most intensive electrification of any nation in the world. The supply of power had been kept *in advance* of need. The nation had been "interconnected" so as to avoid any breakdown in supply, and the rates under state regulation were the lowest in the world. There were rotten practices in some groups, but it is not necessary for the government to take over brickmaking because someone is murdered by a brickbat.

It should be said at once that the Federal government must from time to time undertake the construction of large dams, for the purposes of water conservation, flood control, and navigation. Power is invariably a by-product. The point of departure into socialism in these opera-

[1] George Creel, *Rebel at Large,* p. 306.

tions is simply illustrated by the set-up of the great Colorado River dam. Here, during my administration, we made a forty-year contract selling the power and its operation at the dam to the existing utilities and municipalities for a charge that returned the capital and interest on the full cost, and the states regulated the rates to protect the public. Thus the government did not engage in the power business. I have already related that during my administration we did the engineering planning for a number of great dams but with no idea of nationalizing the nation's electrical power.

The first of the New Deal undertakings was the Tennessee Valley Authority (TVA), established by an Act of Congress of May 18, 1933. This organization became a radiating headquarters for socialism. Dams were built and power was sold direct to consumers by the government. "Cooperatives" were set up with government funds to buy and sell electrical appliances. It engaged in manufacturing fertilizer and other chemicals, and even established canneries and knitting mills. By threat of government competition where government money in effect subsidized its rates, the TVA absorbed neighboring private power companies. It made and sold its fertilizers at a loss in competition with private suppliers.

The TVA was purported to be a "yardstick" of performance for the private companies. In reality it proved the case against, instead of for, public power. Its capital was furnished by the Federal government, and no interest charge was included in the construction costs. A larger part of the capital investment was charged to flood control and navigation than was warranted. Comptroller General J. R. McCarl stated to the House of Representatives, "While the properties operated cost $132,-792,294, they are listed on the books at $51,000,000." [2] According to the *New York Times,* he "questioned the authority of Tennessee Valley Associated Cooperatives, Inc., to buy dairy cattle, open up canneries, do forestry work, buy seed potatoes, conduct knitting projects and buy a flour mill." If the TVA paid interest and amortization on its real capital and the same taxes the private utilities pay, its rates would probably be higher than the neighboring utilities. The TVA authorities, instead of practicing accounting principles in the same way as private companies

[2] *New York Times,* May 22, 1935.

are required by law to do, developed their own accounting procedures, which made comparisons with the "yardstick" difficult. These accounting principles even violated the requirements of the Comptroller General of the United States.

The Public Works Administration under Ickes energetically promoted either gifts or loans to municipalities at government rates of interest with which to purchase and expand municipal ownership and operation of electrical power. These loans, by crowding out the local power companies, laid foundations for the wide expansion of the central power plants of the government.

A typical statement of this indirect coercion of private enterprise is contained in one of Roosevelt's notes where he said:

Where duplication, unnecessary competition, and loss of legitimate investments would result from the distribution of TVA electricity, the TVA has consistently urged upon municipalities the purchase of privately-owned distributing facilities. Out of a series of multi-party contracts signed by the utility companies, the TVA, and cooperative associations and municipalities, there has resulted an almost complete transfer of electric properties to public ownership in Tennessee, northern Alabama, and northeast Mississippi.[3]

Senator W. Warren Barbour of New Jersey gave a prime example of its coercive methods:

Last summer the Tennessee Valley Authority sought to acquire a private company in Knoxville—the Tennessee Public Service Co. Armed with the threat of the establishment of a municipal power plant, the T.V.A. approached this company—capitalized at $17,780,000—with an offer of $6,000,-000. The utility company declined to sell at first, but T.V.A. carried the day by arranging with the P.W.A. to allot the municipality $2,600,000—$600,000 of which was outright gift for the construction of its plant. It is interesting to note that shortly before that the State board of the P.W.A. had refused to lend any money to the city on the ground that the latter's credit did not justify a loan.[4]

[3] *Public Papers and Addresses of Franklin D. Roosevelt,* 1937 volume (Macmillan Company, New York, 1941), pp. 17–18.
[4] *New York Herald Tribune,* Aug. 12, 1935.

Raymond Moley records an interesting commentary on what was in the wind. He describes a conversation with Thomas Corcoran, one of Roosevelt's legislative and political counsellors at this time:

I turned the subject to the utilities. Tom assured me that the utilities were "licked." I asked whether that meant that the T.V.A. was going to try to take over the Commonwealth and Southern.

"You're damned right it will—and all the rest of them, too," Tom said.
"You realize what that means?"

"Well, we're going to squeeze them for a couple of years, at any rate," Tom said.

I remarked that you don't do that kind of thing for "a couple of years." If you did, it stayed done.

"Yes, I suppose so," was the answer. "It won't come fast, but twenty years from now the government will own and operate all the electrical utilities in the country." [5]

A whole series of socialist electrification activities were initiated with presumed authority from various acts of Congress. They stemmed partly from the Reclamation Acts, together with Title II of the NRA of June 16, 1933, the Federal Emergency Relief Act of May 12, 1934, the Emergency Relief Appropriation Act of April 6, 1936, and the use of RFC funds and relief funds.

Title II of NRA was the basis for various government invasions of private enterprise. It specifically provided for "development of water power, transmission of electrical energy. . . ." In addition, the President was given power to "establish such agencies . . . as he may find necessary," and to "delegate any of his functions and powers under this title to such agents . . . as he may designate or appoint."

From this authority stemmed a long series of activities encroaching upon private enterprise. They included not only the TVA but government operations resulting from the Grand Coulee and Bonneville dams on the Columbia, the Shasta and Friant dams in California, and the Flat Rock Dam in Montana. They finally developed into a plan of a government grid of hydroelectric power and transmission lines that were to envelop the eleven western states.

On May 11, 1935, the President established, by Executive Order, the

[5] Raymond Moley, *After Seven Years*, p. 354.

Rural Electrification Administration. It was sanctioned by an act of Congress on May 30, 1936. Under an "Administrator" it was empowered to make loans to "furnish electrical energy," for "rural electrification" and "wiring premises." The RFC was to furnish the money up to 85 per cent of the cost at 3 per cent per annum; but the Rural Electrification Administration, another government agency, furnished the other 15 per cent. There was apparently no liability upon anybody except the taxpayer.

On February 24, 1937, Roosevelt recommended to Congress the expansion of the Bonneville project on the Columbia, saying:

> In order to encourage the widest possible use of available electric energy, to provide reasonable outlets therefor, and to prevent the monopolization thereof by limited groups or localities, the administrator should be authorized to provide electric transmission lines, substations, and other facilities as may be necessary to bring electric energy, available for sale, from Bonneville project to existing and potential markets, and to interconnect Bonneville project with other Federal projects, now or hereafter constructed, for the interchange of electric energy.
>
> To accomplish these ends, the administrator should be authorized to acquire, by eminent domain if need be, such real and personal property, franchises, electric transmission lines, and facilities as may be necessary.

The Bonneville Power Administration was set up by the Congress on August 20, 1937, and started at once to drive the private power companies to the wall. It exercised powers of eminent domain to take over local power in municipalities, built transmission lines to them, and gave preference to these "public bodies" in the sale of its power—subsidized by the taxpayers.

On August 13, 1937, the Congress made an attempt to place these authorities in the hands of the Army Engineers instead of the socialist-minded civilians then prevalent. Roosevelt vetoed the bill.

In line with building up these Federal power administrations, Roosevelt issued an Executive Order on August 26, 1940:

> The Bonneville Power Administrator is hereby designated, under the supervision and direction of the Secretary of the Interior, as agent for the sale and distribution of electrical power and energy generated at the Grand

Coulee Dam Project and not required for operation of that Project, including its irrigation features.

The Administrator shall construct, operate, and maintain the transmission lines and substations and appurtenant structures and facilities necessary for marketing the power and energy delivered to him from the Grand Coulee Dam Project; except that the Bureau of Reclamation may construct, operate, or maintain such transmission facilities as the Secretary of the Interior, in his discretion, deems necessary or desirable.

On January 25, 1936, Governor Alfred E. Smith summed up the situation with the remark:

Just get the platform of the Democratic party and get the platform of the Socialist party and lay them down on your dining-room table, side by side, and get a heavy lead pencil and scratch out the word "Democratic" and scratch out the word "Socialist," and let the two platforms lay there, and then study the record of the present administration up to date.

After you have done that, make your mind up to pick up the platform that more nearly squares with the record, and you will have your hand on the Socialist platform; you would not dare touch the Democratic platform.

And incidentally, let me say that it is not the first time in recorded history that a group of men have stolen the livery of the church to do the work of the devil.

The effect of socialistic government competition was to stifle finance in the private electrical utility field. This is indicated by the fact that for the seven years before the New Deal (including the bad years) new construction in electrical power averaged $728,235,000 per annum. In the seven years of the New Deal, the utilities' credit was so threatened by government competition that they were able to expand at an average of only $303,857,000 per annum.

Note

In 1948–1949 I served as chairman of a bipartisan commission set up by the Congress to advise that body on the reorganization of the executive branch of the government. In the course of the work of that commission, I appointed a leading firm of auditors to examine these electrical enterprises. This examination, and the direct investigations of the commission, showed that more progress had been made in socializing the power industry than the public had any knowledge of. At that time the total electrical power capacity of the country was about 52,000,000 kilowatts. The government had completed fifty-six power plants, and had thirty-seven more under construction. Congress had authorized seventy-nine further plants, all of which, when completed, would produce some 20,000,000 kilowatts, or more than 30 per cent of the whole national output. More than 14,000 miles of transmission lines had been built, and an additional 10,000 were under construction or authorized. These plants were located in more than forty different states. Every one of them became a center of threat to neighboring private industry because of the ability either to force a sell-out or to invoke the powers of eminent domain.

By the time these plants were scheduled for completion (in, say, ten years) the degree of socialization would be far more than 30 per cent. They are mostly tax-free, have unlimited Federal money available at less than 3 per cent interest, their cost is based upon fictitious write-offs for navigation and irrigation, and yet they are unable to undersell power companies by more than the tax differential. Our investigation proved that practically none of them will repay the promised amortization in fifty years with 3 per cent interest. The scandals, inroads of socialization, and indirect control of private enterprise are enormous.

At the time of this investigation, the government also operated nearly one hundred business enterprises in various other fields. Total government invested capital in competitive business was more than $15,000,-000,000. It was engaged in the sale of fertilizers, farm products, minerals, building and renting houses as well as extensive lending operations of all kinds.

Constant exposure of corruption, graft and inefficiency has followed in their wake. None is as beneficial to the national health as the swallowed up or thwarted private enterprise.

CHAPTER 41

DIRECT RELIEF AND PUBLIC WORKS

Another illustration of the specific workings of the New Deal pattern of collectivism occurred in the field of relief of the destitute unemployed.

Relief of the destitute unemployed is not "collectivist" action in the ideological sense. In some form the American people, from colonial days, have provided for the destitute and unfortunate. Starvation has never existed in our country if the neighbors were aware of it.

The collectivist character of this phase of the New Deal and "planned economy" included the deliberate centralization of relief in the Federal government, thus undermining state and local responsibility; the creation of a huge Federal political bureaucracy; and, above all, the securing of votes out of fear of discrimination or from favors given people receiving relief. Congressional investigations repeatedly exposed such evils. This method of relief thus became an instrument for the creation and perpetuation of a one-party form of government. Such lines of action and such accumulations of power are symbolic of all collectivist movements.

To clarify the discussion, I must again distinguish between "direct" and "indirect" relief. The direct relief was actual support given to persons—families in distress. The indirect relief was that given to enable people to support themselves through public works and the action of industry to share work among its employees, etc.

In order to further clarify what happened when the New Deal took over direct relief, I must summarize the method for handling it during my administration. This was to organize, in cooperation with the governors, a relief committee in each state and, through the state committees, to set up a committee in every municipality and county where need existed.

Some three thousand state and local committees were organized over the whole country during 1930. At the lower levels they coordinated local charity and received municipal, county, and state grants-in-aid. The committees were non-partisan and were made up of leading men and women serving without pay.

We organized a national appeal for funds for their support each year. Furthermore, my administration organized employers to accept the responsibility for their normal working staffs. We supplemented these aids by a large expansion of Federal public works and active construction in the industries.

Early in 1932 I gave public assurance that, if committee resources failed, I would favor grants-in-aid from the Federal government to the state committees, on the basis that states and counties, or municipalities, should also contribute. As the depression deepened, I secured, after some delays by the Democratic Congress, authority for the RFC to make such Federal advances; and they were in progress when Roosevelt took over. I also secured authority to divert Farm Board surpluses of wheat and cotton to the relief committees.

My determined objective was to avoid concentration of power in the Federal government with its inevitable corruption, by maintaining local responsibility, with a non-partisan action to insure freedom from politics in so human a service. The local organizations, knowing their towns-people, were able to administer with sympathy and according to need. Our Washington organization kept inspectors in the field to see that there were no failures. Moreover, during the entire period we kept careful check upon the public health which is the immediate criterion of the degree of nourishment and warmth of a people. The sickness in the country steadily diminished during my entire administration, and above all, the community solicitude for children, upon which we were so insistent, resulted in constant decrease each year of the infant death rate until by 1932 we had the lowest in the whole history of the country. It increased when the New Deal took over.

When the Roosevelt administration began, some 18,000,000 persons were thus receiving direct or indirect relief. We estimated that the

MR. HOOVER AND HIS SONS HERBERT, JR. AND ALLAN

local and state cost of direct relief was about $1,300,000,000 during 1932 (not including "indirect" relief such as public works).

That the system was working effectively is amply proven by the fact that in the 1932 campaign neither Roosevelt nor any Democratic opponent uttered any word of criticism. Had there been any failure, they would not have overlooked the chance to make an issue of it.

Immediately upon taking over, Roosevelt secured huge appropriations from the Congress. He dismissed all our relief machinery—national, state, and local—replacing it with a great politically appointed Federal bureaucracy, the Civil Service requirements having been suspended in the Congressional acts.

The cost of relief to the country at once increased enormously. This was due not only to the gigantic paid bureaucracy, but to the establishment of Federal standards of payment or dole, irrespective of actual individual need, and to the fact that employers faced with paying for relief by taxes at once ceased their own relief activities, which we had insisted they maintain for their own working people. It can be easily demonstrated that more than 500,000 breadwinners with, say, 2,000,000 dependents, were thus thrown upon public relief.

Various investigations demonstrated that the total annual cost of the relief was increased by more than 250 per cent through the change in the basis of organization—exclusive of the genuine public works with less effective distribution of relief. The New Dealers, appalled at the rising costs, soon began imposing part of the burden of their huge organization upon the states. The cost—Federal and local—exceeded $3,000,000,000 per annum. Better care could have been given under our system for half that amount. Although that is the official figure, the amount was really much greater because a great part of the "indirect relief" public-works programs was of no importance as public works. Being "made work," it should have been charged to "direct relief."

The money was, however, the least of the public losses. The neighborly interest and responsibility for those in distress were destroyed, resulting in loss both to the unemployed and to the spiritual inspirations of the community.

The number of persons dependent upon public aid remained constant during Roosevelt's entire first eight years at between 16,000,000 and 20,000,000.

Senator Carter Glass said in the Senate in June, 1937:

More economic blunders, if not in some instances economic crimes, have been perpetrated by Congress in the name of starving people who never starved, and freezing people not one of whom has ever frozen, than the imagination can conjure up.

During the four years of my administration, we had expended more than $2,380,000,000 on public works, such as roads, rivers, and buildings. As I have explained in Chapter 27, we came to realize that useful works of this type were about exhausted. As a substitute, I had recommended the "reproductive public works" through the RFC and other agencies, such as toll bridges and power dams which would repay their cost from earnings.

Mr. Roosevelt had attacked our program in the 1932 campaign. He secured from the Congress large powers and appropriations to continue nonproductive public works. Various alphabetic organizations were set up under Harry Hopkins and Secretary Ickes. Huge signs decorated the highways near every works explaining the Federal connection, with Ickes's and Roosevelt's names on them so that all the electorate could see. Public ridicule gave new impetus to an old expression—"boondoggling."

The organization of Roosevelt's public works has been pungently described by George Creel, who occupied several offices from which he could be an eyewitness:

Now, however, came . . . the Civil Works Administration, that bumptious, feckless organization that was to take four million off the relief rolls and put them on federal, state, and local public projects. The idea was a good one, . . . but from the outset millions were squandered on trivial undertakings of every sort. . . .

Then, in late December [1933], came the notice of a brand-new organization—the National Emergency Council—that was to "coordinate" the activities of the NRA, the CWA, the Federal Emergency Relief Administration, and every other New Deal agency. . . . I was to assume the administration of the California division, along with my other duties. . . . It was, of course, the last word in absurdity, for each board, bureau, and commission claimed independent power, and thumbed its nose at any suggestion of control. All that it did was to create fresh angers and confusions.

There were . . . chilling notes. This was particularly true of the growing influence of the campus experts with their glee-club approach to problems. Another thing that brought out the cold sweat was the enormous increase in the federal pay roll and the reckless expenditure of public money. Every day saw the creation of new boards and commissions; and after a modest start with five or ten people, the end of the month saw them with hundreds. The Works Progress Administration was the Abou ben Adhem that led all the rest, both in size and squandering; and as I had been sharply critical, it came as a surprise to have Harry Hopkins offer me the chairmanship of a National Advisory Board.

 . . . Owing to the speed and bewildering variety of Harry's operations, any effort at analysis was about as futile as trying to pass judgment on the colors in a kaleidoscope. When we reported on one set of policies, it was to find that they had been discarded weeks before in favor of brand-new activities, all involving the expenditure of more millions. As a consequence, the National Advisory Board faded out of the picture in five or six months, and the funeral was strictly private. On handing in my resignation, I told Harry quite frankly that the pace was too hot for me. . . .

The trouble with Harry, as with so many others that Franklin Roosevelt gathered around him, and even with the President himself, was that he had never spent his own money. A social worker throughout his adult life, he had obtained his funds from municipal treasuries or foundations, so that dollars were never associated in his mind with work and thrift. Just figures in a budget.[1]

Senator Glass was not lacking in criticism, although he claimed his share of any appropriations. Secretary Ickes had made a speech in Tacoma, saying that Glass was typical of "political hypocrites that bite the hand that feeds them":

The reactionary press hails this "rugged individual" as another Horatius at the bridge because of his bitter attacks on economic policies of the government. Yet no Senator comes oftener and with more insistence for W.P.A. grants than does this same Senator Glass.

[1] George Creel, *Rebel at Large* (G. P. Putnam's Sons, New York, 1947), pp. 278–279, 295–296.

Glass replied:

Secretary Ickes has become a confirmed blackguard, saturated with hate for every member of Congress who voted against spendthrift practices of the New Deal authorities and against projecting the government into every conceivable species of business. . . . Horatius at the bridge stood and fought; he did not go 3000 miles across the continent to lie about his adversaries . . . but assuming the Secretary's assertion to be true, instead of maliciously false, why should I not advocate so-called "grants" to Virginia projects and in what respect is such advocacy "hypocritical"?

Over my protest and contrary to my vote, Congress decided on this fatuous policy of doing business and inasmuch as Virginia must repay on foolish borrowings, why should not Virginia Senators and Representatives ask Federal "aid" for her projects without being offensively and falsely accused of hypocrisy by one of the most prolific spenders of the taxpayers' money? [2]

I reviewed the whole subject of relief and public works in an address at St. Louis on December 16, 1935. On September 23, 1936, I delivered another address in New York on reform in the administration of relief giving further and more complete details.[3]

[2] Smith and Beasley, *Carter Glass,* p. 395.
[3] *Addresses upon the American Road* (1933–1938), pp. 87–100, 186–192.

CHAPTER 42

COLLECTIVISM BY THOUGHT CONTROL
AND SMEAR

An essential technique of collectivism is thought control. It is the natural instinct as well as a necessity of bureaucracy for self-preservation and expansion. Propaganda is its first weapon. The public mind must be conditioned, through government propaganda, into common denominators of thought. No private agency has the funds to contend with government money in this field.

Also criticism must be silenced. Physical concentration camps are not necessary. Repeated defamation, constant attack, and smearing of objectors can create intellectual concentration camps.

Every New Deal bureau was promptly staffed with "public relations" men under various titles. Senator Byrd, a Democrat, stated on May 24, 1939, that 30,000 employees were engaged in propaganda activities. It was an understatement. Their amiable methods were floods of mimeographed statements to the press, to long lists of bureaucrats and supporters; preparation of speeches for their superiors and members of the Congress; guidance to their radio commentators and columnists. The Administration in power, by the greater prominence of its leaders, gets more time on the radio than the opposition. The volume of printed matter sent out was but a small part of the mass of material. But here there is some statistical indication. The free mailing of the executive departments cost $9,200,000 in 1932 and $32,200,000 in 1936. This amounted to 670,000,000 pieces of mail.[1]

---

[1] Annual Report of the Postmaster General, 1932, 1936. A study by a Congressional committee in 1947 showed that expenditures upon "information" and "public relations" had exceeded $74,000,000 in the fiscal year 1946. It was probably under 5 per cent of that amount in 1932.

Stanley High, one of Mr. Roosevelt's early "public relations" advisers and speech-writer, later on gave this item:

Between 1933 and 1937 between five and ten million dollars have been spent by the government in the production of motion pictures. More than forty separate Federal agencies are engaged in motion picture operations.[2]

But propaganda techniques are not always amiable self-glorification. As indicative of the smearing and defamation technique, I cite three incidents: the Liberty League; the renaming of Boulder Dam; the attempted conviction of Andrew Mellon.

THE AMERICAN LIBERTY LEAGUE

One of the humors of the times was the formation of the American Liberty League, announced in August, 1934. The leaders were John J. Raskob, Jouett Shouse, Irénée du Pont, Pierre du Pont, Alfred E. Smith, John W. Davis, Joseph Proskauer, A. A. Sprague, Mrs. Charles Sabin, and Mrs. Henry B. Joy. They had been ardent supporters and, in some cases, managers of Roosevelt's 1932 campaign. A number of big-business Republicans and Democrats plus the usual "joiners" were added to the membership. They originally believed that Roosevelt was being misled by the men and women around him, and that his old friends would correct things by expressing themselves. For a year they uttered no criticism of Roosevelt.

It so happened that some of the members of this group had financed the smearing campaign waged against me during the whole time I was in the White House. Unbelievable as it may be, Raskob wrote asking me to join. My opinion of the organization is indicated by my reply on September 3rd to a friend's request for advice on joining it:

This is the group that financed the Democratic smearing campaign, both directly through the Democratic National Committee and indirectly through various other organizations which they established at that time. Also, this is the group who supported the election of the New Deal. If this group had told the truth, either during the Republican Administration or during the campaign, as they . . . now acknowledge it to be, the country would not be in this situation. They are, therefore, hardly the type of men to lead the cause of Liberty. . . .

[2] Stanley High, *Roosevelt—and Then?* pp. 120–121.

I could go into what is in the minds of this group. I do not do so, but I may state emphatically that I have no more confidence in the Wall Street model of human liberty, which this group so well represents, than I have in the Pennsylvania Avenue model upon which the country now rides.

In the end, the League determined to attack Roosevelt. Governor Smith, in a speech at their meeting at Washington in January, 1936, copiously denounced the whole New Deal and announced, "I am going to take a walk"—out of the Democratic party. The New Deal promptly turned its smear guns upon him, connecting him with the du Ponts.

As to Governor Smith's speech, James A. Farley writes:

In late January, Smith made his "I'm going to take a walk" Liberty League speech. Our strategy board debated about finding someone to answer him and finally chose his 1928 running mate, Senator Joseph T. Robinson of Arkansas.[3]

Certainly Senator Robinson's speech, later alleged to have been written by Charles Michelson, reached great depths in personal smearing. This was especially so as Governor Smith had made no personal attack on Roosevelt, and Roosevelt owed to Smith his whole rise in the political world.

The League set up a great clatter, but the personalities that ran it were so out of favor in the country that it boomeranged to aid Roosevelt. It soon effectively died, although its funeral was not officially announced until some years later.

BOULDER DAM

During my administration, Secretary Wilbur had named the Colorado River dam "Hoover Dam," in accordance with the custom of naming great water conservation dams after the Presidents in whose administrations they were undertaken. That had been the case with Theodore Roosevelt, Taft, Wilson, and Coolidge.

The name Hoover Dam had been accepted generally and had appeared in various official contracts and Congressional appropriations when, on May 8, 1933, Secretary Ickes, under orders from Roosevelt, ordered it changed to Boulder Dam.

On September 30th, Roosevelt dedicated the dam under the name Boulder Dam, never mentioning that I had been especially responsible

[3] James A. Farley, *Jim Farley's Story*, p. 59.

for the enterprise through the chairmanship of the Colorado River Commission which had paved the way for its construction, nor my personal guidance of its engineering, nor the legislation authorizing it, which had been largely prepared by me, nor the fact that two-thirds of the works were completed in my administration.

On April 30, 1947, the name was restored by unanimous action of the House, and only a trifling opposition in the Senate. Ickes expressed poignant misery in the press.

I had made no protest over the matter, but when Congressman Jack Z. Anderson, who had introduced the bill, notified me of its passage, I wrote to him:

March 10, 1947

My dear Mr. Congressman:

Thank you for yours of March seventh.

Confidentially, having had streets, parks, school houses, hills, and valleys named for me, as is done to all Presidents, I have not thought this item of great importance in the life of a nation. But when a President of the United States tears one's name down, that is a public defamation and an insult. Therefore, I am grateful to you for removing it.

Yours faithfully,

HERBERT HOOVER

THE ATTEMPTED CONVICTION OF ANDREW MELLON

A notable instance of smear tactics occurred in 1935 when the New Deal Department of Justice sought to indict former Secretary of the Treasury Mellon for fraudulent income-tax returns. The action was widely heralded in the press as bringing the "reactionaries" to book. Mr. Mellon was to be the prime example. He was one of the richest men in the country. His fortune, partly inherited, had been made by the building up of new industries. In his day that profession was regarded as a worthy calling. The following anecdotes provide an indication of his character. During the time I was in the White House, we had occasion to recommend an increase in taxes. I suggested to Mr. Mellon that the upper brackets of the income and estate taxes be increased and mentioned a very substantial increase. "That is not enough," Mr. Mellon replied.

I had known Mr. Mellon intimately. Not only was he a man of

the most scrupulous integrity, but I knew that in the period when he was supposed to have defrauded the taxpayers, he was the backbone of support of the unemployed in the Pittsburgh area. His expenditure on this and other charities during that time far exceeded his purported gain from evasion of income taxes. Moreover, it was known to the Roosevelt administration that he was preparing a gigantic gift to the nation of one of the greatest art galleries in the world. The site for Mr. Mellon's gift had been reserved both by my administration and by the Roosevelt administration. Despite the attempted indictment, he went ahead with this and other gifts which amounted to somewhere around $100,000,000—the larger part of his great fortune.

At one time it looked as if this very old, feeble, and innocent man would have to stand trial for defrauding the government to which he had given years of able service, and before a people to whom he was passionately devoted. But, to the surprise of the administration, the grand jury refused to bring in an indictment.

An interesting sidelight on all this was given by former Tax Commissioner Elmer Irey in his recital to William J. Slocum of a renewed attempt to indict Mr. Mellon after the first attempt had failed:

"The Roosevelt administration made me go after Andy Mellon," he [Irey] said. "I liked Mr. Mellon and they knew it, so the F.B.I. took the first crack and got tossed out of the Grand Jury room.

"Bob Jackson was made chief counsel of the Internal Revenue Department and he said to me: 'I need help on that Mellon thing. The F.B.I. investigation was no good. You run one on him.'"

Irey said to Jackson, "If I wasn't to be trusted before, why now?"

Jackson's answer was, "I don't know anything about that. You are qualified and I need help. I'll have to see the Secretary."

In a short time Irey got a telephone call from Henry Morgenthau, Jr., Secretary of the Treasury. The Secretary said, "Irey, you can't be 99⅔ per cent on that job. Investigate Mellon. I order it."

. . . Irey explained his personal viewpoint that Mellon was innocent, although admitting it was not his place to judge. Morgenthau's answer was, "I'm directing you to go ahead, Irey." [4]

They failed again.

[4] As reported by Slocum in his Introduction to Irey's book, *The Tax Dodgers* (Greenberg, New York, 1948), pp. xii–xiii.

CHAPTER 43

SOME GOOD ACTIONS

The New Deal brought into being a number of long needed reforms and some constructive actions. Some were completion of efforts started in the previous administrations, and many were possible only because the President and the Congress were of the same party. However, the patterns and principles set up often defeated the full measure of these reforms.

Much of the legislation we had urged was carried to completion. The further needed authorities were given to the RFC, the Home Loan Banks and the Federal Farm Banks. Mortgage relief was expanded. Among the new acts urged during my administration were the Banking and Stock Exchange reforms and the regulation of electric power companies.

FURTHER RELIEF FROM MORTGAGE PRESSURES

All depressions unduly lower equity values and thus jeopardize honest holdings of property that may be under mortgage. Also bankruptcy can end the life of an important productive agency. Beyond this, mortgage foreclosure can bring the greatest of tragedies to home life.

The relief of such mortgage pressure during a world-wide hurricane of depression is not necessarily collectivism, depending on how it is done. To prevent foreclosure for lack of credit due to faulty government regulation of credit institutions was a national necessity.

During the campaign of 1932 Roosevelt said on September 29th: "Today I read in the papers that for the first time, so far as I know, the Administration of President Hoover has discovered that there is such a thing as a farm mortgage or a home mortgage."

As evidence to the contrary, I have given in previous chapters the long list of institutions created and actions taken in this field during my administration.

Mr. Roosevelt properly instituted further measures for relief of mortgage pressure on homes and farms. But the New Deal undertook its mortgage relief direct to the citizen through the Federal agencies, by taking over mortgages from the banks and loan companies, thus relieving them of any risk. Our method was to act through the institutions that held the mortgages, so that they should take some part of the risks and thus avoid the waste and corruption that comes from personal contacts by the government and the cost of a great bureaucracy. The New Deal, however, by centralizing power in the hands of Federal officials gave the citizen full appreciation of the benevolence of the Great White Father. It created a further great political clientele which drove further toward one-party government.

There were none of these provisions which could not have been accomplished by expansion of government credit and guarantees to existing public and private institutions with much smaller losses and less expense to the taxpayer.

Their methods resulted in the taking of a multitude of bad mortgages from the banks, which should have carried at least part of the risk. One of these agencies, the Home Owners' Loan Corporation, thus absorbed probably two billions of such mortgages and in time found itself foreclosing on the home owner. The organization at one time or another foreclosed on over 200,000 homes. Here is an indication at least that banks had been relieved of a lot of their own bad loans.

EXPORT-IMPORT BANK OF WASHINGTON

The Export-Import Bank was created by Executive Order on February 8, 1934, for the purpose of expanding trade with the Soviet Union. No substantial trade, however, eventuated.

A second Export-Import Bank was created on March 4th for promoting trade with Cuba, but expanded on June 30th to include all foreign countries except the Soviet Union. The two were ultimately consolidated.

Not until the Export-Import Bank Act of 1945 was the principle formulated that the Bank should supplement and not compete with private capital, and that loans should be for specific purposes and offer reasonable assurance of repayment. Prior to 1945 it was used for all kinds of political, economic, and diplomatic pressures by the Office of Economic Warfare. Since 1945 it has served proper and legitimate purposes.

SOCIAL SECURITY ACTS

On August 14, 1935, Congress passed the Social Security Act, providing (a) unemployment compensation by a tax on pay rolls, remittable as to 90 per cent against any payments to state funds; (b) old-age pensions by grants to states not in excess of $15 a month equal to similar state action; (c) tax for old-age insurance, equal amounts on employers and employees, commencing at 1 per cent and increasing to 3 per cent. Out of this the government was to pay pensions commencing January 1, 1942, ranging from $10 to $85 per month at sixty-five, depending on the length of participation in the fund; (d) aid to dependent children and the blind, provided through grants to states on matching basis, not exceeding $15 a month; (e) extension of public health services provided through grants to states on matching basis; and (f) vocational rehabilitation.

The broad objective in this act was meritorious. The method of financing of old-age pensions, however, was unsound, as the cash receipts were used to pay current expenses of the government, and government bonds were earmarked for the amount. Consequently, many of those insured under Social Security will have to pay twice, because they will sometime have to put up the money to redeem the bonds.

BUSINESS REGULATION

Distinction must be made between (a) the regulation of business activities, which has been part of the American system of individualism, (b) dictation of business activities, which is fascism, and (c) government operation of competitive business, which is socialism.

My opposition was against collectivism, not against regulation. I had created several regulatory agencies myself during my period in public office.

The major regulatory steps in Roosevelt's administration were:

The banking reform bill, constantly recommended to the Democratic

Congress by my administration, was enacted. To its provisions the Congress in 1933 added Federal deposit insurance, at the suggestion of Republicans and over the objections of Roosevelt.

Congress enacted the consolidation of certain existing Interstate Commerce Commission powers over telegraph and telephone with the Radio Commission, forming the Federal Communications Commission. Both were of Republican origin. There have been repeated charges of favoritism and coercion of business agencies.

I had secured from Congress the creation of the Federal Power Commission. I had urged these extensions of its regulatory powers. But the Democratic Congress refused. Mr. Roosevelt, however, secured them.

A Federal Securities Commission was created by Mr. Roosevelt to regulate stock exchanges and security issues, the foundations for which had been laid during my administration by the Senate investigations which I inspired. The method of regulation was different from my proposals, but it was a public necessity. I had proposed controls through the Courts instead of through a Commission of "Administrative Law."

A Fair Labor Standards Act was passed on June 25, 1938, providing for minimum wages in goods subject to interstate commerce. This was generally approved. Sweated labor then going on in the southern states was barbaric as well as ruinous to industry everywhere.

I may recall some paragraphs on "Business and American Liberty" from an address I made to an important conference in Colorado Springs on March 7, 1936, on regulation as distinguished from dictation and operation of business:

We have three alternatives.

First: Unregulated business.

Second: Government-regulated business, which I believe is the American System.

Third: Government-dictated business, whether by dictation to business or by government in business. This is the New Deal choice. These ideas are dipped from cauldrons of European Fascism or Socialism.

Unregulated Business

While some gentlemen may not agree, we may dismiss any system of unregulated business. We know from experience that the vast tools of technology and mechanical power can be seized for purposes of oppression. They have been used to limit production and to strangle competition and opportunity. We can no more have economic power without checks and balances than we can have political power without checks and balances. Either one leads to tyranny.

And there must be regulation of the traffic even when it is honest. We have too many people and too many devices to allow them to riot all over the streets of commerce. But a traffic policeman must only enforce the rules. He will block the traffic if he stands on the corner demanding to know their business and telling them how to run it.

THE AMERICAN SYSTEM OF REGULATION

. . . The only system which will preserve liberty and hold open the doors of opportunity is government-regulated business. And this is as far from government-dictated business as the two poles. Democracy can regulate its citizens through law and judicial bodies. No democracy can dictate and survive as a democracy. The only way to preserve individual initiative and enterprise is for the government to make the same rules for everybody and act as umpire.

But if we are to preserve freedom we must face the fact that ours is a regulatory system.

And let us be definite once and for all as to what we mean by a system of regulation. It looms up more clearly against the past three years.

1. A great area of business will regulate its own prices and profits through competition. Competition is also the restless pillow of progress. But we must compel honest competition through prevention of monoplies and unfair practices. That is indirect regulation.

2. The semi- yet natural monopolies, such as railways and utilities, must be directly regulated as to rates to prevent the misuse of their privilege.

3. Banking, finance, public markets, and other functions of trust must be regulated to prevent abuse and misuse of trust.

The failure of the States, particularly New York, to do their part during the boom years has necessitated an extension of Federal action. The New Deal regulations of stock and security promotion in various aspects have the right objectives. They were hastily and poorly formed without proper consideration by Congress. But they point right.

4. Certain groups must be appropriately regulated to prevent waste of natural resources.

5. Labor must have the right to free collective bargaining. But it must have responsibilities as well as rights.

6. At one time we relied upon the theory of "shirt sleeves to shirt sleeves in three generations" to regulate over-accumulations of wealth. This is now guaranteed by our income and inheritance taxes. Some people feel these taxes take the shirt also.

But there are certain principles that must run through these methods.

1. The first principle of regulation is the least regulation that will preserve equality of opportunity and liberty itself. We cannot afford to stifle a thousand honest men in order to smother one evil person.

2. To preserve Liberty the major burden of regulation must fall upon the States and local government. But where the States hopelessly fail or when the problem grows beyond their powers we should call upon the Federal government. Or we should invoke the machinery of interstate compacts.

3. Regulation should be by specific law, that all who run may read. That alone holds open the doors of the courts to the citizen. This must be "a government of laws and not of men."

4. And the American System of Liberty will not function solely through traffic policemen. The fundamental regulation of the nation is the Ten Commandments and the Sermon on the Mount.

Incidentally, the government might regulate its own business by some of the standards it imposes on others.

There are certain humanities which run through all business. As we become more experienced, more humane, as conditions change, we recognize things as abuses which we once passed over. There are the abuses of slums, child-labor, sweated hours, and sweated wages. They have been diminishing for decades before the New Deal. They have not been solved yet. They must be solved. We must not be afraid to use the powers of government to eliminate them.

There will be periodic unemployment in any system. It is even so in the self-declared economic heavens of Socialism and Fascism. With common sense we could provide insurance programs against it. We could go further and prevent many causes of depressions.

Out of medical and public-health discoveries we have in eighty years increased the number of people over sixty years of age from four per cent to eight per cent. That imposes another problem upon us.

This American System has sprung from the spirit of our people. It has been developing progressively over many generations. However grave its faults may be they are but marginal to a great area of human well-being. The test of a system is its comparative results with others and whether it has the impulses within to cure its faults. This system based on ordered liberty alone answers these tests.

The doors of opportunity cannot be held open by inaction. . . .

These doors are partly closed by every gentleman who hatches some special privilege. They are closed to somebody by every betrayal of trust. But because brickbats can be used for murder we do not need stop building houses. These doors are partly shut by every needless bureaucrat. And there is the tax collector. He stands today right in the door.

Every new invention, every new idea, every new war shifts and changes our economic life. That greatest instrument of American joy, the automobile, has in twenty years shifted regulation in a hundred directions.

Many obstructions and abuses have been added by the New Deal. Many of them are older but no worse. While the inspiration to reform comes from the human heart, it is achieved only by the intellect. Enthusiastic hearts have flooded us with illusions. Ideals without illusions are good. Ideals with illusions are no good. You may remember that youth with a banner of strange device. Was it "Excelsior" or was it "Planned Economy"? He froze to death.[1]

[1] *Addresses upon the American Road* (1933–1938), pp. 132–135.

CHAPTER 44

THE EXPENDITURES, ACCOUNTING AND STATISTICS

We now come to the question of what all these actions cost the taxpayer and some questions of intellectual honesty in government bookkeeping.

During the campaign of 1932, one of Roosevelt's great themes was the extravagant spending of my administration. He repeatedly promised a reduction of 25 per cent. The violence, bitterness, and misrepresentation in these matters is set out in my account of the Campaign of 1932.

Before an analysis of Roosevelt's actions can be made, there must be an understanding of the changes in accounting methods. Under all previous accounting, the moneys paid out of the Treasury, even for good recoverable loans by the RFC and other agencies, were entered on one side of the ledger simply as expenditures. The actual cash receipts were entered on the other side. That method also included the trust accounts, the District of Columbia income and expenditures, the income and outgo of the Post Office, all of which were on our books, and we included retirement of the public debt.

Mr. Roosevelt at once revised this "horse and buggy" accounting by excluding trust accounts, income and expenditures of the postal services, presenting only the Post Office deficit in the budget. He likewise excluded the income and expenses of the District of Columbia, including only the deficit. Also, in his reports, the statutory debt redemption is omitted. He divided expenditures into "ordinary" and "emergency." His "emergency" expenditures included relief, public works, and loans on security by government or capital subscriptions. He claimed the public works and loans were assets, not expenditures. On the expenditure side, the New Deal had the advantage of not showing most of its loans, which were made by special corporations and were not reflected to the Treasury until liquidation. Of the expenditures in my administration, $2,459,000,000 were recoverable loans, which were later recovered and therefore were not a burden on the taxpayer. There was no fraud in the New Deal form of accounting. The effect, however, was to make their expenditures look smaller.

In order to make a correct comparison, I give the expenditures of my administration calculated upon the New Deal method of accounting, the recasting of which was undertaken for me by one of our former budget officers. The President's term of office does not correspond to the fiscal years (ending June 30); and, as it is impossible from government accounts to split the balances, I have given the amounts (in millions of dollars) for the fiscal years following the date of the Presidential years:

ADMINISTRATION	FISCAL YEAR	TAX RECEIPTS	EXPENDITURES		
			Ordinary	Extraordinary	Total
Hoover	1929	4,983	2,910	279	3,189
	1930	4,045	2,864	446	3,310
	1931	3,189	2,965	706	3,671
	1932	2,006	3,011	1,691	4,702
Roosevelt (1st term)	1933	2,079	2,850	1,779	4,629
	1934	3,116	2,651	3,360	6,011
	1935	3,800	3,457	3,553	7,010
	1936	4,116	5,309	3,357	8,666
Roosevelt (2nd term)	1937	5,294	4,663	3,779	8,442
	1938	6,242	4,646	2,980	7,626
	1939	5,625	5,221	3,845	8,066
	1940	5,739	6,219	2,780	8,999

These comparisons on the New Deal basis can be summarized as follows:

	1929–1932 (Hoover)	1933–1936 (Roosevelt)	1937–1940 (Roosevelt)
Total tax receipts	14,223	13,111	22,900
Total ordinary expenditures	11,750	14,267	20,749
Total extraordinary expenditures	3,122	12,049	13,384
Total expenditures	14,872	26,316	33,133
Total deficit	649	13,205	11,233
National debt at end of term	22,500	38,300	48,500

In tax receipts, Mr. Roosevelt had the advantage of the increased taxes imposed in the latter part of my administration.

Included in the receipts shown above are the Social Security deductions from pay rolls. Some $2,000,000,000 collected from these taxes were, as I have mentioned, used for current expenses by the expedient of placing government bonds to that amount in the social security till—to be collected from the taxpayer again when the social security payments became due.

The New Deal conducted a large number of organizations by loans from the RFC. An astonishing juggle in this particular was the act of February 16, 1938, which provided:

That the Secretary of the Treasury is authorized and directed to cancel notes of the Reconstruction Finance Corporation . . . and all sums due and unpaid upon or in connection with such notes at the time of such cancellation.

This act canceled debts of ten New Deal agencies to the RFC for moneys advanced for New Deal spending. The bill passed in less than three minutes. The total thus wiped off the books exceeded $2,700,-000,000.

Later Senator Vandenberg said:

In about three seconds this afternoon under pressure of the Vice President's gavel, we passed House bill 9379, and I confess that few of us understood what had happened until about a half an hour afterward. H. R. 9379 happens to be a bill which cancels $2,700,000,000 . . . without exercise of any discretion on the part of the officials of the Reconstruction Finance Corporation.[1]

Senator Vandenberg, however, missed the main point in this operation. This $2,700,000,000 avoided the whole procedure of examination and check by Congressional appropriations committees. Thus the whole

[1] *Congressional Record,* Feb. 16, 1938.

Congressional responsibility for the "purse" was by-passed. Expenditures from 1933 to 1938 were thus obscured. What all this juggling added up to is difficult to determine, but it probably obscured some $4,000,-000,000 expenditure of taxpayers' money.

One test of all this was the amount of national debt less the recoverable loans at different periods. On this basis, the debt was about $20,000,-000,000 at the end of my administration, and about $47,000,000,000 at the end of Roosevelt's eight years.

On the basis of Roosevelt's promise in the 1932 campaign of a 25 per cent reduction of expenses, his record in eight years should have been less by about $38,000,000,000. By his second term he had increased the expenditures by more than 225 per cent.

The New Dealers further increased and rearranged the taxes supposedly to take the burden from the poor and place it upon the rich. The following table, in which are given the percentages of taxes falling upon the higher income groups, is illuminating.

(Hoover)	1929....................	69.6
	1930....................	70.5
	1932....................	60.6
(Roosevelt)	1933....................	47.9
	1934....................	37.3
	1935....................	38.7
	1936....................	48.7

Lewis Douglas resigned as Roosevelt's Director of the Budget on August 30, 1934. He informed me he was utterly at variance with Roosevelt's expenditure, monetary, and other economic policies, and could not conscientiously continue in his position.

The only campaign promises to reduce expenditures that Roosevelt made good fell upon the defense and veterans' services, where the record shows:

	Fiscal Year	Defense Services	Veterans
(Hoover)	1931	$734,000,000	$953,000,000
	1932	752,000,000	985,000,000
(Roosevelt)	1933	679,000,000	863,000,000
	1934	531,000,000	557,000,000
	1935	689,000,000	607,000,000

The reduction of military defense expenditures in 1934 came at a time when Hitler, Stalin, the Japanese and Mussolini were loudly threatening the peace of the world.

The effect of Roosevelt's reductions on the number of veterans aided was as follows:[2]

	Fiscal Year	Veterans Aided
(Hoover)	1932	994,000
(⅔ Hoover)	1933	998,000
(Roosevelt)	1934	581,000
	1935	586,000
	1936	601,000
	1937	599,000
	1938	601,000
	1939	603,000
	1940	610,000

Periodically the President issued urgent messages on economy, as on April 13, 1937:

The heads of the executive departments and independent establishments of the Government will immediately cause a survey to be made of the expenditure requirements of their departments . . . the deficit will be far greater than was anticipated unless there is an immediate curtailment of expenditures.

I made an analysis of New Deal manipulation of accounts in an address at Philadelphia on October 16, 1936. Anyone interested in the humors of such accounting will find the full text in my *Addresses upon the American Road,* 1933–1938.

INDEX NUMBERS

One of the intellectual operations of the New Deal was the manipulation of statistics founded on index numbers.

Index numbers are made up from either a single item like wages or component parts where several elements are concerned, such as the cost of living. They are an expression of percentages and are a vital indicator of economic trends.

[2] Annual Reports of the Veterans Administration.

With progress and change in economic life, indexes which are made of component parts must be readjusted so as to include new products, such as was the case in electric power or automobiles. In itself, altering the base of an index is not a dishonest procedure. The adjustment, however, can be used to change the whole appearance of economic progress.

An example of the juggling of a component index was the Federal Reserve index of industrial production. The changed index altered all comparisons about 14 per cent in favor of the New Deal. The purpose seems to have been to delude the public into believing that the New Deal had caused an unprecedented increase in production.

The Cleveland Trust Company *Bulletin* of September, 1940, observed:

> The recent increases are so large that they challenge our credulity, for they seem to indicate that in recent years our volume of production per capita of our population has been about as large as it was in the years of booming prosperity before the depression, and this despite our huge unemployment and shrunken national income.

The original index showed a recovery from the low point in July, 1932, and a rise until the Maine election in September, after which it fell rapidly. The changes made it appear that there had been little improvement in production until after the New Deal came into power.

This juggling extended even to the indexes containing only one component, such as factory pay rolls, and hourly wages. This was accomplished by shifting the base of 1923–1925 to a base of 1939. As the result of the shift, the rise in both hourly and weekly wages since the beginning of World War I was disguised. If the former index had been carried through, the index for the years 1935 through 1939 would have been 273 for hourly wages and 237 for weekly wages. By starting again with 100, wages appeared to have had only minor rises. Similar shifts in base, and other alterations were made in wholesale, retail, and farm prices and a multitude of other business indexes.

The net result of these operations was to manipulate economic history.

CHAPTER 45

THE CONSEQUENCES

I shall try, by the cold application of statistics, to sum up the final proof:

1. That the Great Depression extended from 1929 to 1941;

2. That recovery from the Great Depression came quickly to other nations of free economy; but, as a consequence of the New Deal devices, it never came to the United States under Roosevelt during peacetime;

3. That the primary cause of this failure was the New Deal attempt to collectivize the American system of life;

4. That the Great Depression was ultimately in name ended only by war.

The indexes of the number of unemployed, the number on relief, and the subnormal productivity are the infallible proof that the Great Depression extended until the man power and energies of the American people were absorbed in military action.

The currently published American Federation of Labor figures on unemployment show:

July, 1932	Depression low point	12,300,000
October, 1932	Roosevelt's election	11,586,000
January, 1933		13,100,000
1934		13,282,000
1935		12,058,000
1936		12,646,000
1937		10,002,000
1938		10,926,000
1939		11,369,000
1940		10,656,000

After January, 1940, war production and large mobilization for the armed forces began to have some effect; but even at Pearl Harbor (December, 1941) more than 8,000,000 were still unemployed.

Different authorities vary greatly on the number of unemployed at any one time. I have chosen the American Federation of Labor's currently reported January figures because the only real census of unemployment during this period, taken in November, 1939, corroborated their estimates. Roosevelt stated this census as follows:

This check-up indicated that there were, as of November, 1937, about 11,000,000 totally unemployed or emergency workers. . . .

The number of partly unemployed determined after the check-up census was placed at 5,500,000. . . .[1]

Thus at this time the actual number unemployed was greater than 11,000,000 totally unemployed, and compares with the A. F. of L. estimate of two months later of 10,926,000 unemployed.

The contention is made that New Deal measures were a success because there was an annual increase in the number of workers for whom jobs were provided. That explanation hardly holds water because the increase of workers came from the increase of population; therefore more services, and jobs, were required to support the increase.

It might be observed that the 1940 figure was only about 1,000,000 less than the number unemployed the day Mr. Roosevelt was elected, eight years before.

THE NUMBERS ON RELIEF

The failure to solve unemployment is indicated by the constant numbers of persons on relief.

The number of persons receiving some sort of relief remained fairly constant throughout Roosevelt's eight years. The following table, compiled from the WPA Statistical Bulletin, gives the number of people carried on relief by all agencies, Federal and local. It will be seen that they diminished very little in these years:[2]

[1] *The Public Papers and Addresses of Franklin D. Roosevelt,* 1937 volume, p. 373.

[2] My administration did not compute the numbers, and those given for 1932 are the estimate of the Roosevelt administration when they took over. The number of persons for 1937–1940 is estimated at 4 persons per family. (Source: Federal Security Agency.)

		Households	Estimated Persons
(Hoover)	1932	4,155,000	16,620,000
(Roosevelt)	1933	5,176,000	19,677,000
	1934	6,633,000	23,846,000
	1935	6,370,000	22,354,000
	1936	5,867,000	19,550,000
	1937	3,810,000	15,240,000
	1938	5,790,000	23,160,000
	1939	4,912,000	19,648,000
	1940	4,227,000	16,908,000

There are other facts which amply confirm the failure of planned economy to secure recovery. The four-year period, 1925–1928, prior to the depression contrasted with the four-year period of Roosevelt's second term, 1937–1940, yields the following comparisons of national productivity:[3]

	1925–1928	1937–1940	Decrease
Total value new business equipment....	$34,950,000,000	$26,780,000,000	23%
Total value farm marketings...........	43,380,000,000	32,760,000,000	24
Total fire insurance written............	37,590,000,000	25,920,000,000	31
Total private construction, all kinds....	34,648,000,000	14,510,000,000	58
Total private residential construction....	17,425,000,000	7,891,000,000	55
New dwelling units in non-farm areas..	3,349,000,000	1,638,000,000	50

COMPARISON WITH OTHER COUNTRIES

A further test of all this New Deal failure to end the Great Depression lies in a comparison of our recovery and our unemployment with that of other countries.

Recovery of employment above that of the pre-depression year, 1929, quickly took place in all nations of free economies. The only laggards were the United States and France, hobbled by their "New Deals," and Canada, whose economy was locked to that of the United States.

National income in Britain, where there was then a free economy without a New Deal, almost completely recovered during the first two years of Roosevelt's administration. A comparison shows the following:

HOOVER ADMINISTRATION

	U. S. National Income		British National Income	
	$ Billions	Per Cent of 1929	$ Billions	Per Cent of 1929
1929	79.4	100.0	19.0	100.0
1932	46.3	58.3	11.7	61.0

[3] Source: The National Industrial Conference Board *Economic Almanac*.

ROOSEVELT ADMINISTRATION

1933	43.3	54.5	14.7	77.1
1934	48.7	63.4	18.8	98.8
1935	53.0	66.7	19.6	102.9
1936	59.0	74.4	21.5	113.5

Four years after Roosevelt was elected, not only had other countries of free economy recovered, but their productivity and employment exceeded the boom levels of 1929.[4] For instance

	PER CENT CHANGE 1929 to 1936	
	Industrial Production	Employment
Norway	+ 15	+ 4
Denmark	+ 25	+ 33
Estonia	+ 20	+ 26
Finland	+ 33	+ 2
Greece	+ 39	+ 10
United Kingdom	+ 6	+ 7

During this same period, three countries beset by economic planners had failed to restore production and employment to the 1929 level:

	PER CENT CHANGE 1929 to 1936	
	Industrial Production	Employment
United States	− 12	− 12
France	− 30	− 29
Canada	− 10	− 13

In June, 1939, seven years after Roosevelt was elected, the free economy nations had still further exceeded the boom year, 1929, production and employment figures while the United States still lagged, as shown by the following percentages:[5]

RECOVERY IN INDUSTRIAL PRODUCTION, PER CENT OF CHANGE FROM 1929		RECOVERY IN EMPLOYMENT, PER CENT OF CHANGE	
Bulgaria	+ 83	Japan	+ 75
Japan	+ 81	Estonia	+ 61
Latvia	+ 75	Latvia	+ 46
Finland	+ 56	Norway	+ 29

[4] *Statistical Year Book of the League of Nations* (1936–1937).
[5] Source: *Monthly Bulletin of Statistics,* League of Nations.

Sweden	+ 56	Hungary	+ 25
Estonia	+ 49	Yugoslavia	+ 24
Denmark	+ 46	Australia	+ 21
Norway	+ 39	United Kingdom	+ 17
Chile	+ 35	Finland	+ 9
Poland	+ 27	Poland	+ 8
United Kingdom	+ 24	Sweden	+ 7
Netherlands	+ 8	Netherlands	+ 5
Canada	− 2	Canada	− 5
France	− 8	France	− 18
UNITED STATES	− 18	UNITED STATES	− 7

A further analysis of the comparative British situation six years after Roosevelt's election is of interest:[6]

	United States National Income	Per Cent of 1929	United Kingdom National Income	Per Cent of 1929
1929	$79,395,000,000	100.	$19,029,000,000	100.
1937	71,500,000,000	85.8	23,672,000,000	124.3
1938	64,200,000,000	77.0	21,587,000,000	113.4

CAUSES OF THE UNITED STATES' FAILURE TO RECOVER

The reasons for this failure of the United States to recover were obvious. The first was the setback caused by the wholly unnecessary bank panic. More important than this temporary blow was the whole New Deal collectivism. There is no middle road between any breed of collectivist economy and our American system. Aside from any question as to whether such high productivity as that of the United States could be maintained under either pure communism, fascism, or socialism, even parts of these systems certainly cannot be mixed with free enterprise. The reasons why there can be no mixture are clear. In the American kind of free economy, production and distribution are generators from which flow long transmission lines of initiative, employment, and opportunity. Once these lines are interfered with at any point the whole current is weakened.

[6] The reader should not confuse the European economy during the period 1933–1939 with the period 1945–1951 after the Second World War. In this latter period of demoralization resulting from the war, Europe, except for some small countries such as Belgium, Denmark, Sweden and Switzerland, went deeply into the collectivist mire with the usual dire economic consequences. The small countries, by maintaining free economies, showed much greater prosperity than their collectivist neighbors.

The American system is based upon the confidence, hopes and the judgment of each man in conducting his business affairs upon his judgment. He determines his prices in relation to demand, supply and competition. His policies are based upon endless chains of contracts and agreements. If only one link be touched, the whole chain weakens and the expected results are frustrated. Also, under "planned economy" the actions of government and bureaucrats are unpredictable. At once men become hesitant and fearful. Every time the planners inject their dictation into some region of private enterprise, somehow, somewhere, men's minds and judgments become confused. Initiative and enterprise slacken; production and consumption slow down. At once unemployment is increased, and every fear is accelerated. Then more drastic powers and more government agencies are demanded by the planners. And thus the cancer of power over men grows by creating its own emergencies.

An examination of our economy during the depression indicates the precise spot of stagnation. And in locating this spot we give proof of the destructive forces which were induced by New Deal collectivism.

Our economic front consists of two segments which are, on one hand, the consumer goods including services and, on the other hand, the durable goods. For this discussion the consumer goods and services are defined as those things we quickly use up. They include food, drink, clothing, gasoline, electric power, cosmetics, lawyers' fees, movies, and such like.

Durable goods consist of our equipment for living, working, and making consumer goods. They are homes, buildings, machinery, railways, factories, schoolhouses and such. Every time the population gains a single baby, we need more of them.

Any examination shows we produced a large portion of the needed consumer goods during the whole depression, from 1929 to 1941, including the eight years of Roosevelt. The deficiency was in the production of durable goods. People have to consume to live; but they can postpone for long periods the production or use of durable goods.

The Federal Reserve Board indexes of production over a number of years computed with 1929 as 100 show the difference in the economic status of each of these two categories of production:

		Durable Goods	Consumer Goods
(Coolidge)	1925	80	81
	1926	86	85
	1927	80	89
	1928	88	91
(Hoover)	1929	100	100
	1930	74	90
	1931	50	85
	1932	31	75
(Roosevelt)	1933	42	86
	1934	49	87
	1935	65	96
	1936	81	107
	1937	92	113
	1938	59	102
	1939	82	117

In 1939 and after, the figures were influenced by European war orders. Thus, while the consumer goods improved, as would be natural with increasing population, the durable goods' production lagged. The great unemployment problem, therefore, obviously lay in that segment, and unemployment of necessity somewhat reduced the demand for consumer goods. The figures of the construction industries are ample proof of this.

Mr. Roosevelt constantly used the year 1926 as his economic ideal. If we use 1926 as 100, we find:

	Construction Activity Including Work Relief	Per Cent
1926	$11,130,000,000	100
1937	5,549,000,000	43
1938	5,254,000,000	40
1939	6,302,000,000	48
1940	7,295,000,000	55

The activity in 1940 was artificially increased by European war orders.

It cannot be said that the country did not need the full volume of construction. For instance it was short of houses. The number of dwelling units constructed under a free economy averaged 750,000 per annum from 1921 to 1929. The numbers constructed under the New

Deal were: 1934, 126,000; 1935, 221,000; 1936, 319,000; 1937, 336,000; 1938, 406,000; 1939, 515,000.

If we calculate in money the amount of the lag in the production of durable goods over these years and turn that amount of money into wages, and then add something for the consumer goods that would be bought by these extra wages, we come out with jobs for all the 11,000,000 unemployed.

It may be repeated that the durable goods industries are the area of our economy which especially requires initiative, enterprise, and risk. When men become fearful of the future, they first become hesitant and then postpone action, particularly in this area.

The reasons for the hesitation are simple to explain. During 1930–1932 we were under the influences of the failing banks and the degenerating foreign economic situation. It was a period of fear and consequent postponements. By the time Roosevelt took office the fears from abroad had disappeared. A new line of domestic fears was at once created. They came from tinkering with currency and credit, from creeping fascist dictation to industry, labor, and agriculture. We entered areas of socialism through government production and distribution. We witnessed great centralization of power with a huge bureaucracy. We began a vast increase in government expenditures and debt. We witnessed great forces of moral corruption and intellectual dishonesty. We saw the legislative arm reduced to a rubber stamp, and the Supreme Court subjugated. We saw the development of class hatred at the hands of the government. There was ample reason to fear, to hesitate, and to postpone commitments.

It has been the technique of all collectivist leaders to single out some element of the community for concentrated hate. Lenin directed hate toward the "bourgeoisie"; Hitler, toward the Jews; Mussolini, toward the Communists and democrats; Mr. Roosevelt concentrated his denunciation on a generalized class which he called "economic royalists." Whatever merit this technique may have politically, its result is the discouragement of good men and slowing up of the economy of the nation. Throughout Roosevelt's first eight years, the New Dealers contended that we were not in a "depression"—it was merely a "recession." This sounded better.

However, the chilling result was 11,000,000 unemployed and 16,000,-000 on relief until we entered the path of war. But cold statistics are no measure of the stream of frustrated lives and human tragedy. Neither do they measure the frantic demand for more and more power by the planners, nor their relief from their gigantic failure by the war.

MR. ROOSEVELT'S COMFORTING OPTIMISM

It is of some interest to examine Roosevelt's attitude of mind amidst his long failure to overcome the depression.

During the 1932 campaign he had rubbed in some hopeful remarks of mine made in the early months of 1930 and 1931. (I did not say, "Prosperity is around the corner.") In those times we were strongly started on the way to recovery; but we had a relapse with the European collapse, and I was proved wrong.

Mr. Roosevelt also became periodically most optimistic. For instance, in his annual message to Congress on January 4, 1934, he said, "Now that we are definitely in the process of recovery . . ."

Despite this, the organ of the American Federation of Labor said three months later, in April, 1934:

It is significant that we are at present making no progress whatever in putting the unemployed to work in industry. Prospects for further reemployment before next fall are slight.

Four months later, as the situation looked very gloomy indeed to the public, Roy Howard, a prominent publisher, proposed a breathing spell from attacks upon the American system of life. He wrote the President on August 26th, "There can be no real recovery until the fears of business have been allayed." Roosevelt replied on September 6th:

It is a source of great satisfaction that at this moment conditions are such as to offer further substantial and widespread recovery. . . .

On April 28, 1935, Mr. Roosevelt said:

Never since my Inauguration in March, 1933, have I felt so unmistakably the atmosphere of recovery. . . . Fear is vanishing and confidence is growing on every side, faith is being renewed. . . .

On October 23, 1935, he said:

Yes, we are on our way back—not just by pure chance, my friends, not just by a turn of the wheels, of the cycle. We are coming back more soundly than ever before *because we are planning it that way. Don't let anybody tell you differently.*

At various times in 1936 he said:

Our policy is succeeding. The figures prove it. (January 3rd.)

Results proven by facts and figures show that we are on our way. (April 25th.)

Prosperity is coming back. (September 4th.)

Employment and weekly pay envelopes have increased steadily in the past three years. (September 6th.)

We are heartened by clear evidences of returning prosperity. (September 16th.)

I see an enormous difference . . . in the prosperity of the country as a whole and in every part of it that I have visited. (October 9th.)

I tell you and you will agree that we are around the corner. (October 12th.)

The train of American business is moving ahead. (October 14th.)

The national recovery we have had in the past three years. . . . (October 16th.)

There is no question but things are better in every part of the country. (October 17th.)

Prosperity measured in dollars is coming back. . . . A nation more greatly prosperous, more definitely on the way to recovery. (October 21st.)

Prosperity is back with us again and believe me it is going to stay. (October 22nd.)

These bursts of optimism brought Mr. Roosevelt the same uncomfortable remarks as had come to me. But I can say in his defense that Presidents must be cheerful and optimistic. To be the reverse would bring new disasters. Apparently Roosevelt was not plagued with the fact that unemployment had not greatly diminished since the day of his election. He constantly fooled himself by using as his statistical base his induced bank panic of March 4, 1933.

Now the New Dealers around Roosevelt took another tack—that unemployment was a natural condition for the nation. Aubrey W. Williams, one of Roosevelt's principal administrators, said in February, 1936:

Unemployment—or better, disemployment—is, like the airplane, the radio, the weather and taxes, here to stay. Millions of those now out of jobs will never find jobs again. Thousands of young men and women leaving our schools each year are destined never to become self-supporting and independent in the sense that your and my generation were led to believe was our due.

The supply of workers exceeds the demand. Manpower is a drug on the market.[7]

The New Deal was not unaware of its failure to secure recovery. There had been a small boomlet in business in 1936 which resulted in this great burst of oratorical triumph. But it faded early in 1937 and reached another low point in mid-1938.

The President charged it to a gigantic conspiracy of business against him.

James Farley wrote of their miseries:

At the Cabinet meeting that afternoon, October 8, 1937, Roosevelt . . . [said]:

. . . "I know that the present situation is the result of a concerted effort by big business and concentrated wealth to drive the market down just to create a situation unfavorable to me. . . . The whole situation is being manufactured in Wall Street." [8]

But worse was to come. In ten days the stock market blew up still further. Its effect on the New Dealers is best described by Henry Morgenthau:

Seven million shares changed hands while prices skidded amid a hysteria resembling a mob in a theater fire. . . . The production index started to decline. Panic overcame the business community. . . .[9]

[7] *American Federationist*, Vol. 43, p. 147 (Feb., 1936).
[8] James A. Farley, *Jim Farley's Story*, p. 101.
[9] Henry Morgenthau, Jr., "The Morgenthau Diaries, II—The Struggle for a Program," *Collier's*, Oct. 4, 1947, p. 20.

I could weep with them when I recalled a Black Friday in October, 1929.

Farley tells of a Cabinet meeting about November 10, 1938, at which the discussion centered on government policy toward business in the depression. In the course of it he said to the President:

> ... I think the situation would be helped materially if you did say something to alleviate the fears which no one can deny exist in the business world today. . . . there is a feeling that you have no sympathy or confidence in business—big or little. . . .

The President made the general answer:

> ... I know who's responsible for the situation. Business, particularly the banking industry, has ganged up on me.[10]

That a few thousand or even ten businessmen conspired to bring about an economic slump was preposterous. It becomes even more preposterous when one thinks of the losses such action would have projected upon every one of them. Business never favors a depression. Henry Morgenthau's diary demonstrates the usual New Deal political alibi:

> ... I called F. D. R. that night (November 3, 1937). He got very excited and disagreeable and quoted at great length a man he described as a "wise old bird" who had said that business was deliberately causing the depression in order to hold a pistol to his head and force a retreat from the New Deal.

The President could feel even more gloomy from his November, 1937, unemployment census which I have mentioned above, showing 11,-000,000 totally unemployed and more than 3,000,000 only partly employed—a worse situation than that existing when he was elected five years before.

However, the New Dealers found the answer again. It originated in Keynes' bright young disciples who arose from the colleges mostly around Boston. In the spring of 1938 a committee of them emitted an involved mumbo-jumbo, partially Keynes' in origin, in which they traced depression to excessive saving by the people. Therefore, the gov-

[10] James A. Farley, *Jim Farley's Story*, pp. 104, 106.

ernment must tax the savings away and spend them. As an alternative they proposed the government, in order to avoid harassing the taxpayers, should borrow the people's savings and spend them. They further contended that the government debts were not debts at all because they were owed to the people by the people! There was no need, therefore, to bother about the size of the debt any more.

All this was joyful news to the President. It had other appeals to his political soul as well, as it could be helpful in the forthcoming Congressional election. The net of all this was an appropriation of $5,000,-000,000 by the Congress.

It is of little purpose to argue here that this thesis ignored the fact that the savings of the people are sources of the improvement of production facilities and creation of new industries. The savings of the people build houses and equip them with a long train of other durable goods. The government cannot create reproductive industry. I have already demonstrated the fallacy of the government's being able to fill the gaps in the durable goods industries by public works, and this mumbo-jumbo only increased fears and postponements.

Morgenthau in his diary confirms this embracing of Keynes:

Theories, based in part on the reasoning of . . . John Maynard Keynes, had come into vogue. These theories transformed spending from a temporary expedient to a permanent instrumentality of government. Whenever private investment declined, the Keynesians favored the expansion of government economic activity in order to fill the gap and maintain the level of production and employment.

In a note of explanation in his published papers upon this new program, Roosevelt gave an economic explanation of the "recession" which certainly exonerated the wicked bankers. He said:

. . . This decline was reflected in varying degrees throughout the entire field of American business—in distribution, in transportation, and in the service industries. And with it, of course, had come a progressive decline in employment, and in prices of farm products, raw materials, wholesale commodities, and common stocks.

The reasons for this severe recession were . . . overproduction of materials of all kinds, which outran the buying power of the consuming public, resulting in large inventories . . . Together with this overproduction had come an unwarranted rise in prices, going beyond the ability or willingness of buyers to buy.[11]

It would be difficult for any economist to reconcile all these conflicting economic ideas. The idea that overproduction resulted in higher prices seems a little fantastic. Also, Roosevelt's original thesis had been to raise prices as the road to salvation. With the approaching election of 1940, he said on August 31st:

On this Labor Day of 1940 not only the Nation's wage earners but farmers and business also can look with satisfaction on the improvement in their lot and that of our Nation in the last seven years largely as a result of a far-reaching economic and social program conceived in democratic principles and dedicated to the common good.

However, the dragon of 10,000,000 unemployed and 16,000,000 people on relief was not so easily brushed away.

At the end of eight years of the New Deal, any examination of the causes of its failure to secure economic recovery must needs consider its own seeds of destruction.

The recognition of Russia on November 16, 1933, started forces which were to have considerable influence in the attempt to collectivize the United States, particularly through the labor unions. We saw government conducted by "emergencies," purges, propaganda, bureaucracy, hate, the turmoil of class conflict—all of collectivist pattern. We saw an era of the deepest intellectual dishonesty in public life. We saw the growth of executive power by the reduction of the legislative arm, with few exceptions, to a rubber stamp. We saw the Congressional powers over the purse practically abandoned. We saw the subjection of the Supreme Court to the collectivist ideas of the executive. We saw the independence and responsibility of the states undermined by huge Federal subsidies directly to the citizens.

Thus the four great pillars of free men were weakened. As a result of eight years of the New Deal, there was not more but less liberty in

[11] *Public Papers and Addresses of Franklin D. Roosevelt,* 1938 volume (Macmillan Company, New York, 1941), p. 233.

America. And, unique among the nations of the world free of collectivism, we had not ended the Great Depression. Its vast unemployment and its huge numbers on relief were only ended by war. But out of these years of New Dealism and the necessary expansion of control measures by the war came a partial redemption of America from collectivism.

From this and the necessary expansion of collectivist measures during the war, there came a revulsion in the public mind. A first real turning away from collectivism came with the Congressional election after the war (1946). In the new Congress, Republicans with the aid of conservative Democrats repealed—according to an estimate by a responsible member—some 70,000 New Deal and war rules, regulations and orders, which went far to restore the American system. It has since had some setbacks, but that the American system has survived at all is proof of its vitality.

INDEX

Accounting methods (Federal), Roosevelt's change of, 465–466, 469

Acheson, Dean G., 352

Adams, Alva B., Senator, 380

Agricultural Act (1936), 417

Agricultural Adjustment Act (1933), 408–411, 417

Agricultural credit banks, proposed, 98, 107, 156

Agricultural Production Banks, 110, 162, 264, 306

Agriculture, credit needs of, 22–23, 91, 93; depression aid to, 31, 32, 41; Federal Farm Board program for, 50–51, 52; and 1930 drought in Midwest and South, 51–52, 55, 56, 57; and Soviet government short selling of wheat, 52–53; marketing help by Federal Farm Board, 95; aid to, intended in projected RFC, 98, 107; new help planned by Federal Land Banks and Federal Farm Board, 99; RFC program for, 108, 110, 156; aid to, and the budget, 132, 133; general relief program for, 156–158; 1932 campaign discussion of policies toward, 235, 244, 263, 264, 266, 267, 268, 288–292 *passim*, 296–300 *passim*, 302–309; under Roosevelt, 408–419

Agriculture Department, 52, 156, 304

Allen, George E., WPA Administrator, 426

American Federation of Labor, 45–46, 166, 197, 435, 436–437

American Legion, 83

American Liberty League, 454–455

American Red Cross, drought relief by, 52, 54–55; relief distribution of wheat and cotton, 152–153

American system, 24–28, 252, 324, 329, 336, 337, 338–343; no middle road between collectivism and, 475–476; breathing spell for, proposed, 479; vitality of, 484

Anderson, Jack Z., Congressman, 456

Anti-trust acts, value of, 420; repeal of, 421, 430, 431

Apple sellers, 195

Appropriation bills, 194–195

Arkansas, "riot" of "starving people" in, 55, 224

Armaments, European, 4, 13, 61, 63 n., 71, 89, 105

Astor, Vincent, 202, 220

Austria, customs union with Germany forbidden by Britain and France, which brings pressure through short-term bills of Austrian banks presented by French banks for payment, 61, 62, 64 n.; panic in, 63, 64 n., 65, 68, 72–73, 74

Austrian National Bank, 63 n., 65

Autographs, 344–345

Ayres, Leonard P., 3, 5 n., 164

Baker, Newton D., 168, 174

Ballantine, Arthur A., 207

Baltimore *Sun*, 141, 184, 204

Bank acceptances, 68, 73, 74. *See also* Short-term bills

Bank depositors' panic (Feb., 1933), 40, 202–216, 357, 358–359

Bank deposits, proposed Federal guarantee of, 211, 212; guarantee enacted, 461

Bank failures, American callousness to, 21; evidence of a weak banking system, 23–24, 122; in Apr.–July, 1931, 39; in Jan.–Mar., 1931, 59; menace of, following Central Europe economic collapse, 75; after British collapse, 82; suggested preventive and corrective for, 87; mixture of functions as cause of, 94; yield in Nov., 1931, to re-